The INGRES Papers:

Anatomy of a Relational Database System

Michael Stonebraker, Editor
University of California, Berkeley

ADDISON-WESLEY PUBLISHING COMPANY
Reading, Massachusetts ● Menlo Park, California ● Don Mills, Ontario
Wokingham, England ● Amsterdam ● Sydney ● Singapore ● Tokyo ● Mexico City
Bogotá ● Santiago ● San Juan

This book is in the Addison-Wesley Series in Computer Science.

Consulting Editor: Michael A. Harrison

Library of Congress Cataloging in Publication Data
Main entry under title:

The INGRES papers.

Bibliography: p.
Includes index.
1. Data base management--Addresses, essays, lectures.
2. INGRES (Computer system)--Addresses, essays, lectures. I. Stonebraker, Michael.
II. Title: Relational database system.
QA76.9.D3I535   1986   001.64'2   84-24584
ISBN 0-201-07185-1

Reproduced by Addison-Wesley from camera-ready copy supplied and approved by the author.

ABCDEFGHIJ-HA-898765

Preface

This book summarizes the work of the INGRES project at the University of California, Berkeley over the years 1973-1983. The project was initiated by Professor Eugene Wong and myself in late 1973 and has been in existence since that time. Professor Lawrence Rowe joined the project in 1976.

Initially, the project goal was to construct a working relational database system. In 1970, Ted Codd proposed the relational model as a better foundation on which to build a database system. His ideas (as reported in [CODD70, CODD71, CODD72]) were widely debated in the early 1970s. The critics insisted that a relational database system could not run efficiently. Moreover, even if one could be built, no REAL programmers could be taught to use the novel languages which were being proposed. On the other hand, Codd's supporters claimed that older technologies (e.g., network and hierarchical data models) were too complex, too difficult to program and offered insufficient insulation from changing data structures. The issues were hotly discussed at annual SIGFIDET (now SIGMOD) conferences, and formally debated at the 1974 conference. Eugene Wong and I had begun reading papers in database management in 1972, and it was apparent to us that the relational model offered simplicity and elegance. It seemed to us that this had to be the way of the future, and we embarked on an implementation project to prove that an efficient, easy-to-use system could be built.

The INGRES system first ran in 1975. During 1976 and 1977, we produced increasingly reliable and functional systems. Because our software worked in a UNIX environment, and there were few other database alternatives available, we were able to convince a substantial collection of outside users to try INGRES. By 1978 we had considerable user feedback and were aware of the benefits and shortcomings of our software. Fixing the drawbacks would involve a lot of work and did not seem like a reasonable research project. Hence, active development of the University of California INGRES prototype tapered off in 1979. Since then, several companies (including Amdahl, ELXSI, Computer Associates, Relational Technology, and

NBI) have produced commercial products based on the University of California code.

The first section of this book contains a collection of three papers that chronicle the development of the INGRES system. The papers were written in 1976, 1978, and 1984. The final paper in the trilogy describes the experience of one company, Relational Technology, in correcting the earlier drawbacks.

During the University of California development phase, we made many engineering tradeoffs in the design of INGRES. Many of these issues were concurrently investigated formally by members of the INGRES team. The second section of this book contains a representative collection of supporting studies on issues faced in building a database system. Two of the papers cover the traditional topics of concurrency control and query optimization. The third paper uses INGRES as a vehicle to investigate what database machine architectures might be feasible. The fourth paper uses INGRES to study compilation, microcode, a fast file system, and a special purpose operating system as performance enhancement techniques. The final paper in Section 2 contains a collection of complaints and frustrations concerning the services provided by contemporary operating systems.

In 1977, we enlarged our development sights to include managing data distributed across multiple computer systems in a computer network. Although fraught with implementation problems, Distributed INGRES worked in a two-site configuration over a 9600 baud RS232 interface in 1981 and worked with an arbitrary number of sites over an Ethernet in 1983. The third section of this book includes four papers that discuss this development project, and the lessons we learned from it. The first one indicates the general characteristics of our design, and some performance numbers, and a backward look at problems encountered. Then, two papers which are representative of our thoughts have been included on query processing in a distributed environment. The last paper discusses protocols necessary to correctly recover from crashes in a distributed environment.

During the development of INGRES, we have designed and/or implemented several user interfaces to database systems. Our first programming language interface, EQUEL, remains today as a reasonable mechanism for coupling an existing host language to a database system. Initial use of this interface convinced us that any host language coupling would be fraught with impossible dilemmas. To explore alternative solutions to these problems, we designed and implemented a new programming language, RIGEL, which performed both general purpose computation and database access in one environment. A processor for RIGEL was constructed between 1977 and 1979. More than a dozen external users tried RIGEL in 1979 and 1980. The second paper in Section 4 discusses constructs in this language. A third user interface which we constructed in 1981-83 was oriented toward forms. All real database applications spend an inordinate amount of code manipulating the screen, and we attempted to reduce this effort by an order of magnitude. The third paper in this section discusses the design of the resulting system,

FADS. The last paper in this section proposes a new programming language interface, which may someday replace EQUEL. This interface was motivated by the special needs of application programs which allow users to browse through a collection of data making random changes.

Many researchers and practitioners agree that relational database systems are well suited to business data processing applications. However, there are many other kinds of users with database problems. For lack of a better word, we will term them "non-traditional" applications, and it is evident that their database needs are somewhat different than business ones. Many researchers in the database community are engaged in a "group grope" for ideas that address the issues of this community. Section 5 contains a set of four papers that propose various extensions to the relational model appropriate in nonbusiness environments. At the moment, the INGRES project is attempting to release a new version of the system (Version 8), which contains many of these ideas. We have always prototyped our ideas, and now seems an appropriate time to integrate the more valuable ones, so others can try them out. It is hoped that such research eventually results in a small set of powerful primitives that can address the needs of such clients, and do so with the same robustness that relational database systems have addressed the needs of business data processing applications.

One of the most difficult database problems faced by any real world application designers is to specify his "schema," and then make access path choices to generate good performance for his application. The twin problems of logical database design and physical database design must be overcome. Section 6 contains two papers which represent our insights into this important area.

The future directions of the project are primarily in the area of database support for nontraditional applications. We are pursuing ideas to support text processing, expert systems, and spatial data applications in a database context. We have decided not to attempt a release of Distributed INGRES because the code is not reliable enough to be useful to others.

Because the project is at a crossroads, it seems appropriate to summarize past successes and failures at this time. The papers in this book have been selected with this goal in mind, and were all written by students and professors at the University of California who were associated with the INGRES project.

The INGRES project has always been organized as a chief programmer supported by a team of four to six people. The chief programmer was the only full-time employee; all other people associated with the project have been students intent on passing courses and obtaining degrees. The chief programmers have been:

Dr. Gerald Held   (1973-1975)
   now Director of Strategic Planning at Tandem Computers, Inc.

Mr. Peter Kreps   (1975-1977)
  now Member of the Technical Staff at Relational Technology Inc.
Dr. Robert Epstein   (1977-1980)
  now Vice President at SYBASE
Mr. Eric Allman   (1980-1982)
  now Member of the Technical Staff at Britton-Lee, Inc.
Mr. Joseph Kalash   (1982-1985)
  now Program Manager at Unisoft

Whatever success the project has had rests largely on the contributions of these people. Each was the "keeper" of the INGRES knowledge (i.e., how the system really worked) and was the ultimate authority on how to fix bugs. Moreover, large portions of the system were written by them. It would be impossible to list all of the students who have been associated with the INGRES project but I feel that it is important to acknowledge the contributions that some of them have made to developing the various systems that we have built.

The following students were largely responsible for implementing the early versions of the INGRES system:

Mr. James Ford   (1973-1975)
  now Principal Member of the Technical Staff at CXC Corp.
Mr. William Zook   (1973-1975)
Mr. Rick Berman   (1973-1975)
  now Section Manager at Tandem Computers, Inc.
Mr. Nick Whyte   (1976-1978)
  now Manager of Data Base Development at ELXSI Computers, Inc.
Mr. Peter Rubinstein   (1975-1977)
Ms. Iris Schoenberg   (1974-1975)
Ms. Angela Go   (1974-1975)
Ms. Carol Joyce   (1974-1976)
  now Member of the Technical Staff at Relational Technology Inc.
Dr. Karel Yousseffi   (1973-1976)
  now Member of the Technical Staff at Tandem Computers, Inc.
Dr. Nancy McDonald   (1973-1975)
  now Senior Scientist at GTE Data Services
Mr. Michael Ubell   (1975-1977)
  now Director of IDM Software at Britton-Lee, Inc.
Dr. Daniel Ries   (1975-1978)
  now Director, End User Product Development at Computer Corporation of America, Inc.
Dr. Paula Hawthorn   (1976-1979)
  now Director of Product Development at Britton-Lee, Inc.
Ms. Polly Siegal   (1976-1978)
  now Development Engineer at Hewlett-Packard

Mr. Marc Meyer   (1978-1981)
  now an independent consultant
Dr. Randy Katz   (1977-1980)
  now Professor of Computer Science at the University of California,
  Berkeley

Distributed INGRES was largely coded by the following students:

Mr. John Woodfill   (1979-1983)
  now a graduate student in Computer Science at Stanford University
Mr. Jeff Ranstrom   (1979-1982)
  now Member of the Technical Staff at Altos Computers, Inc.

In addition, the following students contributed various modules to later versions of the code:

Ms. Nadene Lynn   (1981-1982)
  now OEM Support Manager at Relational Technology Inc.
Mr. Robert McCord   (1980-1982)
  now Project Manager, Database Systems at Tolerant Systems, Inc.
Mr. Dennis Fogg   (1981-1982)
  now a graduate student in Computer Science at M.I.T.
Mr. James Ong   (1981-1982)
  now a graduate student in Computer Science at Yale
Ms. Heidi Stettner   (1981-1982)
  now Audio Systems Programmer at Lucas Films, Ltd.

RIGEL was primarily coded under the supervision of Larry Rowe by the following students:

Dr. Kurt Shoens   (1979-1981)
  now Member of the Technical Staff at IBM Research
Mr. Dan Brotsky   (1978-1979)
  now a graduate student at M.I.T.
Mr. Joseph Cortopassi   (1978-1980)
  now Manager of User Interfaces at Relational Technology Inc.
Mr. Doug Doucette   (1978-1980)
  now Member of the Technical Staff at Tolerant Systems, Inc.

FADS was primarily coded by Kurt Shoens as a portion of his Ph.D. dissertation with assistance from:

Mr. Mark Hanner
  now a product marketing engineer for Relational Technology Inc.

The INGRES project has been supported primarily by research grants from various federal agencies. The support of Mr. John Machado of the Naval Electronics Systems Command, Captain William Price of the Air Force Office of Scientific Research, Dr. Jimmie Suttle of the Army Research Office, and Dr. Rick Adrion and Dr. Bernard Chern of the National Science Foundation are especially appreciated.

This book was edited using UNIX document processing facilities primarily by Beatrice Dryfoos and Beth Rabb to whom I am deeply indebted. Typesetting was expertly done by Beatrice Dryfoos.

Berkeley, California   *M.S.*

Contents

1

Design of Relational Systems

This section of the book contains a trilogy of papers describing the design and implementation of INGRES. The first paper describes INGRES as it existed in early 1976. This paper sketches the original design principles and the reasoning behind them. It was written when the original system was emerging and appeared in the September 1976 issue of *Transactions on Data Systems* (TODS).

The second part of the trilogy was written in late 1978 when initial performance tests on the code had been done and we discovered some major design flaws. At this point, it was clear that major problems existed with the code, and the INGRES project was having a "what's next" crisis. The original title of the paper (Chapter two here) was "Requiem for a Data Base System," but the TODS reviewers thought the title was too somber. It appeared as "Retrospection on a Database System" in the September 1980 issue of TODS.

The last paper in the trilogy was written in early 1984 and describes the changes to INGRES since 1978. Since the majority of the work on the code has been done at Relational Technology Inc., the paper is aptly named "The Commercial INGRES Epilogue."

Keep the following thoughts in mind as you read these papers. First, notice some of the naive comments in the first paper. There are remarks that the UNIX kernal will be used for buffer management and that a multiple process database system should execute as fast as a single process one. Such comments reflected the inexperience of the designers concerning the real operating system costs of various functions. The second paper discusses the extreme cost of such operations once INGRES was running and benchmark testing had been performed.

Notice the discussion in the three papers concerning the tradeoff of space for speed. The earlier system was constrained to a small address space machine and all tradeoffs were forced to the "small space" alternative. The third paper indicates the ways in which the code was speeded up by trading space for time (e.g., caching the "state" of past commands).

Then, notice the willingness of the design team to rethink past decisions and to rewrite major pieces of the system, if appropriate. The adage that it is never too late to throw everything away and begin again with a clean slate should always be kept in mind.

Notice also the desire to use the operating system facilities intact for the purposes for which they were designed, regardless of the performance consequences. Notice that INGRES continues to use the operating system scheduler, messages, and file system. Although loud complaints appear in a later section about operating system services, it is clear that we had no desire to redo such services if we could avoid it.

In the first paper note the defense of single statement transactions and a single level of delegation in the protection system. Such remarks reflect our absence of maturity about these issues.

Finally, notice that the theme of rapid prototyping is prevalent throughout the three papers. The second paper describes an early INGRES user using the now popular technique for application design. Moreover, it is evident that the INGRES design team used this approach for all their development.

From the third paper, one can note the direction in which INGRES is moving. Tactics include generating a query plan by examining all (or most) of the possibilities and saving the plan for reuse if possible. Plans should include both merge-sort and tuple substitution as possible tactics. These decisions are ones that the System R designers also arrived at [SELI79] and are commonly believed correct in 1984.

One might ask, "what implementation issues are not well understood at the moment?" The rest of this introduction addresses this question. First, there is a trend by operating system designers to move transaction management inside the operating system. This topic is briefly addressed in the next section, and it appears that there are substantial implementation problems to be overcome [STON84]. Hence, the proper place of transaction management is still an open issue.

Secondly, most database management systems peak at 50 or fewer transactions per second in large transaction-processing applications. The reason is not insufficient CPU horsepower or I/O bandwidth but a variety of software bottlenecks. For example, while a lock is being set, the lock table is temporarily in an inconsistent state. As a result, a process to set a lock must get exclusive control of the lock table for the duration of its modification to the data structure. In applications with a very large number of terminals (say 1000), there may be queuing delays to access the lock table. Another problem is that standard database practice requires that a log record be written out to disk at the conclusion of a transaction. Many database systems have a single log file per database; hence, one must write 50 log records to a single file in one second in order to commit 50 transactions per second. This is difficult to do with most contemporary operating systems. How to overcome this myriad of software bottlenecks and achieve dramatic increases in transaction throughput (say 1000 per second) remains an open question.

A third issue is storage of complex objects in a database system. This topic is extensively discussed in Section 5.0 for engineering applications. However, one should note that data dictionaries for relational database systems are being enlarged to hold information on reports, forms, graphs, application programs, and so forth, as well as information on relations and storage structures. The information about a form includes the layout of its fields, the position of trim elements, which fields are protected, and so forth. Such information does not naturally fit the relational model. I feel that extending the semantics for the relational model to handle such complex objects is one of the most pressing open issues.

Nowadays, computers are being sold with increasing amounts of main memory, and buffer pools with a size of several megabytes are becoming commonplace. Clearly, database systems must change over the current decade to manage a database that is partly on disk and partly in main memory. This possibility suggests for example that hash-join algorithms may be a viable query processing tactic [DEWI84]. Re-engineering current systems to take advantage of massive amounts of main memory is a challenging open issue.

Lastly, I predict that optical disks will finally see the light of day and become commercially significant. A "write once" device with a very large capacity has considerable appeal. Clearly, one can put the database log on such a device. However, one might be able to build a data structure in which data records are never overwritten. This would allow all past values of all items in the database to be accessible and would allow one to ask questions of the database as of some particular point of time in the past. Building such a data structure on a write-once medium is a challenging open issue.

## CHAPTER ONE

The Design and Implementation of INGRES

Michael Stonebraker / Peter Kreps / Eugene Wong / Gerald Held

1.0. INTRODUCTION

INGRES (Interactive Graphics and Retrieval System) is a relational database system which is implemented on top of the UNIX operating system developed at Bell Telephone Laboratories [RITC74a] for Digital Equipment Corporation PDP 11/40, 11/45, and 11/70 computer systems. The implementation of INGRES is primarily programmed in C, a high level language in which UNIX itself is written. Parsing is done with the assistance of YACC, a compiler-compiler available on UNIX [JOHN74].

The advantages of a relational model for database management systems have been extensively discussed in the literature [CODD70, CODD74, DATE74] and hardly require further elaboration. In choosing the relational model, we were particularly motivated by the high degree of data independence that such a model affords, and the possibility of providing a high level and entirely procedure-free facility for data definition, retrieval, update, access control, support of views, and integrity verification.

1.1. Aspects Described in This Paper

In this paper we describe the design decisions made in INGRES. In particular we stress the design and implementation of:

1) the system process structure (see Section 2.0 for a discussion of this UNIX notion);

2) the embedding of all INGRES commands in the general purpose programming language C;

3) the access methods implemented;

4) the catalog structure and the role of the database administrator;

5) support for views, protection, and integrity constraints;

6) the decomposition procedure implemented;

7) implementation of updates and consistency of secondary indices;

8) recovery and concurrency control.

In Section 1.2 we briefly describe the primary query language supported, QUEL, and the utility commands accepted by the current system. The second user interface, CUPID, is a graphics-oriented, casual-user language which is also operational [MCDO75a, MCDO75b] but not discussed in this paper. In Section 1.3, we describe the EQUEL (Embedded QUEL) precompiler, which allows the substitution of a user-supplied C program for the "front-end" process. This precompiler has the effect of embedding all of INGRES in the general purpose programming language C. In Section 1.4 a few comments on QUEL and EQUEL are given.

In Section 2.0 we describe the relevant factors in the UNIX environment which have affected our design decisions. Moreover, we indicate the reasoning behind the choices implemented.

In Section 3.0 we indicate the catalog (system) relations which exist and the role of the database administrator with respect to all relations in a database. The implemented access methods, their calling conventions, and, where appropriate, the actual layout of the data pages in secondary storage are also presented.

Sections 4.0, 5.0, and 6.0 discuss, respectively, the various functions of each of the three "core" processes in the system. Also discussed are the design and implementation strategy of each process. Finally, Section 7.0 draws conclusions, suggests future extensions, and indicates the nature of the current applications run on INGRES.

Except where noted to the contrary, this paper describes the INGRES system operational in March 1976.

1.2. QUEL and the Other INGRES Utility Commands

QUEL (QUEry Language) has points in common with Data Language/ALPHA [CODD71], SQUARE [BOYC73], and SEQUEL [CHAM74b], in that it is a complete query language which frees the programmer from concern for how data structures are implemented and what algorithms are operating on stored data [CODD71]. As such, it facilitates a considerable degree of data independence [STON74a].

The QUEL examples in this section all concern the following relations:

EMP (NAME, DEPT, SALARY, MANAGER, AGE)
DEPT (DEPT, FLOOR#)

A QUEL interaction includes at least one RANGE statement of the form

   RANGE OF variable-list IS relation-name

The purpose of this statement is to specify the relation over which each variable ranges. The variable-list portion of a RANGE statement declares variables which will be used as arguments for tuples. These are called "tuple variables."

   Moreover, an interaction includes one or more statements of the form:

   Command [result-name](target-list)
      [WHERE Qualification]

Here "Command" is either RETRIEVE, APPEND, REPLACE, or DELETE. For RETRIEVE and APPEND, "result-name" is the name of the relation which qualifying tuples will be retrieved into or appended to. For REPLACE and DELETE, "result-name" is the name of a tuple variable which, through the qualification, identifies tuples to be modified or deleted. The target-list is a list of the form

   result-domain = QUEL Function,
   result-domain = QUEL Function, . . .

Here the result-domains are domain names in the result relation which are to be assigned the values of the corresponding functions.

   The following suggest valid QUEL interactions. A complete description of the language is presented in [HELD75b].

Example. Compute salary divided by age-18 for employee Jones.

   RANGE OF E IS EMP
   RETRIEVE INTO W (COMP = E.SALARY/(E.AGE-18))
      WHERE E.NAME = "Jones"

Here E is a tuple variable which ranges over the EMP relation, and all tuples in that relation are found which satisfy the qualification E.NAME = "Jones." The result of the query is a new relation W, which has a single domain COMP that has been calculated for each qualifying tuple.

   If the result relation is omitted, qualifying tuples are written in display format on the user's terminal or returned to a calling program.

Example. Insert the tuple (Jackson, candy, 13000, Baker, 30) into EMP.

   APPEND TO EMP (NAME = "Jackson",
               DEPT = "candy", SALARY = 13000,
               MGR = "Baker", AGE = 30)

Here the result relation EMP is modified by adding the indicated tuple to the relation. Domains which are not specified default to zero for numeric domains and null for character strings. A shortcoming of the current implementation is that 0 is not distinguished from "no value" for numeric domains.

Example. Fire everybody on the first floor.

```
RANGE OF E IS EMP
RANGE OF D IS DEPT
DELETE E WHERE E.DEPT = D.DEPT
                    AND D.FLOOR# = 1
```

Here E specifies that the EMP relation is to be modified. All tuples are to be removed which have a value for DEPT which is the same as some department on the first floor.

Example. Give a 10-percent raise to Jones if he works on the first floor.

```
RANGE OF E IS EMP
RANGE OF D IS DEPT
REPLACE E(SALARY = 1.1*E.SALARY)
            WHERE E.NAME = "Jones"
            AND E.DEPT = D.DEPT AND D.FLOOR# = 1
```

Here E.SALARY is to be replaced by 1.1*E.SALARY for those tuples in EMP where the qualification is true.

In addition to the above QUEL commands, INGRES supports a variety of utility commands. These utility commands can be classified into seven major categories.

1) Invocation of INGRES:

INGRES database-name

This command executed from UNIX "logs in" a user to a given database. (A database is simply a named collection of relations with a given database administrator who has powers not available to ordinary users.) Thereafter the user may issue all other commands (except those executed directly from UNIX) within the environment of the invoked database.

2) Creation and destruction of databases:

CREATEDB database-name
DESTROYDB database-name

These two commands are called from UNIX. The invoker of CREATEDB must be authorized to create databases (in a manner to be described presently), and he automatically becomes the database administrator. DESTROYDB successfully destroys a database only if invoked by the database administrator.

3) Creation and destruction of relations:

CREATE relname(domain-name IS format,
                    domain-name IS format, . . .)
DESTROY relname

These commands create and destroy relations within the current database. The invoker of the CREATE command becomes the "owner" of the relation created. A user may only destroy a relation that he owns. The current formats accepted by INGRES are 1-, 2-, and 4-byte integers, 4- and 8-byte floating point numbers, and 1- to 255-byte fixed length ASCII character strings.

4)   Bulk copy of data:

COPY relname(domain-name IS format,
                       domain-name IS format, . . .)
              direction "filename"

PRINT relname

The command COPY transfers an entire relation to or from a UNIX file whose name is "filename." Direction is either TO or FROM. The format for each domain is a description of how it appears (or is to appear) in the UNIX file. The relation relname must exist and have domain names identical to the ones appearing in the COPY command. However, the formats need not agree, and COPY will automatically convert data types. Support is also provided for dummy and variable length fields in a UNIX file.

PRINT copies a relation onto the user's terminal, formatting it as a report. In this sense it is a stylized version of COPY.

5)   Storage structure modification:

MODIFY relname TO storage-structure ON (key1, key2, . . .)
INDEX ON relname IS indexname (key1, key2, . . .)

The MODIFY command changes the storage structure of a relation from one access method to another. The five access methods currently supported are discussed in Section 3.0. The indicated keys are domains in relname which are concatenated left to right to form a combined key which is used in the organization of tuples in all but one of the access methods. Only the owner of a relation may modify its storage structure.

INDEX creates a secondary index for a relation. It has domains of key1, key2, . . ., pointer. The domain "pointer" is the unique identifier of a tuple in the indexed relation having the given values for key1, key2, . . . An index named AGEINDEX for EMP might be the binary relation shown in Table 1.1 (assuming that there are six tuples in EMP with appropriate names and ages).

The relation "indexname" is in turn treated and accessed just like any other relation, except it is automatically updated when the relation it indexes is updated. Naturally, only the owner of a relation may create and destroy secondary indexes for it.

6)   Consistency and integrity control:

INTEGRITY CONSTRAINT is qualification

	Age	Pointer
	25	identifier for Smith's tuple
AGEINDEX	32	identifier for Jones's tuple
	36	identifier for Adams's tuple
	29	identifier for Johnson's tuple
	47	identifier for Baker's tuple
	58	identifier for Harding's tuple

TABLE 1.1. Binary Relation

INTEGRITY CONSTRAINT LIST relname
INTEGRITY CONSTRAINT OFF relname
INTEGRITY CONSTRAINT OFF (integer, . . . , integer)
RESTORE database-name

The first four commands support the insertion, listing, deletion, and selective deletion of integrity constraints which are to be enforced for all interactions with a relation. The mechanism for handling this enforcement is discussed in Section 4.0. The last command restores a database to a consistent state after a system crash. It must be executed from UNIX and its operation is discussed in Section 6.0. The RESTORE command is only available to the database administrator.

7) Miscellaneous:

HELP [relname or manual-section]
SAVE relname UNTIL expiration-date
PURGE database-name

HELP provides information about the system or the database invoked. When called with an optional argument which is a command name, HELP returns the appropriate page from the INGRES reference manual [ZOOK75]. When called with a relation name as an argument, it returns all information about all relations in the current database.

SAVE is the mechanism by which a user can declare his intention to keep a relation until a specified time. PURGE is a UNIX command which can be invoked by a database administrator to delete all relations whose "expiration-dates" have passed. This should be done when space in a database is exhausted. (The database administrator can also use the DESTROY command to remove any relations from his database using the DESTROY command, regardless of who their owners are.)

Two comments should be noted at this time:

1) The system currently accepts the language specified as $QUEL_1$ in [HELD75b]; extension is in progress to accept $QUEL_n$.

2) The system currently does not accept views or protection statements. Although the algorithms have been specified [STON74c, STON75], they are not yet operational. For this reason no syntax for these statements is given in this section; however, the subject is discussed further in Section 4.0.

1.3. EQUEL

Although QUEL alone provides the flexibility for many data management requirements, there are applications which require a customized user interface in place of the QUEL language. For this as well as other reasons, it is often useful to have the flexibility of a general purpose programming language in addition to the database facilities of QUEL. To this end, a new language, EQUEL (Embedded QUEL), which consists of QUEL embedded in the general purpose programming language C, has been implemented.

In the design of EQUEL the following goals were set:

1) The new language must have the full capabilities of both C and QUEL.

2) The C program should have the capability for processing each tuple individually that satisfies the qualification of a RETRIEVE statement. (This is the "piped" return facility described in Data Language/ALPHA [CODD71].)

With these goals in mind, EQUEL was defined as follows:

1) Any C language statement is a valid EQUEL statement.

2) Any QUEL statement (or INGRES utility command) is a valid EQUEL statement as long as it is prefixed by two number signs (**##**).

3) C program variables may be used anywhere in QUEL statements except as command names. The declaration statements of C variables used in this manner must also be prefixed by double number signs.

4) RETRIEVE statements without a result relation have the form

```
    RETRIEVE (target-list)
              [WHERE qualification]
##{
C-block
##}
```

which results in the C-block being executed once for each qualifying tuple.

Two short examples illustrate EQUEL syntax.

Example. The following program implements a small front-end to INGRES which performs only one query. It reads in the name of an employee and prints out the employee's salary in a suitable format. It continues to do this as long as there are names to be read in. The functions READ and PRINT have the obvious meaning.

```
main ( )
{
## char EMPNAME[20];
## int SAL;

while (READ(EMPNAME))
        {
##          RANGE OF E IS EMP
##          RETRIEVE (SAL = E.SALARY)
##          WHERE E.NAME = EMPNAME
                ##{
                PRINT("The salary of", EMPNAME, "is", SAL);
                ##}
        }
}
```

In this example the C variable EMPNAME is used in the qualification of the QUEL statement, and for each qualifying tuple the C variable SAL is set to the appropriate value and then the PRINT statement is executed.

Example. Read in a relation name and two domain names. Then, for each of a collection of values which the second domain is to assume, do some processing on all values which the first domain assumes. (We assume the function PROCESS exists and has the obvious meaning.) A more elaborate version of this program could serve as a simple report generator.

```
main ( )
{
## int VALUE;
## char RELNAME[13], DOMNAME[13], DOMVAL[80];
## char DOMNAME2[13];

READ(RELNAME);
READ(DOMNAME);
READ(DOMNAME2);
##RANGE OF X IS RELNAME
while (READ(DOMVAL))
        {
##      RETRIEVE (VALUE = X.DOMNAME)
##          WHERE X.DOMNAME2 = DOMVAL
```

```
                              ##{
                              PROCESS(VALUE);
                              ##}
                  }
        }
```

Any RANGE declaration (in this case the one for X) is assumed by INGRES to hold until redefined. Hence only one RANGE statement is required, regardless of the number of times the RETRIEVE statement is executed. Note clearly that anything except the name of an INGRES command can be a C variable. In the above example, RELNAME is a C variable used as a relation name, while DOMNAME and DOMNAME2 are used as domain names.

1.4. Comments on QUEL and EQUEL

In this section a few remarks are made indicating differences between QUEL and EQUEL and selected other proposed data sublanguages and embedded data sublanguages.

QUEL borrows much from Data Language/ALPHA. The primary differences are:

1)   Arithmetic is provided in QUEL; Data Language/ALPHA suggests reliance on a host language for this feature.

2)   No quantifiers are present in QUEL. This results in a consistent semantic interpretation of the language in terms of functions on the crossproduct of the relations declared in the RANGE statements. Hence, QUEL is considered by its designers to be a language based on functions and not on a first order predicate calculus.

3)   More powerful aggregation capabilities are provided in QUEL.

The latest version of SEQUEL [ASTR76] has grown rather close to QUEL. The reader is directed to Example 1(b) of [ASTR76], which suggests a variant of the QUEL syntax. The main differences between QUEL and SEQUEL appear to be:

1)   SEQUEL allows statements with no tuple variables when possible using a block-oriented notation.

2)   The aggregation facilities of SEQUEL appear to be different from those defined in QUEL.

System R [ASTRA76] contains a proposed interface between SEQUEL and PL/1 or other host language. This interface differs substantially from EQUEL and contains explicit cursors and variable binding. Both notions are implicit in EQUEL. The interested reader should contrast the two different approaches to providing an embedded data sublanguage.

■■■■■ 2.0. THE INGRES PROCESS STRUCTURE

INGRES can be invoked in two ways. It can be directly invoked from UNIX by executing "INGRES database-name," or it can be invoked by executing a program written using the EQUEL precompiler. We discuss each in turn and then comment briefly on why two mechanisms exist. Before proceeding, however, a few details concerning UNIX must be introduced.

2.1. The UNIX Environment

Two points concerning UNIX are worthy of mention in this section.

1) The UNIX file system. UNIX supports a tree-structured file system similar to that of MULTICS. Each file is either a directory (containing references to descendant files in the file system) or a data file. Each file is divided physically into 5l2-byte blocks (pages). In response to a read request, UNIX moves one or more pages from secondary memory to UNIX main memory buffers and then returns to the user the actual byte string desired. If the same page is referenced again (by the same or another user) while it is still in a buffer, no disk I/O takes place.

   It is important to note that UNIX pages data from the file system into and out of system buffers using a "least recently used" replacement algorithm. In this way, the entire file system is managed as a large virtual store.

   The INGRES designers believe that a database system should appear as a user job to UNIX. (Otherwise, the system would operate on a nonstandard UNIX and become less portable.) Moreover, the designers believe that UNIX should manage the system buffers for the mix of jobs being run. Consequently, INGRES contains no facilities to do its own memory management.

2) The UNIX process structure. A process in UNIX is an address space (64K bytes or less on an 11/40, 128K bytes or less on an 11/45 or 11/70) which is associated with a user-id and is the unit of work scheduled by the UNIX scheduler. Processes may "fork" subprocesses; consequently, a parent-process can be the root of a process subtree. Furthermore, a process can request that UNIX execute a file in a descendant process. Such processes may communicate with each other via an interprocess communication facility called "pipes." A pipe is a one direction communication link which is written into by one process and read by a second one. UNIX maintains synchronization of pipes so no messages are lost. Each process has a "standard input device" and a "standard output device." These are usually the user's terminal, but may be directed by the user to be files, pipes to other processes, or other devices.

   Last, UNIX provides a facility for processes executing reentrant code to share procedure segments if possible. INGRES takes advantage of this facility, so the main memory space overhead of multiple concurrent users is only that required by data segments.

2.2. Invocation from UNIX

Issuing INGRES as a UNIX command causes the process structure shown in Figure 1.1 to be created. In this section the functions of the four processes will be indicated. The justification of this particular structure is given in Section 2.4.

Process 1 is an interactive terminal monitor which allows the user to formulate, print, edit, and execute collections of INGRES commands. It maintains a workspace with which the user interacts until he is satisfied with his interaction. The contents of this workspace are passed down pipe A as a string of ASCII characters when execution is desired. The set of commands accepted by the current terminal monitor is indicated in [ZOOK75].

As noted above, UNIX allows a user to alter the standard input and output devices for his processes when executing a command. As a result the invoker of INGRES may direct the terminal monitor to take input from a user file (in which case he runs a "canned" collection of interactions) and direct output to another device (such as the line printer) or a file.

Process 2 contains a lexical analyzer, a parser, query modification routines for integrity control (and, in the future, support of views and protection), and concurrency control. Because of size constraints, however, the integrity control routines are not in the currently released system. When process 2 finishes, it passes a string of tokens to process 3 through pipe B. Process 2 is discussed in Section 4.0.

Process 3 accepts this token string and contains execution routines for the commands RETRIEVE, REPLACE, DELETE, and APPEND. Any update is turned into a RETRIEVE command to isolate tuples to be changed. Revised

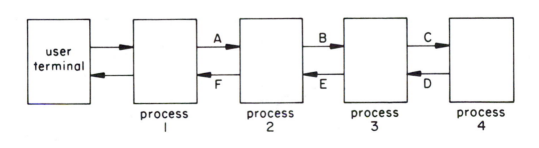

FIGURE 1.1. INGRES Process Structure

copies of modified tuples are spooled into a special file. This file is then processed by a "deferred update processor" in process 4, which is discussed in Section 6.0.

Basically, process 3 performs two functions for RETRIEVE commands.

1)   A multivariable query is decomposed into a sequence of interactions involving only a single variable.

2)   A one-variable query is executed by a one-variable query processor (OVQP). The OVQP in turn performs its function by making calls on the access methods. These two functions are discussed in Section 5.0; the access methods are indicated in Section 3.0.

All code to support utility commands (CREATE, DESTROY, INDEX, etc.) resides in process 4. Process 3 simply passes to process 4 any commands which process 4 will execute. Process 4 is organized as a collection of overlays which accomplish the various functions. Some of these functions are discussed in Section 6.0.

Error messages are passed back through pipes D, E, and F to process 1, which returns them to the user. If the command is a RETRIEVE with no result relation specified, process 3 returns qualifying tuples in a stylized format directly to the "standard output device" of process 1. Unless redirected, this is the user's terminal.

2.3. Invocation from EQUEL

We now turn to the operation of INGRES when invoked by code from the precompiler.

In order to implement EQUEL, a translator (precompiler) was written to convert an EQUEL program into a valid C program with QUEL statements converted to appropriate C code and calls to INGRES. The resulting C

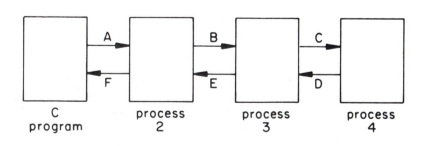

FIGURE 1.2. The Forked Process Structure

program is then compiled by the normal C compiler, producing an executable module. Moreover, when an EQUEL program is run, the executable module produced by the C compiler is used as the front end process in place of the interactive terminal monitor, as noted in Figure 1.2:

During execution of the front end program, database requests (QUEL statements in the EQUEL program) are passed through pipe A and processed by INGRES. Note that unparsed ASCII strings are passed to process 2; the rationale behind this decision is given in [ALLM76]. If tuples must be returned for tuple at a time processing, then they are returned through a special data pipe set up between process 3 and the C program. A condition code is also returned through pipe F to indicate success or the type of error encountered.

The functions performed by the EQUEL translator are discussed in [ALLM76].

2.4. Comments on the Process Structure

The process structure shown in Figures 1.1 and 1.2 is the fourth different process structure implemented. The following considerations suggested this final choice:

1)   Address space limitations. To run on an 11/40, the 64K address space limitation must be adhered to. Processes 2 and 3 are essentially their maximum size; hence they cannot be combined. The code in process 4 is in several overlays because of size constraints.

Were a large address space available, it is likely that processes 2, 3, and 4 would be combined into a single large process. However, the necessity of 3 "core" processes should not degrade performance substantially for the following reasons.

If one large process were resident in main memory, there would be no necessity of swapping code. However, were enough real memory available (~300K bytes) on a UNIX system to hold processes 2 and 3 and all overlays of process 4, no swapping of code would necessarily take place either. Of course, this option is possible only on an 11/70.

On the other hand, suppose one large process was paged into and out of main memory by an operating system and hardware which supported a virtual memory. It is felt that, under such conditions, page faults would generate I/O activity at approximately the same rate as the swapping/overlaying of processes in INGRES (assuming the same amount of real memory was available in both cases).

Consequently, the only sources of overhead that appear to result from multiple processes are the following:

a)   Reading or writing pipes require system calls which are considerably more expensive than subroutine calls (which could be used in a single-process system). There are at least eight such system calls needed to execute an INGRES command.

b) Extra code must be executed to format information for transmission on pipes. For example, one cannot pass a pointer to a data structure through a pipe; one must linearize and pass the whole structure.

2) Simple control flow. The grouping of functions into processes was motivated by the desire for simple control flow. Commands are passed only to the right; data and errors only to the left. Process 3 must issue commands to various overlays in process 4; therefore, it was placed to the left of process 4. Naturally, the parser must precede process 3.

Previous process structures had a more complex interconnection of processes. This made synchronization and debugging much harder.

The structure of process 4 stemmed from a desire to overlay little-used code in a single process. The alternative would have been to create additional processes 5, 6, and 7 (and their associated pipes), which would be quiescent most of the time. This would be required added space in UNIX main memory tables for no real advantage.

The processes are all synchronized (i.e., each waits for an error return from the next process to the right before continuing to accept input from the process to the left), simplifying the flow of control. Moreover, in many instances, the various processes *must* be synchronized. Future versions of INGRES may attempt to exploit parallelism where possible. The performance payoff of such parallelism is unknown at the present time.

3) Isolation of the front end process. For reasons of protection the C program which replaces the terminal monitor as a front end must run with a user-id different from that of INGRES. Otherwise it would tamper directly with data managed by INGRES. Hence, it must be either overlaid into a process or run in its own process. The latter was chosen for efficiency and convenience.

4) Rationale for two process structures. The interactive terminal monitor could have been written in EQUEL. Such a strategy would have avoided the existence of two process structures which differ only in the treatment of the data pipe. Since the terminal monitor was written prior to the existence of EQUEL, this option could not be followed. Rewriting the terminal monitor in EQUEL is not considered a high priority task given current resources. Moreover, an EQUEL monitor would be slightly slower because qualifying tuples would be returned to the calling program and then displayed rather than being displayed directly by process 3.

3.0. DATA STRUCTURES AND ACCESS METHODS

We begin this section with a discussion of the files that INGRES manipulates and their contents. Then we indicate the five possible storage structures (file formats) for relations. Finally we sketch the access method language used to interface uniformly to the available formats.

3.1. The INGRES File Structure

Figure 1.3 indicates the subtree of the UNIX file system that INGRES manipulates. The root of this subtree is a directory made for the UNIX user "INGRES." (When the INGRES system is initially installed such a user must be created. This user is known as the "superuser" because of the powers available to him. This subject is discussed further in [STON76b].) This root has six descendant directories. The AUX directory has descendant files containing tables that control the spawning of processes (shown in Figures 1.1 and 1.2) and an authorization list of users who are allowed to create databases. Only the INGRES superuser may modify these files (by using the UNIX editor). BIN and SOURCE are directories indicating descendant files of respectively object and source code. TMP has descendants which are temporary files for the workspaces used by the interactive terminal monitor. DOC is the root of a subtree with system documentation and the reference manual. Last, there is a directory entry in DATADIR for each database that exists in INGRES. These directories contain the database files in a given database as descendants.

These database files are of four types:

1) Administration file. This contains the user-id of the database administrator (DBA) and initialization information.

2) Catalog (system) relations. These relations have predefined names and are created for every database. They are owned by the DBA and constitute the system catalogs. They may be queried by a knowledgeable user issuing RETRIEVE statements; however, they may be updated only by the INGRES utility commands (or directly by the INGRES superuser in an emergency). (When protection statements are implemented the DBA will be able to selectively restrict RETRIEVE access to these relations if he wishes.) The form and content of some of these relations will be discussed presently.

3) DBA relations. These are relations owned by the DBA and are shared in that any user may access them. When protection is implemented the DBA can "authorize" shared use of these relations by inserting protection predicates (which will be in one of the system relations and may be unique for each user) and deauthorize use by removing such predicates. This mechanism is discussed in [STON76b].

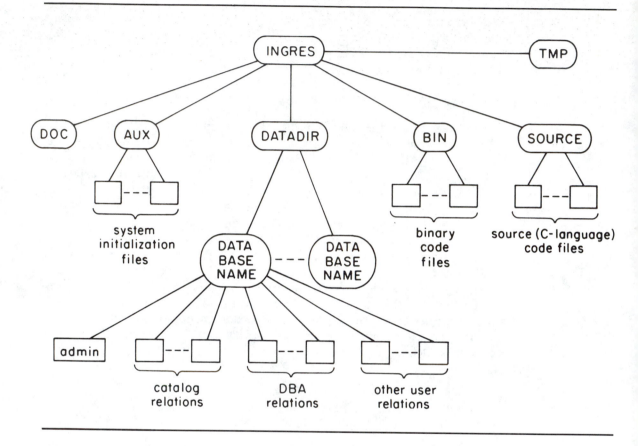

FIGURE 1.3. The INGRES Subtree

4) Other relations. These are relations created by other users (by RE-
    TRIEVE INTO W or CREATE) and are *not shared*.

    Three comments should be made at this time.

1) The DBA has the following powers not available to ordinary users: the
    ability to create shared relations and to specify access control for them;
    the ability to run PURGE; the ability to destroy any relations in his da-
    tabase (except the system catalogs).

    This system allows "one-level sharing" in that only the DBA has
    these powers, and he cannot delegate any of them to others (as in the
    file systems of most time sharing systems). This strategy was imple-
    mented for three reasons:

    a) The need for added generality was not perceived. Moreover, added generality would have created tedious problems (such as making revocation of access privileges nontrivial).

b) It seems appropriate to entrust the DBA with the duty (and power) to resolve the policy decision which must be made when space is exhausted and some relations must be destroyed or archived. This policy decision becomes much harder (or impossible) if a database is not in the control of one user.

c) Someone must be entrusted with the policy decision concerning which relations are physically stored and which are defined as "views." This "database design" problem is best centralized in a single DBA.

2) Except for the single administration file in each database, every file is treated as a relation. Storing system catalogs as relations has the following advantages:

a) Code is economized by sharing routines for accessing both catalog and data relations.

b) Since several storage structures are supported for accessing data relations quickly and flexibly under various interaction mixes, these same storage choices may be utilized to enhance access to catalog information.

c) The ability to execute QUEL statements to examine (and patch) system relations where necessary has greatly aided system debugging.

3) Each relation is stored in a separate file, i.e., no attempt is made to "cluster" tuples from *different* relations which may be accessed together on the same or on a nearby page.

Note clearly that this clustering is analogous to DBTG systems which allow a record type to be accessed via a set type which associates records of that record type with a record of a different record type. Current DBTG implementations usually attempt to physically cluster these associated records.

Note also that clustering tuples from one relation in a given file has obvious performance implications. The clustering techniques of this nature that INGRES supports are indicated in Section 3.3.

The decision not to cluster tuples from different relations is based on the following reasoning.

a) UNIX has a small (512-byte) page size. Hence it is expected that the number of tuples which can be grouped on the same page is small. Moreover, logically adjacent pages in a UNIX file are *not necessarily* physically adjacent. Hence clustering tuples on "nearby" pages has no meaning in UNIX; the next logical page in a file may be further away (in terms of disk arm motion) than a page in a different file. In keeping with the design decision of *not* modifying UNIX, these considerations were incorporated in the design decision not to support clustering.

b)   The access methods would be more complicated if clustering were supported.

c)   Clustering of tuples only makes sense if associated tuples can be linked together using "sets" [CODA71], "links" [TSIC75], or some other scheme for identifying clusters. Incorporating these access paths into the decomposition scheme would have greatly increased its complexity.

It should be noted that the designers of System R have reached a different conclusion concerning clustering [ASTR76].

3.2. System Catalogs

We now turn to a discussion of the system catalogs. We discuss two relations in detail and indicate briefly the contents of the others.

The RELATION relation contains one tuple for every relation in the database (including all the systems relations). The domains of this relation are:

RELID
   the name of the relation.

OWNER
   the UNIX user-id of the relation owner; when appended to relid it produces a unique file name for storing the relation.

SPEC
   indicates one of five possible storage schemes or else a special code indicating a virtual relation (or "view").

INDEXD
   flag set if secondary index exists for this relation. (This flag and the following two are present to improve performance by avoiding catalog lookups when possible during query modification and one variable query processing.)

PROTECT
   flag set if this relation has protection predicates.

INTEG
   flag set if there are integrity constraints.

SAVE
   scheduled lifetime of relation.

TUPLES
   number of tuples in relation (kept up to date by the routine "closer" discussed in the next section).

ATTS
   number of domains in relation.

WIDTH
  width (in bytes) of a tuple.

PRIM
  number of primary file pages for this relation.

The ATTRIBUTE catalog contains information relating to individual domains of relations. Tuples of the ATTRIBUTE catalog contain the following items for each domain of every relation in the database:

RELID
  name of relation in which attribute appears.

OWNER
  relation owner.

DOMAIN-NAME
  domain name.

DOMAIN-NO
  domain number (position) in relation. In processing interactions, INGRES uses this number to reference this domain.

OFFSET
  offset in bytes from beginning of tuple to beginning of domain.

TYPE
  data type of domain (integer, floating point, or character string).

LENGTH
  length (in bytes) of domain.

KEYNO
  if this domain is part of a key, then KEYNO indicates the ordering of this domain within the key.

These two catalogs together provide information about the structure and content of each relation in the database. No doubt items will continue to be added or deleted as the system undergoes further development. The first planned extensions are the minimum and maximum values assumed by domains. These will be used by a more sophisticated decomposition scheme being developed, which is discussed briefly in Section 5.0 and, in detail, in [WONG76]. The representation of the catalogs as relations has allowed this restructuring to occur very easily.

Several other system relations exist which provide auxiliary information about relations. The INDEX catalog contains a tuple for every secondary index in the database. Since secondary indices are themselves relations, they are independently cataloged in the RELATION and ATTRIBUTE relations. However, the INDEX catalog provides the association between a primary relation and its secondary indices and records which domains of the primary relation are in the index.

The PROTECTION and INTEGRITY catalogs contain respectively the protection and integrity predicates for each relation in the database. These predicates are stored in a partially processed form as character strings. (This mechanism exists for INTEGRITY and will be implemented in the same way for PROTECTION.) The VIEW catalog will contain for each virtual relation, a partially processed QUEL-like description of the view in terms of existing relations. The use of these last three catalogs is described in Section 4.0. The existence of any of this auxiliary information for a given relation is signaled by the appropriate flag(s) in the RELATION catalog.

Another set of system relations consists of those used by the graphics subsystem to catalog and process maps, which (like everything else) are stored as relations in the database. This topic has been discussed separately in [GO75].

3.3. Storage Structures Available

We will now describe the five storage structures currently available in INGRES. Four of the schemes are keyed, i.e., the storage location of a tuple within the file is a function of the value of the tuple's key domains. They are termed "hashed," "ISAM," "compressed hash," and "compressed ISAM." For all four structures the key may be any ordered collection of domains. These schemes allow rapid access to specific portions of a relation when key values are supplied. The remaining nonkeyed scheme (a "heap") stores tuples in the file independently of their values and provides a low overhead storage structure, especially attractive in situations requiring a complete scan of the relation.

The nonkeyed storage structure in INGRES is a randomly ordered sequential file. Fixed length tuples are simply placed sequentially in the file in the order supplied. New tuples added to the relation are merely appended to the end of the file. The unique tuple identifier for each tuple is its byte-offset within the file. This mode is intended mainly for

1) very small relations, for which the overhead of other schemes is unwarranted;

2) transitional storage of data being moved into or out of the system by COPY;

3) certain temporary relations created as intermediate results during query processing.

In the remaining four schemes the key-value of a tuple determines the page of the file on which the tuple will be placed. The schemes share a common "page-structure" for managing tuples on file pages, as shown in Figure 1.4.

A tuple must fit entirely on a single page. Its unique tuple identifier (TID) consists of a page number (the ordering of its page in the UNIX file) plus a line number. The line number is an index into a line table, which grows upward from the bottom of the page, and whose entries contain pointers to the tuples on the page. In this way the physical arrangement of tuples on a page can be reorganized without affecting TIDs.

Initially the file contains all its tuples on a number of primary pages. If the relation grows and these pages fill, overflow pages are allocated and chained by pointers to the primary pages with which they are associated. A schema for page layout is shown in Figure 1.4. Within a chained group of pages no special ordering of tuples is maintained. Thus in a keyed access which locates a particular primary page, tuples matching the key may actually appear on any page in the chain.

As discussed in [HELD75c], two modes of key-to-address transformation are used: randomizing (or "hashing") and order preserving. In a "hash" file

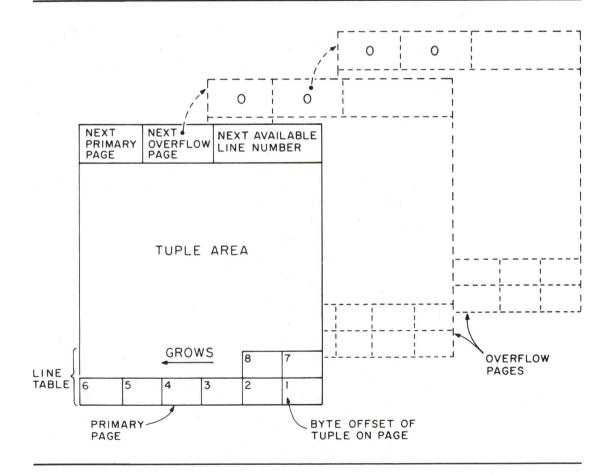

FIGURE 1.4. Page Layout for Keyed Storage Structures

tuples are distributed randomly throughout the primary pages of the file according to a hashing function on a key. This mode is well suited for situations in which access is to be conditioned on a specific key value.

As an order preserving mode, a scheme similar to IBM's ISAM [IBM66] is used. The relation is sorted to produce the ordering on a particular key. A multilevel directory is created which records the high key on each primary page. The directory, which is static, resides on several pages following the primary pages within the file itself. A primary page and its overflow pages are *not* maintained in sort order. This decision is discussed in Section 4.2. The "ISAM-like" mode is useful in cases where the key value is likely to be specified as falling within a range of values, since a near ordering of the keys is preserved. The index compression scheme discussed in [HELD75c] is currently under implementation.

In the above-mentioned keyed modes, fixed length tuples are stored. In addition, both schemes can be used in conjunction with data compression techniques [GOTT75] in cases where increased storage utilization outweighs the added cost of encoding and decoding data during access. These modes are known as "compressed hash" and "compressed ISAM."

The current compression scheme suppresses blanks and portions of a tuple which match the preceding tuple. This compression is applied to each page independently. Other schemes are being experimented with. Compression appears to be useful in storing variable length domains (which must be declared their maximum length). Padding is then removed duing compression by the access method. Compression may also be useful when storing secondary indices.

3.4. Access Methods Interface

The Access Methods Interface (AMI) handles all actual accessing of data from relations. The AMI language is implemented as a set of functions whose calling conventions are indicated below. A separate copy of these functions is loaded with processes 2, 3, and 4.

Each access method must do two things to support the following calls. First, it must provide some linear ordering of the tuples in a relation so that the concept of "next tuple" is well defined. Second, it must assign to each tuple a unique tuple-id (TID).

The nine implemented calls are as follows:

1) OPENR(descriptor, mode, relation-name)

Before a relation may be accessed it must be "opened." This function opens the UNIX file for the relation and fills in a "descriptor" with information about the relation from the RELATION and ATTRIBUTE catalogs. The descriptor (storage for which must be declared in the calling routine) is used in subsequent calls on AMI routines as an input parameter to indicate which relation is involved. Consequently, the AMI data accessing routines need not themselves check the system catalogs for the description of a relation. "Mode" specifies whether the relation is being opened for update or for retrieval only.

2) GET(descriptor, tid, limit-tid, tuple, next-flag)

This function retrieves into "tuple," a single tuple from the relation indicated by "descriptor." "Tid" and "limit-tid" are tuple identifiers. There are two modes of retrieval, "scan" and "direct." In "scan" mode GET is intended to be called successively to retrieve all tuples within a range of tuple-ids. An initial value of "tid" sets the low end of the range desired and "limit-tid" sets the high end. Each time GET is called with "next-flag" = TRUE, the tuple following "tid" is retrieved and its tuple-id is placed into "tid" in readiness for the next call. Reaching "limit-tid" is indicated by a special return code. The initial settings of "tid" and "limit-tid" are done by calling the FIND function. In "direct" mode ("next-flag" = FALSE), GET retrieves the tuple with tuple-id = "tid."

3) FIND(descriptor, key, tid, key-type)

When called with a negative "key-type," FIND returns in "tid" the lowest tuple-id on the lowest page which could possibly contain tuples matching the key supplied. Analogously, the highest tuple-id is returned when "key-type" is positive. The objective is to restrict the scan of a relation by eliminating tuples from consideration which are known from their placement not to satisfy a given qualification.

"Key-type" also indicates (through its absolute value) whether the key, if supplied, is an EXACTKEY or a RANGEKEY. Different criteria for matching are applied in each case. An EXACTKEY matches only those tuples containing exactly the value of the key supplied. A RANGEKEY represents the low (or high) end of a range of possible key values and thus matches any tuple with a key value greater than or equal to (or less than or equal to) the key supplied. Note that only with an order preserving storage structure can a RANGEKEY be used to successfully restrict a scan.

In cases where the storage structure of the relation is incompatible with the "key-type," the "tid" returned will be as if no key were supplied (that is, the lowest or highest tuple in the relation). Calls to FIND invariably occur in pairs, to obtain the two tuple-ids which establish the low and high ends of the scan done in subsequent calls to GET.

Two functions are available for determining the access characteristics of the storage structure of a primary data relation or secondary index, respectively.

4) PARAMD(descriptor, access-characteristics-structure)

5) PARAMI(index-descriptor, access-characteristics-structure)

The "access-characteristic-structure" is filled in with information regarding the type of key which may be utilized to restrict the scan of a given relation. It indicates whether exact key values or ranges of key values can be used, and whether a partially specified key may be used. This determines the "key-type" used in a subsequent call to FIND. The ordering of domains in the key is also indicated. These two functions allow the access optimization routines to be coded independently of the specific storage structures currently implemented.

Other AMI functions provide a facility for updating relations.

6)   INSERT(descriptor, tuple)

The tuple is added to the relation in its "proper" place according to its key value and the storage mode of the relation.

7)   REPLACE(descriptor, tid, new-tuple)

8)   DELETE(descriptor, tid)

The tuple indicated by "tid" is either replaced by new values or deleted from the relation altogether. The tuple-id of the affected tuple will have been obtained by a previous GET.

Finally, when all access to a relation is complete it must be closed:

9)   CLOSER(descriptor)

This closes the relation's UNIX file and rewrites the information in the descriptor back into the system catalogs if there has been any change.

3.5. Addition of New Access Methods

One of the goals of the AMI design was to insulate higher level software from the actual functioning of the access methods, thereby making it easier to add different ones. It is anticipated that users with special requirements will take advantage of this feature.

In order to add a new access method, one need only extend the AMI routines to handle the new case. If the new method uses the same page layout and TID scheme, only FIND, PARAMI, and PARAMD need to be extended. Otherwise new procedures to perform the mapping of TIDs to physical file locations must be supplied for use by GET, INSERT, REPLACE, and DELETE.

4.0. THE STRUCTURE OF PROCESS 2

Process 2 contains four main components:

1)   a lexical analyzer;

2)   a parser (written in YACC [JOHN74]);

3)   concurrency control routines;

4)   query modification routines to support protection, views, and integrity control (at present only partially implemented).

Since (1) and (2) are designed and implemented along fairly standard lines, only (3) and (4) will be discussed in detail. The output of the parsing process is a tree structured representation of the input query used as the internal form in subsequent processing. Furthermore, the qualification portion of the query has been converted to an equivalent Boolean expression in conjunctive normal form. In this form the query tree is then ready to undergo what has been termed "query modification."

4.1. Query Modification

Query modification includes adding integrity and protection predicates to the original query and changing references to virtual relations into references to the appropriate physical relations. At the present time only a simple integrity scheme has been implemented.

In [STON75] algorithms of several levels of complexity are presented for performing integrity control on updates. In the present system, only the simplest case, involving single-variable, aggregate free integrity assertions, has been implemented, as described in detail in [SCHO75].

Briefly, integrity assertions are entered in the form of QUEL, qualification clauses to be applied to interactions updating the relation over which the variable in the assertion ranges. A parse tree is created for the qualification and a representation of this tree is stored in the INTEGRITY catalog together with an indication of the relation and the specific domains involved. At query modification time, updates are checked for any possible integrity assertions on the affected domains. Relevant assertions are retrieved, rebuilt into tree form, and grafted onto the update tree so as to AND the assertions with the existing qualification of the interaction.

Algorithms for the support of views are also given in [STON75]. Basically a view is a virtual relation defined in terms of relations which physically exist. Only the view definition will be stored, and it will be indicated to INGRES by a DEFINE command. This command will have a syntax identical to that of a RETRIEVE statement. Thus legal views will be those relations which it is possible to materialize by a RETRIEVE statement. They will be allowed in INGRES to support EQUEL programs written for obsolete versions of the database and for user convenience.

Protection will be handled according to the algorithm described in [STON74c]. Like integrity control, this algorithm involves adding qualifications to the user's interaction. The details of the implementation (which is in progress) are given in [STON76b], which also includes a discussion of the mechanisms being implemented to physically protect INGRES object code. Last, [STON76b] distinguishes the INGRES protection scheme from the one based on views in [CHAM75] and indicates the rationale behind its use.

In the remainder of this section we give an example of query modification at work.

Suppose at a previous point in time all employees in the EMP relation were under 30 and had no manager recorded. If an EQUEL program had been written for this previous version of EMP which retrieved ages of employees coded into 5 bits, it would now fail for employees over 31.

If one wishes to use the above program without modification, then the following view must be used:

RANGE OF E IS EMP
DEFINE OLDEMP (E.NAME, E.DEPT., E.SALARY, E.AGE)
        WHERE E.AGE < 30

Suppose that all employees in the EMP relation must make more than 8000. This can be expressed by the integrity constraint:

RANGE of E IS EMP
INTEGRITY CONSTRAINT IS E.SALARY > 8000.

Last, suppose each person is only authorized to alter salaries of employees whom he manages. This is expressed as follows:

RANGE OF E IS EMP
PROTECT EMP FOR ALL (E.SALARY; E.NAME)
        WHERE E.MANAGER = *

The * is a surrogate for the logon name of the current UNIX user of INGRES. The semicolon separates updatable from nonupdatable (but visible) domains.

Suppose Smith through an EQUEL program or from the terminal monitor issues the following interaction:

RANGE OF L IS OLDEMP
REPLACE L(SALARY = .9*SALARY)
        WHERE L.NAME = "Brown"

This is an update on a view. Hence, the view algorithm of [STON75] will first be applied to yield:

RANGE OF E IS EMP
REPLACE E(SALARY = .9*E.SALARY)
        WHERE E.NAME = "Brown"
        AND E.AGE < 30

Note Brown is only in OLDEMP if he is under 30. Now the integrity algorithm in [STON75] must be applied to ensure that Brown's salary is not being cut to as little as 8000. This involves modifying the interaction to:

RANGE OF E IS EMP
REPLACE E(SALARY = .9*E.SALARY)
        WHERE E.NAME = "Brown"
        AND E.AGE < 30
        AND .9*E.SALARY > 8000

Since .9*E.SALARY will be Brown's salary after the update, the added qualification ensures this will be more than 8000.

Last, the protection algorithm of [STON76b] is applied to yield:

```
RANGE OF E IS EMP
REPLACE E(SALARY = .9*E.SALARY)
        WHERE  E.NAME = "Brown"
        AND E.AGE < 30
        AND .9*E.SALARY > 8000
        AND E.MANAGER = "Smith"
```

Notice that in all three cases more qualification is ANDed onto the user's interaction. The view algorithm must in addition change tuple variables.

In all cases the qualification is obtained from (or is an easy modification of) predicates stored in the VIEW, INTEGRITY, and PROTECTION relations. The tree representation of the interaction is simply modified to AND these qualifications (which are all stored in parsed forms).

It should be clearly noted that only one-variable, aggregate free integrity assertions are currently supported. Moreover, even this feature is not in the released version of INGRES. The code for both concurrency control and integrity control will not fit into process 2 without exceeding 64K words. The decision was made to release a system with concurrency control.

The INGRES designers are currently adding a fifth process (process 2.5) to hold concurrency and query modification routines. On PDP 11/45s and 11/70s that have a 128K address space this process will not be required.

4.2. Concurrency Control

In any multiuser system provisions must be included to ensure that multiple concurrent updates are executed in a manner such that some level of data integrity can be guaranteed. The following two updates illustrate the problem.

```
        RANGE OF E IS EMP
U1      REPLACE E (DEPT = "toy")
            WHERE  E.DEPT = "candy"

        RANGE OF F IS EMP
U2      REPLACE F(DEPT = "candy")
            WHERE F. DEPT = "toy"
```

If U1 and U2 are executed concurrently with no controls, some employees may end up in each department and the particular result may not be repeatable if the database is backed up and the interactions re-executed.

The control which must be provided is to guarantee that some database operation is "atomic" (occurs in such a fashion that it *appears* instantaneous and before or after any other database operation). This atomic unit will be called a "transaction."

In INGRES there are five basic choices available for defining a transaction:

1) something smaller than one INGRES command;
2) one INGRES command;
3) a collection of INGRES commands with no intervening C code;
4) a collection of INGRES commands with C code but no system calls;
5) an arbitrary EQUEL program.

If option 1 is chosen, INGRES could not guarantee that two concurrently executing update commands would give the same result if they were executed sequentially (in either order) in one collection of INGRES processes. In fact, the outcome could fail to be repeatable, as noted in the example above. The situation is clearly undesirable.

Option 3 is, in the opinion of the INGRES designers, impossible to support. The following transaction could be declared in an EQUEL program.

> BEGIN TRANSACTON
>> first QUEL update
>> system calls to create and destroy files
>> system calls to fork a second collection of INGRES processes to which commands are passed
>> system calls to read from a terminal
>> system calls to read from a tape
>> second QUEL update (whose form depends on previous two system calls)
> END TRANSACTION

Suppose T1 is the above transaction and runs concurrently with a transaction T2 involving commands of the same form. The second update of each transaction may well conflict with the first update of the other. Note that there is no way to tell apriori that T1 and T2 conflict, since the form of the second update is not known in advance. Hence, a deadlock situation can arise which can only be resolved by aborting one transaction (an undesirable policy in the eyes of the INGRES designers) or attempting to back out one transaction. The overhead of backing out through the intermediate system calls appears prohibitive (if it is possible at all).

Restricting a transaction to have no system calls (and hence no I/O) cripples the power of a transaction in order to make deadlock resolution possible. This was judged undesirable.

For example, the following transaction requires such system calls:

BEGIN TRANSACTON
    QUEL RETRIEVE to find all flights on a particular day from San
        Francisco to Los Angeles with space available
    Display flights and times to user
    Wait for user to indicate desired flight
    QUEL REPLACE to reserve a seat on the flight of the user's choice
END TRANSACTION

If the above set of commands is not a transaction, then space on a flight may not be available when the REPLACE is executed even though it was when the RETRIEVE occurred.

Since it appears impossible to support multi-QUEL statement transactions (except in a crippled form), the INGRES designers have chosen Option 2, one QUEL statement, as a transaction.

Option 3 can be handled by a straightforward extension of the algorithms to follow and will be implemented if there is sufficient user demand for it. This option can support "triggers" [ASTR76] and may prove useful.

Supporting Option 4 would considerably increase system complexity for what is perceived to be a small generalization. Moreover, it would be difficult to enforce in the EQUEL translator unless the translator parsed the entire C language.

The implementation of 2 or 3 can be achieved by physical locks on data items, pages, tuples, domains, relations, etc. [GRAY75] or by predicate locks [STON74b]. The current implementation is by relatively crude physical locks (on domains of a relation) and avoids deadlock by not allowing an interaction to proceed to process 3 until it can lock all required resources. Because of a problem with the current design of the REPLACE access method call, all domains of a relation must currently be locked (i.e., a whole relation is locked) to perform an update. This situation will soon be rectified.

The choice of avoiding deadlock rather than detecting and resolving it is made primarily for implementation simplicity.

The choice of a crude locking unit reflects our environment where main memory storage for a large lock table is not available. Our current implementation uses a LOCK relation into which a tuple for each lock requested is inserted. This entire relation is physically locked and then interrogated for conflicting locks. If none exist, all needed locks are inserted. If a conflict exists, the concurrency processor "sleeps" for a fixed interval and then tries again. The necessity to lock the entire relation and to sleep for a fixed interval results from the absence of semaphores (or an equivalent mechanism) in UNIX. Because concurrency control can have high overhead as currently implemented, it can be turned off.

The INGRES designers are considering writing a device driver (a clean extension to UNIX routinely written for new devices) to alleviate the lack of semaphores. This driver would simply maintain core tables to implement desired synchronization and physical locking in UNIX.

The locks are held by the concurrency processor until a termination message is received on pipe E. Only then does it delete its locks.

In the future we plan to experimentally implement a crude (and thereby low CPU overhead) version of the predicate locking scheme described in [STON74b]. Such an approach may provide considerable concurrency at an acceptable overhead in lock table space and CPU time, although such a statement is highly speculative.

To conclude this section, we briefly indicate the reasoning behind not sorting a page and its overflow pages in the "ISAM-like" access method. This topic is also discussed in [HELD78].

The proposed device driver for locking in UNIX must at least ensure that read-modify-write of a single UNIX page is an atomic operation. Otherwise, INGRES would still be required to lock the whole LOCK relation to insert locks. Moreover, any proposed predicate locking scheme could not function without such an atomic operation. If the lock unit is a UNIX page, then INGRES can insert and delete a tuple from a relation by holding only one lock at a time if a primary page and its overflow page are unordered. However, maintenance of the sort order of these pages may require the access method to lock more than one page when it inserts a tuple. Clearly deadlock may be possible given concurrent updates, and the size of the lock table in the device driver is not predictable. To avoid both problems these pages remain unsorted.

5.0. PROCESS 3

As noted in Section 2.0, this process performs the following two functions, which will be discussed in turn:

1) Decomposition of queries involving more than one variable into sequences of one-variable queries. Partial results are accumulated until the entire query is evaluated. This program is called DECOMP. It also turns any updates into the appropriate queries to isolate qualifying tuples and spools modification into a special file for deferred update.

2) Processing of single-variable queries. The program is called the one-variable query processor (OVQP).

5.1. DECOMP

Because INGRES allows interactions that are defined on the crossproduct of perhaps several relations, efficient execution of this step is of crucial importance in searching as small a portion of the appropriate crossproduct space as possible. DECOMP uses three techniques in processing interactions. We describe each technique, and then give the actual algorithm implemented followed by an example which illustrates all features. Finally, we indicate the role of a more sophisticated decomposition scheme under design.

1) Tuple substitution. The basic technique used by DECOMP to reduce a query to fewer variables is tuple substitution. One variable (out of possibly many) in the query is selected for substitution. The AMI language is used to scan the relation associated with the variable one tuple at a time. For each tuple the values of domains in that relation are substituted into the query. In the resulting modified query, all previous references to the substituted variable have now been replaced by values (constants) and the query has thus been reduced to one less variable. Decomposition is repeated (recursively) on the modified query until only one variable remains, at which point the OVQP is called to continue processing.

2) One-variable detachment. If the qualification Q of the query is of the form

$$Q1 \ (V1) \ AND \ Q1(V1, \ldots, Vn)$$

for some tuple variable V1, the following two steps can be executed:

(a) Issue the query

RETRIEVE INTO W (TL[Vl])
WHERE Q1[V1]

Here TL[V1] are those domains required in the remainder of the query. Note that this is a one-variable query and may be passed immediately to OVQP.

(b) Replace Rl, the relation over which Vl ranges, by W in the range declaration and delete Q1[V1] from Q.

The query formed in step (a) is called a "one-variable, detachable subquery," and the technique for forming and executing it is called One-Variable Detachment (OVD). This step has the effect of reducing the size of the relation over which V1 ranges by restriction and projection. Hence it may reduce the complexity of the processing to follow.

Moreover, the opportunity exists in the process of creating new relations through OVD, to choose storage structures, and particularly keys, which will prove helpful in further processing.

3) Reformatting. When a tuple variable is selected for substitutions, a large number of queries, each with one less variable, will be executed. If OVD is a possible operation after the substitution for some remaining variable V1, then the relation over which V1 ranges, R1, can be reformatted to have domains used in Q1(V1) as a key. This will expedite OVD each time it is executed during tuple substitution.

We can now state the complete decomposition algorithm. After doing so, we illustrate all steps with examples.

Step 1. If the number of variables in the query is 0 or 1, call OVQP and then return; else go on to step 2.

Step 2. Find all variables, [V1, . . ., Vn], for which the query contains a one-variable clause. Perform OVD to create new ranges for each of these variables. The new relation for each variable V1 is stored as a hash file with key K, chosen as follows:

> 2.1. For each j select from the remaining multivariate clauses in the query the collection Cij which have the form Vi.di = Vj.dj where di and dj are domains in Vi and Vj.

> 2.2. Form the key Ki to be the concatenation of domains di1, di2, . . . of Vi appearing in clauses of Cij.

> 2.3. If more than one j exists for which Cij is nonempty, one Cij is chosen arbitrarily for forming the key. If Cij is empty of all j, the relation is stored as an unsorted table.

Step 3. Choose the variable Vs with the smallest number of tuples as the next one for which to perform tuple substitution.

Step 4. For each tuple variable Vj for which Cjs is nonnull, reformat if necessary the structure of the relation Rj over which it ranges so that the key of Rj is the concatenation of domains dj1, . . . appearing in Cjs. This ensures that when the clauses in Cjs become one-variable after substituting for Vs, subsequent calls to OVQP to restrict further the range of Vj will be done as efficiently as possible.

Step 5. Iterate the following steps over all tuples in the range of the variable selected in step 3 and then return.

> 5.1. Substitute values from the tuple into the query.

> 5.2. Invoke decomposition recursively on a copy of the resulting query which now has been reduced by one variable.

> 5.3. Merge the results from 5.2 with those of previous iterations.

We use the following query to illustrate the algorithm:

> RANGE OF E, M IS EMP
> RANGE OF D IS DEPT
> RETRIEVE (E.NAME)
>   WHERE E.SALARY > M.SALARY
>   AND E. MANAGER = M.NAME
>   AND E. DEPT = D.DEPT
>   AND D.FLOOR# = 1
>   AND E.AGE > 40

This request is for employees over 40 on the first floor who earn more than their manager.

LEVEL 1

Step 1. Query is not one variable.

Step 2. Issue the two queries:

> RANGE OF D IS DEPT
> RETRIEVE INTO T1(D.DEPT)
>> WHERE D.FLOOR# = 1   (1)

> RANGE OF E IS EMP
> RETRIEVE INTO T2(E.NAME, E.SALARY, E.MANAGER, E.DEPT)
>> WHERE E.AGE > 40   (2)

T1 is stored hashed on DEPT; however, the algorithm must choose arbitrarily between hashing T2 on MANAGER or DEPT. Suppose it chooses MANAGER. The original query now becomes:

> RANGE OF D IS T1
> RANGE OF E IS T2
> RANGE OF M IS EMP
> RETRIEVE (E.NAME)
>> WHERE E.SALARY > M.SALARY
>> AND E.MANAGER = M.NAME
>> AND E.DEPT = D.DEPT

Step 3. Suppose T1 has smallest cardinality. Hence D is chosen for substitution.

Step 4. Reformat T2 to be hashed on DEPT; the guess chosen in step 2 was a poor one.

Step 5. Iterate for each tuple in T1 and then quit:

> 5.1. Substitute value for D.DEPT yielding

>> RANGE OF E IS T1
>> RANGE OF M IS EMP
>> RETRIEVE (E.NAME)
>>> WHERE E.SALARY > M.SALARY
>>> AND E.MANAGER = M.NAME
>>> AND E. DEPT = value

> 5.2. Start at step 1 with the above query as input (Level 2 below).

> 5.3. Cumulatively merge results as they are obtained.

LEVEL 2

Step 1. Query is not one variable.

Step 2. Issue the query

> RANGE OF E IS T2
> RETRIEVE INTO T3 (E.NAME, E.SALARY, E.NAME)
>> WHERE E.DEPT = value   (3)

T3 is constructed hashed on MANAGER. T2 in step 4 in Level 1 above is reformatted so that this query (which will be issued once for each tuple in T1) will be
done efficiently by OVQP. Hopefully the cost of reformatting is small compared to
the savings at this step. What remains is

RANGE OF E IS T3
RANGE OF M IS EMP
RETRIEVE (E.NAME)
    WHERE E.SALARY > M.SALARY
    AND E.MANAGER = M.NAME

Step 3. T3 has less tuples than EMP; therefore choose T3.

Step 4. [unnecessary]

Step 5. Iterate for each tuple in T3 and then return to previous level:

    5.1. Substitute values for E.NAME, E.SALARY, and E.MANAGER, yielding:

        RANGE OF M IS EMP
        RETRIEVE (VALUE 1)
            WHERE Value2 > M.SALARY
            AND Value3 = M.NAME   (4)

    5.2. Start at step 2 with this query as input (Level 3 below).

    5.3. Cumulatively merge results as obtained.

LEVEL 3

Step 1. Query has one variable; invoke OVQP and then return to previous level.

The algorithm thus decomposes the original query into the four prototype,
one-variable queries labeled (1)-(4), some of which are executed repetitively with
different constant values and with results merged appropriately. Queries (1) and
(2) are executed once, query (3) once for each tuple in T1 , and query (4) the
number of times equal to the number of tuples in T1 times the number of tuples in
T3.

    The following comments on the algorithm are appropriate.

  1)   OVD is almost always assured of speeding processing. Not only is it possi-
      ble to choose the storage structure of a temporary relation wisely, but also
      the cardinality of this relation may be much less than the one it replaces as
      the range for a tuple variable. It only fails if little or no reduction takes
      place and reformatting is unproductive.

          It should be noted that a temporary relation is created rather than a
      list of qualifying tuple-id's. The basic tradeoff is that OVD must copy quali-
      fying tuples but can remove duplicates created during the projection. Stor-
      ing tuple-id's avoids the copy operation at the expense of reaccessing quali-
      fying tuples and retaining duplicates. It is clear that cases exist where each
      strategy is superior. The INGRES designers have chosen OVD because it
      does not appear to offer worse performance than the alternative, allows a

2)   Tuple substitution is done when necessary on the variable associated with the smallest number of tuples. This has the effect of reducing the number of eventual calls on OVQP.

3)   Reformatting is done (if necessary) with the knowledge that it will usually replace a collection of complete sequential scans of a relation by a collection of limited scans. This almost always reduces processing time.

4)   It is believed that this algorithm efficiently handles a large class of interactions. Moreover, the algorithm does not require excessive CPU overhead to perform. There are, however, cases where a more elaborate algorithm is indicated. The following comment applies to such cases.

5)   Suppose that we have two or more strategies ST*,ST1,. . . STn, each one being better than the previous one but also requiring a greater overhead. Suppose further that we begin an interaction on ST* and run it for an amount of time equal to a fraction of the estimated overhead of ST1. At the end of that time, by simply counting the number of tuples of the first substitution variable which have already been processed, we can get an estimate for the total processing time using ST*. If this is significantly greater than the overhead of ST1, then we switch to ST1. Otherwise we stay and complete processing the interaction using ST*. Obviously, the procedure can be repeated on ST1, to call ST2 if necessary, and so forth.

The algorithm detailed in this section may be thought of as ST*. A more sophisticated algorithm is currently under development [WONG76].

5.2. One-Variable Query Processor (OVQP)

This module is concerned solely with the efficient accessing of tuples from a single relation given a particular one-variable query. The initial portion of this program, known as STRATEGY, determines what key (if any) may be used profitably to access the relation, what value(s) of that key will be used in calls to the AMI routine FIND, and whether access may be accomplished directly through the AMI to the storage structure of the primary relation itself or if a secondary index on the relation should be used. If access is to be through a secondary index, then STRATEGY must choose which *one* of possibly many indices to use.

Tuples are then retrieved according to the access strategy selected and are processed by the SCAN portion of OVQP. These routines evaluate each tuple against the qualification part of the query, create target list values for qualifying tuples, and dispose of the target list appropriately.

Since SCAN is relatively straightforward, we discuss only the policy decisions made in STRATEGY.

First STRATEGY examines the qualification for clauses which specify the value of a domain, i.e., clauses of the form

> domain op constant
>
> or
>
> constant op domain

where "op" is one of the set {=, <, >, ≤, ≥}. Such clauses are termed "simple" clauses and are organized into a list. The constants in simple clauses will determine the key values input to FIND to limit the ensuing scan.

Obviously, a nonsimple clause may be equivalent to a simple one. For example, E.SALARY/2 = l0000 is equivalent to E.SALARY = 20000. However, recognizing and converting such clauses requires a general algebraic symbol manipulator. This issue has been avoided by ignoring all nonsimple clauses.

STRATEGY must select one of two accessing strategies:

1) issuing two AMI FIND commands on the primary relation followed by a sequential scan of the relation (using GET in "scan" mode) between the limits set, or

2) issuing two AMI FIND commands on some index relation followed by a sequential scan of the index between the limits set. For each tuple retrieved the "pointer" domain is obtained; this is simply the tuple-id of a tuple in the primary relation. This tuple is fetched (using GET in "direct" mode) and processed.

To make the choice, the access possibilities available must be determined. Keying information about the primary relation is obtained using the AMI function PARAMD. Names and indices are obtained from the INDEX catalog and keying information about indices is obtained with the function PARAMI.

Further, a compatibility between the available access possibilities and the specification of key values by simple clauses must be established. A hashed relation requires that a simple clause specify equality as the operator in order to be useful; for combined (multidomain) keys, all domains must be specified. ISAM structures, on the other hand, allow range specifications; additionally, a combined ISAM key requires only that the most significant domains be specified.

STRATEGY checks for such a compatibility according to the following priority order of access possibilities: (1) hashed primary relation, (2) hashed index, (3) ISAM primary relation, (4) ISAM index. The rationale for this ordering is related to the expected number of page accesses required to retrieve a tuple from the source relation to each case. In the following analysis the effect of overflow pages is ignored (on the assumption that the four access possibilities would be equally affected).

In case 1, the key value provided locates a desired source tuple in one access via calculation involving a hashing function. In case 2, the key value similarly locates an appropriate index relation tuple in one access, but an additional access is required to retrieve the proper primary relation tuple. For an ISAM-structured scheme, a directory must be examined. This lookup itself incurs at least one access but possibly more if the directory is multilevel. Then the tuple itself must be accessed. Thus case 3 requires at least two (but possibly more) total accesses. In case 4, the use of an index necessitates yet another access in the primary relation, making the total at least three.

To illustrate STRATEGY, we indicate what happens to queries (l)-(4) from Section 5.1.

Suppose EMP is an ISAM relation with a key of NAME, while DEPT is hashed on FLOOR#. Moreover a secondary index for AGE exists which is hashed on AGE, and one for SALARY exists which uses ISAM with a key of SALARY.

Query (1): One simple clause exists (D.FLOOR# = 2). Hence Strategy 1 is applied against the hashed primary relation.

Query (2): One simple clause exists (E.AGE>40). However, it is not usable to limit the scan on a hashed index. Hence a complete (unkeyed) scan of EMP is required. Were the index for AGE an ISAM relation, then Strategy 2 would be used on this index.

Query (3): One simple clause exists and T1 has been reformatted to allow Strategy 1 against the hashed primary relation.

Query (4): Two simple clauses exist (value2 > M.SALARY; value3 = M.NAME). Strategy 1 is available on the hashed primary relation, as is Strategy 2 for the ISAM index. The algorithm chooses Strategy 1.

6.0. UTILITIES IN PROCESS 4

6.1. Implementation of Utility Commands

We have indicated in Section 1 several database utilities available to users. These commands are organized into several overlay programs as noted previously. Bringing the required overlay into core as needed is done in a straightforward way.

Most of the utilities update or read the system relations using AMI calls. MODIFY contains a sort routine which puts tuples in collating sequence according to the concatenation of the desired keys (which need not be of the same data type). Pages are initially loaded to approximately 80 percent of capacity. The sort routine is a recursive N-way merge-sort where N is the maximum number of files process 4 can have open at once (currently eight). The index-building occurs in an obvious way. To convert to hash structures, MODIFY must specify the number of primary pages to be allocated. This parameter is used by the AMI in its hash scheme (which is a standard modulo division method).

It should be noted that a user who creates an empty hash relation using the CREATE command and then copies a large UNIX file into it using COPY creates a very inefficient structure. This is because a relatively small default number of primary pages will have been specified by CREATE, and overflow chains will be long. A better strategy is to COPY into an unsorted table so that MODIFY can subsequently make a good guess at the number of primary pages to allocate.

6.2. Deferred Update and Recovery

Any updates (APPEND, DELETE, REPLACE) are processed by writing the tuples to be added, changed, or modified into a temporary file. When process 3 finishes, it calls process 4 to actually perform the modifications requested and any updates to secondary indices which may be required as a final step in processing. Deferred update is done for four reasons.

1) Secondary index considerations. Suppose the following QUEL statement is executed:

> RANGE OF E IS EMP
> REPLACE E(SALARY = 1.1*E.SALARY)
>   WHERE E.SALARY > 20000

Suppose further that there is a secondary index on the salary domain and the primary relation is keyed on another domain.

   OVQP, in finding the employees who qualify for the raise, will use the secondary index. If one employee qualifies and his tuple is modified and the secondary index updated, then the scan of the secondary index will find his tuple a second time since it has been moved forward. (In fact, his tuple will be found an arbitrary number of times.) Either secondary indexes cannot be used to identify qualifying tuples when range qualifications are present (a rather unnatural restriction), or secondary indices must be updated in deferred mode.

2) Primary relation considerations. Suppose the QUEL statement

> RANGE OF E, M IS EMP
> REPLACE E(SALARY = .9*E.SALARY)
>   WHERE E.MGR = M.NAME
>   AND E.SALARY > M.SALARY

is executed for the following EMP relation:

NAME	SALARY	MANAGER
Smith	10K	Jones
Jones	8K	
Brown	9.5K	Smith

Logically Smith should get the pay cut and Brown should not. However, if Smith's tuple is updated before Brown is checked for the pay cut, Brown will qualify. This undesirable situation must be avoided by deferred update.

3) Functionality of updates. Suppose the following QUEL statement is executed:

> RANGE OF E, M IS EMP
> REPLACE E(SALARY = M.SALARY)

This update attempts to assign to each employee the salary of every other employee, i.e., a single data item is to be replaced by multiple values. Stated differently, the REPLACE statement does not specify a function. In certain cases, (such as a REPLACE involving only one tuple variable) functionality is guaranteed. However, in general the functionality of an update is data dependent. This nonfunctionality can only be checked if deferred update is performed.

To do so, the deferred update processor must check for duplicate TIDs in REPLACE calls (which requires sorting or hashing the update file). This potentially expensive operation does not exist in the current implementation, but will be optionally available in the future.

4) Recovery considerations. The deferred update file provides a log of updates to be made. Recovery is provided upon system crash by the RESTORE command. In this case, the deferred update routine is requested to destroy the temporary file if it has not yet started processing it. If it has begun processing, it reprocesses the entire update file in such a way that the effect is the same as if it were processed exactly once from start to finish.

Hence the update is "backed out" if deferred updating has not yet begun; otherwise it is processed to conclusion. The software is designed so the update file can be optionally spooled onto tape and recovered from tape. This added feature should soon be operational.

If a user from the terminal monitor (or a C program) wishes to stop a command he can issue a "break" character. In this case, all processes reset except the deferred update program, which recovers in the same manner as above.

All update commands do deferred update; however the INGRES utilities have not yet been modified to do likewise. When this has been done, INGRES will recover from all crashes which leave the disk intact. In the meantime, there can be disk-intact crashes which cannot be recovered in this manner (if they happen in such a way that the system catalogs are left inconsistent).

The INGRES "superuser" can checkpoint a database onto tape using the UNIX backup scheme. Since INGRES logs all interactions, a consistent system can always be obtained, albeit slowly, by restoring the last checkpoint and running the log of interactions (or the tape of deferred updates if it exists).

It should be noted that deferred update is a very expensive operation. One INGRES user has elected to have the updates performed directly in process 3, cognizant that he must avoid executing interactions which will run incorrectly. Like checks for functionality, direct update may be optionally available in the future. Of course, a different recovery scheme must be implemented.

7.0. CONCLUSION AND FUTURE EXTENSIONS

The system described herein is in use at about fifteen installations. It forms the basis of an accounting system, a system for managing student records, a geo-data system, a system for managing cable trouble reports and maintenance calls for a large telephone company, and assorted other smaller applications. These applications have been running for periods of up to nine months.

7.1. Performance

At this time no detailed performance measurements have been made, as the current version (labeled Version 5) has been operational for less than two months. We have instrumented the code and are in the process of collecting such measurements.

The sizes (in bytes) of the processes in INGRES are indicated below. Since the access methods are loaded with processes 2 and 3 and with many of the utilities, their contribution to the respective process sizes has been noted separately.

access methods (AM)	11K
terminal monitor	10K
EQUEL	30K + AM
process 2	45K + AM
process 3 (query processor)	45K + AM
utilities (8 overlays)	160K + AM

7.2. User Feedback

The feedback from internal and external users has been overwhelmingly positive. In this section we indicate features that have been suggested for future systems.

1) Improved performance. Earlier versions of INGRES were very slow; the current version should alleviate this problem.

2) Recursion. QUEL does not support recursion, which must be tediously programmed in C using the precompiler; recursion capability has been suggested as a desired extension.

3) Other language extensions. These include user defined functions (especially counters), multiple target lists for a single qualification statement, and if-then-else control structures in QUEL; these features may presently be programmed, but only very inefficiently, using the precompiler.

4) Report generator. PRINT is a very primitive report generator and the need for augmented facilities in this area is clear; it should be written in EQUEL.

5) Bulk copy. The COPY routine fails to handle easily all situations that arise.

7.3. Future Extensions

Noted throughout the paper are areas where system improvement is in progress, planned, or desired by users. Other areas of extension include:

- a multicomputer system version of INGRES to operate on distributed databases;
- further performance enhancements;
- a higher level user language including recursion and user defined functions;
- better data definition and integrity features;
- a database administrator advisor.

The database administrator advisor program would run at idle priority and issue queries against a statistics relation to be kept by INGRES. It could then offer advice to a DBA concerning the choice of access methods and the selection of indices. This topic is discussed further in [HELD75c].

ACKNOWLEDGEMENTS

The following persons have played active roles in the design and implementation of INGRES: Eric Allman, Rick Berman, Jim Ford, Angela Go, Nancy McDonald, Peter Rubinstein, Iris Schoenberg, Nick Whyte, Carol Williams, Karel Youssefi, and Bill Zook.

## CHAPTER TWO

Retrospection on a Database System

Michael Stonebraker

ABSTRACT

This paper describes the implementation history of the INGRES database system. It focuses on mistakes that were made in progress rather than on eventual corrections. Some attention is also given to the role of structured design in a database system implementation and to the problem of supporting nontrivial users. Lastly, miscellaneous impressions of UNIX, the PDP-11 and data models are given.

1.0. INTRODUCTION

This paper was written in response to several requests to know what really happened in the INGRES database management system project [STON76a] and why. To the extent that it contains practical wisdom for other implementation projects, it serves its purpose. To the extent that it is a self-righteous defense of the existing design, the author apologizes in advance.

It may be premature to write such a document, since INGRES has only been fully operational for three years and user experience is still somewhat limited. Hence, the ultimate jury, real users, has not yet made a full report. The reason for reporting now is that we have reached a turning point. Until now (late 1978), the goal was to make INGRES "really work," i.e., efficiently, reliably and without surprises (bugs) for users. There are now only marginal returns to pursuing that goal. Consequently, the project is taking new directions, which are discussed below.

This paper is organized as follows. In Section 2.0, we trace the history of the project through its various phases and highlight the more significant events that took place. Then, in Section 3.0, we discuss several lessons that we had to learn the hard way. Section 4.0 takes a critical look at the current

M. Stonebraker, *ACM Transactions on Database Systems*, vol. 5, no. 2, June 1980. Copyright 1980, Association for Computing Machinery, Inc.; reprinted by permission.

design of INGRES and discusses some of the mistakes. Next, Section 5.0 consists of an assortment of random comments. Lastly, Section 6.0 outlines the future plans of the project.

2.0. HISTORY

The project can be roughly decomposed into three periods:

1) the early times − 3/73-6/74;
2) the first implementation − 6/74-9/75;
3) make it really work − 9/75-present.

2.1. The Early Times

The project began in 1973 when Eugene Wong and I agreed to read and discuss literature relating to relational databases. From the beginning we were both enthusiastic about an implementation. It did not faze either one of us that we possessed no experience whatsoever in leading a nontrivial implementation effort. In fact, neither of us had ever written a sizable computer program.

Our first task was to find a suitable machine environment for an implementation. It became clear quickly that no machine to which we had access was appropriate for an interactive database system. Through various mechanisms (mainly engineered by Eugene Wong and Pravin Varaiya), we obtained about $90,000 for hardware. The liability that we obtained was a commitment to write a geo-data system for the Urban Economics Group led by Pravin Varaiya and Roland Artle.

Our major concerns in selecting hardware were in obtaining large (50 or 100 megabytes at the time) disks and a decent software environment. After studying the UNIX CACM paper [RITC74b], I was convinced that we should use UNIX and buy whatever hardware we could afford to make it run. We placed a hardware order in February of 1974 and had a system in September of the same year.

We decided to offer a seminar running from September 1973 to June 1974 in which a design would be pursued. Somewhat symbiotically the seminar split into two groups: One, led by Gene, would plan the user language; the other, led by me, would plan the support system. The language group converged quickly on the retrieval portion of the data sublanguage QUEL. It was loosely based on DSL/Alpha [CODD71] but had no notion of quantifiers.

As soon as UNIX was chosen, my group laid out the system catalogs (data dictionary) and the access method interface. Initially, we considered a nonrelational structure for the catalogs as that would make them somewhat more efficient. However, it quickly became clear that providing a specialized access facility for the system catalogs involved code duplications and would ruin the possibility of using QUEL to query the system catalogs. The latter feature would, in essence, provide a data dictionary system for free. Hence, the system catalogs became simply more relational data for the system to manage.

An idea from the very start had been to have several implementations of the access method interface. Each would have the same calling conventions for simplicity and would function interchangeably. We were committed to the relational principle that users see nothing of the underlying storage structure. Hence, no provisions were made to allow a user to access a lower level of the system (as is done in some other database systems).

During the winter of 1974 a lot of effort went into the tactics we would use for "solving" QUEL commands (query processing). The notion of tuple substitution [WONG76] as a strategy for decomposing QUEL commands into simpler command in QUEL itself was developed at this time. This notion of decomposition strongly influenced the resulting design. For example, having a level in the system that corresponded to the "one-variable query processor" occurred because decomposition required it.

In summary, the salient features of INGRES at the time were:

1) QUEL retrieval was defined;
2) an integrated data dictionary was proposed;
3) multiple implementations of the access methods were suggested;
4) a "pure" relational system was agreed on;
5) decomposition was developed.

This first period ended with the delivery of a PDP-11 in June 1974 which could be used on an interim basis for code development. Hence, we could begin implementing before our own machine arrived. The project was organized as a chief programmer team of four persons under the direction of Gerry Held. This same organizational structure remains today.

2.2. The First Implementation

We expected to exploit the natural parallelism which multiple UNIX processes allowed. Hence, decomposition would be a process to run in parallel with the one-variable query processor (OVQP). The utilities (e.g., to create relations, destroy them and modify their storage structure) would be several overlays but nobody was exactly sure where they would go. By this time, we had decided to take protection seriously and that a database administrator (DBA) was an appropriate concept. He or she would own all the physical UNIX files in which relations for a given database were stored. In addition, the INGRES object code would use the "set user id" facility of UNIX so that it would run on behalf of any user with an effective user id of the DBA. This was the only way we could see to guarantee that nobody (except the DBA) could touch a database except by executing INGRES. Any less restrictive scheme would allow other programs to tamper with the database, which we thought undesirable.

Because the terminal monitor allowed the user to directly edit files, we had to protect the rest of INGRES from it. Hence, it had to be a separate process. The notion of query modification for protection, integrity control and views was developed during this time. It would be implemented with the parser but no thought was given to the form of this module. During the summer of 1974, the process structure changed several times. Moreover, no one could coherently check any code because everyone needed the access methods as part of their code and they did not work yet.

About this time another version of QUEL was developed which included updates and more general aggregates. This version survives today except for the keyword syntax, which was changed in early 1975.

By the end of the summer, we had some access method code, some routines to access the data dictionary (to create and destroy relations for example), and a terminal monitor, along with pieces of DECOMP and OVQP. In September, the department arranged to invite Ken Thompson (the creator of UNIX in conjunction with Dennis Ritchie) to Berkeley for a two week visit. Ken was instrumental in getting UNIX to run on the INGRES machine and introduced us to YACC [JOHN74] as a parser generator.

In January of 1975, we invited Ted Codd to come to Berkeley in early March to see a demonstration of INGRES. The final two weeks before his visit everyone worked night and day so that we would have something to show him. What we demonstrated was a very "buggy" system with the following characteristics:

1) The access methods "sort of" worked. Retrieves worked on all five implementations of the access methods (heap, hash, compressed hash, index and compressed index). However, only heaps could be updated without fear of disaster.

2) Decomposition was implemented by brute force.

3) A primitive database load program existed but few other services.

4) All the messy interprocess problems had been ignored. For example, there was no way to reset INGRES so it would stop executing the current command and be ready to do something new. Instead, "reset" simply killed all the INGRES processes and returned the user to the operating system command language interpreter.

5) There were many bugs. For example, boolean operators sometimes worked incorrectly. The average function applied to a relation with no tuples produced an inappropriate response, etc.

At this point, it became clear that the punctuation-oriented syntax for QUEL was horrible and it was scrapped in favor of a keyword-oriented approach. The designers of SEQUEL [CHAM74b] saw this important point sooner than we did. This was the last significant change to the user language.

During this time, we spent a lot of time discussing the pros and cons of dynamic directory facilities (e.g., B-tree-like structures) and static directories (e.g., ISAM). The basic issue was whether the index levels in a keyed sequential access method were read-only or not. At the time we opted for static directories and wrote the paper "B-trees Reexamined" [HELD78]. This is one of the mistakes discussed in Section 4.0.

Lastly, it became clear that we needed a coupling to a host language. Moreover, C was the only possible candidate, since it alone allowed interprocess communication, a fact essential for INGRES operation. As a result, we began work on a preprocessor EQUEL [ALLM76], to allow convenient access to INGRES from C.

The end of this initial implementation period occurred when we acquired a user. Through Ken Thompson, to whom a tape of an early system had been sent, and through a group at Bell Labs in Holmdel, Mr. Dan Gielan of New York Telephone Company became interested in using our system. After a trial period using our machine, he obtained his own computer and set about tailoring INGRES to his environment and fixing its flaws (many bugs, bad performance, no concurrency control, no recovery, shaky physical protection, EQUEL barely usable). In a sense, he was duplicating much of the effort at Berkeley during the next year, and the two systems quickly and radically diverged.

Issues resolved during this period included:

1) QUEL syntax for updates was specified;

2) the final syntax and semantics of QUEL were defined;

3) protection was figured out;

4) EQUEL was designed;

5) concurrency control and recovery loomed on the horizon as big issues. Initial discussions on these subjects started.

2.3. Make It Really Work

The current phase of INGRES development began during the latter part of 1975. At this time, the system "more or less" worked. There were lots of bugs and it was increasingly difficult to get them out. The system had performance problems due to convoluted and inefficient code everywhere. The code was in bad shape; it had been constructed haphazardly by several people, not all of whom were still with the project. Each had his own coding style, way of naming variables, and library of common routines. In short, the system was unmaintainable.

The objective of the current phase was to make the system efficient, reliable, and MAINTAINABLE. At the time, we didn't realize that this amounted to a total rewrite. We began to operate with more so-called "controls." There was no more arbitrary tampering with the "current" copy of the code; rudimentary testing procedures were constructed, and rigid coding conventions were enforced. We began to operate more like a production software house and less like a free wheeling, unstructured operation.

During the current phase, concurrency control and recovery were seriously addressed. We took a long time to decide whether to take concurrency control seriously and write a sophisticated locking subsystem (such as the one in SYSTEM-R [GRAY76, GRAY78]) or to do a quick and dirty subsystem using either coarse physical locks (say on files or collections of files) or predicate locks [ESWA76]. We also gave considerable thought to the size of a transaction. Should it be larger than one QUEL statement? If so, the simple strategy of demanding all needed resources in advance and avoiding deadlock was not possible.

The transaction size was eventually decided largely based on simplicity. Once one QUEL statement was selected as the atomic operation for concurrency control and recovery, our hunch was that coarse physical locking would be best. This was later verified by simulation experiments [RIES77, RIES79].

Recovery code was postponed as long as possible because it involved major changes to the utilities. All QUEL statements went through a "deferred update" facility which made recovery from soft crashes (i.e., the disk remains intact) easy if a QUEL statement was being executed. The more difficult problem was to survive crashes while the utilities were running. Each utility performed its own manipulation of the system catalogs in addition to other functions. Leaving the system catalogs in a consistent state required being able to back up or run forward each command. The basic idea was to create an algorithm which would pass the system catalogs once (or at most twice), find all the inconsistencies regardless of what commands were running, and take appropriate action. Creating such a program required iron-clad protocols on how the utilities manipulated the system catalogs. Installing such protocols was a lot of work, most of it in the utilities, which everyone by this time regarded as boring code in enormous volume.

The parser had finally become so top heavy from patches that it was rewritten from scratch. Decomposition was improved and the system became progressively faster. In addition, the system was instrumented (no performance hooks were built in from the start). As a result we caught several serious performance botches. Elaborate tracing facilities were retrofitted to allow a decent debugging environment. In short, the entire system was rewritten.

During this time we also started to support a user community. There are currently some one hundred users − all requesting better documentation, more features and better performance. These became a serious time drain on the project.

Some of our early users appeared to be contemplating selling our software. We had taken no initial precautions to safeguard our rights to the code. It became necessary to prepare a license form and to pull everyone's lawyers into the act. This became a headache that could not easily be deflected, but which made technically supporting users look easy by comparison.

3.0. LESSONS

The following section discusses some of the lessons that have been learned from the INGRES project.

3.1. Goals

Our goals have expanded several times (always when we were in danger of achieving the previous collection). Thus we added features which were not thought about in the initial design (such as concurrency control and recovery) and began worrying about distributed databases (which were NEVER even talked about earlier). The effect of this goal expansion has been to force us to rewrite a lot of INGRES, in some cases more than once.

3.2. Structured Design

The current wave of structured programming enthusiasts suggests the following implementation plan. Starting with the overall problem, one successively refines it until one has a tree structure of subproblems. Each level in such a tree serves as a "virtual machine" and hides its internal details from higher level machines. We have encountered several problems in attempting to follow this seemingly sound advice. We discuss four of them.

1) It presumes that one knows what one is doing from the outset. There were many times when we were confused concerning how to proceed. In all cases we chose to do something as opposed to doing nothing, feeling that this was the most appropriate way to discover what we should have done. This philosophy has caused several virtual machines to be dead wrong. Whenever this happened, a lot of redesign was inevitable. One example is the access method interface. This level was designed before it was completely understood how optimization concerning restricting scans of relation would be handled. It turned out that the interface chosen initially was ultimately not what we needed.

2) We have had to contend with a 64K address space limitation. Initially we did not have a good understanding of how large various modules would be. On more than one occasion we have run out of space in a process, which has forced us into the unpleasant task of restructuring the code on space considerations alone. Moreover, since interprocess communication is not fast, we could not always structure code in the "natural" way because of performance problems.

3) There was a strong temptation not to think out all of the details in advance. Because the design leaders had many other responsibilities, we often operated in a mode of "plan the general strategy and rough out the attack." In the subsequent detailed design, flaws would often be uncovered which we had not thought of, and corrective action would have to be taken. Often, major redesigns were the result.

4)   It was sometimes necessary to violate the information hiding of the virtual machines for performance reasons. For example, there is a utility which loads indexed sequential (ISAM-like) files and builds the directory structure. It is not reasonable to have the utility create an empty file and then add records one at a time through the access method. This strategy would result in a directory structure with unacceptable performance because of bad balance. Rather, one must sort the records, then physically lay them out on the disk and then, as a final step, build the directory. Hence, the program which loads ISAM files must know the physical structure of the ISAM access method. When this structure changed (and it did several times), the ISAM loader had to be changed.

All these problems created a virtually constant rewrite/maintenance job of huge magnitude. In four years there have been between two and five incarnations of all pieces of the system. Roughly speaking, we rewrote the majority of the system each year since the project began. Only now is code beginning to have a longer lifetime.

Earlier, there was hesitation on the part of the implementors to document code because it might have a short lifetime. Hence, documentation has been almost nonexistent until recently.

3.3. Coding Conventions

The necessity of this task was a very important lesson to us. As mentioned earlier, the equivalent of one total rewrite resulted from our initial failure in this area. We found that pieces of code which had a nontrivial lifetime were unmaintainable except by the original writer. Also, every time we gave someone responsibility for a new module he or she would rewrite it according to his or her standards (allegedly to clean up the other person's bad habits). This process never converges and I feel that it is similar to the dog or wolf who stakes out his "turf" by urinating on each bush on its perimeter.

Only coding conventions stop this process.

3.4. User Support

There are lessons which we have learned about users in three areas.

Serious Users

There are a few serious users (5-10). All have been extremely bold and forward-looking people and have exercised our system extensively before committing to use it. All of these users first chose UNIX (which says something about their not being a random sample of users) and then obtained INGRES.

Most have made modifications to personalize INGRES to their needs, viewed us as a collection of goofy academicians and were pretty skeptical that our code was any good. All were very concerned about support, future enhancements and how much longer our research grants would last.

All have developed end user facilities using EQUEL and have given us a substantial wish list of features. The following is typical:

1) the system is too slow (especially for trivial interactions);

2) the system is too slow for very large databases (whatever this means);

3) protection, integrity constraints and concurrency control are missing (true for earlier versions);

4) the EQUEL interface is not particularly friendly;

5) the system should have partial string matching capabilities, a data type of "bit," and a macro facility. (The wish list of such features is almost unbounded.)

Surprisingly, nobody has ever complained about the crash recovery facilities. Also, a concurrency control scheme consisting of locking the whole database would be an acceptable alternative for most of our users.

The biggest problem that these users have faced is the problem of understanding some 500,000 bytes of source code, most of it free of documentation (other than comments in the code).

The merits of INGRES that most of these users claim rest on

1) Ease of use. The system is easy to use after a minor amount of training. The "startup" cost is much lower than for other systems.

2) The high level language allows applications to be constructed incredibly fast, as much as 10 times faster than originally anticipated.

This short coding cycle allowed at least one user to utilize a novel approach to application design. The conventional approach is to construct a specification of the application by interacting with the end user. Then, programmers go into their corner to implement the specifications. A long time later they emerge with a system and the users respond that it is not really what they wanted. Then, the rounds of retrofitting begin.

The novel approach was to do application specification and coding in parallel. In other words, the application designer interacted with end users to ascertain their needs and then coded what they wanted. In a few days he returned with a working prototype (which of course was not quite what they had in mind). Then the design cycle iterated. The important point is that end users were in the design loop and their needs were met in the design process. Only the ability to write database applications quickly and economically allowed this to happen.

Casual Users

There are about 90 more "casual" users. We hear less from these people. Most are universities who use the system in teaching and research applications. These users are less disgruntled with performance and unconcerned about support.

Performance Decisions

Users are not always able to make crucial performance decisions correctly. For example, the INGRES system catalogs are accessed very frequently and in a predictable way. There are clear instructions concerning how the system catalogs should be physically structured (they begin as heaps and should be hashed when their size becomes somewhat stable). Even so, some users fail to hash them appropriately. Of course, the system continues to run; it just gets slower and slower. Finally, we removed this particular decision from the users' domain entirely. It makes me a believer in automatic database design (e.g., [HAMM76b])!

4.0. FLAT OUT MISTAKES

This section will discuss what we believe to be the major mistakes in the current implementation.

4.1. Interpreted Code

The current prototype interprets QUEL statements even when these statements come from a host language program. An interpreter is reasonable when executing ad-hoc interactions. However, the EQUEL interface processes interactions from a host language program as if they were ad-hoc statements. Hence, parsing and finding an execution strategy are done at run time, interaction by interaction.

The problem is that most interactions from host languages are simple and are done repetitively. (For example, giving a 10 percent raise to a collection of employee names read in from a terminal amounts to a single parameterized update inside a WHILE statement.) The current prototype has a fixed overhead per interaction of about 400 msec. (400,000 instructions). Hence, throughput for simple statements is limited by this fixed overhead to about 2.5 interactions per second. Parsing at compile time would reduce this fixed overhead somewhat.

At least as serious is the fact that the interpreter consumes a lot of space. The "working set" for an EQUEL program is about 150K bytes plus the program. For systems with a limited amount of main memory this presents a terrible burden. A compiled EQUEL would take up much less space (at least for EQUEL programs with fewer than 10 interactions per program). Moreover, a compiled version of EQUEL would require less operating system processes, saving us some interprocess communication overhead. This issue is further discussed in Section 4.3.

The interpreter was built with the notion of ad-hoc interactions in mind. Only recently did we realize the importance of a programming language interface. Now we are slowly converting INGRES to be alternately compiled and interpreted. We were clearly naive in this respect.

4.2. Validity Checking

This mistake is related to the previous one. When an interaction is received from a terminal or an application program, it is parsed at run time. Moreover, (and at a very high cost) the system catalogs are interrogated to validate that the relation exists, that the domains exist, that the constants to which the domains are being compared are of the correct type or are converted correctly, etc. This costs perhaps 100 msec. of the 400 msec. fixed overhead, and no effort has been made to minimize its impact. This makes the "do nothing" overhead high and, from a performance viewpoint, is the really expensive component of interpretation.

4.3. Process Problems

The "do nothing" overhead is greatly enlarged by our problems with a 16 bit address space. The current system runs as 5 processes (and the experimental system at Berkeley as 6) and processing the "nothing" interaction requires that the flow of control go through 8 processes. This necessitates formatting 8 messages, calling the UNIX scheduler 8 times and invoking the interprocess message system (pipes) 8 times. This generates about 150-175 msec. of the 400 msec. of fixed overhead.

In addition, code cannot be shared between processes. Hence, the access methods must appear in every process. This causes wasted space and duplicated code. Moreover, some of the interprocess messages are the internal form of QUEL commands. As such, we require a routine to linearize a tree-structured object to pass through a pipe and the inverse of the routine to rebuild the tree in the recipient process. This is considerably more difficult than a procedure call passing as an argument a pointer to the tree. Again, the result is extra complexity, extra code and lower performance.

Besides this performance problem, the previous section noted that the process structure has changed several times because of space considerations. As a result, a considerable amount of energy has gone into designing new process structures, writing the code which correctly "spawns" the right run-time environment and handling user interrupts correctly.

In retrospect, we had no idea how serious the performance problems associated with being forced to run multiple processes would be. It would have been clearly advantageous to choose a 32-bit machine for development; however, there was no affordable candidate to be obtained at the time we started. Also, perhaps we should have relaxed the 64K address limitation once we obtained a PDP-11/70 (which has a 128K limitation). This would have cut the number of processes somewhat. However, many of our 100 users have 11/34s or 11/40s and we were reluctant to cut them off. Lastly, we could have opted for less complexity in the code. However, to effectively cut the number of processes and the resulting overhead, the system would have to be reduced by at least a factor of two. It is not clear that an interesting system could be written within such a constraint. The bottom line is that this has been an enormous problem, but one for which we see no obvious solution, other than to buy a PDP-11/780 and correct the situation now that a 32-bit machine is available which can run our existing code.

4.4. Access Methods

The decision was made very early that we were not going to write our own file system to get around UNIX performance (as SYSTEM-R elected to do for VM/370 [ASTR76]). Instead, we would simply build access methods on top of the existing file system.

The reasoning behind this decision was to avoid duplicating operating system functions. Also, exporting our code would have been more difficult if it contained its own file system. Lastly, we underestimated the severity of the performance degradation that the UNIX file system contributes to INGRES when it is processing large queries. This topic is further discussed in [HAWT79]. In retrospect, we probably should have written our own file system.

The other problem with the access methods is that they were designed under the supposition that INGRES would be I/O bound. Our initial assumption was that it would never take INGRES more than 30 msec. to process a 512-byte page. Since it takes UNIX about this long to fetch a page from the disk, INGRES would always be I/O bound for systems with a single disk controller (the usual case for PDP-11 environments). Although INGRES is sometimes I/O bound, there are significant cases where it is CPU bound [HAWT79].

The following three situations are bad mistakes when INGRES is CPU bound:

1) An entire 512-byte page is always searched even if one is looking only for one tuple (i.e., a hash bucket is a UNIX page).

2) A tuple may be moved in main memory one more time than is strictly necessary.

3) A whole tuple is manipulated rather than just desired fields.

Although we have corrected points 2 and 3, point 1 is fundamental to our design and is a mistake.

4.5. Static Directories

INGRES currently supports an indexing access method with a directory structure which is built at load time and never modified thereafter. The arguments in favor of such a structure are presented in [HELD78]. However, we
would implement a dynamic directory (as in B-trees) if the decision were
made again. Two considerations have influenced the change in our thinking.

The database administrator has the added burden of periodically re-
building a static directory structure. Also, he can achieve better performance
if he indicates to INGRES a good choice for how full to load data pages initially. In the previous section, we indicated that database administrators
often had trouble with performance decisions, and we now believe that they
should be relieved of all possible choices. Dynamic directories do not require
periodic maintenance.

The second fundamental problem with static directories is that buffer requirements are not predictable. In order to achieve good performance,
INGRES buffers file system pages in user space when advantageous. However, when overflow pages are present in a static directory structure, INGRES
should buffer all of them. Since, our address space is so limited, a fixed
buffer size is used and performance degrades severely when it is not large
enough to hold all overflow pages. On the other hand, dynamic directories
have known (and nearly constant) buffering requirements.

4.6. Decomposition

Although decomposition [WONG76] is an elegant way to process queries,
which is easy to implement and optimize, there is one important case which
it cannot handle. For a two-variable query involving an equi-join, it is sometimes best to sort both relations on the join field and then merge the results
to identify qualifying tuples [BLAS77]. Consequently, it would be desirable
for us to add this as a tactic to apply when appropriate. This would require
modifying the decomposition process to look for a special case (which is not
very hard) and in addition restructuring the INGRES process structure (since
query processing is in two UNIX processes and this would necessarily alter
the interface between them). Again, the address space issue rears its ugly
head!

4.7. Protection

It appears much cleaner to protect views as in [GRIF76] rather than base relations as in [STON74c, STON76b]. It appears that sheer dogma on my part
prevented us from correcting this.

4.8. Lawyers

I would be strongly tempted to put INGRES into the public domain and delete our interactions with all attorneys (ours and everyone else's). Whatever revenue the University of California derives from license fees may well not compensate for the extreme hassle which licensing has caused us. Great insecurity and our egos drove us to force others to recognize our legal position. This was probably a big mistake.

4.9. Usability

Insufficient attention has been paid to the INGRES user interface. We have learned much about "human factors" during the project and have corrected many of the botches. However, there are several which remain. Perhaps the most inconvenient is that updates are "silent." In other words, INGRES performs an update and then responds a "done." It never gives an indication of the tuples that were modified, added or deleted (or even how many there were). This "feature" has been soundly criticized by almost everyone.

5.0. COMMENTS

This section contains a collection of comments about various things which do not fit easily into the earlier sections.

5.1. UNIX

As a program development tool, we feel that UNIX has few equals. We especially like the notion of the command processor, the notion of pipes, the ability to treat pipes, terminals and files interchangeably, the ability to spawn subprocesses and the ability to fork the command interpreter as a subprocess from within a user program. UNIX supports these features with a pleasing syntax, very few "surprises," and most unnecessary details (e.g., blocking factors for the file system) remain hidden.

The use of UNIX has certainly expedited our project immeasurably. Hence, we would certainly choose it again as a operating system.

The problems which we have encountered with UNIX have almost all been associated with the fact that it was envisioned as a general purpose time-sharing system for small machines and not as a support system for database applications.

Hence, there is no concurrency control and no crash recovery for the file system. Also, the file system does not support large files (16 Mbytes is the current limit) and uses a small (512 bytes) page size. Moreover, the method used to map logical pages to physical ones is not very efficient. In general, it appears that the performance of the file system for our application could be dramatically improved.

5.2. The PDP-11

Other than the address space problems with a PDP-11, I have only two other comments regarding the hardware. First, there is no notion of "undefined" as a value for numeric data types supported by the hardware. Allowing such a notion in INGRES would require taking some legal bit pattern and by fiat making it equal undefined. Then, we would have to inspect every arithmetic operation to see if the chosen pattern happened inadvertently. This could be avoided by simple hardware support (such as found on CDC 6000 machines).

Second, there is no machine instruction which can move a string in main memory. Consequently, data pages are moved in main memory one word at a time inside a loop. This is a source of considerable inefficiency.

5.3. Data Models

There has been a lot of debate over the efficiency of the various data models. In fact, a major criticism of the relational model has been its (alleged) inefficiency.

There are (at least) two ways to compare the performance of database systems:

1) The overhead for small transactions. This is a reasonable measure for how many transactions per second can be done in a typical commercial environment.

2) The cost of a given big query.

It should be evident that the first has nothing to do with the data model used (at least in a PDP-11 environment). It is totally an issue of the cost of the operating system, system calls, environment switches, data validity costs, etc. In fact, if INGRES were a network-oriented system and ran as five processes, it would also execute 2.5 transactions per second.

The cost of a big query is somewhat data-model dependent. However, even here this cost is extremely sensitive to the cost of a system call, the operating system decisions concerning buffering and scheduling, the cost of shuffling output around and formatting it for printing, and the extent to which clever tuning has been done. In addition, the design of a database management system is often very sensitive to the features (and quirks) of the operating system on which it is constructed (at least INGRES is). These are probably much more important in determining performance than what data model is used.

In summary, I would allege that a comparison of two systems using different data models would result primarily in a test of the underlying operating system and the implementation skill (or man years allowed) of the designers and only secondarily in a test of the data models.

▮▮▮ 6.0. INGRES PROJECT PLANS

INGRES appears to be at least potentially commercially viable. However, a commercial version would require at least:

1) Someone to market it;

2) Much better documentation;

3) Someone willing to guarantee maintenance (whether or not we do it, the University of California will not promise to fix bugs);

4) A pile of boring utilities (e.g., a report generator, a tie in to some communications facilities, and access to the system from other languages than C).

Even so, we would not have a good competitive position because UNIX is not supported and because no COBOL exists for UNIX.

There has been a clear decision on the part of the major participants not to create a commercial product (although that decision is often re-examined). On the other hand, the project cannot simply announce that it has accomplished its goals and close shop. Hence, we have gone through a (sometimes painful) process of self examination to decide "what next." Here are our current plans.

1) Distributed INGRES

We are well into designing a distributed database version of INGRES which will run on a network of PDP-11s. The idea here is to hide the details of location of data from the users and fool them into thinking that a large unified database system exists [EPST78, STON77].

2) A distributed database machine

This is a variant on a distributed database system in which we attempt only to improve performance. It has points in common with "back-end machines" and depends on customizing nodes to improve performance.

3) A new database programming language

Obviously, starting with C and an existing database language QUEL and attempting to glue them together into a composite language is rather like interfacing an apple to a pancake. It would clearly be desirable to start from scratch and design a good language. Initial thoughts on this language are presented in [PREN78].

4) A data entry facility

An application designer must write EQUEL programs to support his customized interface. The portion of such programs that can be attributed to the database system has shrunk to near zero (by the high level language facilities of QUEL). Hence, we are left with transactions that have virtually no database code and are entirely what might be called "screen definition, formatting and data entry." We are designing a facility to help in this area.

5)   Improved integrity control

Currently, INGRES is not very smart in this area. Other than integrity constraints [STON75] (which do something, but not as much as might be desired), we have no systematic means to assist users with integrity/validation problems. We are investigating what can be done in this area.

It is pretty clear that all of the above will require substantial changes in the current software. Hence, we can remain busy for a seemingly arbitrary amount of time. This will clearly continue until we get tired or are again in danger of meeting our goals.

ACKNOWLEDGEMENTS

The INGRES project has been directed by Professors Eugene Wong and Larry Rowe in addition to myself. The role of chief programmer has been filled by Gerald Held, Peter Kreps, Eric Allman and Robert Epstein. The following persons worked on the project at various times: Richard Berman, Ken Birman, James Ford, Paula Hawthorn, Randy Katz, Nancy MacDonald, Marc Meyer, Daniel Ries, Peter Rubinstein, Polly Siegel, Michael Ubell, Nick Whyte, Carol Williams, John Woodfill, Karel Yousseffi and William Zook.

CHAPTER THREE

The Commercial INGRES Epilogue

Lawrence A. Rowe / Michael Stonebraker

ABSTRACT

This paper describes the founding of Relational Technology Inc. and the development of INGRES during the period 1980-1984. It focuses on the evolution of the INGRES system into a commercial product and discusses what we learned as result of this experience.

1.0. INTRODUCTION

In 1978, we first contemplated starting a commercial enterprise based on the INGRES system [HELD75b]. There were several factors that encouraged us to move in this direction. First, we wanted INGRES to be widely used but most organizations would not consider using the system because it was an unsupported research prototype running on an unsupported operating system (UNIX). Even when we could overcome these obstacles, the data processing community was unwilling to use the system because we did not provide the application development tools they required (e.g., a report writer and a COBOL interface).

The second factor was that it was becoming increasingly difficult to keep the students on the University project working on research ideas. INGRES had been distributed to over 150 sites and we were providing very limited, but extremely popular, technical support over the phone. Unfortunately, user demands (bug fixes, new features, and improved performance) in most cases did not qualify as research. The students were anxious to satisfy these demands because they thought it would reduce the phone calls and contribute to the fame of INGRES. Moreover, like most programmers, they took pride in "their system" and they wanted to make it the best possible DBMS. From a research perspective, this development was unrewarding and we wanted to move on to new ideas. It was imperative the University research project get out of the "software support" business.

Lastly, the window was rapidly closing on the opportunity to make

INGRES a commercial product. Several companies with large development groups were beginning to develop relational systems. Independent of how good INGRES was at the time, other systems would soon surpass its function and performance and it would only be of "historical interest."

It is mildly surprising in 1984 that the University of California version of INGRES, which is basically the same as it was in 1979, is still reasonably competitive against other commercial offerings [BITT83]. In retrospect, we overestimated the ability of others to build relational systems and bring them to market.

For these reasons we decided to start a company. This paper describes our experiences starting a company and turning INGRES into a commercial product. We have divided the presentation into four time periods:

1)   In the Beginning (July 1979 - September 1980)

2)   Struggle in the Basement (October 1980 - June 1981)

3)   An Engineering Company (July 1981 - June 1983)

4)   A Real Company (July 1983 - June 1984)

The next four sections chronicle each period. Following this, we describe the future plans for the commercial product and some things we have learned from managing a commercial development group.

2.0. IN THE BEGINNING (JULY 1979 - SEPTEMBER 1980)

During the summer of 1979 Eugene Wong and the authors decided to form a company to market INGRES. We approached Jon Nackerud (then Vice President and Western Regional Sales Manager for Cullinet Corporation), whose office was in Berkeley, to ask his advice on how to get our venture off the ground. Jon was enthusiastic about our idea and we invited him to join us. He brought sales and marketing skills, which we did not have.

Between the four of us we wrote a business plan. A business plan explains the product, describes why it is better than other products that are available, describes how the product will be marketed and sold, and forecasts revenues and expenses for the first few years. We sent our plan around to the venture capital community (affectionately known as the "land sharks") to solicit funds.

Selling the plan to the land sharks was our first real sales experience. Of course, one of us (Stonebraker) had been selling the concept of INGRES for several years to the research community at conferences. However, people in that community are technical experts and are able to evaluate technical issues. The land sharks were business experts not software experts, so we spent most of the time explaining to them why it is hard to build a relational DBMS and why someone would want to buy one.

After many meetings with different venture capitalists, we reached a "handshake" agreement with one. After a three-month delay while their lawyers produced several hundred pages of legalese for us to sign, Relational Technology Inc. (RTI) was incorporated in October 1980. Of course, the five-figure bill from the lawyers came out of the capital put up by the venture firm.

The venture capitalists encouraged us to hire a "numbers man" who had more financial experience than any of the founders and helped us find Gary Morgenthaler, who was, at the time, a consultant for McKinsey, Inc. Gary wore a suit, "talked to bankers," and could make numbers dance across electronic spreadsheets, all of which were important as we grew larger.

3.0. STRUGGLE IN THE BASEMENT (OCTOBER 1980 - JUNE 1981)

This period began when we incorporated and continued until we moved into our first real offices. Corporate headquarters started out in Jon Nackerud's basement to conserve money and to set the proper tone for "leaness." We had actually been in business informally since June 1980. We had hired Derek Frankforth, then a student at Berkeley, to begin converting the INGRES code from UNIX to the standard DEC operating system (VMS).

By May of 1981, we had completed the conversion and were trying to sell the system. Potential customers told us that the major limitations of the system were:

1) performance on short queries was too slow,

2) performance on long queries was too slow,

3) no hard crash recovery,

4) only single-statement transactions,

5) no report writer,

6) no easy-to-use end-user interfaces,

7) no nested queries, and

8) INGRES databases could only be accessed from C.

Other than these problems, they thought INGRES was great! So we set out to correct the problems with the manpower available at the time, which was four people.

The basic tenets that we adopted were to make small incremental steps and to maximize the results delivered per unit effort. We believed that a startup company might not survive a mistake so we took small steps to minimize the chances of a failure. Moreover, it was critical that we produce results quickly, so we worked on projects that could achieve a noticeable result fast. Projects that were hard (e.g., multi-statement transactions) were deferred.

We made dramatic progress during the first year. The projects we completed are described in the following subsections.

3.1. Improve the Performance of the System

INGRES had two performance problems. First, short queries (i.e., single record retrievals and updates) that run repetitively were much too slow. They were slow because the query was parsed, validated, and optimized every time it was run and because the inner loop that tests whether a tuple satisfies the query predicate was interpreted.

The generic benchmark of short query performance is to have a program insert records into a relation and time how many inserts can be done per second. University INGRES could insert a little over 2 records per second on a VAX 11/780.

The second performance problem was that long queries (e.g., 3-way joins) were too slow. These queries were slow because the query optimizer did not use a sort-merge tactic. However, in a customer benchmark INGRES ran only twice as slow as a BASIC program with a hand-coded algorithm to join three files, so we were optimistic that this problem could be solved.

We elected to concentrate on short query performance during the first year and to defer work on long queries until later. INGRES was changed to parse a query only on the first execution. The basic idea was to store the parsed and validated query, called a *query tree*, in virtual memory the first time it was run. On subsequent executions, only a query identifier and parameters for the query were sent to the DBMS process. INGRES would validate the parameters and substitute them into the query tree. Then, the command would be optimized and executed. This technique saved the time to parse and validate the query on repeated executions. This optimization eliminates about one-fourth of the total overhead. This change was coded in about two months and together with other changes in the I/O library improved the performance of short queries by a factor of two.

We would have preferred to compile queries as is done in System R [ASTR76]. However, this change would have required major surgery on the code, which violated our tenet to take small steps, so we deferred query compilation to later.

3.2. Develop a Report Writer

It is impossible to compete in the commercial marketplace without a report writer. A report writer implements a fairly complex language that is a cross between a text formatting language (such as Nroff/Troff [OSSA79] or Tex [KNUT84]) and a programming language with embedded data manipulation commands. Most report writer languages are not particularly friendly, and we wanted to do better. Our approach was to make the report writer an output formatting language. We intentionally left out local variables and control flow (if-then-else and goto). Unfortunately, the marketplace expects report writers to be programming languages, so we have been forced to add these features to the INGRES Report Writer.

In our opinion, report writers suffer a serious identity problem. Users demand a programming language but they refuse to acknowledge it. It would be relatively straightforward to add text formatting features to an existing database programming language such as EQUEL. Unfortunately, this is considered unacceptable, and every vendor is forced to develop a reasonably complex programming language "from scratch."

3.3. Develop EQUEL Preprocessors

EQUEL preprocessors were developed for the major programming languages available on the VAX. We found a potential customer that used each language as their primary development tool. As a result we have had to implement an EQUEL preprocessor for BASIC, C, COBOL, FORTRAN, and Pascal. Each of these preprocessors, except C, was completed under extreme time pressure because a potential customer had agreed to buy INGRES if it supported his favorite language.

Each preprocessor is different because each language has different data types, syntax for variable declarations, and name visibility rules (i.e., scope rules). EQUEL must parse the host language declarations so that database values can be assigned to program variables and vice versa. Consequently, a substantial code maintenance problem is generated, namely several different flavors of the same basic code.

This period of the company history ended when we moved to real office space. At the time of the move we had sold our first system and had 8 full-time employees.

4.0. AN ENGINEERING COMPANY (JULY 1981 - JUNE 1983)

During the next two years we made dramatic progress. The development staff grew from 4 to 32 people and the company grew from 8 to 52 people. Most product decisions were being made in engineering because we did not have a marketing organization. The company operated with little structure, which meant engineering performed a variety of functions including technical support, sales support, documentation, and quality assurance in addition to doing product development.

During this period, we added two new product lines: VAX/UNIX INGRES and M68000/UNIX INGRES. We decided to enter these markets because the development effort required was minimal, customers were willing to pay us to do them, and we believed they would grow to sizable markets. We also decided not to enter the IBM PC market, at least for the time being, for the following reasons:

1) our full-function product was too large,

2)   the segmented address space on the INTEL 8086 would require us to write a software overlaying mechanism, which would make the code less portable and harder to maintain,

3)   we had no expertise in the consumer software business (i.e., selling through retail stores), and

4)   it was expensive to enter, and, we believed, extremely risky.

At the time, we were also hoping to have only one version of the source code to reduce the cost of development and maintenance. We realized that we could not develop one system that would be a full-function and high performance product on large machines and simultaneously be a space-efficient product on small machines.

Making strategic marketing decisions is difficult because they are subjective decisions based on incomplete and often wrong information. Moreover, a lot of emotional energy was consumed making such decisions because an error could lead to the failure of the company.

On the technical front, we completed many projects. These projects are described in the remainder of this section.

4.1. Query-By-Forms

It was clear to everyone that ordinary mortals did not want to use QUEL for data manipulation. All textual query languages, of which QUEL is an example, have two fundamental flaws. They are too verbose when performing the same task repetitively and they do not forgive errors by a novice user. For example, consider appending 10 records to a relation by repeating the following command:

    APPEND TO EMP (NAME = ''xxx'', AGE = yyy,
            SALARY = zzz, DEPT = ''aaa'')

Only the data for the four constants changes for each insertion. The user must know the syntax of the append command and the names of the attributes in EMP and must spell everything correctly or he gets an unfriendly error message.

To rectify these problems, we constructed a browser, called Query-By-Forms (QBF), that was modeled after a similar program developed by one of us (Rowe) as part of the FADS project at the University [ROWE82]. With QBF a user can enter, query, and update data through a form. The form is displayed on a CRT screen with a menu of operations listed across the bottom, as shown in Figure 3.1. Together a form and a menu of operations is called a *frame*. The user enters data into the fields of the form and executes operations to accomplish some task. The frame in the figure has been filled in with a query to retrieve employees who are under 25 and make more than $30,000. At this point, if the user executes the **Go** operation the data will be retrieved and displayed through the form one record at a time.

This example shows the default form that would be generated for the

```
┌─────────────────────────────────────────────┐
│                                               │
│      TABLE IS EMP                             │
│                                               │
│      name:                    age: <25        │
│                                               │
│      salary: >30000      dept:                │
│                                               │
│                                               │
│              Help    Query   Go   End         │
│                                               │
└─────────────────────────────────────────────┘
```

FIGURE 3.1. Sample Query Specification

EMP relation. During this period, we also developed a visual forms editor that allows a user to customize the form. For example, he can change the field labels and the trim (e.g., the title on the first line of the frame) and add display enhancements (e.g., inverse video, blinking, and so forth) and edit checks (e.g., salary must be positive). With QBF and the forms editor, a user could "get going" quickly on his project. Moreover, it is possible to build a wide variety of custom database interfaces with no programming.

The first version of QBF was an extremely limited product. It only displayed one record at a time on the screen, worked on only a single table, and did not allow OR's between clauses in the query predicate. Nevertheless, QBF has been our most successful end-user product because even the most naive user can use it to solve his data management problems.

4.2. Extend QUEL

Many people have objected to the use of range variables in QUEL. For example, one must declare a range variable to specify even a single relation query as illustrated by

```
RANGE OF E IS EMP
RETRIEVE (E.SALARY) WHERE E.NAME = "Mike"
```

Users objected to range variables because they were hard to explain to naive users and required too much typing. We decided to implement default range variables, which allow a relation name to be used as the range variable. As a result, the example above could be specified as follows

> RETRIEVE (EMP.NAME) WHERE EMP.NAME = "Mike"

This change, suggested independently by Zaniolo [ZANI83], required only a few days to implement and was enthusiastically received by everyone.

Default range variables do, however, have one unpleasant side effect. Consider the query

> RANGE OF E IS EMP
> REPLACE EMP (SALARY = 1000) WHERE E.NAME = "Mike"

which is translated internally to

> RANGE OF E IS EMP
> RANGE OF EMP IS EMP
> REPLACE EMP (SALARY = 1000) WHERE E.NAME = "Mike"

This query sets the salary of everyone in the EMP relation to 1000 and not the salary of Mike to 1000, which is probably not what the user wanted.

4.3. Rewrite Query Processing

The decomposition algorithm, called DECOMP, that is described in [WONG76] was replaced by a new query optimizer. The new optimizer, called JOINOP, is different than DECOMP in two ways. First, JOINOP develops a complete plan to implement a query before any part of the query is executed. DECOMP, on the other hand, constructed the first step of a plan and executed it. After the first step was finished, the optimizer resumed and constructed the next step. In other words, DECOMP uses an iterative solution. The iterative solution has two advantages: it reduces the size of the search space, and it has better information on which to make decisions because the size of intermediate results is known. As it turns out, for queries that users actually run, the search space is small and the estimates of the intermediate result sizes are good enough.

The second difference between DECOMP and JOINOP is that DECOMP uses nested iteration to implement a join operation, and JOINOP uses nested iteration or sort-merge as a tactic. A sort-merge tactic is a clear winner for many queries.

The JOINOP optimizer is quite similar to the optimizer used in System R that is described in [SELI79]. One difference between JOINOP and the System R optimizer is the terminating condition. JOINOP terminates when the time spent searching for a query implementation is greater than the estimated time for the best plan or the search space is exhausted. The System R optimizer essentially does an exhaustive search.

The query optimizer was tuned by running it on a set of queries taken from the benchmarks that RTI had been asked to perform. Whenever the optimizer chose a poor strategy, its cost function was changed to fix the mistake. Over time the optimizer has become extremely good, and INGRES is rarely beaten on long queries.

JOINOP has another advantage over DECOMP. JOINOP creates a control block, called a *query execution plan* (QEP), that represents the query implementation which is to be executed. As described below, this structure allowed us to cache QEP's after optimization as another performance enhancement. This structure also made it possible to modify INGRES to "stack" its environment, so that it can interrupt a query being executed and begin work on another one (i.e., nested queries). In both cases, a QEP stored in a data structure is easier to save and restore than a DECOMP plan that was stored in local variables dispersed throughout the code.

4.4. Other Forms Interfaces

The success of QBF confirmed our opinion that forms-interfaces were a good interface for both naive and expert users. They are simultaneously user-friendly to naive users and economical in keystrokes for an expert user. Hence, we decided to use forms-interfaces for all of our products.

Two other forms-based user-interfaces were developed during this period: Graph-By-Forms (GBF) and Report-By-Forms (RBF). GBF allows a user to display data through standard business graphs (e.g., scatter and line plots and bar and pie charts) and RBF is a visual editor for defining reports. RBF was targeted for naive users, so it did not provide all the features in the full-function report writer because we believed that if it did the interface would be too complex.

The emphasis on forms ultimately led to Application-By-Forms (ABF), an end-user application generator. ABF allows a user to build an application by putting together QBF frames for querying and updating data, report frames for displaying data in a report, and graph frames for displaying data in a graph. In addition, users can define their own frames in which the operations are coded in an extended version of QUEL. One use of user-defined frames is to define menu frames that allow a user to select the function they want to perform next. A user defines an ABF application by filling in forms just like the other user-interfaces. Eventually, ABF will be a complete application development environment with interactive debuggers and version control.

ABF was based on the Forms Application Development System (FADS) which had been built at the University of California [ROWE82, SHOE82]. FADS had a performance problem because application descriptions (e.g., the definitions of frames, forms, and operations) were stored in the database in Third Normal Form [CODD71]. To retrieve the definition of a frame from the database required over 200 queries and took over 2 minutes to execute.

No matter how fast a database system can execute queries, this approach requires unreasonable overhead. In ABF, we compiled frames into an executable image so they did not have to be retrieved from the database at run-time. This approach reduced the time to call a frame by over a factor of 100, yielding acceptable performance.

We have learned several things as a result of building forms-interfaces.

First, little details in a user interface can make a big difference. For example, an operation is invoked by typing an escape character, a correct prefix of the desired operation, and a return character. Users quickly learn to enter just the first character of an operation because it is fast and in most cases sufficient. Frames that have several operations that start with the same letter are frustrating to use because the user enters just the first letter of the operation and the system prints an error message. As a result those frames that have been carefully designed with unique, intuitive operation names are qualitatively nicer. This point seems very small, but the effect on the user's perception can be dramatic.

The second thing we have learned is that frames are like procedures. The constant part of a frame (e.g., the trim, labels, and field masks) corresponds to the code for a procedure and the variable part of a frame (e.g., the values in the fields and the operation menus) corresponds to the data for a procedure. On large time-shared systems, the constant frame data should be separated from the variable frame data and the constant data should be shared among concurrent users just like procedure code is separated from data and is shared.

Finally, applications built using a tool like ABF can be developed very quickly. A simple resource scheduler was written both in EQUEL C with embedded screen input/output commands [RTI83a] and in ABF. The EQUEL program was about 300 lines of code as compared with about 50 lines in the ABF.

4.5. Portable Code

During this period the system was modified so that it could be easily ported to new machines and operating systems. The biggest problem we encountered making the system portable was that INGRES uses numerous operating system primitives that are semantically different on every system. For example, INGRES uses a *sleep* primitive when it starts up the multi-process environment in which it runs. We used a primitive on VMS that takes as its argument the number of milliseconds to sleep. The analogous primitive on UNIX interprets its argument as the number of seconds to sleep. The first bug encountered when we ported the system back to UNIX was that INGRES would start-up and nothing would happen. In fact, the code encountered the call *sleep(1000)* and suspended for about 15 minutes rather than one second. There are numerous examples of similar problems.

We solved this problem by designing a "compatibility library" (CL) that includes all operating system calls that INGRES makes and changing the system to call these routines rather than the operating system directly. To port INGRES to a new environment, the CL is converted and the rest of the system recompiled. The CL is composed of 60 routines and is less than 5% of the lines of code so that the effort required to port it to a new environment is minimal.

The second problem we encountered when trying to make the code portable was that C is not standardized. Consequently, different implementations of the language would not always compile the system. For example, different compilers and linkers allow different length identifier names. We solved this problem by restricting all identifiers to 6 character names, which is acceptable by all implementations that we know of.

Finally, the flexibility of UNIX caused some problems because users insist on changing sensitive internal data structures and commands. For example, INGRES stores relations in files and the directory containing these files corresponds to a database. In an early release we deleted a database by using an option to the "remove file" command that deleted a directory and all of the files in it. One customer site decided this option was too error prone so they removed the option and recompiled the command. Of course, the result was that they could not delete a database. The solution to this problem was to remove from the code as many dependencies on the local environment commands as possible.

The bottom line is that making a complex program portable that uses numerous operating system facilities such as INGRES is hard but it can be done.

4.6. Transaction Management

To compete successfully in the commercial marketplace, a DBMS must support fine granularity locks (page or record level), multi-statement transactions, and recovery from both soft crashes (i.e., data on a disk is not lost) and hard crashes (i.e., data on a disk is lost). The University of California INGRES supported relation level locks, single-statement transactions, and soft crash recovery, so a complete rewrite of the transaction management system was required.

We adopted a conventional solution, similar to the one described in [GRAY78], with the exception that INGRES does deferred update rather than direct update. Deferred update changes the database in two phases. In the first phase, changes are written to a log. After all changes are logged, the second phase re-reads the log and updates the data relations. Direct update, on the other hand, writes changes to the data relations and the log simultaneously using a "write ahead" log protocol.

The advantage of deferred update is that it guarantees a consistent answer to all updates. For example, the update

```
RANGE OF E IS EMP
RANGE OF M IS EMP
REPLACE E (SALARY = .9 * E.SALARY)
        WHERE E.MGR = M.NAME
        AND E.SALARY > M.SALARY
```

gives a 10 percent pay cut to all employees who earn more than their managers. This query is the "generic" example of a reflexive join query. When run on a relation with the following data

NAME	SALARY	MANAGER
Smith	2000	Jones
Jones	1900	
Brown	900	Smith

deferred update reduces only Smith's salary. Direct update reduces either Brown's and Smith's salary or just Smith's salary. Brown's salary is reduced only if Smith is updated before Brown. Consequently, direct update produces a random answer on this command and other commands like it. To avoid this semantic ambiguity, INGRES does deferred update.

The disadvantage of deferred update is that it requires additional I/O operations (reading the log in the second phase). However, it appears that a carefully tuned implementation can be as efficient as direct update. Examples of possible optimizations are: do direct update for single record updates, use read-ahead and write-behind I/O operations, and cache data and log pages appropriately.

4.7. More Improvements to the Performance of Short Queries

As described previously, parsing and validating a query at first execution is a way to gain speed at a cost in address space. There are many other similar optimizations, and we exploited as many of them as we could. For example, while processing a query, INGRES calls a function which opens a relation and creates a data structure which describes the relation. When the query is finished, the data structure, called a *relation descriptor*, is discarded. If the next command accesses the same relation, the descriptor is reconstructed, which costs approximately 15000 instructions and one or two I/O operations. By using a ''descriptor cache'' this overhead can be eliminated.

Another way the system was improved was to eliminate CPU overhead. An embarrassing example was found in the scanner which required four procedure calls per input character read. By expanding the *getcharacter* routine in-line, the scanner ran a factor of two faster. Notice that this tactic also consumes address space.

5.0. A REAL COMPANY (JULY 1983 - JUNE 1984)

This period began when we hired sales and marketing Vice Presidents. They brought a new perspective to the scene including the need for

1)   an active public relations program,

2)   more training and consulting for customers, and

3)   a more aggressive marketing program aimed at our competitors.

Marketing hired a public relations firm and worked to get more visibility for the company and the product. They wrote articles for the trade press and developed glossy brochures to advertise the product. We were surprised to learn that most papers that appear in the trade press (e.g., ComputerWorld) are ghost written and placed by marketing people and public relations firms.

During this period, the company grew from 52 to 130 people and engineering grew from 32 to 71. The following table lists the different groups in engineering and the headcounts.

Group	Headcount
Computing Facility	6
Conversions	22
Customer Support	17
Product Development	20
Quality Assurance	6

This phase of the company's growth has been easier for engineering because the marketing and sales departments have taken over many of the tasks engineering used to perform. It is now also possible to get reasonable market information (e.g., what customers of flavor X think about Y). Consequently, the development staff can concentrate on development.

The major projects completed during this period are described in the following sections.

5.1. More Performance Improvements

The major performance enhancement completed during this period was to cache repeat queries after query optimization rather than after parsing and validation. This saves the time it takes to optimize the query on subsequent executions. With this improvement, INGRES now runs approximately 10 insertions per second on a VAX 11/780, which is five times faster than University INGRES.

We are approaching the stage where performance improvements are harder to achieve. Either the improvement affects only a small set of queries or the effort required to change the system will be large relative to the performance improvement achieved. The techniques that we have to apply include counting instruction path lengths, monitoring the code for frequently executed code segments, and hand optimizing critical sections. The changes possible produce only small percentage improvements rather than the "order of magnitude" improvements possible with algorithm changes. This effect is expected from a more mature system.

5.2. B-Trees

A B-tree storage structure was added to the system. We have discovered two additional reasons why B-trees are good storage structures. First, some applications have relations keyed on a sequence number that is always increasing (e.g., a timestamp). Over time, the older tuples are deleted from the relation. A B-tree is the only reasonable storage structure for this data because the key set that is indexed is always an increasing interval. Only a dynamic index can adapt to such changes.

The second reason a B-tree is a good storage structure is that the sort-merge join strategy works best when the data is already sorted. If the join attribute is the key attribute of the B-tree, the data is in sort order. The ISAM storage structure does not keep the data on a leaf page, and its associated overflow pages, sorted. Consequently, the sort-merge implementation sometimes has to re-read pages while processing the data in one ISAM bucket.

5.3. Multi-Table QBF

QBF was an extremely successful product. However, as one would expect, our customers wanted more features, including multiple records on the screen at one time and forms that map data to more than one table (e.g., a *master-detail* form like a purchase order). A major enhancement of QBF was recently completed that includes these features. The user describes the mapping between the form and the data in the database by filling in forms, and then he can use an interface similar to the one provided by the earlier product.

One nice feature of the master-detail QBF is that it is possible to retrieve data based on a predicate specified in the master part and the detail part as shown in Figure 3.2. This query requests all purchase orders for the "XYZ Bolt Company" that have a line item for washers. Even though the data is stored in two relations, the user views purchase orders as single entities.

5.4. INGRES on Small Machines

The demand for a compatible DBMS that runs on small machines (less than .75 megabyte and swap-based) and large machines is very strong. To satisfy this demand we developed a subset of INGRES that would run efficiently on these smaller machines. Our goal was to produce a product, called INGRES/CS for INGRES/Compact Systems, that supports the forms-based user-interfaces and requires less than 500K bytes of memory. We also insisted on upward compatibility with the version INGRES that runs on larger machines, which meant that any user-interface that runs on INGRES/CS also runs on full-function INGRES.

INGRES/CS was developed by starting with the University code and modifying it to save space. We also added functions that are required by the user-interfaces.

This product has just recently been completed and early indications are

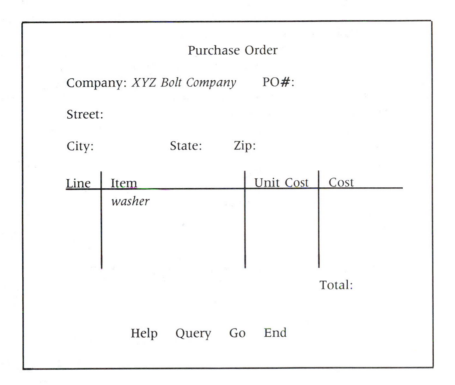

FIGURE 3.2. Master-Detail Query Specification

that it will be successful. Unfortunately, we now have two copies of the source code and two parallel development groups. We will have to manage these groups very carefully to keep the systems compatible.

6.0. WHAT COMES NEXT?

This section describes our future plans for INGRES. We plan to

1) enter the IBM market,

2) develop a distributed DBMS, and

3) develop a new integrated environment to access data in an INGRES database.

These plans are discussed briefly in the remainder of this section.

From the very beginning, many people advised us to enter the IBM market as soon as possible. Their rationale was that more money could be made in that market because the customers are conditioned to paying high prices for software and because there are more potential customers. We delayed entering this market because we thought it would require more function and performance than University INGRES had and because IBM-land was an alien environment. Another company has been able to sell a product into the IBM market that we believe is essentially University INGRES so we may have been wrong about the function/performance issue. Nevertheless, we have now completed the necessary features and so it is time to do the conversion.

INGRES will be converted to run on the prevalent operating systems for IBM machines. The major problems to be faced are:

1)   SQL compatibility,

2)   half-duplex terminal I/O, and

3)   a hostile operating system environment.

In our opinion, SQL [IBM81] is inferior to QUEL. Our major complaints stem from the fact SQL is a non-uniform language and QUEL is more powerful. The following example illustrates a non-uniformity in SQL. The query

```
SELECT NAME
FROM EMP
WHERE SALARY > (SELECT AVG(SALARY) FROM EMP)
```

is legal whereas the query

```
SELECT NAME
FROM EMP
WHERE (SELECT AVG(SALARY) FROM NAME) < SALARY
```

is illegal because the nested-select must be the right operand to the relational operator. A non-uniform language is harder to learn because there are many special cases and more error prone because users do not remember the exact rules.

QUEL is more powerful because it allows nested aggregates and because a table can be updated with values from another table. An example of the latter problem is shown by the following query that gives an employee a raise based on the percentage increase for his job title which is given in another table.

```
REPLACE EMP (SALARY = RAISE.PERCENT * EMP.SALARY)
      WHERE EMP.JOBTITLE = RAISE.JOBTITLE
```

This query cannot be done in SQL.

Lastly, SQL has some constraints that may make sense to programmers familiar with block-structured languages (e.g., Pascal) but not to novice users. A range variable defined in an outer block can be referenced in an inner block but not vice versa. For example, the following query is illegal:

```
SELECT NAME
FROM EMP
WHERE SALARY > M.SALARY
    AND MGR =
        (SELECT NAME
        FROM EMP M)
```

A more complete discussion of the relative merits of the two languages is given elsewhere [DATE84, ROWE83].

Regardless of the technical issues, SQL will be very popular because IBM supports it. Consequently, we are developing SQL interfaces to INGRES databases.

The second problem with IBM systems is that they support only half-duplex terminals. "What you see is what you get" interfaces become "what you see *may be* what you get" because the display is not updated in response to an arbitrary keystroke. Consequently, we will have to change all our interfaces to use function keys for commands rather than mnemonic ordinary keys. The eventual salvation will come when all 3270s are replaced by PCs and we can move our application programs into the terminal.

The third problem in IBM-land is that the operating systems do not provide the higher-level functions we are used to in the VAX environment. For example, it is difficult to have two VM (virtual machines) update the same file concurrently. These problems can be solved but the "pain factor" may be high.

The second major technical direction we are pursuing is distributed INGRES. Customers want to run applications that can access data stored on other machines. For example, many large organizations have a centralized DP center that runs the corporate database on large mainframe computers. Departments often have a super-mini on which they run decision-support and end-user databases. The problem faced by these organizations is how to allow applications to access data from both sources simultaneously. A second example is that users at a personal workstation want to access data stored on different file servers connected to a local network. From a technical standpoint, the answer to both problems is a distributed database system.

The third major technical direction we are pursuing is to develop a new visual interface, called the *relational shell*, to access and display data in a database. The relational shell will be similar to the UNIX shell [BOUR78] in that it will be possible to execute commands and to "pipe" the output of one command (e.g., a query) into the input of another command (e.g., a report). The relational shell should have two advantages over the UNIX shell. First, the data passed between two commands is a stream of records rather than an unstructured byte stream. Moreover, the commands can access the same database process so that the overhead to open a database does not have to be paid each time a command is run.

With the relational shell, the user is able to specify a query in QUEL, SQL, or QBF and display the data in a table, a report, or a graph. It is also possible to display data in different output formats on the screen at the same time (i.e., display windows). For example, a user is able to display data through a report and, at the same time, be browsing it with QBF. Simultaneous access to data through different windows allows a user to switch rapidly between different interfaces and to examine different relationships between the data (e.g., summary versus detail data).

Lastly, we will add new interfaces to the environment (e.g., spreadsheet and word processing) and new data types to the database (e.g., icon and geometric data).

7.0. WHAT WE LEARNED

This section describes what we have learned about managing the development of a software product in a "real-world" company. We discuss how products are developed and what schedules really mean.

During the first two years, we would sketch out an idea that would be refined and implemented by the person(s) assigned to the project. On a regular basis, we would meet individually with each project group and review their progress. As a product limped into existence, everyone in the company would experiment with it and suggest changes that would improve it. These changes would be incorporated into the interface as it was being developed. When everyone was pleased with the design and the bugs were removed, the product would be released. Hence, we essentially prototyped a new product, gave it to a sample user community (us!), and then refined the prototype into a product.

This methodology corresponds closely to the design philosophy that we use at the University [ALLM82]. Note clearly that no design documentation was produced, design reviews were informal discussions on how things were going, and no formal software development methodologies were used (e.g., structured walkthroughs).

During 1983, we instituted formal design reviews because the development group became too large for us to review the details of every project. Products are sketched out by us or someone in marketing and then the developer writes a document (encouraged to be less than 5 pages long) that describes what he plans to build and any difficult implementation problems that must be solved. This document is reviewed by a committee, including representatives from engineering and marketing, who evaluate the proposal to ensure that the product can be built and is competitive in the marketplace.

The basic contract that a development group makes with the rest of the company is "I will deliver X on date Y." It is usually reasonable to deliver less than X, but potential customers and the sales force get upset if you slip Y. Because a start-up company must move quickly, one cannot spend a great deal of time to study the difficulty of achieving X. Consequently, one must produce the best estimate possible on the available information and then promise to deliver to the estimated schedule.

Of course in many cases the completion date for a project was bounded by other factors (e.g., the company requesting a conversion or the planned delivery date for a release). One problem we had managing the conversion process was the continuous stream of requests of the form "can you port INGRES to system X by Y." Most requests were never undertaken but you could never tell which ones were real. Consequently, we spent a tremendous amount of time planning and revising schedules.

The project scheduling process forces an organization to make the hard decisions about what projects will be completed during the next development period. Projects that are "on the schedule" will be completed and those that are not can be completed only by adding resources (people and computing) or deferring another project that is scheduled. The scheduling process works as follows. First, everyone puts forth their "wish list." Then everyone's list is combined and ordered by priority. The third step is to assign people to projects until the current staff and expected new hires are committed. It is a challenge to schedule the last few projects because there are typically many contenders, each approximately equally worthy. Someone has to make this decision and up to this point engineering has made it.

Once the schedule is fixed and people are working on their projects, a new opportunity may present itself or an external market pressure may change the priority of the projects. At this point, we have to figure out how to complete everything that is scheduled and add the previously unscheduled project to the schedule. We have tried to resist moving people to a different project once they had started another, but we have not always been successful. We believe frequently changing the schedule reduces productivity and morale, so it must be done only under the most dire circumstances.

Finally, as the product and the company have gotten larger, it has been more difficult to make significant enhancements to the product quickly. Several factors contribute to this slowdown. First, we have already completed most of the "quick and easy" enhancements. The tasks remaining are more complicated and require more substantial changes to the code. Consequently, it takes more people and time to complete them.

Second, the system is getting larger. University INGRES and its user-interfaces (the terminal monitor and EQUEL C) are approximately 100K lines of code. In contrast, release 3.0 of RTI INGRES is approximately 350K lines of code. As the system gets larger, it takes more time to integrate and test new releases, particularly when they involve substantial changes.

Lastly, as the company has grown, more technical resources have been allocated to converting the code to new environments because the marginal return is higher. For example, adding a new data type or storage structure to the system generates less revenue than porting INGRES to a new machine. The latter opens a new market while the former influences only a few sales.

ACKNOWLEDGEMENTS

It would be impossible for us to acknowledge all of the people who have made significant contributions to commercial INGRES. However, we would like to recognize some of the engineering staff at RTI whose dedication and effort made it possible for us to write this paper. They include Greg Batti, Paul Butterworth, Joe Cortopassi, Derek Frankforth, Bob Kooi, John Newton, and Peter Schmitz.

2

Supporting Studies on Relational Systems

In this section, we present a collection of papers that report on simulation or experimental studies that were conducted to examine INGRES design decisions. Also included is one paper that complains about operating system support for database systems.

The paper on locking granularity was motivated by the necessity of choosing lock sizes for our prototype. The 1976 INGRES design paper in the previous section claims that coarse granularity would work best. Dan Ries implemented a simulation model to study the issue, and, in 1977, we published a paper arguing that coarse granularity is optimal [RIES77]. This paper drew close scrutiny from the research community and considerable skepticism. Jim Gray was among the people who said it could not be correct. The paper included in this section was a more careful analysis that included alternative assumptions which were more realistic in transaction processing environments. The ultimate conclusion is that multiple granularities are the best option.

The 1980 retrospection paper indicates that we were surprised to find that INGRES was usually CPU bound. In the early 1970s it seemed to be a common belief that all database systems were I/O bound, and we were surprised to discover contrary behavior. Furthermore, since we were experts on INGRES processing algorithms, we knew that standard buffer management schemes would not work well in our environment. Paula Hawthorn instrumented INGRES with performance monitoring software to discover where the system spent CPU time and what kind of buffer reference patterns were actually occurring. The second paper in this section reports on this study. A sidelight of this analysis was comments on what sorts of database machine architectures would be viable. This comment was in reaction to a common belief at the time that so-called "associative disks" were the way to speed up any database system.

During this study, I became convinced that the way to build a database machine was to assemble a collection of "vanilla" computers on a local area network. My paper [STON79] elaborates on the architecture desired. Marguerite Murphy embarked on a project to attempt to prove this hypothesis. Unfortunately the project became bogged down in implementation difficulties, and only a paper design was completed. At the same time, three other studies were performed to examine a faster file system, a microcoded version of INGRES, and compilation as a performance tactic. These four studies were merged and published in TODS in 1981.

The compilation and file system studies were directly motivated by performance problems noted in the 1980 retrospection paper. It was no surprise that a dramatic win could be obtained from relatively modest investments of effort. The conclusion is that a "raw" file system is not very hard to write and enhances performance markedly. Given the interpretive overhead of INGRES, the dynamic compiler is equally beneficial. On the other hand, our microcode study showed little improvement. The standard wisdom at the time was to buy a user-writable control store and move the inner loop of one's computation into microcode. Very large numbers (e.g., 50%) were being suggested as the anticipated improvement. Our experience was contrary. The TODS referees were unconvinced by the microcode numbers and cited positive microcode experiences by Cullinet, Britton-Lee, and others. Personally, I am very dubious about the potential for microcode on machines designed after 1970. Recent designs have included in the instruction sets all the functions (e.g., string move, string compare, queue management, and so forth) that a database system wants most. Such function is absent from older machines and appears to result in noticeable speed increases. However, I expect further improvements will be much harder to realize.

The paper on query processing arose from a desire to understand the consequences of our rather ad-hoc decisions in implementing the initial heuristics. The paper carefully considers all the options easily available to us, and suggests that most of our initial hunches were good ones. In fact, our query processor remains surprisingly competitive against systems of considerably newer vintage [BITT83]. The only significant shortcoming to the query processor (noted in the Commercial INGRES Epilogue) is the absence of merge-sort as a tactic. Although the viability of this tactic had been pointed out in 1976 [BLAS76], inserting this strategy would have necessitated a substantial rethinking of decomposition, and it was never attempted.

The last paper discusses operating system support for database systems. It summarizes several years of assorted frustration with the design of most time-sharing systems. Since the paper was written, I have learned several more reasons why the interface between the database system and the operating system is tricky. For example, the "server" model for a database system should be avoided because it requires writing a scheduler and task manager in user code. However, the "process per user model" suffers the following problem in addition to the ones mentioned in the paper. If one puts a single relation in a file and wishes to have multiple database processes access this file, the file must be physically opened by each process. This extra overhead is painful, and the impossibility of "caching" open files across multiple operating system processes is very frustrating.

## CHAPTER FOUR

Locking Granularity Revisited

Daniel R. Ries / Michael Stonebraker

ABSTRACT

Locking Granularity refers to the size and hence the number of locks used to ensure the consistency of a database during multiple concurrent updates. In an earlier simulation study we concluded that coarse granularity, such as area or file locking, is to be preferred to fine granularity such as individual page or record locking.

However, alternate assumptions than those used in the original paper can alter that conclusion. First, we changed the assumptions concerning the placement of the locks on the database with respect to the accessing transactions. In the original model the locks were assumed to be well-placed. Under a worst-case and random placement assumptions, when only very small transactions access the database, fine granularity is preferable.

Second, we extended the simulation to model a lock hierarchy where large transactions use large locks and small transactions use small locks. In this scenario, again under the random worst-case lock placement assumptions, fine granularity is preferable if all transactions accessing more than 1% of the database use large locks.

Finally, we simulated database systems which support a "claim-as-needed" locking strategy together with the resultant necessity for deadlock detection and resolution. In the original study all locks were claimed in one atomic operation at the beginning of a transaction. The claim-as-needed strategy does not change the conclusions on the desired granularity.

1.0. INTRODUCTION

In a previous paper [RIES77], we examined the effects of using locks of various sizes (or "granules") for concurrency control in a database management

D. R. Ries and M. Stonebraker, *ACM Transactions on Database Systems*, vol. 4, no. 2, June 1979. Copyright 1979, Association for Computing Machinery, Inc.; reprinted by permission.

system. In this paper, we report three significant extensions that affect the conclusions of that study. We first briefly review some aspects of concurrency control in a database system and present an overview of the results in the original paper.

1.1. Database Concurrency Control

The concurrency control mechanism in a database management system is responsible for ensuring some level of consistency [ESWA76] during the processing of concurrent updates. A variety of concurrency control mechanisms have been suggested [CHAM74a, GRAY76, MACR76, STEA76], which lock required portions of a database while a transaction is in progress.

Some mechanisms require the notion that certain units of the database can be locked. We shall refer to a unit of the database which can be locked by the concurrency mechanism as a "granule". The size of the granule in different database management systems varies. In some systems (CODASYL [CODA73], System R [ASTR76], DMS-1100 [GRAY75]), the granule may be as small as one record. Other systems, e.g., IMAGE [HEWL77], support one granule covering the entire database. Still other systems (DBMS-11 [DIGI77], LSL [LIPS76]) support intermediate sized granules such as files or areas.

1.2. Previous Results

In the previous paper [RIES77] we described a simulation model which was used to examine the effects of different granule sizes on the efficiency of the database management system. It is clear that fine granularity allows a higher degree of parallelism at a greater cost in managing locks. Conversely, coarse granularity decreases parallelism but minimizes lock management costs. The simulation model gave insight into the tradeoffs between the increased parallelism and the locking overhead.

In the simulation, a fixed number of transactions were cycled continuously around the model shown in Figure 4.1. In this model, the database was an abstract collection of entities. An entity can be thought of as the unit of data moved by the operating system into the database system buffers.

The number of entities "touched" or accessed by a given transaction completely determined the amount of I/O, CPU and lock resources required by the transaction. The I/O and CPU resources required for processing a transaction were respectively equal to the number of entities touched times an I/O cost per entity and a CPU cost per entity. The proportion of available locks required was equal to the percentage of the entities touched by the transaction.

Initially, the transactions arrived one time unit apart and were put on the pending queue. A transaction then went through the following stages.

1) The transaction was removed from the PENDING queue and all required locks were requested. If the locks were granted, the transaction

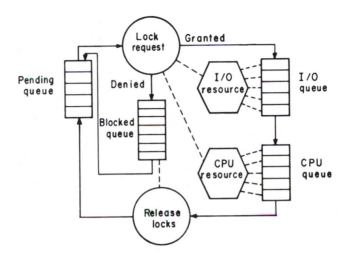

FIGURE 4.1. The Simulation Model

was placed on the bottom of the I/O queue. If the locks were denied, the transaction was placed on the bottom of a BLOCKED queue. The blocking transaction was recorded. Note that no locks are held while on the blocked queue so deadlock was impossible.

2) After completing the I/O required, the transaction was placed on the bottom of the CPU queue.

3) After completing the required CPU, the transaction released its locks and joined the end of the PENDING queue. Note that each transaction went through one I/O phase and one CPU phase. Although they were sequential in the model, the result would be the same if each transaction went through many I/O - CPU phases in a single cycle. All transactions that were blocked by the completed transaction were placed on the front of the PENDING queue.

The major parameters in the model were:

1) The number of transactions.

2) The number of entities "touched" by a transaction.

3) The distribution of the entities touched by transactions.

4) The I/O cost of processing an entity.

5) The CPU cost of processing an entity.

6)   The number of granules or locks.

7)   The I/O cost of setting one lock.

8)   The CPU cost of setting one lock.

The simulation was run varying the size of the granules while holding other factors fixed. Figure 4.2 shows a typical output from the model. In this figure, the average transaction "touched" 10% of the database, the I/O cost for accessing an entity was four times the CPU costs for manipulating the data within one entity (simulating I/O bound transactions), the I/O cost for setting a lock was equal to the I/O cost for accessing an entity, while the CPU cost for setting a lock was 1/5 of the CPU cost for manipulating an entity.

Note that machine utilization increases as the number of granules increases then levels off and falls. Also note that maximum utilization occurs at a relatively small number of granules and that utilization is within 1% of this optimum for 10 granules. The conclusion can be drawn that crude locking schemes with coarse granularity are nearly optimal. Since a crude

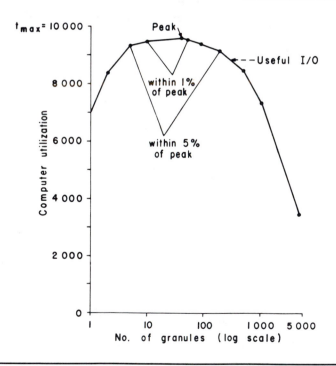

FIGURE 4.2. Computer Time Versus Number of Granules

locking system may be easier to implement than a sophisticated finer granularity scheme, it is preferred. This conclusion was tested against many changes in model parameters. These experiments included changing the ratio of I/O time to CPU time required by a transaction; changing the CPU and I/O resources required for locking; and changing the number of I/O channels. The model was also changed to reflect not keeping all of the locks for the entire duration of transaction processing and to reflect the keeping of locks for a "think period" during which no useful I/O or CPU activity for the given transaction took place. In all cases curves similar to Figure 4.2 resulted.

Three situations, however, did favor somewhat finer granularity than shown in Figure 4.2. First, reducing the costs associated with locking, particularly keeping all locks in core (i.e., I/O lock cost was set to zero), significantly reduced the heavy overhead costs associated with fine granularity. The second case was using very small transactions. In this case, the optimum granularity in Figure 4.2 was moved to the right. Finally, a balance between the I/O and CPU costs for processing each entity needed by a transaction also moved the optimum to the right. Such a "balanced" system creates the greatest potential for I/O and CPU overlap. However, even in these cases coarse granularity would have served almost as well (i.e., within 5%).

1.3. Model Extensions

Several people have questioned the validity of some of our model assumptions. In particular our assumption concerning the number of locks that must be obtained for each transaction is sometimes suspect. Potentially, many more granules may be required to lock a given number of entities than allowed in the original model. Alternate assumptions concerning these numbers are explored in Section 2.0. Also, a lock hierarchy [GRAY76] could have significantly changed our results. In a lock hierarchy, different transactions use different size granules for locking. With such a hierarchy, the costs of locking may be greatly reduced since it would be cheaper to set one large lock than to set many small locks. This alternative is explored in Section 3.0. Finally, in our original model, all locks were requested at the beginning of a transaction. In some database locking mechanisms, locks are requested during the transaction processing. These claim-as-needed mechanisms can result in more concurrency since locks are not held during the entire lifetime of a transaction. However, the possibility of deadlock is introduced. This case is discussed in Section 4.0. In Section 5.0, we present our overall conclusions.

2.0. GRANULE PLACEMENT

In the original model, the number of locks required by a given transaction was exactly proportional to the percentage of the database "touched" or accessed by the transaction. Hence, a transaction which touched half of the entities in the database would require half of the possible database locks. Note that this amounts to assuming that the granules are "well placed," i.e., that the entities needed by the transactions are packed into as few "lockable" granules as possible. This assumption is reasonable for transactions which access the database sequentially. Although sequential processing in database applications has been observed [RODR76], actual transactions may require a combination of sequential and random accesses to the database. Robert Fabry was the first to suggest that we explore the effects of assumptions other than "well placed" granules on the locking granularity.

2.1. Alternative Granule Placement Assumptions

In order to study the effects of different lock placement assumptions, two alternatives to "well placed" locks were explored.

1) Worst case access:

    Each transaction requires the maximum number of granules possible. If the total number of entities touched by a given transaction, say NE, is greater than the number of locks covering the entire database, say NL, then in the worst case all of the locks might have to be set to access the needed entities. If NE is less than NL, on the other hand, the number of locks that have to be set is bounded by the number of entities NE. Thus the number of locks required is the minimum of the number of locks for the entire database and the number of entities touched by the transaction. This assumption simulates an "uncooperative" transaction; i.e., one whose access pattern is the worst possible one from the point of view of the locking mechanism. This scenario is the opposite extreme of the "well placed" assumption.

2) Random access:

    For each transaction, a mean-value formula is used to estimate the number of locks required. Let s be the number of records in the database; nlks be the total number of locks; and p be the number of records per block (= s/nlks). Then a transaction which accesses r records will require

    $$\text{nlks}*\left[1 - \frac{C_r^{s-p}}{C_r^s}\right]$$

    locks. The C_r^{s-p} and C_r^s represent the number of different ways r records can be selected from $s-p$ and s records respectively. The number of locks required under the random access assumption is analogous to the number of blocks accessed when randomly selecting records from a blocked file. A mean-value formula for this number and its derivation are given in [YAO77]. This model accurately reflects random processing where the probability of accessing any entity is the same, and is independent of any previous entities accessed.

Which model is more accurate depends on the nature of transactions in a given application. However, our experience is that is it will normally be somewhere between well-placed and random depending on how much sequential processing is done. Which model is chosen affects our original results. If the "worst case" is chosen, the following intuitive analysis applies. The graph in Figure 4.3 assumes that all transactions touch the same number of entities NE. The machine utilization measures decreased as the number of locks for the entire database increased from one to NE. The decrease is because each transaction will require more and more locks, thus increasing the locking overhead. However, there is no additional parallelism because each transaction locked the entire database.

The utilization increases, however, as the number of locks increases from NE to the total number of entities in the database because the cost of the locking overhead will remain constant while the allowed concurrency increases. The locking overhead remains constant since each transaction can never set more than NE locks. Consequently, the optimum number of locks is very dependent on the transaction sizes in the worst case placement lock

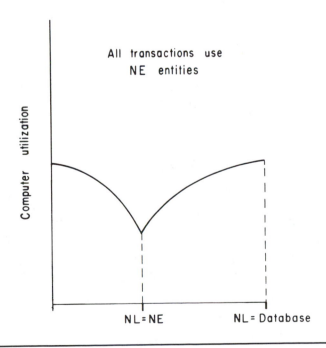

FIGURE 4.3. Worst Case Lock Placement

assumption. Moreover, it will always occur at one granule or the maximum number of granules (corresponding to one lock per entity) if all the transactions are the same size.

The effects of having varying transaction sizes will be discussed below.

2.2. Simulation Extension

The simulation model was run for each of the three placement assumptions under a wide variety and combination of parameter values. Figures 4.4 and 4.5 diagram some of the results. In Figure 4.4, the transaction sizes were determined by an exponential distribution but with a mean value of 500 entities (10% of the database). In Figure 4.5, the transaction sizes were also determined by an exponential distribution but with a mean value of 5 entities (0.1% of the database). For these runs, the locks were assumed to be in main memory (no lock I/O required) and the I/O and CPU time required by the transactions were equal. These conditions were chosen as the ones most

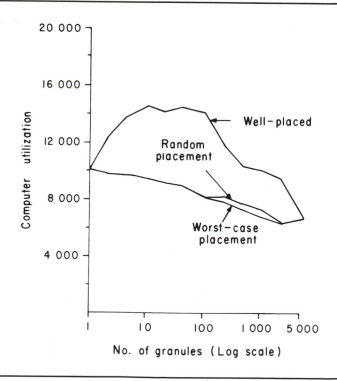

FIGURE 4.4. Large Transactions

favorable to finer granularity. The other parameters were similar to those described in the original paper. The top curve in both figures is consistent with the results in our original paper. The bottom two curves represent the worst case and random access assumptions.

For large transactions requiring about 10% of the database (see Figure 4.4) a smaller number of granules was still to be preferred to a lock for each entity. For small transactions requiring about 0.1% of the database (see Figure 4.5) one lock per entity produced the greatest machine utilization under the worst case and random placement assumptions. However, even with small transactions, the degree of improvement was small as the granularity increased beyond a certain limit. With 200 locks, for example, 90% of the maximum machine utilization was reached.

Next, the simulation was run with mixed size transactions (the size being generated by hyper-exponential distributions, also suggested by Robert Fabry) using the best case, the worst case and random access assumptions. Intuitively, this simulates a few large transactions and many small ones. As

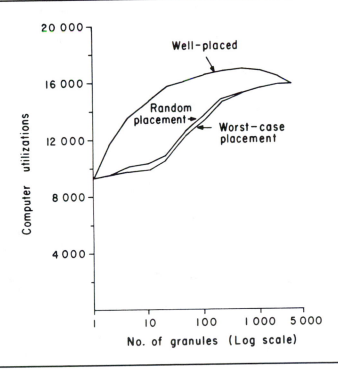

FIGURE 4.5. Small Transactions

in the original paper, under the well-placed assumption a small number of granules was best. A relatively flat curve relating machine utilization and the number of locks was observed for the worst case and random access assumptions. Thus, in these two cases, fine granularity did not interfere with useful I/O and CPU time, but more coarse granularity would have served as well. In fact, 98% of the maximum utilization was achieved by 10 granules. The basic problem with fine granularity is that the expense of running just a few large transactions seems to outweigh the gain due to the increased concurrency experienced by the small transactions.

2.3. Conclusions

These studies do change our original conclusions somewhat. Fine granularity may be best if the following two conditions are met: 1) almost all of the transactions are small and 2) access patterns are random with no sequentiality. Under these conditions, the greater the number of locks, the greater the machine utilization. However, the rate of increase drops dramatically after a certain level of granularity is obtained (about 200 granules in our simulation). Hence "medium" granularity does almost as well as fine granularity; coarse granularity is unacceptable in this case.

If too many of the transactions access a large portion of the database, fine granularity produces too much locking overhead and coarse granularity is again to be preferred.

Regardless of the transaction sizes, if the data access patterns are primarily sequential, coarse granularity is still most effective.

3.0. LOCK HIERARCHY

One way a large transaction can avoid the expense of locking many small granules might be to have the large transactions lock large granules while the small transactions continue to use the small locks [GRAY76]. An extension of our simulation model to study the effects of such a lock hierarchy on the desired granularity was first suggested by Richard Karp.

3.1. The Model Extension

In the simulation extension a two level hierarchy was implemented. A transaction, depending on its size, either requested a set of small locks or one global lock which covered the entire database. With this extension, we explored the interactions between any two levels of a more general hierarchy.

The simulation was modified by adding "pending" and "blocked" queues for the global lock. If a transaction is "small", it sets the global lock in shared mode and is placed on the original pending queue. From that queue the "small" transactions must compete for the small locks as in the original model. If the transaction is "large," the global lock is set for exclusive access and the transaction waits for all active transactions to finish. With the global lock set for exclusive use, new transactions, regardless of size would also wait in the blocked queue. Once the large transaction is allowed to proceed, it goes directly to the I/O queue bypassing the small lock control.

The simulation was used to study the effects of certain parameters of such a hierarchy on the desired granularity. One of the main areas of interest was the criteria for deciding whether the small locks or the global lock should be used. An input parameter was added to the simulation which specified the threshold percentage, tp, of the database which must be touched by a transaction before it is declared "large." If a transaction used less than tp percent of the database, the small locks would be used. Otherwise, only the global lock would be set.

3.2. The Simulation Results

The simulation was run with threshold percentages of 0.1%, 0.2%, 0.5%, 1%, 2%, 5%, 25%, 50%, and 100% for each of a large number of other parameter settings in order to find the value of tp which maximized machine utilization. The optimum threshold observed was dependent on the number of small locks, the assumptions concerning the placement of those locks, the number of entities touched by the transactions, and the size of the database.

Figures 4.6 and 4.7 compare the threshold percentages with the number of small locks. The depicted results represent simulation runs with a data-base of 5000 entities and transaction sizes determined by a hyper-exponential distribution with 90% of the transactions touching an average of 5 entities and 10% touching an average of 500 entities. Again, the I/O lock costs were assumed zero (locks kept in main memory), and the CPU and I/O costs for a given transaction were equal — two factors favoring finer granularity in our original study. The results in Figure 4.6 reflect the best case assumption that the transactions are sequential. Random access of the database is assumed for the simulation runs for Figure 4.7.

Each of the graphs is divided into three areas based on machine utiliza-tion. The "optimum" line represents the threshold value, tp, at which the maximum I/O and CPU utilization was observed for a fixed number of small locks. With threshold values in area B, the hierarchical locking produced results within 2% of that maximum utilization. In area A, the utilization was less than in area B. In this case, too few transactions used the global lock, i.e., the threshold, tp, was set too high. In area C, the machine utilization was also less than in area B. In this case, however, too many transactions have used the global lock, i.e., the threshold, tp, was too low.

For example, consider Figure 4.6 with 1000 small locks. The machine utilization increased as the threshold percentage was increased from 0.1% to 5%, but decreased as the threshold increased from 5% to 100%. However, simulation runs with threshold percentages between 1% and 25% produced within 2% of the machine utilization observed with the optimum threshold.

In Figure 4.6, "well placed" granules are assumed. With more than

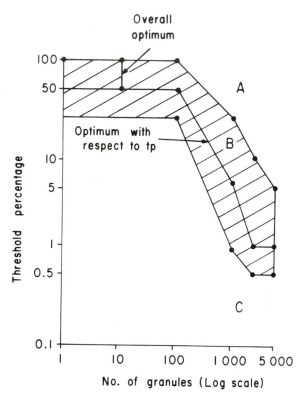

Area A: tp too high
Area B: highest machine utilization
Area C: tp too low

FIGURE 4.6. Well Placed Locks in a Lock Hierarchy

1000 small locks the optimum value of tp was between 1% and 5%. With the number of locks between 10 and 100, tp values of 50% to 100% were optimal. In this granularity interval, the 2% area included the case where all transactions used only the small locks. The overall maximum machine utilization occurs in Figure 4.6 with 10 locks and tp values greater than 50%. In these cases, almost all of the transactions used the small locks. Hence, the value of a lock hierarchy under the well-placed locks assumption is very small.

However, in Figure 4.7, the random access patterns for each transaction are assumed. With coarse granularity, the optimum threshold occurred at

0.5% With a higher threshold, more of the smaller transactions would use the small locks, and consequently would lock a large portion of the database. As a result, these transactions would expend more resources for locking than if the global lock were used without significantly increasing the concurrency allowed.

In Figure 4.7, the differences in computer utilization between areas A, B, and C is small for coarse granularity. For 10 granules, for example, no matter what value of tp is used, the computer utilization is within 3% of the maximum observed for that granularity. Similarly, for 100 granules, the computer utilization was within 15% of the maximum observed for any value of tp. Thus even with random access transactions, a hierarchy with a small number of small locks can at best provide slight improvement over a single

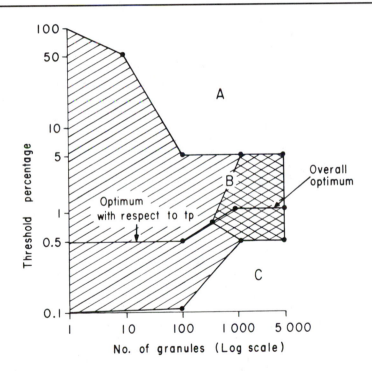

Area A: tp too high
Area B: highest machine utilization
Area C: tp too low

FIGURE 4.7. Random Lock Access in a Lock Hierarchy

level locking system.

Under the random access assumptions, the overall maximum machine utilization occurred with 5000 granules and a tp of 1%. The cross-hatched area in Figure 4.7 represents those combinations of tp and number of small locks which resulted in machine utilization within 2% of the overall maximum. Hence, fine granularity is to be preferred. The lock hierarchy effectively prevents excessive locking overhead for large transactions.

For fine granularity, the B areas in Figures 4.6 and 4.7 have considerable overlap. For example, in Figure 4.6, with 2500 small locks, the 2% of optimum interval occurred with a tp between 0.5% and 10%. In Figure 4.7, with the same number of small locks, the interval occurred with tp values between 0.5% and 5%. Thus, at this granularity, a tp between 0.5% and 5% and can safely be chosen regardless of the randomness of the data access patterns.

Other simulation experiments used the worst case data access assumption and produced results very similar to those in Figure 4.7.

In still other simulation runs, as the average transaction size decreased, the range of acceptable tp values (area B) also decreased. With fine granularity, regardless of the transaction sizes, a threshold between 1 and 2% always produced machine utilization within 2% of the maximum.

With coarse granularity, however, changes in the size of the transactions created non-overlapped intervals of acceptable tp values. In other words, no one value of tp could be chosen that would be correct for vastly different sized transactions. Thus much greater care must be applied to a hierarchy with coarse granularity. Furthermore, a stable transaction size environment must be assumed.

The size of the database was also varied. For example, we ran the simulation with a database consisting of only 16 entities. In this scenario, we examined the possible interaction of a page/record hierarchy. An entity corresponds to one record in a page which holds 16 records. In our simulation, we were then testing the effects of locking the whole page by the global lock, or locking individual records by the small locks. Some increase in machine utilization was observed with a threshold of 50%; but the increase over using no hierarchy at all was less than 4%. Again it appears that a lock hierarchy covering only a small number of smaller locks is not worth implementing.

We also ran the simulation with databases of up to 100,000 entities. The results were similar to the results produced with a database of 5,000 entities. For example, we ran cases where the average transaction size of most of the transactions was just 0.05% of a 100,000 entity database and the average size of a few large transactions was 1% of the database. In these cases, with the finest granularity (100,000 small locks), a threshold of 1% was still optimal.

3.3. Conclusions

A locking hierarchy should be implemented when the small locks are of a fine granularity; a low threshold is used to separate the large and small transactions, and random data access patterns are anticipated. With this model the increase in machine utilization over a single level locking scheme is potentially significant. Furthermore, a threshold of about one percent can be selected independent of the granule placement or transaction size assumptions.

With coarse granularity, on the other hand, a locking hierarchy should not be used. The potential again is not significant and is only realized in certain cases. Another problem with the coarse granularity/locking hierarchy model is that the optimum value for the threshold percentage is extremely sensitive to the placement of the locks with respect to the transaction.

4.0. CLAIM-AS-NEEDED LOCKING

Another difference between our model and some database concurrency control implementations deals with when the locks are actually acquired. In the original study, a ''pre-claim'' model was assumed where all of the locks were acquired before any transaction processing took place. In some database systems, a lock is not acquired until the related entities are actually needed by a transaction. These ''claim-as-needed'' schemes are used either to reduce the total time locks are held and/or because the locks to be acquired cannot be anticipated. In these cases, some locks may have to be held while other locks are requested, and deadlock can occur [GRAY76]. In this section we examine the effects of the optimum granularity of a claim-as-needed scheme.

4.1. The Model Extension

The simulation was modified by cycling each transaction through the I/O and CPU queue (see Figure 4.1) once for each lock required. The total I/O and CPU times required for a transaction are the same as in the original model and are equally distributed among each of a transaction's cycles.

Between each cycle, a transaction requests one lock. If the lock is granted, the transaction goes on the active queue. When a transaction has completed its last cycle on the active queues, all its locks are released as in the original model.

If the lock is denied, the requesting transaction is placed on the blocked queue. The lock can be denied due to locks held by other active transactions, or by blocked transactions. If the blocking transaction is on the blocked queue, a deadlock condition can exist. If deadlock occurs, a victim is picked for backout. The locks held by the victim are released, any blocked transactions are freed, and any time spent on the active queues by the victim is added to a ''lost time'' total.

4.2. The Simulation Results

The modified simulation was run varying the sizes of the transactions, changing the lock placement assumptions, and with or without a lock hierarchy. Again we assumed that there is no I/O cost associated with locking and that the transactions required equal amounts of CPU and I/O resources.

The results of these simulation runs are very similar to those in [RIES77] and those presented above for the pre-claim strategy. In all cases, a claim-as-needed strategy does not change the granularity required for maximum machine utilization.

For example, Figure 4.8 shows the results of running the simulation with no hierarchy, well placed granules and transaction sizes determined by a hyper-exponential distribution (see Section 3.2). The lost time area represents the machine utilization by transactions that had to be restarted due to deadlock. The useful computing includes only the I/O and CPU resources used by successfully completed transactions.

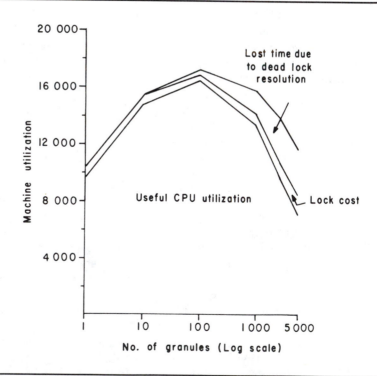

FIGURE 4.8. Claim-as-needed Locking

The locking cost in the preclaim model is greater than the locking cost in the claim-as-needed locking model. This difference is because in the case of a lock request failure, in the preclaim model all of the locks must be requested again. In many cases, any decrease in lock costs, however, was more than offset by the lost time due to deadlock resolution. Thus the useful machine utilization was greater under the preclaim model than under the claim-as-needed strategy. Many other cases with different transaction sizes and lock placement assumptions were also tested and produced similar results.

For example, Figure 4.9 compares the useful machine utilization between the two models under the assumptions that all transactions are small and that each transaction has random data access patterns. In both of these runs, the average transaction size was 0.1% of the database. Note that with the possibility of deadlock, the machine utilization curve does not flatten out as the granularity increased, in contrast to our observation in Section 2.3. In these cases, we thus conclude that with a claim-as-needed model, the finest granularity may be mandatory. Note however, that the claim-as-needed scheme again produced less useful I/O and CPU utilization than the preclaim model.

However, as the average transaction size became even smaller, the last observation does not hold. With an average transaction size of less than 0.05% of the database, random data access patterns, and the finest granularity, the claim-as-needed scheme resulted in greater useful machine utilization. Under these conditions, the claim-as-needed strategy allowed the greatest concurrency since locks were held for a shorter period of time. In contrast to our other runs, very few transactions had to be backed out and the cost of rerunning such small transactions was insignificant.

The modified simulation was also run with a lock hierarchy and various threshold percentage values. A similarity in the shapes of the curves between the preclaim and claim-as-needed strategies was also observed. Under the random access assumptions, for example, the maximum machine utilization is again reached with the finest granularity and a threshold value of 1 to 2 percent.

4.3. Conclusions

The acquisition of locks throughout the processing of a transaction does not significantly change the other conclusions of this paper. However, two observations should be made. First, deadlock detection and resolution appears to be generally more expensive than the release and rerequest used in the preclaim strategy. When locks are known at the start of a transaction a preclaim algorithm is suggested.

Second, if all of the transactions are small and a random access pattern is present (see Figure 4.9), an algorithm allowing for deadlock makes the finest possible granularity essential.

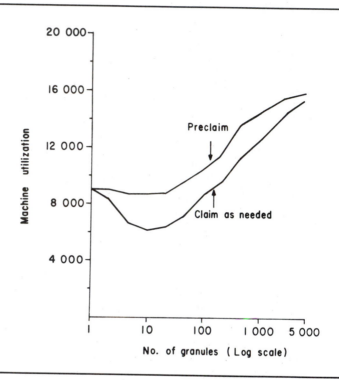

FIGURE 4.9. Preclaim versus Claim-as-needed

5.0. SUMMARY

In a previous study, we concluded that for concurrency control locking in a database management system, coarse granularity, such as file, area or database locking, was almost always preferable to fine granularity such as individual page or record locking.

In this extension of the study, several alternative assumptions showed that there are cases where this conclusion doesn't hold. In particular, if ALL transactions are randomly accessing small parts of the database, then finer granularity is to be preferred.

However, if several of the transactions are large, a lock hierarchy must be used if the fine granularity is still to be supported. Such a hierarchy was shown to be beneficial mainly for fine granularity and random data access patterns. In these cases, all transactions touching more than 1% of the database should use a few large locks rather than many small locks. If the data access patterns were sequential, however, single level locking with coarse granularity was still to be preferred.

Both of these results hold, regardless of whether a preclaim or claim-as-needed strategy is used for lock acquisition. In general, a preclaim strategy produced better machine utilization than the claim-as-needed model.

Our overall conclusions are that the optimum locking granularity is somewhat application dependent. In many cases, coarse granularity, such as file or relation locking, with a preclaim strategy is to be preferred. Such a coarse granularity can be augmented with a lock hierarchy using very small granules, such as record or page locking within a file, at the lower level of the hierarchy. Then the concurrency control can be tuned to allow for a wider class of transactions that randomly access just a few records of a given file. However, any gains of such a hierarchy are still application dependent and must be weighed against increased implementation and locking overhead costs.

## CHAPTER FIVE

The Use of Technological Advances to Enhance Database System Performance

Paula Hawthorn / Michael Stonebraker

ABSTRACT

The effect of the performance of data management systems on the use of extended storage devices, multiple processors and prefetching data blocks is analyzed with respect to one system, INGRES. Benchmark query streams, derived from user queries, were run on the INGRES system and their CPU usage and data reference patterns traced. The results show that the performance characteristics of two query types, data-intensive queries and overhead-intensive queries, are so different that it may be difficult to design a single architecture to optimize the performance of both types. It is shown that the random access model of data references holds only if references to system catalogs are not considered data references. Significant sequentiality of reference was found in the data-intensive queries. It is shown that back-end data management machines that distribute processing toward the data may be cost effective only for data-intensive queries. It is proposed that the best method of distributing the processing of the overhead-intensive queries is

P. Hawthorn and M. Stonebraker, *ACM-SIGMOD Conference Proceedings*, ACM-SIGMOD International Conference on Management of Data, Boston, Massachusetts, June 1979. Copyright 1979, Association for Computing Machinery, Inc.; reprinted by permission.

through the use of intelligent terminals. A third benchmark set, multi-relation queries, was devised, and proposals are made for taking advantage of the locality of reference which was found.

1.0. INTRODUCTION

1.1. Background

Two technological advances that may have substantial impact on data management system performance are low cost, fast processors and extended storage devices such as CCDs, bubbles and semiconductor memories. Low cost processors should lead to machines with distributed intelligence; extended storage devices should lead to systems with improved I/O performance due to buffering techniques. What is not clear is the most effective use of these advances: what CPU functions to distribute; and when and how to buffer I/O.

The problem of determining how to buffer I/O is essentially the problem of determining data reference patterns. If the data is referenced randomly across the database, the buffer size must approach the size of the database in order to increase performance by obtaining a large percentage of hits in the buffer. Therefore, in order to effectively use the increased buffer size made possible by extended storage devices, there must exist sequentiality and/or locality of access in the data.

If the I/O references are known to be sequential, the data can be stored sequentially on the disk and read into main memory or an extended storage device an entire track or cylinder at a time, thus dramatically reducing access time. This read-ahead tactic is often employed by operating systems when processing sequential files. If there is locality of reference in the I/O requests, then data pages should be buffered in faster memory and a replacement algorithm used. Such pages should be treated in much the same way as program pages are handled in virtual memory machines [DENN68].

There are several studies of data management system I/O reference patterns which deal with buffer replacement algorithms [SHER76, TUEL76, LANG77], but do not directly address the question of under what conditions there is locality or sequentiality in the I/O references. In studies of an IMS trace [RODR76], sequentiality was found in the data references, and in [SMIT76], read-ahead strategies to take advantage of that sequentiality were analyzed. The trace analyzed in [RODR76] also exhibited some inter-query locality of reference.

CPU usage patterns have not been previously considered in published performance evaluations of data management systems. It is often assumed that the CPU time in a data management system is insignificant compared to the I/O time [YAO78b]. However, the CPU can become the bottleneck in data management systems. This may become a critical problem if I/O time is reduced through the use of extended storage devices or read-ahead tactics.

One method of lessening a CPU bottleneck is to distribute the processing of the queries through the use of intelligent terminals and/or back-end machines. We will indicate under what circumstances one database management system is CPU bound and what forms of distributed processing appear to be beneficial.

1.2. Description of this Study

The performance of the data management system INGRES [STON76a] was analyzed to determine its CPU usage and data reference patterns. The study was done using a software trace facility and benchmark query streams.

It is impossible to assess the generality of the results of any performance evaluation of a real system unless it is known precisely why the stated results occur. Therefore, INGRES, the benchmark programs, and the results are explained in detail. The description of INGRES and the trace are in Section 2.0.

In Section 2.0 the benchmark query streams are described. We did not attempt to trace a "typical user" for a "typical week" but, instead, constructed a series of benchmarks. This technique was used because the goal was to identify and analyze the performance patterns of general types of queries, not to determine the mixture of these queries in any one user's query stream. Three sets of benchmarks were developed from user query streams. These were overhead-intensive, data-intensive, and multi-relation queries. Since all updates in INGRES are physically implemented by executing a RETRIEVE command to isolate qualifying tuples followed by lower level shuffling, we treat only retrieval commands in this study.

Section 3.0 also contains the results of the analysis of the benchmarks. It is shown that the performance patterns of the overhead-intensive queries differ greatly from the data-intensive queries. There is locality of reference to INGRES system files for overhead-intensive queries; moreover, they are CPU bound. It is shown that data-intensive queries exhibit a high degree of sequentiality, and cyclic sequentiality. In addition there is intraquery locality of reference in INGRES only when processing aggregate functions or multi-relation queries. The CPU usage patterns of INGRES are analyzed to determine the most efficient distribution of the functions of the CPU. Lastly, Section 4.0 summarizes our conclusions.

2.0. INGRES

2.1. Descriptive Summary

The following is a brief description of INGRES. Complete descriptions of the INGRES data management system are contained in [STON76a, WONG76, EPST77].

INGRES supports three structures for a relation: it may be an unordered collection of tuples (heap); it may be hashed on any domain or any combination of domains (hash); or it may be stored indexed sequential on any or in any combination of domains.

A query such as

```
RANGE OF E IS EMP
RETRIEVE (E.NAME) WHERE E.EMP# = 1234
```

results in the searching of the employee relation for all tuples with EMP# = 1234. In the above query, if the EMP relation is stored as a heap, the entire relation will be scanned, each tuple tested for EMP# = 1234, and the NAME domain in the qualifying tuples returned to the user. The relation is read in logically sequential order, one page at a time.

If the relation is hashed on EMP#, the hash function (which is selected automatically by INGRES and has a bucket size equal to one UNIX page) is used to determine the main page the tuples satisfying the qualification would fall on. That page is read, then each tuple on that page is tested and the data in the qualifying tuples returned to the user.

The case where more tuples hash to a location than can fit on one page is handled by chaining overflow pages. If there are overflow pages, they are also read as above.

If the relation is ISAM, the index associated with the relation is first searched to determine the main page that the tuples would fall on, and then processing continues as in a hashed relation.

If the relation is not structured on EMP#, but has a secondary index on EMP#, the secondary index is searched to find the logical page number and offset within the page of the qualifying tuples. All pages containing a qualifying tuple are read, and the data in the qualifying tuples returned to the user. Note in this case that the secondary index identifies qualifying tuples. Hence, unlike ISAM and hash, a data page does not have to be exhaustively searched.

2.2. Significant Considerations about the INGRES Environment

2.2.1. The Process Structure

Because DEC PDP-11 computers have an address space limitation of 64K bytes per process, INGRES is separated into 5 processes. These processes are the terminal monitor, parser, decomposition (DECOMP), single relation query processor (OVQP), and the database utilities (DBU). INGRES is an interpretive system. The terminal monitor fields the user's query and passes it to the parser. The parser parses the query and passes it to the decomposition process, which decomposes the query into single relation queries, which are executed by OVQP. The database utilities include such functions as creating relations and modifying storage structures. The processes communicate by using UNIX protocols.

This five process structure has considerable impact on the performance of INGRES. The CPU time per query is increased by the cost of interprocess communication (approximately 0.2 sec. per query for the five processes). Both CPU and I/O time are increased by the same validity checking which must be done independently by more than one process. This extra cost is unavoidable in a 16 bit machine.

It is estimated that the CPU time of INGRES, since it is interpreted rather than compiled, is substantially greater than the CPU time of a compiled system. If the system were compiled, almost all of the cost in the parser and DECOMP could be paid at compile time rather than runtime. Additionally, the OVQP time might be reduced by a factor of two or three.

2.2.2. Terminal Monitor

INGRES supports two interfaces to users: a stand alone terminal monitor for interactively formulating and executing queries and a programming language interface, EQUEL [ALLM76]. In effect, the latter interface replaces the terminal monitor with a custom host language program. Production use of INGRES involves both executing terminal commands through the terminal monitor and running EQUEL programs.

The benchmarks which follow use the terminal monitor since they result from scripts of terminal commands. However, it should be noted that the terminal monitor was designed to provide a large class of services and is not particularly efficient. The single feature of user defined macros can require as much as 2 seconds per command in the terminal monitor. This cost is not present for EQUEL applications. In fact, the time spent in the EQUEL host program can be easily kept under 100 msec. per query.

2.2.3. UNIX

The costs of using the UNIX operating system for I/O are that pages are constrained to be 512 bytes long, and logically sequential pages in a file are not necessarily stored physically sequentially. There is a facility for defining page sizes longer than 512 bytes, but the operating system will, in fact, store the larger pages as two or more disjoint 512-byte pages. A page is read into UNIX process space and then copied into INGRES process space, which also increases the CPU time.

The performance data which follows reflects all these costs. Note very clearly that some of the costs are inevitable (e.g., address space), some reflect design decisions (e.g., interpretation), and some reflect the choice of the user program which "drives" INGRES (e.g., terminal monitor rather than EQUEL program).

2.3. The Software Trace

Software probes placed in the operating and data management systems consist of calls to a system trace subroutine with the relevant data as parameters. The subroutine reads a clock with 0.0001 second resolution and appends that time to the data. It then writes the package to one of three 1K byte buffers, checking to see if the buffer is full. If it is, the buffer is written to tape. The trace adds about 10% to the normal running time of the query stream. For this report, the probes placed in INGRES traced the logical page numbers and relation names for each read and write, and the total CPU time for each process. The probes placed in the operating system traced the disk read and write times. The trace information was then analyzed to produce the following results.

3.0. PERFORMANCE ANALYSIS

3.1. Overview

Three sets of benchmark programs were developed: sets of overhead-intensive, data-intensive, and multi-relation queries. Overhead-intensive and data-intensive are general types of queries which appear in other data management systems. The differentiation is similar in concept to the differentiation between "simple" and "batch" queries defined in [GRAY78].

We will define an overhead-intensive query as one for which data processing time is less than system (operating and data management) overhead to process the query. The overhead is the time to communicate with the user, parse and verify the query, and issue the command to fetch the data. The data processing time is the time to actually fetch and manipulate the data. Therefore, the overhead-intensive query is a query which references little data. This case arises when the query inherently references little data and the database has been previously optimized to support the query. For instance,

RETRIEVE (E.NAME) WHERE E.EMP# = 1234

will be an overhead-intensive query if there are few employees with E.EMP# = 1234 and if a useful storage structure involving EMP# is available. Such a structure exists if the employee relation is hashed on EMP#, ISAM on EMP#, or has a secondary index on EMP#.

The performance pattern expected of an overhead-intensive query was that it would contain no locality of reference within the query, because by definition it references little data. It was not known initially whether the overhead was CPU or I/O bound.

A data-intensive query is defined as a query for which the time to process the data is much greater than the overhead. It references a large quantity of data, and is the other end of the continuum from overhead-intensive to data-intensive queries. A data-intensive query arises from two causes:

1) the query is inherently data-intensive.

   If in the above example there were two million employees with E.EMP#= 1234, the query would be a long, data-intensive query.

   Inherently data-intensive queries are produced any time there is a complete scan of a large portion of the data, as in the production of periodic reports, billing of large sections of customer accounts, and statistical analysis of large amounts of data for such applications as management information systems.

2) queries for which the database is not well-structured.

In the above example, if the employee relation is not structured on EMP# or if it does not have a secondary index on EMP#, the entire EMP relation will be read.

This situation arises in poorly designed databases and in data management systems, such as INGRES, that support ad hoc queries. The performance pattern expected of data-intensive queries was that they would be I/O bound, and that there would be little re-referencing of data.

Data-intensive ("long") queries and overhead-intensive ("short") queries exist in other data management systems. The third set of benchmarks, multi-relation queries, are specific to relational systems. Due to the particular implementation of INGRES, the results from these queries may not generalize to other relational systems. They are queries which reference more than one relation, and, because of the INGRES implementation were expected to show significant locality of I/O references.

3.2. Results

The benchmarks were run single-user on a DEC PDP 11/70. This is a 16-bit minicomputer, with a 2K byte cache, and will perform 3.15 million register increments per second. The databases were on a disk with an average access time of .030 seconds per 512-byte block.

3.2.1. Overhead-Intensive Queries

Three query streams were developed to determine the performance patterns for overhead-intensive queries. The three benchmarks were taken from a collection of user queries from an application used by the UC Berkeley EECS Department. The application is course and room scheduling, where the database contains 24704 pages of data in 102 relations. The data is information about courses taught: instructor's name, course name, room number, type of course, etc.

The application programmer used the INGRES macro facility to define a query:

```
DESTROY TEMP
RETRIEVE INTO TEMP
    (COURSENN.INFO1, . . ., COURSENN.INFO13)
    WHERE COURSENN.INSTRUCTOR = "name"
PRINT TEMP
```

The terminal operator merely specified a query number, course number, and professor's name, and the above query was executed with the appropriate substitutions made (namely, course number for COURSENN, professor's name for name). In the script used to form the benchmark SHORT1, the above query was duplicated, exactly as the user wrote it, with 76 professor's names substituted for "name" and any one of eight courses (picked at random) substituted for COURSENN. Since the names were all unique, and the courses were picked at random, the queries are guaranteed to generate random references to data. This was done to study the performance patterns of short, random queries as would normally be found in this application.

The COURSENN relations were hashed on instructor name. The data is stored in one relation per quarter. Since the same relations were used for room scheduling, there is an entry for each course for each day the course is taught.

First, any relation named TEMP that happens to be in the database is destroyed. Then the data needed from the COURSENN relation is put into TEMP, where the implicit actions of removing duplicates and sorting on the first field take place. Then the data is printed. The only reason for using this "destroy - retrieve into - print" technique, according to the user, was to remove the duplicates introduced by having an entry per day per course. That technique is probably not generally necessary for overhead-intensive queries, as it is simply a way to get around the absence of a RETRIEVE UNIQUE command for INGRES. Therefore, the benchmark SHORT2 was created. It is the query stream SHORT1 except the destroy - retrieve into - print set is replaced by

> RETRIEVE (COURSENN.INFO1, . . ., COURSENN.INFO13)
>   WHERE COURSENN.INSTRUCTOR = "name"

This prints directly to the terminal without removing duplicates.

It was decided that the general user also probably will want fewer than 13 items of information per query, so SHORT3 was created. It is:

> RETRIEVE (COURSENN.INFO1, COURSENN.INFO2)
>   WHERE COURSENN.INSTRUCTOR = "name"

Table 5.1 summarizes some of the trace analysis results for the overhead-intensive query streams. The first column is the query stream name, the second the number of queries in the query stream. The third column, the I/O time per query, was obtained by multiplying the number of page references by the average measured physical I/O time per block for the query stream, and dividing by the number of queries. The average physical I/O time per block for each query stream varies slightly from one query stream to another, depending on the placement of data on the disk. The trace analysis program reports the total number of references to each of the relations. These are then separated into system and data references, divided by the number of queries, and presented in columns four and five. The trace analysis also keeps track of logically sequential references. A page reference is a logically sequential reference if the logical page number is one plus the logical page number of the previous reference to that file. The percentage of the references that were logically sequential are reported in column six.

We note from Table 5.1 that the number of queries in SHORT1 is three times that of SHORT2 and SHORT3, a direct result of the way the query streams were formed.

We will refer to a "destroy - retrieve into - print" collection of queries as a query set, and for SHORT1, the average I/O time for the query set was 3.06 seconds. Most of this time (98%) was spent reading and writing INGRES system relations. The relation that contains information about the relations in the database (the RELATION relation) is referenced to destroy TEMP and create it again, and to retrieve information about COURSENN. The relation that contains information about each attribute in the database, the ATTRIBUTE relation, is referenced once per attribute in the relation to be destroyed or created, and once per attribute of COURSENN in the query. It should be noted that a cache of the system catalog information could be used to substantially decrease the number of system catalog references. This is not currently done.

The data referenced per query set in SHORT1 includes three data pages

	SHORT1	SHORT2	SHORT3
number of queries	228	76	76
I/O time per query	3.06*	.55	.25
number of system references	170*	13	8
number of data references	5*	3	3
percent sequential references	13.3	18.8	21.8

* quantities given for each query set consisting of three operations (DESTROY, RETRIEVE INTO, PRINT)

TABLE 5.1. I/O Reference Pattern for Overhead Intensive Queries

from COURSENN read, and one page written to and read from the relation TEMP. The references to sort the data are not included.

Comparing the Table 5.1 entries for SHORT1 and SHORT2 we conclude that the user is paying a lot for duplicate suppression. The I/O time for SHORT2 is significantly less than the time for SHORT1 because the system relations do not have to be referenced as often. The data references are now the three pages read from the COURSENN relation. There remain an average of 13 references per query to the system relations because the ATTRIBUTE and RELATION relations must still be read for verification. The cost of that verification is apparent in SHORT3, where the only difference between that query and SHORT2 is that it references fewer attributes.

The high percentages of sequential references we see in Table 5.1 are the result of reading strings of overflow pages in the system relations. The user's database was copied from the user's machine to the test machine, so the overflow pages in the relations were formed when the relations were first created. In that case, strings of overflow pages tend to be sequential. That would not be the case if the data had been added a little at a time, through updates. It would be the case whenever the queries were run on newly modified system relations. Therefore, the sequentiality observed in Table 5.1 cannot be assumed to be true for overhead-intensive queries in general, and cannot even be assumed to be generally true for overhead-intensive queries.

A commonly accepted measure of locality is the hit-ratio curve. The hit ratio curves for overhead-intensive queries are presented in Figures 5.1 and 5.2.

The vertical axes are the percentage of requests that would have been buffer hits if the buffer were the size given on the horizontal axes. These curves were calculated by taking the output from the software trace, the logical reads and writes, and simulating the effect of increasing the buffer size. The LRU algorithm for buffer replacement was used.

In this query stream, because each query references so little data, we are only interested in inter-query locality. Figure 5.1 is the hit ratio for the overhead-intensive query streams. There is a sizeable hit ratio for even a small number of buffers for all three query streams because of the large number of reads and writes to system relations. This is confirmed by Figure 5.2, which shows the same curves, but with the references to the system relations removed. The line for SHORT1 in Figure 5.2 is higher than those for SHORT2 and SHORT3 because SHORT1 is writing and reading small temporary relations.

Since the hit ratios for SHORT2 and SHORT3 are nearly zero, it is apparent that there is no inter-query locality in the data references. The data references for the overhead-intensive queries therefore conform to the random reference models of data references, which is not surprising since the query script that made up the benchmark was chosen to be random. When the system relations are included, the hit ratios become high. The straight lines of the hit ratio curves indicate that there is no advantage to adding

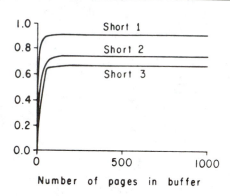

FIGURE 5.1. Overhead Intensive Queries

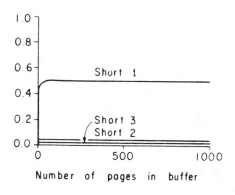

FIGURE 5.2. Overhead Intensive Queries

buffers after the few needed for the system references are provided because the references are random.

Whether there is locality of data reference in general in overhead-intensive queries depends on the application. In applications such as customer information systems and banking applications, there is little locality of data reference. However, there are systems such as airline reservations systems that may naturally have much locality of data reference (i.e., there is more activity for a plane about to leave than one scheduled for next week).

Therefore, for overhead-intensive queries, the only reliable locality of reference appears to be the references to the system relations. It is clear that caching the system relations would be very beneficial. However, this results directly from the interpretive nature of INGRES and would not be applicable to a compiled system.

INGRES has a heavier use of system relations than most other data management systems for two reasons. First, the process structure forces greater referencing of system relations because of validity checking in each process. Second, INGRES is interpretive. Many other data mangement systems are compiled, and do only minimal run-time validity checking of system catalogs. However, as long as successive queries are to the same database, and there is run-time validity checking, caching system catalogs should produce performance improvements for any data management system.

Table 5.2 contains the CPU usage patterns for overhead-intensive queries. The CPU time for each process is indicated along with the total time spent in OVQP as well as the portion of OVQP time spent on actual data manipulation (dp).

The time spent in the terminal monitor is a function of the number of characters in the query and is mostly spent looking for macros. The time spent in the parser process for SHORT1 is less than the time spent for SHORT2 because some functions to print the output are done by the parser process for a RETRIEVE in SHORT2 and are done by the print utility DBU for a PRINT in SHORT1. It is greater for SHORT2 than SHORT3 because SHORT3 has fewer domains for verification and because the query in SHORT3 is smaller, thus easier to parse.

Decomposition is the process that breaks the query apart into single

	SHORT1	SHORT2	SHORT3
monitor	1.91	1.75	.88
parser	.30	.98	.26
decomp	.21	.11	.05
OVQP total	.52	.38	.28
(dp)	.16	.15	.12
DBU	4.48		
total	7.42	3.22	1.47
total-monitor	5.51	1.47	.59

TABLE 5.2. CPU Time for Overhead Intensive Queries (all times are in seconds)

relation queries. It must also be called to pass data through the pipes from one process to the next in line. Since the utilities are at the end of the line, it must be called several times per query set in SHORT1. Therefore, the time in the process DECOMP is longer in SHORT1. The time difference between SHORT2 and SHORT3 for DECOMP is accounted for by the difference in length of the message passed.

The total OVQP time includes the data processing time in the column in the table marked dp. The time is greater for SHORT1 because OVQP must open two relations (TEMP and EMP) and write the data to one of them. The time difference between SHORT2 and SHORT3 occurs because there are fewer domains in SHORT3. The data processing time, dp, is the time to process the three pages. The time in DBU is the time to destroy, create, sort, and print the relation TEMP.

Except for SHORT1, which is probably not a general query stream, the terminal monitor requires the largest percentage of the overhead time − 54% for SHORT2. The actual data processing time in all cases is much less than the time for setting up the query. The total CPU time per query found in Table 5.2 is, for all three cases, greater than the total I/O time per query found in Table 5.1. We therefore conclude that INGRES is always CPU bound when handling overhead-intensive queries. Moreover, this statement is true even if terminal monitor time is zero, as noted in the last row, which represents a "super efficient" EQUEL program. In such a circumstance, INGRES will execute about 1.6 queries from SHORT3 per second and use less than half the available disk transfers.

Distributed processing at the data level (as in DIRECT [DEWI78] and RAP [OZKA77]) will not speed the processing of overhead-intensive queries at all, since they spend little time processing data. In fact, an extra staging device between the I/O device and the user, as in DIRECT, or the inability to support access to a single item through a key, as in RAP, will slow the processing of short queries. Instead, either the processing must be distributed toward the user, through use of intelligent terminals and front-end machines, or the amount of processing must be reduced through use of a less functional terminal monitor or through compilation of queries. In the overhead-intensive queries in the benchmark query streams, the relocation of the terminal monitor functions would clearly be a performance improvement.

The INGRES terminal monitor provides many functions for the user (e.g., macro definitions, abbreviations) and is certainly not a minimal terminal monitor. However, if these functions are to be provided to the user, it is clear they can best be provided through intelligent terminals.

3.2.2. Data-Intensive Queries

The data-intensive query streams were developed from an accounting application, the UC Berkeley EECS Department's Cost Account and Recharge System. As in the overhead-intensive query case, we use the technique of making the first benchmark correspond exactly to the user queries, the third benchmark correspond exactly to our idea of what a "typical query stream" for data-intensive queries would be, and the second benchmark is in between.

The query stream LONG1 is exactly as the user wrote it. It consists of 58 queries which reference 14 relations which contain a total of 822 pages of data. This query stream prints accounting reports by creating temporary relations in which the domains are both projections of existing relations in the database and zero or blank summary domains. The summary domains are then filled in by using multi-relation aggregate functions, and then the temporary relations reprinted. There are an average of 14 domains referenced per query in LONG1. LONG2 is LONG1 with all multi-relation aggregate functions removed, and the RETRIEVE INTO constructs replaced by RETRIEVE commands. LONG2 contains single-relation aggregate functions. LONG3 is LONG2 with all aggregate functions removed, and with the average number of domains referenced by each query reduced to two. There was no attempt to do the same work in LONG1, LONG2 and LONG3.

The query:

```
RETRIEVE (ACCT.ACCT#, ACCT.FUND,
          ENCUMB = SUM (ACCT.ENCUMB
          BY ACCT.ACCT#, ACCT.FUND))
```

is a query from the accounting application and included in LONG1 and LONG2. The relation ACCT has information about the department's outstanding accounts. The query results in a list of the totals of the outstanding encumbrances grouped by account number and fund. INGRES processes the aggregate function SUM by creating a temporary relation TEMP1 which contains three domains: ACCT#, FUND, and SUM. It will be hashed on (ACCT#, FUND) and is initially empty. The relation ACCT is read once, and for each tuple the (ACCT#, FUND) pair evaluated, the tuple from TEMP1 for that pair read, the sum updated, and the totals replaced in the TEMP1 relation. After the last tuple of ACCT is read, the TEMP1 relation is read and the results printed on the user's terminal.

Table 5.3 presents the results of the query analysis of the data-intensive query streams with respect to I/O usage. The number of queries in LONG1 is greater than the number of queries in LONG2 because the multi-relation queries in LONG1 were not included in LONG2, and because the "destroy - retrieve into - print" queries were replaced by a single RETRIEVE. LONG3 contains fewer queries than LONG2 because the aggregates were dropped to create LONG3. The I/O time per query is the total I/O time for the query stream divided by the total number of queries in the stream. It is greater for LONG2 than for LONG1 because the queries that were dropped from LONG1 in forming LONG2 were queries that reference little data. The queries that form the LONG3 subset of LONG2 reference much less data because the aggregates were dropped from LONG2 to create LONG3.

The number of system references per query is a direct result of the

	LONG1	LONG2	LONG3
number of queries	58	18	13
I/O time per query	15.0	16.7	5.1
number of system references	129	73	15
number of data references	290	484	155
percent sequential references	30	28	84

TABLE 5.3. I/O References for Data-Intensive Queries (all times are in seconds)

number of temporary relations created and the number of attributes referenced per query.

The percentage of sequential accesses is high in all three cases. It is apparent that the INGRES processing of aggregates is dominating the I/O references, because when the aggregates are removed, the sequentiality dramatically increases. This sequentiality is the result of reading entire relations, either to print selected attributes, or to print summary statistics.

In Figures 5.3 and 5.4 we present the hit ratio curves for these benchmarks. Note that LONG1 is a gently rising curve in both figures, while LONG2 is nearly flat. The rising nature of LONG1 appears to be due entirely to the INGRES implementation of aggregate functions where random re-referencing of (relatively small) temporaries is taking place.

In LONG3 we see the result of sequentiality and locality. The same relation was referenced sequentially in several queries; when the buffer size was large enough to hold both that relation and the relations referenced by intervening queries, there was a sharp jump, at 350 pages, in the hit ratio curve.

In Figure 5.4 we see that this locality is not caused by references to system relations. This is not because system relations are referenced less in data-intensive queries than in overhead-intensive queries, but that the proportion of system references to data references has changed. Therefore, although caching system relations will not hurt the performance of the data-intensive query, it will not greatly improve it either.

There was a high degree of sequentiality found in all three reference traces. There were two types of locality found. One type, the locality resulting from the INGRES implementation of aggregate functions (as seen in the

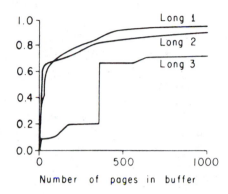

FIGURE 5.3. Data-Intensive Queries

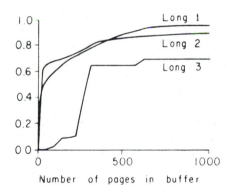

FIGURE 5.4. Data-Intensive Queries, System References Removed

hit-ratio curves for LONG1 and LONG2) is very much like the locality found in program references (Figure 5.7). The buffer size needed to take advantage of this type of locality can be relatively small and is related to the number of values for which aggregates are simultaneously being performed. The second type of locality, the cyclic sequentiality (as seen in the curves for LONG3) would require a buffer size equal to the size of the relation being repeatedly scanned. Since this can be very large, it may not be cost effective to deal with this situation by "blind buffering". Rather, data read-ahead may be especially attractive here. It may be best to simply ignore the cyclic sequential case, and only do the read-ahead that the large amount of sequentiality mandates.

Table 5.4 indicates the CPU usage for the data-intensive queries. The variation between monitor and parser times is as explained in the overhead-intensive queries. The decomposition time for LONG1 is much greater than the others because of the presence of multi-relation queries in LONG1, which means decomposition has work to do. The OVQP time is greater per query in LONG2 because LONG1 includes queries where most of the work is being done in the utilities. When those queries were dropped, the average per-query time in OVQP increased. The time spent in the utilities (DBU) is mostly spent sorting relations and printing them. LONG3 has less time in OVQP because fewer attributes were manipulated in the queries in LONG3.

We note that in all cases the data processing time (dp) in OVQP is the greatest single item of CPU time, and that I/O time is approximately equal to CPU time. It should be consequently noted that both improved buffering and distributing the processing toward the data would be required to improve performance for data-intensive queries. Because INGRES interprets queries CPU time is probably higher than compiled systems. On the other hand, our configuration contains only one disk controller. A multiprogrammed benchmark with multiple I/O controllers could cut the effective I/O time substantially. Hence, both I/O and CPU time are higher than might be the case in an alternate architecture. Database machines (e.g., RAP, DIRECT) should pay careful attention to staging of data as well as to creating a distributed processing environment.

	LONG1	LONG2	LONG3
monitor	1.7	2.1	1.3
parser	.4	.9	.3
decomp	.8	.26	.07
OVQP Total	7.1	11.23	3.73
(dp)	6.9	11.0	3.5
DBU	5.8		
total	15.8	14.39	5.4
total-monitor	14.1	12.4	4.1

TABLE 5.4. CPU Times for Data-Intensive Queries (all times are in seconds)

3.2.3. Multi-Relation Queries

Multi-relation queries are specific to relational systems. The INGRES implementation of them does not necessarily generalize to other relational systems. They were included in this analysis because the potential benefits of extended storage devices, read ahead policies and distributed processing may make a very efficient implementation of multi-relation queries possible.

In INGRES multi-relation queries are processed through the formation of temporary relations and the use of tuple substitution. The technique is described in detail in [WONG76] and [YOUS78] and shall be illustrated by an example. We shall call this example the ROOMS query. It is included in the benchmark, and is from the user application.

The query is:

```
RETRIEVE (ROOMS.BUILDING, ROOMS.RM#, ROOMS.CAPACITY,
        ROOMS.DAY, ROOMS.HOUR)
    WHERE ROOMS.RM# = COURSE.RM#
    AND ROOMS.BUILDING = COURSE.BUILDING
    AND ROOMS.TYPE = "lab"
```

The relation COURSE contains information about all the courses taught by the UC Berkeley EECS Department in the last four years. It contains 11436 tuples in 2858 pages, and is stored in an ISAM storage structure, keyed on instructor name and course number. The relation ROOMS contains information about every room that the EECS Department can use for teaching courses. It contains 282 tuples in 29 pages, and is hashed on room number.

The result of this query is a list which contains the building, room number, capacity, day, and hour of the use of any lab for the last four years.

To process this query, first INGRES will note that there is a one-relation restriction (WHERE ROOMS.TYPE = "lab"), so that restriction will be done first. The query is issued

```
RETRIEVE INTO TEMP1 (ROOMS.BUILDING,
        ROOMS.RM#, ROOMS.CAPACITY)
    WHERE ROOMS.TYPE = "lab"
```

The temporary relation TEMP1 which resulted from the actual query in this case contained 20 tuples in 2 pages.

The relation COURSE is not stored in a way that is helpful to the processing of this query, and only a few domains of each tuple are needed for this query. Hence, INGRES performs the projection of COURSE by issuing the query:

```
RETRIEVE INTO TEMP2 (COURSE.DAY, COURSE.HOUR,
        COURSE.BUILDING, COURSE.RM#)
```

This results in a relation TEMP2 which contains the same number of tuples as COURSE (11436) but less space (867 pages) since the tuples are smaller.

The final step is tuple substitution, where each tuple in TEMP1 is compared to each tuple in TEMP2, and the result printed on the terminal. For instance, the first tuple in TEMP1 is the tuple (cory, 119, 15), so the query is issued:

```
RETRIEVE (BUILDING = "cory", RM# = 119,
        CAPACITY = 15, TEMP2.DAY, TEMP2.HOUR)
    WHERE TEMP2.RM# = 119
    AND TEMP2.BUILDING = "cory"
```

This process of tuple substitution is repeated 20 times, once per tuple in TEMP1. Since TEMP2 is unordered, the result is that the entire TEMP2 relation is scanned 20 times, resulting in 17,340 data pages read in a cyclic sequential fashion. INGRES includes a set of heuristics which dynamically decide when to reformat a temporary relation. TEMP2 could have been reformatted to a relation hashed on (BUILDING, RM#). It was not reformatted because the cost functions associated with modifying the relation to hash showed that cost would be greater than re-scanning the relation 20 times. It should be clearly noted that all 20 queries could have been been processed in parallel with one sequential pass of TEMP2. Unfortunately, the current implementation does not support such a strategy.

The multi-relation benchmark was prepared by assembling a collection of unrelated users' queries which were multi-relation queries and which referenced the same database. The database was the UC Berkeley EECS Department's course and scheduling database. The patterns observed were dominated by the ROOMS query. Most of the queries referenced about 109 pages; the ROOMS query referenced 19000 pages of data. Most of the queries used about 7.25 seconds of CPU time; the ROOMS query used 709.5 seconds of CPU time. Therefore the results are reported without the query ROOMS in MULTI1, and for ROOMS alone.

The I/O reference patterns are presented in Table 5.5. There are few system references compared to the number of data references in ROOMS because the temporary relation is being read so many times. The temporary relation is read sequentially each of the 20 times it is read, which is why the percentage of sequential references is so high. Figures 5.5 and 5.6 show the hit-ratio curves for the multi-relation queries. The hit-ratio curve for for the ROOMS query takes a sharp jump as soon as the window size is above the 867-page size of the relation being continually re-referenced. This is the cyclic sequential referencing found in the query stream LONG3, but with a difference: the size of the cycle is precisely known by INGRES. Hence, this information can be used advantageously in a buffering or read ahead policy.

CPU patterns are presented in Table 5.6. Since these queries are data-intensive as well as multi-relation queries, the CPU time spent in the data-processing portion of the data management system is the greatest component of the CPU time.

	MULTI1	ROOMS
number of queries	24	1
I/O time per query	3.27	505.16
number of system references	23	70
number of data references	86	19023
percent sequential references	35	85

TABLE 5.5. I/O References for Multi-Relation Queries (all times are in seconds)

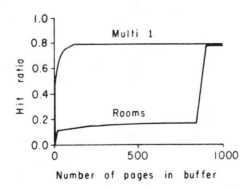

FIGURE 5.5. Multi-Relation Queries

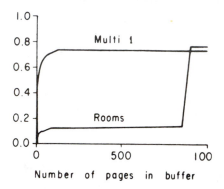

FIGURE 5.6. Multi-Relation Queries, System References Removed

	MULTI1	ROOMS
monitor	1.0	1.37
parser	.25	.81
decomp	.52	.71
OVQP Total	4.33	705.75
(dp)	4.2	705.4
DBU	1.15	1.86
total	7.25	709.5
total-monitor	6.3	708.1

TABLE 5.6. CPU Times for Multi-Relation Queries (all times are in seconds)

It might be claimed that the above numbers simply reflect the INGRES algorithms for handling multi-variable queries and would not be indicative of referencing patterns of the other approaches (e.g., [BLAS76]). We might note that other algorithms often include sorting. Many sorting algorithms involve a limited kind of cyclic sequentiality of referencing, at least to write data, then read it in again. Hence, our results may be representative of such algorithms also.

The CPU time per query in Table 5.6 is greater than the I/O time per query (Table 5.5) so INGRES at this time would see little benefit from caching the relations to be re-referenced. However, combined with the compilation of the queries and/or distributing processing on the data level, using extended storage devices, or an effective read ahead policy would appear very beneficial.

4.0. SUMMARY

4.1. Read Ahead

Comparing the hit ratio curves in Figures 5.1-6 and the typical hit ratio curve for program references in Figure 5.7, we note that INGRES data references are in most cases very different from program references. This difference results from sequentiality of reference. This sequentiality can be used to increase performance by placing pages which are logically sequential in a file physically sequential on the disk. Then, if a relation is being read sequentially, when one page on a disk track is read, several pages or even the remainder of the track can also be read. It is even possible to read an entire cylinder at a time if an extended storage device is available. The amount which should be prefetched depends on available buffer space and whether the database system is I/O bound. In the best case, read ahead would reduce the time to fetch a disk block from about 30 msec to less than 3 msec; an order of magnitude improvement in I/O system performance.

Clearly, it is only wise to read ahead if one knows that additional data will be used. Therefore the system handling I/O and buffer management must have the information that the data is being accessed sequentially. In an analysis of IMS data references, [SMIT76], it is recommended the number of

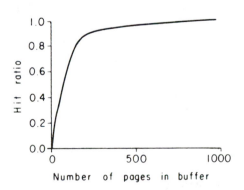

FIGURE 5.7. Typical Hit Ratio Curve for Program References

blocks to be read ahead be based on the number of blocks previously read sequentially. This is a guess, and necessary in IMS because the level of the user interface to the data management system is one record at a time. But in INGRES and other high-level systems the user interface is at least one relation at a time. There is no need to guess; INGRES knows when it must read all or a part of a file sequentially. It can either pass that information to the operating system through a new read command (read sequentially) or do its own I/O management so that read-ahead can be selectively invoked.

4.2. Locality

Locality of reference (as opposed to sequentiality) was found in references to the system catalogs and in processing aggregate functions. Moreover, cyclic sequentiality was found in the processing of multi-relation queries. The locality of reference for system relations can be utilized by permanently storing them on an extended storage device. For a long time operating systems have used the technique of keeping hierarchies of directories in main memory and on fixed head disks. Alternately, INGRES could be redesigned to do minimal run-time checking.

The cyclic sequential locality of reference in multi-relation queries can be used either by implementing a cache or by invoking a read ahead policy. Lastly, the processing of aggregate functions can be expedited only by a buffer cache. INGRES is aware of when a multi-relation query or aggregate function is being processed and can signal the operating system that cyclic sequential or random referencing will be taking place.

4.3. Distributed Processing

In INGRES the performance bottleneck for overhead-intensive queries and for many data-intensive queries is the CPU. Distributed processing is one solution to the CPU-bound problem. Several data management machines have been designed which include distributed processing. We have shown that for data-intensive queries, distributing the processing toward the data certainly will result in a performance improvement and that for overhead-intensive queries distributing the processing toward the user will result in performance improvement.

Although these two solutions do not appear to be in conflict, they are. If distributing the processing toward the data requires overhead that increases the processing time of the overhead-intensive query, and if a substantial portion of the use of the system will be overhead-intensive queries, the performance will degrade.

4.4. Conclusion

The data usage and I/O reference patterns found in the processing of queries by INGRES show that the performance of INGRES may be improved dramatically by using some combination of extended memory, read ahead and multiple processors.

For overhead-intensive queries, this may be done by:

1)   distributing processing at the terminal monitor level.

2)   using extended storage (or main memory) to cache temporary and system relations.

For data-intensive queries, this may be done by:

1)   distributing the processing at the data level.

2)   using main memory or an extended storage device to implement large, read-ahead buffers to take advantage of the sequential reading of data.

3)   using main memory or an extended storage device to cache the temporary relations formed and referenced during the processing of aggregate functions.

For multi-relation queries:

1)   distributing the processing at the data level.

2)   caching the relations to be cyclically re-referenced in an extended storage device or invoking read ahead.

INGRES, in its present form, is CPU bound most of the time. Therefore, the benefits received by improving I/O speed would not appreciably effect the query response time unless the CPU time is decreased. This can be done by distributing the processing or compiling a part of the query processing.

The INGRES system, which is forced into a multi-process structure and which supports a complex terminal monitor, may have a higher overhead than most data-management systems. However, any system that supports a highly functional user interface may benefit from putting as much of the interface as possible into intelligent terminals. Those systems that do run-time checking of system catalogs may benefit from caching them in extended storage.

In the case of data-intensive queries, sequentiality of access has been found in another data management system [RODR76], and may be present in any data management systems that support such facilities as report generators. Therefore, the caching of read-ahead data blocks appears to be a good technique for any system which

1)   has space available in main memory or an extended storage device.

2) has the data organized on the disks to take advantage of sequential reads, so that actual I/O time is saved by reading several disk blocks at once.

3) can communicate with the operating system that data is to be read sequentially.

## CHAPTER SIX

Performance Enhancements to a Relational Database System

Michael Stonebraker / John Woodfill / Jeff Ranstrom / Marguerite Murphy / Marc Meyer / Eric Allman

ABSTRACT

In this paper, we examine four performance enhancements to a database management system. These are: use of dynamic compilation, use of micro-coded routines, use of a special purpose file system and use of a special purpose operating system. All were examined in the context of the INGRES data base management system. Benchmark timings are included which suggest the attractiveness of dynamic compilation and a special purpose file system. Microcode and a special purpose operating system are analyzed and appear to be of more limited utility in the INGRES context.

1.0. INTRODUCTION

Many tactics are available which may improve database system performance. These include compiling commands, enhancing the file system, lowering the cost of commonly used system calls, judicious use of microcode, using special purpose hardware, clustering multiple record types in a single operating system file, etc.

In this paper, we report case studies on the attempted application of four of these tactics in the environment of the INGRES relational database system [STON76a, STON80b]. For each technique studied, we indicate limitations concerning the applicability of our results to other contexts.

M. Stonebraker, J. Woodfill, J. Ranstrom, M. Murphy, M. Meyer, and E. Allman, *ACM Transactions on Database Systems*, vol. 8, no. 2, June 1983. Copyright 1983, Association for Computing Machinery, Inc.; reprinted by permission.

In the next subsections we briefly discuss the INGRES environment and outline the tactics we studied.

1.1. The INGRES Environment

On VAX 11/780 computers INGRES runs as two processes as noted in Figure 6.1. An application program (or the INGRES terminal monitor) runs as a front end UNIX process and the remainder of the run-time system is a second process. This second process contains code that was split into several address spaces in previous PDP-11 versions because of addressing limits on those machines. The INGRES process makes system calls on UNIX [RITC74b] to read and write 1024 byte disk blocks. Database commands are passed between the application program and the INGRES process over the UNIX interprocess message systems (pipes).

UNIX provides a global cache for the file system in the operating system address space. INGRES requests that can be satisfied by data in this cache cause no I/O activity. Moreover, UNIX notes sequential access to a file and prefetches the next block before a process requests it. Each user obtains his own INGRES process which shares a code segment with all other concurrent INGRES processes. Each INGRES process also has a private data segment which contains an additional non-shared buffer pool for each user.

1.2. Compilation

INGRES is currently an interpretive database system. Consequently, database commands are received from an application program as ASCII strings at run time and then parsed, validated and executed. Although ad-hoc commands from a user at a terminal must have these steps performed at run time, commands from a host language program can have some of the above functions done at compile time. As a result, run-time overhead would be reduced. For

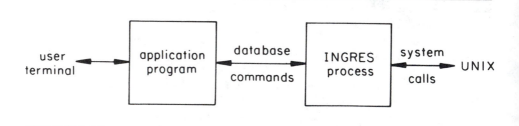

FIGURE 6.1. The INGRES Environment

example, System R [ASTR76, BLAS79b] compiles commands into machine language programs to be executed at run time. The various options have been sketched in [KATZ78] and include several possibilities between the INGRES pure interpreter and the System R pure compiler.

Performance studies in [HAWT79] suggest that parsing and validating an INGRES command at compile time would be advantageous for simple commands. In fact, the parse-at-run-time strategy is one of the major mistakes in the design of INGRES noted in [STON80b], and it is possible that INGRES will be modified to parse at compile time in the future.

However, in longer transactions parsing at compile time would have little impact. The overhead of parsing and validating a command is dominated by the effort needed for data searching. On long commands about 95 percent of the CPU time is spent by INGRES inside an inner loop [HAWT79] which compares a record to a template and reports whether the record satisfies the qualification indicated by the template.

To reduce the overhead of record interpretation we could incorporate a pure compiler in INGRES, but this would involve a complete rewrite of the system and is infeasible. On the other hand, we feel that dynamic compilation is a viable alternate strategy. Hence, we would compile a procedure to perform record selection while processing an individual command. As a result, instead of requiring N interpretations for N records, we need one compilation followed by N executions of the compiled code.

The use of dynamic compilation has several advantages compared to generating machine code at compile time. First, access path selection can continue to be done at run time. The code to accomplish this is very complex, and an interpreter for it is easier to build than a compiler. In addition, access path selection at run time can make use of the actual sizes of partial results when planning the next step to take [EPST80a].

In Section 2.0 of this paper we report on the design of our dynamic compiler and give benchmark results concerning its performance.

1.3. Microcode

The VAX 11/780 computer contains a user writable control store; hence, we can write microcode for commonly executed routines. Microcode has been used successfully by the IDMS and ADABAS database systems for IBM 370 computers and in the IDM 500 [EPST80b] database machine. A performance improvement is possible from two sources. First, one can replace several machine language instructions by a single larger one thereby saving the instruction fetch portion of each execution cycle. In addition, one may be able to code a more compact algorithm in microcode than is possible with the machine instructions provided by the computer designer.

A simple example will clarify both advantages. On a PDP-11 computer one can move 512 bytes (256 words) from an even location in memory (stored in R1) to another even location in memory (stored in R2) with the following code fragment:

```
            MOV #256, R0
      LOOP:  MOV (R1)+, (R2)+
             SOB R0, LOOP
```

First we move the word count to R0 and then execute the two instruction loops 256 times. On each pass 2 bytes are moved from the storage location pointed to by R1 to the storage location pointed to by R2 and both R1 and R2 are incremented by 2. A total of 512 instructions are fetched and executed by this loop.

If a PDP-11 could be microcoded, one could implement a single instruction, BMOVE, with three register operands that would perform the same function. BMOVE would avoid 511 instruction fetches. Moreover, it can request the next two bytes from memory in parallel with decrementing the count register (R0) and performing the conditional branch. Consequently, a large improvement would be anticipated by microcoding this routine.

Of course, the problem with microcode is that few tools are available to assist in its construction. For example, we were unable to locate a microcode assembler which would run under UNIX, and the documentation on how to use the microstore was difficult to read. Moreover, the VAX is a modern machine which corrects many gaps in the PDP-11 instruction set. For example, "block move" has been included in the VAX instruction set. Consequently, many candidate routines have already been microcoded by the VAX system designers.

Because of the poor tools and documentation, we were unsuccessful in producing a microcode version of INGRES which could be benchmarked. However, in Section 3.0, we report on our experiments with profiling INGRES to isolate high traffic routines. Then, we estimate the size and expected speed-up of INGRES with a microcode assist.

1.4. File Systems

The UNIX file system was designed to serve time sharing users [RITC74b, BELL78]. Consequently, it is easy and efficient to create and destroy files and to change their length dynamically. However, UNIX randomly allocates disk blocks to a file. As a result logically adjacent blocks in a file are not necessarily physically close together. Since INGRES does a substantial amount of sequential access [HAWT79], random allocation is undesirable. Moreover, UNIX uses a collection of indirect blocks to map logical pages to physical blocks. These indirect blocks must be read during a page access and increase the overhead associated with reading or writing a file. Lastly, the block size used by UNIX (1024 bytes) appears rather small for database use.

To test the performance consequences of the UNIX file system, we designed a special relation storage module that directly accesses a "raw" disk. This software efficiently supports access to a relation without the overhead of the UNIX file system. In Section 4.0 we briefly discuss the design of this software and then show via benchmark studies the impact which it has on the performance of INGRES.

1.5. General Purpose Operating System

Besides the file system, a DBMS makes use of other operating system services. These include process management and interprocess messages. For example, INGRES uses the UNIX message system to communicate with the application program. Moreover, on each data access that requires an actual disk read, INGRES will be suspended and a task switch will occur to another process. Operating systems usually support processes with considerable state information. As a result switching tasks is often an expensive operation. In addition, on many current systems interprocess messages are expensive. Since a database system must use both facilities extensively or implement its own multitasking system in user space [STON80a], the operating system may stand in the way of efficient database operation.

To study this issue we designed a small special purpose operating system, MANGOS. This software runs on a dedicated machine and supports only the facilities that a database system requires. Such services are specially tuned to database needs.

In Section 5.0, we indicate the design of MANGOS and make estimates concerning its performance. Since it is not yet completely coded, benchmark studies have not been run in this environment.

1.6. The Benchmark

In order to test our dynamic compiler and special purpose file system we constructed the following benchmark. It consisted of two sections, the first was designed to test commands which would sequentially scan a relation stored as a heap while the second tried to illustrate performance when a keyed access path could be used.

The first section consisted of four queries using the following PARTS relation:

PART(P#, PNAME, PCOLOR, PWEIGHT, QOH)

It contained 34 byte tuples and was stored as a heap. Runs were made with 1, 210 and 3360 tuples occupying respectively 1, 8 and 118 pages.

1) RETRIEVE (a = 1)

2) RANGE OF P IS PARTS
   RETRIEVE (P.P#)

3) RETRIEVE (P.PNAME, P.P#)
      WHERE P.P# > 3
      OR P.PNAME = "Processor"
      OR P.PCOLOR = "Black"

    4)   RETRIEVE (P.P#)
           WHERE P.QOH $<$ log (9/5) * P.WEIGHT

Query (1) is intended to show the cost of compilation for a very short query. In this case, the query requires no database accesses and its interpretation is inexpensive. On the other hand, compiling such a query should only generate additional overhead.

Queries (2) through (4) require a sequential scan of the PARTS relation. Moreover, (3) and (4) have a complex qualification which may be costly to interpret. A compiler should perform well in these situations.

The second portion of the benchmark deals with a PARTS relation which has tuples widened to 200 bytes with a filler field. Moreover, PARTS contains 3360 tuples and was stored indexed sequential (ISAM) with P# as a key. The data level of this structure contained 646 1K pages each with 5 tuples and 130 1K overflow pages each with a single record. This situation models a perfectly built keyed structure for 3230 tuples followed by 130 random inserts.

    5)   RETRIEVE (P.QOH) WHERE P.P# $<$ 2500

    6)   RANGE OF Q IS PARTS
           RETRIEVE (P.QOH, Q.QOH)
              WHERE P.P# = Q. P#

    7)   RETRIEVE (P.QOH, Q.QOH)
              WHERE P.P# = Q.P#
              AND P.COLOR = "Black"

    8)   RETRIEVE (P.QOH)
              WHERE P.P# = Q.P#
              AND P.P# $<$ 2500

    9)   RETRIEVE (P.QOH, Q.QOH)
              WHERE P.P# = Q.P#
              AND P.COLOR = "Black"
              AND P.QOH $<$ log (9/5) * P.WEIGHT
              AND Q.QOH $<$ log (9/5) * P.WEIGHT

Query (5) illustrates a range search on a portion of PARTS. Then commands (6) through (9) suggest various natural joins all of which connect PARTS to itself using the keyed field. These queries are intended to be illustrative of complex commands and differ in the amount of added qualification. In all cases, performance numbers were generated for both an ISAM structure and for a PARTS relation hashed on pnum. Since the results are similar, we present only the ISAM numbers.

All numbers will be in seconds and are obtained from a VAX 11/780 computer running the UNIX operating system. In all cases we indicate elapsed wall clock time for the command and total CPU time spent on command processing either by INGRES directly or by UNIX on behalf of INGRES. Moreover, numbers were obtained with the benchmark as the only task executing. In this way there is no variation due to the load generated by other concurrent tasks. Also, the benchmark was submitted from a single application program, and no attempt was made to explore the impact of a multi-user benchmark.

In selecting the benchmark and the timing technique we were motivated by the following considerations. We attempted to choose a collection of commands which would illustrate the behavior of dynamic compilation and a special purpose file system. In addition, the benchmark was chosen to be representative of an ad-hoc query and update environment such as a computer aided design application. Here, an engineer might be editing a circuit design stored in a database. Such scientific applications appear to be typical of current INGRES use.

The benchmark does not contain a large collection of simple commands such as might be submitted concurrently in a banking or airline reservation environment. In such applications there can be extra overhead due to concurrency control conflicts or competition for buffer space. No conclusions can be drawn from our studies for such environments.

2.0. A DYNAMIC COMPILER

In this section we sketch the design of our dynamic compiler and then give results on the performance improvement obtained.

2.1. Design of DC-INGRES

Dynamically Compiled INGRES (DC-INGRES) compiles commands that affect only a single relation. The code to decompose multi-relation commands into a sequence of single relation commands is unaffected.

For example, the following command finds all employees under 30 or in the toy department or who make less than $20,000.

```
RANGE OF E IS EMP
RETRIEVE (E.NAME)
        WHERE E.age < 30
        OR E.dept = "toy"
        OR E.salary < 20000
```

Current INGRES algorithms will scan the employee relation record by record, interpreting the above qualification for each one. Moreover, the target list, in this case the name of an employee, is interpretively constructed for qualifying records.

The implementation is via a stack-oriented interpretation of a postordered list of symbols representing the command. Figure 6.2 illustrates the data structure used for the qualification "WHERE 13 + E.salary = 100". The second entry in the stack indicates that salary is the first field in EMP and is a four-byte floating point number. The other entries are self-explanatory.

```
┌─────────────────────────┐
│         INT, 2          │
│           13            │
├─────────────────────────┤
│     VAR, 1, FLOAT, 4    │
├─────────────────────────┤
│         opPLUS          │
├─────────────────────────┤
│         INT, 2          │
│          100            │
├─────────────────────────┤
│          opEQ           │
└─────────────────────────┘
```

FIGURE 6.2. The Qualification "WHERE 13 + E.SALARY = 100"

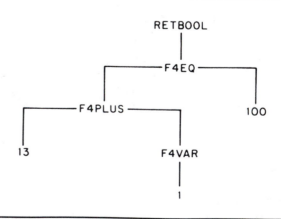

FIGURE 6.3. The Intermediate Code Tree

This is a costly approach to record evaluation. For example, if there are 1000 tuples that must be evaluated, the code for opEQ will check its arguments each of the 1000 times to determine if a conversion is necessary. Consequently, the integer 100 will be converted to a float 1000 times so that opEQ can compare two operands of the same type.

To alleviate this overhead, the DC-INGRES compiler produces a form of code loosely based on direct threaded code [BELL73, DEWA75]. The compiler takes as input a list such as the one in Figure 6.2 and builds a tree-formatted intermediate code data structure. In this tree, shown for the above qualification in Figure 6.3, the nodes are specialized operators, and their descendants are their operands. For example, the node F4PLUS is a pointer to code to add two four-byte floats and return a four-byte floating point number. Hence, no decision-making concerning types is done during tree evaluation. Lastly, DC-INGRES converts all constants to the desired type during tree construction. Consequently, the integers 13 and 100 are converted to floats just once.

Although DC-INGRES does not produce in-line machine code, we feel that the performance penalty for our threaded code solution may not be large. The additional overhead is perhaps two or three instructions per operator in the tree. Since most nodes require several instructions to implement, the threaded code penalty may be as little as 10-20 percent.

Query	Relation Size	DC-INGRES Elapsed Time	INGRES Elapsed Time	IMPROVEMENT
a	0	.9	.9	0%
b	1	.9	.9	0%
b	210	1.2	1.3	8.3%
b	3360	5.0	5.7	14.0%
c	1	1.2	1.2	0%
c	210	1.7	2.0	17.6%
c	3360	7.6	11.5	51.3%
d	1	1.0	1.0	0%
d	210	1.5	1.8	20.0%
d	3360	5.5	11.5	109.1%
e	3360	17.1	18.7	9.4%
f	3360	52.8	63.5	20.3%
g	3360	31.5	33.3	5.7%
h	3360	47.5	54.5	14.7%
i	3360	32.3	34.4	6.5%

TABLE 6.1. Elapsed Time

2.2. The Performance Results

This section discusses the results obtained from the benchmark indicated in Section 1.5 for normal INGRES and DC-INGRES. Two statistics were measured: elapsed wall clock time with the benchmark as the only active task, and CPU time spent by INGRES or by UNIX on behalf of INGRES. These are reported in Tables 6.1 and 6.2.

2.3. Conclusions

The results show that for commands affecting a single tuple the compiler costs somewhat more CPU time (about .012 seconds) but generates the same response time. In general, DC-INGRES cuts the cost of processing a record substantially (from .0031 to .0019 sec. for query c) with 3360 tuples). Consequently, if more than about ten records are evaluated, one would expect DC-INGRES to outperform normal INGRES. The performance improvement is considerable for complex one-relation commands, for example d) and e), when a large number of records are examined.

In general, the improvement in response time is less significant. When a page is requested which is in neither the UNIX cache nor the INGRES cache, both DC-INGRES and normal INGRES must wait about 30 msec. for it to be read into main memory from the disk. This I/O delay adds a constant value to the response time for both versions and reduces the response time improvement of DC-INGRES.

A multi-relation command is decomposed by INGRES into a sequence of one-relation commands. In f) through i), they generally have a qualification of the form

    WHERE P# = constant

and only a few records are evaluated for each one since PARTS is keyed on P#. However, DC-INGRES notes that a sequence of identical commands is generated, differing only in the constant used. Consequently, it reuses the compiled form of the query and substitutes new constants. Hence, the .012 sec. compilation cost is required only once. As a result an improvement is still possible in all multi-relation commands in the benchmark.

It should be noted that these results apply only to environments which interpret record selection. When compiled code is produced prior to run time, e.g., [BLAS79b], or where record evaluation code is part of the application program, e.g., [CODA71], these observations are inapplicable.

3.0. MICRO-INGRES

In order to evaluate the feasibility of a microcode version of INGRES (M-INGRES) we first profiled the INGRES run-time code to find high traffic routines as candidates for conversion to microcode. Then, we hoped to recode

Query	Relation Size	DC-INGRES Total CPU time	INGRES Total CPU time	IMPROVEMENT
a	0	.087	.087	0%
b	1	.123	.112	-9.5%
b	210	.353	.401	13.7%
b	3360	3.88	4.73	21.8%
c	1	.208	.195	-6.4%
c	210	.605	.823	36.1%
c	3360	6.37	10.3	61.9%
d	1	.177	.162	-8.5%
d	210	.433	.812	87.3%
d	3360	4.25	10.6	148.3%
e	3360	6.43	8.96	39.4%
f	3360	42.4	53.1	25.2%
g	3360	10.6	13.1	23.2%
h	3360	33.1	41.9	26.3%
i	3360	11.1	14.1	26.7%

TABLE 6.2. INGRES Total CPU Time

some of them in microcode so we could benchmark M-INGRES to test its performance. In this section we report on our findings.

3.1. Profiling

In order to identify the high traffic routines, we ran the benchmark with the UNIX profiler enabled. This package indicates the percentage of CPU time inside each procedure of the INGRES run-time system. The major portion of INGRES time is spent inside the code that evaluates so-called one variable commands (OVQP). A substantial fraction of this code is the record evaluation code discussed in Section 2.0. Table 6.3 indicates the routines with more than 3.0% of the run-time CPU cycles. Together, they account for 54.3% of total INGRES CPU time in the benchmark.

A brief description of each of these routines now follows.

GETSYMBOL: This routine fetches symbols from the data structure representing the qualification indicated in Figure 6.2. The symbols themselves are triples consisting of a type, a length, and a value. The representation of the value depends on both the type and length. Within the

%Time	Routine	Short Explanation
17.1	GETSYMBOL	get symbol from list
14.8	INTERPRET	interpret list
4.4	LOG	logarithm
4.3	READ	read system call
3.9	BMOVE	block memory move
3.7	GET	get tuple
3.1	FWRITE	write to file
3.0	SCAN	scan a relation

TABLE 6.3. High Traffic Routines

subroutine, the legality of the type and length are checked and an indication of whether the list has been exhausted is returned to the calling routine. This routine is 105 lines of C.

INTERPRET: This is the main routine of OVQP. It processes tuples against a qualification structured as in Figure 6.2 and uses GETSYMBOL to fetch the symbols. The code is structured as a loop which first removes a symbol from the list, then processes it using a series of nested switch statements. This routine is 420 lines of C.

LOG: This is the logarithm function from the C procedure library. It is present only because the benchmark contains commands with a logarithm in them.

READ: This is the C procedure which formats a user disk read and does the operating system call. This time does not include the time spent inside UNIX executing the call.

BMOVE: This routine moves a block of data from one place in main memory to another. It uses the VAX block move instruction.

GET: This is the access method routine to fetch a tuple. It is called by SCAN when another tuple is required for evaluation.

WRITE: This is the C procedure which disposes of output. The benchmark contains RETRIEVE commands whose output is directed to a file using this routine.

SCAN: This routine sets up a scan of a relation as a result of access path selection code. It calls GET to fetch a tuple and then calls INTERPRET to discover if the tuple qualifies.

3.2. Performance of M-INGRES

After extensive effort we successfully implemented an integer add instruction in the user microstore. Most of the problems we encountered concerned inadequate documentation and support tools. However, we gained enough experience to estimate values for the rows of Table 6.4.

In that table we first give an estimate for the number of microwords that we would have to write for the two highest traffic routines. This number was obtained by multiplying the number of assembly language instructions in the routine by 6. This is the number of microwords needed to implement a memory-to-memory add instruction. Because of the nature of the two candidate routines, we felt this was a typical instruction.

The remainder of the table deals with a performance estimate for the resulting microcoded routine. The time savings due to a microcode version were assumed to result primarily from avoiding an instruction fetch on failed branch statements. The one-instruction prefetch mechanism used by the VAX 11/780 was assumed to operate reliably in all other cases. An estimate of the number of failed branch statements was taken to be one half the static count of branch statements in the assembly level code. Since both routines rarely loop, this number appears reasonable. The instruction fetch time was assumed to be 290nsec., which is the average access time to the VAX 11/780 hardware cache. Hence, our estimate of the resulting time savings is obtained by multiplying 290 nsec. by the number of failed branch instructions. Next, we report the average CPU time per call for each routine when the benchmark is processed. The final two rows respectively give our estimate for the percentage speed up of each routine due to microcode and its overall impact on INGRES performance.

3.3. Conclusions

The VAX instruction set has been designed to encompass all of the common high level language constructs. For example, the C switch statement maps directly into the VAX case instruction. Neither candidate routine exhibited constructs not already present in the existing machine language instruction set. It is our assessment that we would not be able to substantially outperform their implementations. Hence, we would not expect to be able to make code improvements which would substantially impact Table 6.4.

As can be seen, we would improve performance about 2.3%. If the VAX did not perform instruction prefetch, we would expect the improvement to double to nearly 5%. Even if we could implement code improvement which would double the gain to 10%, one would find it difficult to justify the complexity of writing nearly 4000 words of microcode. In addition, the overhead to call a microcoded routine (3.3 microseconds) for the VAX 11/780 was not included in the calculations.

It should be clearly noted that this conclusion applies only to the VAX instruction set, and it is likely that older architectures are more amenable to

	GETSYMBOL	INTERPRET
lines of C	105	420
lines of assembler	135	514
expected number of microwords per assembler instruction	6	6
expected number of total microwords	810	3084
number of branches	43	119
half the number of branches	21.5	59.5
instruction fetch time	290 nsec.	290 nsec.
estimated speed up of routine	6.0 usec.	17.0 usec.
execution time per call in the benchmark	70 usec.	360 usec.
percentage speed up of routine	8.6%	4.7%
overall improvement to INGRES	1.6%	0.7%

TABLE 6.4. Performance of M-INGRES

microcode enhancements. Also, the module (OVQP) in which all high traffic routines exist was not originally constructed with a microcode implementation in mind. It is possible that it could be restructured to be more easily microcodable. Moreover, the collection of high traffic routines would change if a compiled version of OVQP were implemented as in Section 2.0. Lastly, a DBMS which does extensive management of a shared buffer pool or a large lock table of small granularity locks might have additional high traffic routines which are candidates for microcoding. No conclusions can be drawn for such environments.

████ **4.0. FS-INGRES**

This section reports on the design of INGRES enhanced with a special purpose file system. This composite is FS-INGRES which is now described.

4.1. The Design of FS-INGRES

The basic objectives of FS-INGRES are:

1) To provide an extent based file system, with a minimum extent size of one track. In this way random allocation of disk blocks will be avoided.

2) To avoid the UNIX requirement of copying data from system buffers to the INGRES cache. This is accomplished by a direct read to the INGRES address space.

To accomplish these objectives, FS-INGRES implements the notion of a relation on top of a "raw" disk. Instead of directories and files, there are only databases and relations. Each relation is stored in up to 8 extents, each of which is a variable size physically contiguous collection of disk blocks. Such extents are allocated as needed, and the minimum extent size is one disk track. Instead of having a file control block, FS-INGRES stores information on the extents of a given relation in the RELATION relation. This relation contains one row of INGRES specific information for each relation in a database.

Free space is managed using a bit map which resides at a known location on the disk. Moreover, start-up information, such as the address of the RELATION relation, is also at hard-wired addresses.

Lastly, UNIX supports only synchronous I/O; i.e., a process which issues a disk read does not get control again until the requested data is in main memory. Therefore, it is impossible for FS-INGRES to implement any prefetching policy because it would require asynchronous I/O. As noted in [STON80a] INGRES usually knows which block it will access next, and an intelligent prefetch could be realized, but only by modifying UNIX.

As an interim approach which would not require operating system changes, FS-INGRES reads an entire track of data at a time in those cases where it is doing sequential processing. In this way it obtains 16 contiguous 1024 byte blocks from each read. It is likely that UNIX will be modified to support asynchronous I/O in the future so that a more sophisticated strategy can be implemented.

4.2. Benchmark Results

Tables 6.5 and 6.6 give benchmark results for standard INGRES and FS-INGRES and indicate elapsed time and total CPU time spent in command processing by INGRES or UNIX with the benchmark as the only executing task.

Query	Size	FS-INGRES	INGRES	IMPROVEMENT
a	0	0.7	0.9	28.6%
b	1	0.8	0.9	12.5%
b	210	1.1	1.3	18.2%
b	3360	5.2	5.7	9.6%
c	1	1.1	1.2	9.1%
c	210	1.9	2.0	5.3%
c	3360	11.2	11.5	2.7%
d	1	1.0	1.0	0%
d	210	1.7	1.8	5.9%
d	3360	11.0	11.5	4.5%
e	3360	10.8	18.7	73.1%
f	3360	54.2	63.5	17.2%
g	3360	18.0	33.0	85.0%
h	3360	46.0	54.5	18.5%
i	3360	19.4	34.4	77.3%

TABLE 6.5. Performance Comparisons for Elapsed Time

4.3. Conclusions

Several conclusions are evident from Tables 6.5 and 6.6. In simple commands FS-INGRES gives better response time than normal INGRES (typically 10-20%) with comparable CPU time. The explanation is probably faster access to the system catalog relations due to track-at-a-time reads. On longer commands which involve sequential access (b, c and d with 3360 tuples) FS-INGRES saves about 10% in CPU time with a lesser response time gain. In these situations UNIX notes sequential access and prefetches the next logical page in advance. Hence, processing the previous page is overlapped with fetching the next one. Since normal INGRES has a comparable amount of CPU and I/O time per page on these commands, it is comparable to FS-INGRES which fetches whole tracks. If normal INGRES were more I/O bound on these commands, a greater performance gain would have been recorded. The 10% CPU time improvement results primarily from the fact that the FS-INGRES storage system is more efficient and has a lesser number of requests to execute.

    Case e shows significant improvement. In this situation INGRES accesses primary pages interspersed with overflow pages. UNIX will note a run of two primary pages and fetch the third one in advance. However, a switch to an overflow page will destroy sequentiality, and UNIX will fail to

Query	Size	FS-INGRES	INGRES	IMPROVEMENT
a	0	.083	.087	4.0%
b	1	.122	.112	-8.2%
b	210	.378	.401	6.2%
b	3360	4.24	4.73	11.6%
c	1	.187	.195	1.0%
c	210	.787	.823	4.7%
c	3360	9.77	10.3	5.5%
d	1	.160	.162	1.0%
d	210	.767	.812	5.9%
d	3360	9.87	10.6	7.0%
e	3360	6.64	8.96	35.0%
f	3360	48.7	53.1	9.2%
g	3360	9.11	13.1	43.8%
h	3360	37.6	41.9	11.4%
i	3360	10.0	14.1	40.3%

TABLE 6.6. Performance Comparisons for Total CPU Time

prefetch both the overflow page and the next two primary pages. Consequently, CPU and I/O activity are not consistently overlapped, and normal INGRES suffers poor response time.

On the other hand, FS-INGRES will read a track at a time and capture a whole run of primary pages. It must wait for overflow pages like normal INGRES but not for the next primary page. As a result, there is a significant gain in response time.

In command g INGRES decomposition will first find all black parts as follows:

RETRIEVE INTO TEMP (P.P#) WHERE P.COLOR = "Black"

This command will involve a sequential scan of PARTS and is accomplished by reading primary pages interspersed with overflow pages. Moreover, since there are few black parts, processing the rest of the query is quite simple. Consequently, the argument for case e applies to this query and a considerable improvement is observed. Case i is a similar command and exhibits the same behavior.

Queries f and h are dominated by the time to do the actual join. Although PARTS is read sequentially as above and an improvement recorded, this speedup must be spread over considerably more CPU time.

Consequently, the percentage improvement is smaller.

In general, FS-INGRES saves 5 to 10% in CPU time and produces a command-dependent improvement in response time. Future experimentation is needed to determine the impact of parameters not considered. These include modifying UNIX to support asynchronous I/O (which should benefit FS-INGRES by allowing an implementation of an accurate prefetching mechanism), modifying UNIX to store pages contiguously and read a track at a time (which might allow normal INGRES to realize most of the gain in query e) and running the benchmark in a multiuser environment (which would add the effects of disk contention and multiprogramming to both systems).

It should be noted that the observations of this section deal only with physical placement of disk blocks, the number of blocks fetched on each access, and the storage system overhead necessary to accomplish read and write operations. To the extent that an operating system efficiently implements facilities in these areas, the conclusions of this section would fail to apply. Moreover, they would not apply to a DBMS, e.g., [ASTR76], which already manages its own disk activity.

5.0. MANGOS

Besides using the services of a file system, INGRES uses the multitasking and interprocess message facilities of an operating system. Moreover, the application program (or INGRES terminal monitor) must communicate with an end user using operating system terminal I/O facilities.

To assess the impact of operating system overhead external to the file system on DBMS performance, we designed MANGOS. This system would include a special purpose file system such as discussed in Section 4.0. Hence, it would automatically obtain the performance improvement of FS-INGRES. In this section we discuss the additional performance improvement which might be obtainable.

There are two possible environments in which MANGOS could run. First, it could be the operating system for a machine dedicated to running only the INGRES process. Application programs would continue to run on a general purpose host. This is the back end architecture used, for example, by the IDM-500 [EPST80b]. Alternatively, one could design a special purpose operating system which included facilities for terminal I/O and ran both application programs and the INGRES process. This is the environment supported, for example, by the Airline Control Program, ACP.

We chose the former environment because it is compatible with our proposal for a database machine [STON79] and because it is easier to build. Consequently, MANGOS is intended to run only the INGRES process on a dedicated VAX 11/780 processor. INGRES commands are received from an application program on another machine. Consequently, a network manager must also run on the dedicated processor to handle all external communication.

The main modules in MANGOS are:

1) A buffer manager which is responsible for the buffer pool.

2) A process manager which co-ordinates processes.

3) A device driver, which performs disk I/O and interrupt handling. This module moves blocks between the disk and the buffer pool in a standard way.

4) INGRES, which executes database commands.

5) A network manager, which receives INGRES commands from another machine and returns the results of such commands. In MANGOS we use a modified version of COCANET [ROWE79a] for this purpose.

These modules run in one large address space and are not protected from each other.

5.1. Buffer Management

A buffer consists of a 4096 byte page-aligned section of memory and an associated header in a separate data structure. Every header appears on one of the following lists: free, owned by the disk, owned by the network, disk I/O in progress and network I/O in progress.

5.2. Process Control

The only processes supported by MANGOS are instantiations of INGRES. Each process contains a fixed size private data area which holds the data structure corresponding to the current command and its state of execution. The number of processes is established at system initialization time, and each has an associated process control block (PCB).

Processes are coordinated by moving their PCB's on and off various queues. Each process is initially on an idle queue, then it is moved to the ready queue when allocated to an arriving INGRES command. Thereafter, it cycles between the ready and blocked queue as it does I/O.

An INGRES process invokes the services of the buffer manager via a subroutine call which returns when the action is complete (except in the case of asynchronous I/O where control is returned after I/O is initiated, but not necessarily complete).

Context switches only occur when a process calls the buffer manager requesting service and is placed on the blocked queue. Since processes all execute in the same address space, we need only save the current processor state, find the processor state of the next ready process and restore it. We have estimated that ten machine instructions are required to accomplish this task.

5.3. Messages

The only messages in MANGOS are communications among INGRES, the network manager and the buffer manager. Messages are implemented by removing a buffer from one list and placing it on another. In essence, a message is a pointer to a 4096 byte block of storage. The overhead to send or receive a message has been estimated at nine instructions.

5.4. Performance Estimates

MANGOS will enhance INGRES performance in two ways. First, it will provide parallelism due to a multiprocessor configuration. Second, it will provide faster system service in the area of task switches, interprocess messages, and I/O. We only estimate the impact of the latter effect.

In normal INGRES, one message is required to receive the command from the front end process. One message per 1024 bytes of returned data is also needed. In MANGOS, we optimistically assume these messages consume minimal CPU time compared to normal INGRES. Hence, we expect to save the UNIX interprocess message cost for the appropriate number of messages.

In normal INGRES, a system call is required for each read or write

Query	Size	Number of System Calls	Number of Messages
a	0	0	2
b	1	5	2
b	210	13	3
b	3360	125	32
c	1	5	2
c	210	13	7
c	3360	125	88
d	1	5	2
d	210	13	3
d	3360	125	23
e	3360	609	59
f	3360	1572	25
g	3360	1210	5
h	3360	1317	25
i	3360	1224	5

TABLE 6.7. Access Statistics for MANGOS

operation. For some reads the required data is in the UNIX cache, and no physical I/O takes place. For other read operations, normal INGRES is blocked, and a task switch to another process occurs. All write operations affect the cache, and data is then aged to disk by an LRU algorithm. Hence, no task switch is required. MANGOS will replace each task switch by one which consumes minimal resources. Consequently, we anticipate saving the cost of a task switch for each physical read that is required in the benchmark. For other I/O operations, we will replace a systems call with a subroutine call to the buffer manager which consumes minimal resources. Hence, we anticipate saving the cost of a systems call in these circumstances. Currently, UNIX on a VAX 11/780 requires 0.270 msec. to perform a task switch [JOY80] and the cost to send a message to another process has been measured to be 1.65 msec. (Extensive tuning has made these numbers nearly a factor of 3 smaller than previous UNIX timings.) Moreover, a system call to obtain the time of day was measured to consume .14 msec.

Table 6.7 contains the number of system calls and number of messages for each command in the benchmark. For each message MANGOS should save nearly 1.65 msec. and for each system call it should save either .14 msec. or .27 msec. depending on whether a task switch is required. Under

Query	Size	MANGOS CPU time	INGRES CPU time	IMPROVEMENT
a	0	.084	.087	3.4%
b	1	.107	.112	4.5%
b	210	.393	.401	2.0%
b	3360	4.64	4.73	1.9%
c	1	.190	.195	2.6%
c	210	.808	.823	1.8%
c	3360	10.12	10.3	1.7%
d	1	.157	.162	3.1%
d	210	.802	.812	1.0%
d	3360	10.53	10.6	0.7%
e	3360	8.70	8.96	2.9%
f	3360	52.64	53.1	0.9%
g	3360	12.77	13.1	2.6%
h	3360	41.5	41.9	1.0%
i	3360	13.76	14.1	2.4%

TABLE 6.8. MANGOS Performance

the optimistic assumption that 1.65 msec. and .27 msec. are consistently realized for the two events, Table 6.8 indicates MANGOS performance compared to that of normal INGRES.

5.5. Conclusions

It can be observed that the expected performance improvement of MANGOS is in the 1-5% range. Prior to UNIX tuning, it would have been nearly three times as large. If needed operating system services have been extensively tuned to DBMS needs, then it appears that a special purpose operating system has limited utility. Note clearly that there may be other reasons for constructing a special purpose operating system, for example, the absence of a needed facility (such as shared segments) in a general purpose operating system. Also, note that this section has discussed only non-file system considerations and only in a back-end dedicated machine context.

6.0. CONCLUSIONS

Our four case studies of performance improvements can be summarized as follows:

Tactic	Effect	Estimated Difficulty
DC-INGRES	no effect for short commands; 25-100% for longer commands	4 man-months
M-INGRES	2.3%	more than 6 man-months
FS-INGRES	5-40% CPU time 5-50% response time	2 man-months
MANGOS	1-5%	6-12 man-months

Clearly, compilation and file system tactics have a high return in our environment and are relatively easy to accomplish. Microcode and a special operating system do provide a performance improvement for our context, but not a large one and at high cost.

Moreover, we benchmarked the combination of DC-INGRES and FS-INGRES and found that the individual impacts of both systems were basically additive. Since they impacted different areas of the code, this outcome was expected. On the other hand, M-INGRES and DC-INGRES affect the same module and only one can be applied. In our environment compilation should be exhausted as a performance tactic before microcode is attempted. It would be an interesting future experiment to profile the combination of DC-INGRES and M-INGRES to study the possibility of microcoding this system.

Lastly, operating system overhead can come from one of three sources, namely:

1)   the file system,

2)   process management and interprocess communication,

3)   terminal I/O and other application program services.

FS-INGRES studied the first source while MANGOS addressed the second. In our environment, the file system proved a much greater cause of overhead than process management.

## CHAPTER SEVEN

Query Processing in a Relational Database Management System

Karel Youssefi / Eugene Wong

1.0. INTRODUCTION

In [WONG76] we presented a general strategy for query processing known as decomposition, which had been designed for the nonprocedural query language QUEL [HELD75b] and was in the process of being implemented in the relational database management system INGRES [STON76a]. In this approach the problem of dealing with a multi-relational query is separated into two stages. First, a query which references several relations is decomposed into simpler components, the main objective at this point being to minimize the combinatorial growth that multi-relational queries entail. The information used to achieve this minimization consists mainly of the structure of the query and size statistics of the relations used. Once the query is decomposed into "sufficiently simple" components, the focus of the strategy shifts from one of structural simplification to that of minimizing data access, and in this "end game" phase of query processing the information associated with storage structure plays a dominant role.

One of the principal tactics that we proposed for breaking up a query into simple pieces was reduction, a process which might be described as separating a query at its natural joints. On both intuitive and theoretical grounds reduction appeared to be a highly advantageous tactic. However, the overall procedure of decomposition was too complex to permit a com-

K. Youssefi and E. Wong, *Proceedings of the Fifth Very Large Data Base Conference*, Rio de Janeiro, 1979. Reprinted with permission of the VLDB Endowment; copyright © 1979.

plete theoretical analysis, and the efficacy of reduction required confirmation by an empirical study. Such a study has now been undertaken [YOUS78], and a summary of its major findings will be reported in this paper.

A second issue to be addressed in this paper is the strategy of the "end game." In contrast to decomposition, a considerable amount of work has already been published on strategies for processing two-variable queries. Our work differs from these both in the way the problem is abstracted and in the specific assumptions concerning the costs that the implementation environment imposes.

In Section 2.0 we shall review the principal features of the decomposition procedures with an emphasis on the tactic of reduction. In Section 3.0 the results of our experiments concerning reduction will be summarized. In Section 4.0, details of the end game strategy together with a summary of some empirical studies will be presented.

2.0. DECOMPOSITION

The principal features of decomposition are easily explained by an example. Consider a database that contains the following relations with the domain names appearing within the parentheses:

    SUPPLIER (S#, SNAME, CITY)
    PARTS (P#, PNAME, SIZE)
    PROJECT (J#, JNAME, CITY)
    INVENTORY (S#, P#, QOH)
    SUPPLY (S#, J#, P#, QTY)

Suppose that we want to find "the names of all those suppliers each of whom supplies #6 bolts to some project located in the same city in quantity greater than 1000 but less than its quantity-on-hand." This query can be expressed in QUEL as follows:

    RANGE OF S IS SUPPLIER
    RANGE OF P IS PARTS
    RANGE OF J IS PROJECTS
    RANGE OF V IS INVENTORY
    RANGE OF Y IS SUPPLY
    RETRIEVE INTO RESULT (S.SNAME)
          WHERE S.S# = Y.S#
          AND S.CITY = J.CITY
          AND J.J# = Y.J#
          AND V.P# = P.P#
          AND J.QTY < V.QOH
          AND V.P# = P.P#
          AND P.PNAME = "bolts"
          AND P.SIZE = 6

The structure of this query is revealed by the following self-explanatory graphical representation in Figure 7.1 [WONG77]. The following tactics for decomposition have been proposed:

1) Query Transformation - The query can be transformed into a number of semantically equivalent forms. Of these, the addition of one-variable conditions by invoking transitivity is probably the most useful. In our example, the conditions (V.QOH > Y.QTY) and (Y.QTY > 1000) imply that (V.QOH > 1000) can be added as a condition. Since every added restriction means smaller intermediate results, one-variable conditions due to transitivity should always be added.

2) Reduction - A query is said to be reducible if it can be separated into two pieces which overlap on a single variable and each of which has at least two variables. An irreducible query is one that is not reducible. In [WONG76] we showed that the irreducible components of a query are unique. For our example, they can be represented graphically as shown in Figure 7.2. Thus, there are three irreducible components in our example, one with three variables and two with two variables.

3) One-Variable Subquery Processing - Often, one or more relations referenced by a query can be reduced in size by both restriction (fewer rows) and projection (fewer columns). Such an operation corresponds to a one-variable subquery which can be detached and processed separately. In our example, there are three such one-variable subqueries, and they can be represented as shown in Figure 7.3.

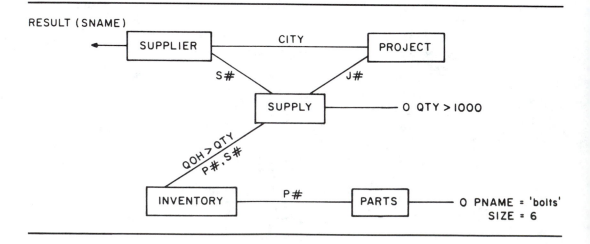

FIGURE 7.1.

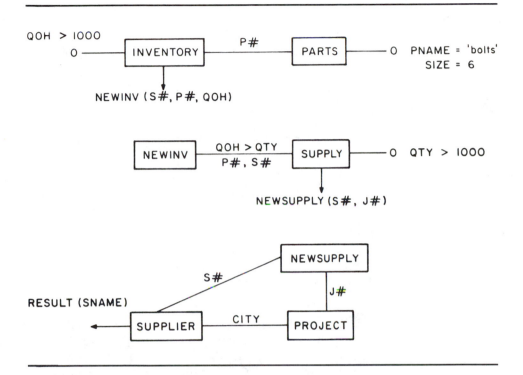

QOH > 1000
O ——————— INVENTORY ——— P# ——— PARTS ——— O   PNAME = 'bolts'
                                                   SIZE = 6

NEWINV (S#, P#, QOH)

NEWINV ——— QOH > QTY ——— SUPPLY ——— O   QTY > 1000
          P#, S#

NEWSUPPLY (S#, J#)

NEWSUPPLY

S#   J#

RESULT (SNAME)

SUPPLIER ——— CITY ——— PROJECT

FIGURE 7.2.

   4)   Tuple-Substitution - Suppose that one of the variables in a query is re-
        placed by the tuples in its range relation, one tuple at a time. What
        results then is a collection of queries (one per substituted tuple) each
        with one less variable.

   On intuitive grounds, the merits and demerits of each of these tactics
can be evaluated. Tuple substitution is a tactic of last resort. Successive substitution for every variable but one in the query is tantamount to constructing
a cartesian product of all the range relations. Such a procedure will always
work, but its inefficiency is deplorable. Reduction, on the other hand,
prevents combinatorial growth at little processing cost and should probably
be undertaken whenever possible. Whether or not a one-variable subquery
should be detached depends on both the storage structure and the semantics
of the query, and it is a decision that is best left to the end game.
   The advantages of reduction were elaborated in [WONG76] and can be
briefly stated. It replaces a query by a sequence of queries with fewer variables and smaller (usually much smaller) relations. It allows the difficult decision of choosing a variable for tuple substitution to be deferred until a time

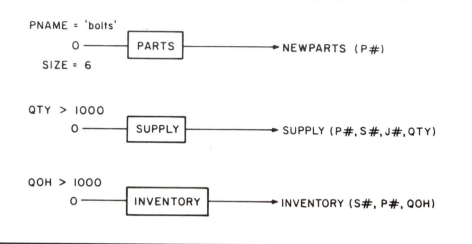

FIGURE 7.3.

when the choice is clearer and the potential for mistakes more limited.

One possible disadvantage of reduction is that it constrains the order in which the relations are accessed. The graphical representation of our example makes this clear. Once reduced, the query consists of three irreducible components which must be processed in the following sequence:

(PARTS, INVENTORY) → (NEWINV, SUPPLY)
→ (NEWSUPPLY, PROJECT, SUPPLIER)

It is conceivable that in some situations such a restriction on the order of processing would prevent an optimum strategy from being realized. Of course, such an optimum strategy may be difficult to discover and may not be realized anyway. Nonetheless, our hypothesis that the constraint on sequential order imposed by reduction rarely entails a major sacrifice in efficiency required empirical verification.

A second possible disadvantage of reduction is that if a joining variable is to be substituted it would appear to be better done prior to reduction, since then a single substitution simultaneously reduces the number of variables in two components. However, a separate component may be an advantage rather than a disadvantage since its range will have been reduced after the first component is processed.

In sum, we found it impossible to completely evaluate the effects of reduction by a theoretical analysis. Thus, a series of experiments was constructed for an empirical assessment.

 3.0. EXPERIMENT ON REDUCTION

Our experiment consisted of running a series of multivariable queries, each of which was free of one-variable subqueries, using every possible strategy which combined reduction and tuple substitution. For each run the total number of data pages accessed was measured, and the strategies was compared solely on the number of pages accessed. Although there are other costs in processing a query, the most significant component for a complex query is the time for accessing the data. Furthermore, other costs such as overhead do not differ significantly from one strategy to another.

A collection of 11 queries was chosen. These range in the number of variables from 3 to 4, and in the sizes of the relations from 15 tuples (2 pages) to 128 tuples (70 pages). The structure of these queries together with the sizes of the relations involved can be represented graphically. Let each relation be represented by a node in a graph, and let an arc between two nodes signify the existence of a conjunction clause in which both relations are referenced. The circled nodes are those which appear in the target list (i.e., in the relations referenced by the result). The queries for which measurements were made can be represented as follows in Figure 7.4.

The queries used in our experiment were free of one-variable subqueries. Hence, the first move in any strategy must be either a tuple-substitution or a reduction. We wanted answers to the following questions from our series of experiments:

1) Since reduction always puts a component containing the target list near the end in the sequence of processing, is it often the case that a target list variable should be substituted for before reduction?

2) Is it often the case that tuple-substitution for a joining variable should precede reduction?

3) Is reduction as the first move a good general strategy?

In Table 7.1 we have tabulated the page counts for the best strategy of each of the following four categories:

1) The first move is substitution for a target list variable.

2) The first move is substitution for a joining variable.

3) The first move is tuple substitution without restriction on the variable.

4) The first move is reduction.

For each case page counts for both keyed and non-keyed storage structures are presented.

The implications of our experiments seem rather clear. First, reduction as the first move is the best in every single case. The difference in some cases (e.g., 11) is rather dramatic. Second, if tuple substitution is to be selected as the first move, then the best choice in every case is a joining variable. Finally, the fact that reduction defers the access for the target list variables till the

Query 1

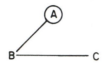

tA = 66   PA = 15
tB = 56   PB = 13
tC = 51   PC = 14

Query 2

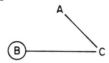

tA = 66   PA = 15
tB = 56   PB = 13
tC = 150   PC = 39

Query 3

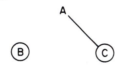

tA = 66   PA = 15
tB = 56   PB = 13
tC = 150   PC = 39

Query 4

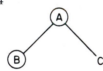

tA = 62   PA = 32
tB = 62   PB = 17
tC = 56   PC = 29

Query 5

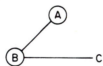

tA = 66   PA = 15
tB = 51   PB = 14
tC = 56   PC = 13

Query 6

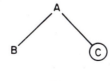

tA = 98   PA = 50
tB = 79   PB = 17
tC = 62   PC = 17
tD = 40   PD = 3

FIGURE 7.4.

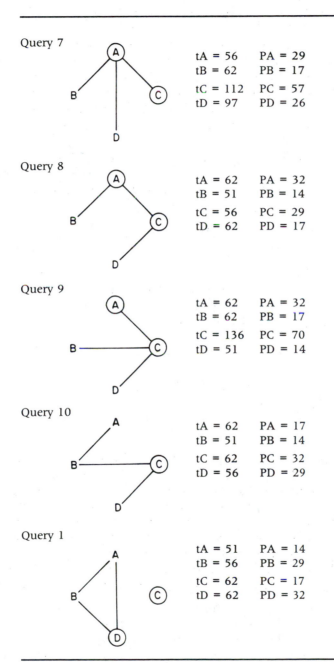

Query 7

tA = 56	PA = 29
tB = 62	PB = 17
tC = 112	PC = 57
tD = 97	PD = 26

Query 8

tA = 62	PA = 32
tB = 51	PB = 14
tC = 56	PC = 29
tD = 62	PD = 17

Query 9

tA = 62	PA = 32
tB = 62	PB = 17
tC = 136	PC = 70
tD = 51	PD = 14

Query 10

tA = 62	PA = 17
tB = 51	PB = 14
tC = 62	PC = 32
tD = 56	PD = 29

Query 1

tA = 51	PA = 14
tB = 56	PB = 29
tC = 62	PC = 17
tD = 62	PD = 32

FIGURE 7.4. (continued)

query	(a) target-list		(b) joining		(c) best-tuple-subs		(d) reduction	
	keyed	non-keyed	keyed	non-keyed	keyed	non-keyed	keyed	non-keyed
1	892	980	255	793	255	793	208	744
2	1450	2265	479	2243	479	2243	263	1888
3	12713	144760	636	2261	636	2261	319	1944
4	540	1986	157	1083	157	1083	354	354
5	2054	2458	469	1015	469	1015	323	578
6	51420	128083	1637	3015	1637	3015	519	519
7	3357	3670	3357	3670	3357	3670	643	957
8	2230	4257	2230	4257	2230	4257	471	1302
9	88470	113296	3145	4329	3145	4329	3042	4458
10	357	927	357	927	357	927	419	655
11	34038	112716	14751	14752	14751	14751	645	1914

TABLE 7.1. Reduction vs. Tuple Substitution

end had no unfavorable effect in any of the queries of our experiment. Indeed, tuple substitution for a target list variable as a first move often had disastrous consequences. (See e.g., queries 3, 6, 9, 11).

We believe that the efficacy of reduction as a decomposition tactic has been well demonstrated by evidence. It is the one tactic which is most responsible for the prevention of combinatorial growth.

4.0. THE END GAME

Decomposition in general and reduction in particular provide a means for reducing the complexity of a query to a point when the effects of storage structure on access efficiency become clearer. An appropriate point at which to stop and focus our attention on the storage structure appears to be when the number of variables is two or less. Indeed, two-variable queries have received a great deal of attention in the literature [ROTH75, BLAS76]. An effort has been made in [YAO78a] to organize the many techniques which have been suggested into a coherent theory. The focus of our attention is somewhat different, our objectives being:

1) to provide a detailed evaluation of two-variable strategies in the specific context of the INGRES system, and

2) to present some experimental results on these strategies.

In INGRES access to stored data is deferred until a one-variable query is encountered. Thus, faced with a two-variable query, we have to make the following decisions.

1) If a one-variable subquery involving restriction and/or projection on one of the relations can be detached, should it be detached and processed before the rest of the query?

2) Since tuple substitution must be made for one of the two variables, how should the selection be made?

3) Should the storage structure for one or both of the relations be modified?

An example will make these issues clear.

Consider the two-variable query shown in Figure 7.5, which is the first irreducible component of the example in Section 2.0.

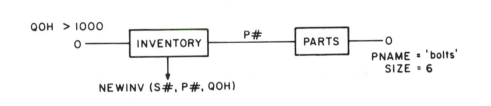

FIGURE 7.5.

Faced with such a query, we have to decide whether to take each of the following possible actions:

1) We can restrict parts according to the condition (PNAME = 'bolts') and (SIZE = 6) and project the result on P# before further processing.

2) We can restrict inventory on (QOH > 100) before further processing.

3) We can tuple substitute for PARTS or for INVENTORY.

4) We can modify the storage structure of PARTS or INVENTORY.

All these decisions are affected by the existing storage structures, and to determine how they are affected, we need to abstract the relevant factors of the storage structures.

Let R be a relation and let B(r), r an element of R, be a truth function on R. Let q(R, E) be the number of tuples in R which satisfy B. Let t(R, B) be the number of tuples which have to be examined to determine the qualifying ones, and P(R, B) be the number of pages which have to be accessed to determine the qualifying ones. Storage structures potentially achieve one or both of two things:

a) Keep t(R, B) as close to q(R, B) as possible.

b) Minimize P(R, B). If t(R, B) $\approx$ q(R, B), we shall say that R is indexed on B, and if F(R, B) $\approx$ q(R, B) $\cdot$ (width of R/page size), we shall say R is clustered on B.

We observe that for R to be clustered on B it is necessarily indexed on B, but the converse is not true. Typically, a secondary index on a domain "indexes" a relation on any condition referencing that domain, but does not cluster it unless the condition is satisfied by at most one tuple.

As an example consider the relation PARTS (P#, PNAME, SIZE) which is hashed on P# with a secondary index on PNAME. We shall assume that a given P# corresponds to at most a single tuple, but that there may be several tuples with the same PNAME. Consider the conditions

B1 : P# = 12345
B2 : PNAME = "bolts"

The relation PARTS is indexed on both B1 and B2, but clustered only on B1 and not B2. However, suppose that the roles of P# and PNAME are reversed in the storage structure, i.e., PARTS is hashed on PNAME with a secondary index on P#. Then PARTS would be clustered on B2 because the primary structure is keyed on PNAME, and also clustered on B1 because there is a secondary index on P# and B1 is satisfied by at most one tuple.

The first issue in the end game that we shall try to resolve is the detachment of one-variable subqueries. A general two-variable query in QUEL has the form:

RANGE OF R IS R1
RANGE OF S IS S1
RETRIEVE INTO RESULT (TL(R, S)) WHERE qualification

TL denotes the target list (i.e., the domains of the result relation), and the qualification has the general form:

C1(R) and C2(S) and C(R,S)

where C1 and C2 are one-variable clauses which can be detached.

Intuitively, the cost of processing a one-variable subquery is linear in the cardinality of the relation involved, while the cost of processing a two-variable query is super-linear in the sum of the cardinalities. This line of reasoning suggests that it is nearly always advantageous to restrict R1 on C1 and S1 on C2. There is one important exception to this rule. Suppose that R1 is not clustered on C1(R) but R1 is clustered on C(R, S) for every S. Then access to R1 is best deferred until a variable is chosen for tuple-substitution because should S be substituted, then access to R1 using C(R,S) and C1(R) together is far more efficient than access using C1(R) alone.

Consider our example:

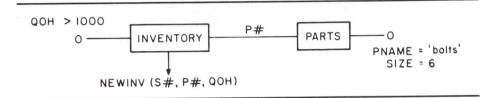

FIGURE 7.6.

Assume that INVENTORY is stored in a keyed-structure with (P#, S#) as key and PARTS is hashed on PNAME. Then, the one-variable subquery

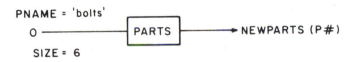

FIGURE 7.7.

clearly should be detached, but the one-variable subquery

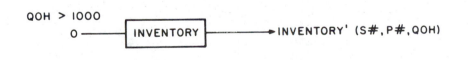

FIGURE 7.8.

should not be detached. Access to INVENTORY is best made using the condition on P# rather than QOH.

The second decision that we have to face is the selection of a variable for substitution. Let Q(R, S) denote a two-variable query, TL(R, S) its target list and C(R, S) its qualification. Let | R | and | S | denote the cardinality of R1 and S1 respectively. Suppose that we substitute for R1, then we get $|R|$ one-variable queries on S1. The total cost measured in pages accessed is

$$\text{cost (substitute for R)} = |R| + |R| \, P(S, Q)$$

where $P(S, Q)$ is the average number of pages accessed to process Q for each substituted R. It follows that

$$\text{cost}_{min} (Q) = \min \, (|R| + |R| \, P(S, Q), \; |S| + |S| \, P(R, Q))$$

and the variable chosen for substitution should correspond to the smaller of the pair

$$\frac{|R|}{P(R,Q) + 1} \quad , \quad \frac{|S|}{P(S,Q) + 1}$$

The difficulty in using this decision rule is that while $|R|$ and $|S|$ can be assumed known, $P(R, Q)$ and $P(S, Q)$ must be estimated. Of the factors which affect $P(R, Q)$, the following are probably the most important:

1) $P(R)$, the number of pages occupied by R1.
2) Whether or not R1 is referenced by the target list.
3) Whether or not R1 is clustered relative to the qualification.

The reason that (2) is important is because in QUEL there is an implied existential quantifier on any variable not referenced in the target list. Hence, in a query (TL(S), C(R, S)) only a single R1 tuple satisfying C needs to be found for each substituted S.

The simplest situation arises when neither R1 nor S1 has a useful storage structure and both appear in the target list. Then, $P(R, Q) = P(F)$, $P(S, Q) = P(S)$ and both are known quantities. In Table 7.2 we have summarized the experimental data on eight queries of this kind. We see that not only is our criterion verified in every case, but the cost is very nearly proportional to the ratio #tuples/(#pages + 1).

The situation becomes more difficult to analyze if only one of the two relations (say R1) is referenced in the target list. In that case $P(S, Q)$ is very likely to be less than $P(S)$ since we only need to find one tuple in S1 which satisfies Q. In Table 7.3 we compare the measured values for $P(S, Q)$ with $P(S)$ for 8 queries in which S is not referenced in the target list. Unfortunately, the results afford us little predictive value for $P(S, Q)$. It is always less than $P(S)$, but beyond that we need additional information about the data to make a useful prediction for $P(S, Q)$.

The situation is equally murky if one or both of the relations has a useful storage structure. Suppose that S1 is clustered on C(R, S) for each fixed R. This means that for a fixed R the S1-tuples which satisfy C(R, S) are on nearly the minimum number of pages. However, if the number of such S1-tuples is not known, estimating $P(S, Q)$ is still difficult. In Table 7.4 we

query	| R | / P(R) + 1	| S | / P(S) + 1	pages (R substituted)	pages (S substituted)
1	1.944	4.125	2104	4633
2	3.444	1.944	4307	2355
3	4.125	5.789	3709	4918
4	3.444	1.931	3538	1950
5	4.125	4.389	1135	1194
6	4.556	4.647	1329	1358
7	3.565	10.125	595	1788
8	1.9375	11.515	2014	11811

TABLE 7.2. Experimental Data

0	P(S)	P(S,Q)	ratio
1	70	2.2	.03
2	70	3.25	.90
3	15	5.33	.35
4	57	11.82	.21
5	15	5.58	.37
6	29	2.48	.08
7	14	10.75	.77
8	29	26.78	.92

TABLE 7.3. Relation Not Referenced in Target List

again compare the measured P(S, Q) with P(S), but this time S1 is always referenced in the target list and is clustered with respect to Q. As in the case of a relation not referenced in the target list, our experimental results afford us little predictive value.

Q	P(S)	P(S,Q)	ratio
1	70	53.2	.76
2	70	.23	.03
3	15	11.4	.76
4	57	44	.77
5	15	9.8	.65
6	17	14	.82
7	22	1.1	.05
8	31	1.4	.05

TABLE 7.4. Effect of Keyed Structure

Suppose that the condition $C(R, S)$ is of the simple form

$R.A = S.B$

where A is a domain in R1 and B a domain in S1, and suppose that we know the quantity

k = number of different A values in R1

Then, we can make a reasonable estimate of $P(S, Q)$ when S1 is not referenced in the target list or when S1 has a keyed storage structure with B as its key.

For each R, there are on the average $|S|/k$ tuples in S1 which satisfy $C(R, S)$. If S1 is not referenced in the target list, only one of these tuples need be found and the average number of pages that would have to be accessed is

a) $P(S, Q) = P(S) / (k |S|)$

On the other hand if S1 is keyed when the number of pages that would have to be accessed is

b) $P(S, Q) = (|S|/k) / \text{\# tuples per page}$
$= P(S) / k$

Our experiments provided a limited amount of data for verifying these formulas. In Table 7.5 we have summarized the results on five queries, each of which involves two relations R1 and S1 such that S1 is not in the target list while R1 is keyed. Thus, the same set of queries can be used to check both of our estimation formulas.

The estimates erred consistently on the low side, but on the whole the agreement was not bad for such simple formulas. What is more significant is that if these estimates had been used in comparing | R | / (P(R, Q) + 1) and | S | /(P(S, Q) + 1) to select a variable for substitution, the correct decision would have been made in every case, and by a comfortable margin.

Tuple substitution for one variable in a two-variable query results in a collection of similar queries on the remaining variable. Since the collection is homogeneous in the form of the qualifying condition, the same storage structure would allow the relation to be clustered for every query in the collection. Specifically, suppose that we substitute for r in R. Then, if S is clustered with respect to C(r, s) for one r it is clustered for every r. Thus, if S is not already clustered with respect to C(R, s) it would probably pay to modify its storage structure. There are three choices in INGRES: modify to ISAM, modify to hash, create secondary index. The cost of creating a secondary index is always less than modifying the primary structure, but the benefit is also less and sometimes down right useless. The relative cost of modification between ISAM and hash is very much a function of the particular implementation environment. Since ISAM involves sorting, its cost must be super linear in terms of the relation size, but surprisingly it is often less than the cost of hashing. As implemented, the costs in pages accessed for modifying to hash and ISAM are:

$$cost (hash) \approx P(S) + 2.888 \mid S \mid$$
$$cost (ISAM) \approx 7.5 \, P(S) + 2P(S) \log 7 \, (P(S)/64)$$

In Table 7.6 we have summarized some empirical results on storage structure modification. For each of 11 two-variable queries, we compare the total cost (in pages accessed) of processing using each of four strategies:

query	P(R,Q)		P(S,Q)	
	estimated	measured	estimated	measured
1	8	12	1	1
2	1	1	30	62
3	56	42	2	5
4	8	13	4	11
5	3	12	2	4

TABLE 7.5. Verification of Estimates

Query	(a) No Modification	(b) Hash	(c) ISAM	(d) Index
1	8748	2101	1356	1026
2	1196	622	972	10478
3	1710	806	937	7654
4	1191	299	500	1204
5	5400	703	536	2181
6	1196	451	404	10478
7	3960	1666	1504	2184
8	17820	1999	1955	2789
9	16170	1976	1486	2255
10	17820	---	916	22595
11	16170	---	504	10344

TABLE 7.6. Comparison of Storage Structure Modification

1) no storage modification,
2) modify S to hash after substitution for r,
3) modify S to ISAM after substitution for r,
4) create secondary index after substitution for r.

The cost includes that of any storage modification which was undertaken.

We note that some general conclusions can be drawn. First, in every case storage modification was useful and in several instances critical. Second, ISAM was the best structure overall, and for queries which involve inequalities in their qualification (e.g., queries 10 and 11) choosing ISAM is of vital importance. Finally, secondary index is rarely the best strategy (only query 1) and often it is down right dangerous (e.g., 2 and 6). All in all, once tuple substitution is undertaken, modifying the remaining relation to ISAM appears to be the clear-cut winning strategy.

5.0. CONCLUSION

This is a follow up to our earlier paper [WONG76] on query processing in the INGRES system. Our two principal goals have been: (a) to verify through an empirical study that "reduction" as a tactic in decomposition is of near panacea quality, and (b) to provide a detailed treatment, by both analytical and empirical means, of the "end game" phase of query processing. Although our experiments have been far from exhaustive, the consistency of the results leads us to believe that the major issues which we have posed are now resolved.

## CHAPTER EIGHT

Operating System Support for Database Management

Michael Stonebraker

ABSTRACT

This paper examines several operating system services with a view toward their applicability to support of database management functions. These services include buffer management, file systems, scheduling, interprocess communication and consistency control.

1.0. INTRODUCTION

In this paper we examine several popular operating system services and indicate whether they are appropriate for support of database management (DBMS) functions. Often we will see that the wrong service is provided or that severe performance problems exist. When possible, we offer some suggestions concerning possible improvements. In the next several sections we treat the services provided by buffer pool management, the file system, scheduling, interprocess communication and consistency control. We then conclude with a discussion of the merits of including all files in a paged virtual memory.

The examples in this paper are primarily drawn from the UNIX operating system [RITC74b] and the INGRES relational database system [STON76a, STON80b]. It appears that most of the points made for this environment have general applicability to other operating systems and data managers.

M. Stonebraker, *Communications of the ACM*, vol. 24, no. 7, July 1981. Copyright 1981, Association for Computing Machinery, Inc.; reprinted by permission.

◼◼◼◼ 2.0. BUFFER POOL MANAGEMENT

Many modern operating systems provide a main memory cache for the file system. For example, UNIX provides a buffer pool whose size is set when the operating system is compiled. Then, all file I/O is handled through this cache. A file read returns data directly from a block in the cache, if possible, else it causes a block to be "pushed" to disk and replaced by the desired block. A file write simply moves data into the cache; at some later time the buffer manager writes the block to the disk. The UNIX buffer manager uses the popular LRU [MATT70] replacement strategy. Lastly, when UNIX detects sequential access to a file, it prefetches blocks before they are requested.

Conceptually, this service is desirable because blocks for which there is so-called "locality of reference" [MATT70, SHAW74] will remain in the cache over repeated reads and writes. However, the following problems arise in using this service for database management.

2.1. Performance

The overhead to fetch a block from the buffer pool manager usually includes that of a system call and a core-to-core move. For UNIX on a PDP-11/70 the cost to fetch 512 bytes exceeds 5000 instructions. To fetch 1 byte from the buffer pool requires about 1800 instructions. It appears that these numbers are somewhat higher for UNIX than other contemporary operating systems. Moreover, they can be cut somewhat for VAX 11/780 hardware [KASH80]. This trend toward lower overhead access will hopefully continue.

However, many DBMS's including INGRES [STON80b] and SYSTEM R [BLAS79b] choose to put a DBMS managed buffer pool in user space to reduce overhead. Hence, each of these systems has gone to the trouble of constructing their own buffer pool manager to enhance performance.

In order for an Operating System (OS) provided buffer pool manager to be attractive, the access overhead must be cut to a few hundred instructions. The trend toward providing the file system as a part of shared virtual memory (e.g., PILOT [REDE80]) may provide a solution to this problem. This topic is examined in Section 7.0.

2.2. LRU Management

Although the folklore indicates that LRU is a generally good tactic for block management, it appears to perform only marginally in a database environment. Database access in INGRES is a combination of:

1) sequential access to blocks which will not be re-referenced,

2) sequential access to blocks which will be cyclically re-referenced,

3) random access to blocks which will not be referenced again,

4) random access to blocks for which there is a non-zero probability of re-reference.

Although LRU works well for case 4), it is a bad strategy for the other situations. Since a DBMS knows which blocks are in each category, it can use a composite strategy. For case 4) it should use LRU while for 1) and 3) it should use "toss immediately." For blocks in class 2) the reference pattern is 1,2,3,...,n,1,2,3,.... Clearly LRU is the worst possible replacement algorithm for this situation. Unless all n pages can be kept in the cache, the strategy should be to "toss immediately." Initial studies [KAPL80] suggest that the miss ratio can be cut 10-15 percent by a DBMS specific algorithm.

In order for an OS to provide buffer management, some means must be found to allow it to accept "advice" from an application program (e.g., a DBMS) concerning the replacement strategy. It appears to be an interesting problem to design a clean buffer management interface with this feature.

2.3. Prefetch

Although UNIX correctly prefetches pages when sequential access is detected, there are important cases where it fails.

Except in rare cases INGRES knows at (or very shortly after) the beginning of its examination of a block EXACTLY which block it will access next. Unfortunately, this block is not necessarily the next one in logical file order. Hence, there is no way for an OS to implement the correct prefetch strategy.

2.4. Crash Recovery

An important DBMS service is to provide recovery from hard and soft crashes. The desired effect is for a unit of work (a transaction) which may be quite large and span multiple files either to be completely done or look like it had never started.

The way many DBMSs provide this service is to maintain an "intentions list." When the intentions list is complete a "commit flag" is set. The last step of a transaction is to process the intentions list making the actual updates. The DBMS makes the last operation idempotent (i.e., it generates the same final outcome no matter how many times the intentions list is processed) by careful programming. The general procedure is described in [GRAY78, LAMP76a]. An alternate process is to do updates directly as they are found and maintain a log of "before images" so that backout is possible.

During recovery from a crash the commit flag is examined. If set, the DBMS recovery utility processes the intentions list to correctly install the changes made by updates in progress at the time of the crash. If the flag is not set, the utility removes the intentions list thereby backing out the transaction. The impact of crash recovery on the buffer pool manager is the following.

The page on which the commit flag exists must be forced to disk AFTER all pages in the intentions list. Moreover, the transaction is not reliably committed until the commit flag is forced out to the disk, and no response can be given to the person submitting the transaction until this time.

The service required from an OS buffer manager is a "selected force out" which would push the intentions list and the commit flag to disk in the proper order. Such a service is not present in any buffer manager known to the author.

2.5. Summary

Although it is possible to provide an OS buffer manager with the required features, none exists currently to this author's knowledge. It would be an interesting exercise to design such a facility with prefetch advice, block management advice and selected force out. This exercise is of interest both in a paged virtual memory context and in an ordinary file system.

The strategy used by most DBMSs (for example, SYSTEM R [BLAS79b] and IMS [IBM74]) is to maintain a separate cache in user space. This buffer pool is manged by a DBMS specific algorithm to get around the problems mentioned in this section. The result is a "not quite right" service provided by the OS going unused and a comparable application specific service being provided by the DBMS. We will see this theme in several service delivery areas throughout this paper.

3.0. THE FILE SYSTEM

The file system provided by UNIX supports objects (files) which are character arrays of dynamically varying size. On top of this abstraction, a DBMS can provide whatever higher level objects it wishes.

This is one of two popular approaches to file systems; the second is to provide a record management system inside the OS (e.g., RMS-11 for DEC machines or Enscribe for Tandem machines). In this approach structured files are provided (with or without variable length records). Moreover, efficient access is often supported for fetching records corresponding to a user supplied value (or key) for a designated field or fields. Multilevel directories, hashing and secondary indexes are used to provide this service.

The point to be made in this section is that the second service, which is what a DBMS wants, is not always efficient when constructed on top of a character array object. The following subsections explain some considerations.

3.1. Physical Contiguity

The character array object can usually be expanded one block at a time. Often the result is blocks of a given file scattered over a disk volume. Hence, the next logical block in a file is not necessarily physically close to the previous one. Since a DBMS does considerable sequential access, the result is considerable arm movement.

The desired service is for blocks to be stored physically contiguous and a whole collection to be read when sequential access is desired. This naturally leads a DBMS to prefer a so-called extent based file system (e.g., VSAM [KEEH74]) to one which scatters blocks. Of course, such files must grow an extent at a time rather than a block at a time.

3.2. Tree Structured File Systems

UNIX implements two services by means of data structures which are trees. The blocks in a given file are kept track of in a tree (of indirect blocks) pointed to by a file control block (i-node). Second, the files in a given mounted file system have a user visible hierarchical structure composed of directories, subdirectories, etc. This is implemented by a second tree. A DBMS such as INGRES then adds a third tree structure to support keyed access via a multilevel directory structure (e.g., ISAM [IBM66], B-trees [BAYE70, KNUT78], VSAM [KEEH74], etc.).

Clearly, one tree with all three kinds of information is more efficient than three separately managed trees. It is suspected that the extra overhead is substantial.

3.3. Summary

It is clear that a character array is not a useful object to a DBMS. Rather it is the abstraction presumably desired by language processors, editors, etc. Instead of providing records management on top of character arrays, it is possible to do the converse; the only issue is one of efficiency. Moreover, editors can probably use records management structures as efficiently as the ones which they create themselves [BIRS77]. It is suspected that OS designers should change their thinking toward providing DBMS facilities as lower level objects and character arrays as higher level ones. This philosophy is already present in [EPST80b].

4.0. SCHEDULING AND PROCESS MANAGEMENT

Often, the simplest way to organize a multi-user database system is to have one OS process per user; i.e., each concurrent database user runs in a separate process. Hopefully, all users share the same copy of the code segment of the database system and perhaps one or more data segments. In particular, a DBMS buffer pool and lock table should be handled as a shared segment. The above structure is followed by System R and in part by INGRES. Since UNIX has no shared data segments, INGRES must put the lock table inside the operating system and provide buffering private to each user.

The alternative organization is to allocate one run time database process which acts as a "server." All concurrent users send messages to this server with work requests. The one run time server schedules requests through its own mechanisms and may support its own multi-tasking system. This organization is followed by IMS [IBM74] and by Enscribe [TAND79].

Although Lauer [LAUE79] points out that the two methods are equally viable conceptually, the design of most operating systems strongly favors the first approach. For example, UNIX contains a message system (pipes) which is incompatible with the notion of a server process. Hence, it forces the first alternative. There are at least two problems with the process-per-user alternative.

4.1. Performance

Every time a run time database process issues an I/O request that cannot be satisfied by data in the buffer pool, a task switch is inevitable. The DBMS suspends waiting for required data to appear and another process is run. It is possible to make task switches very efficient, and some operating systems can perform a task switch in a few hundred instructions. However, many operating systems have "large" processes, i.e., ones with a great deal of state information (e.g., accounting) and a sophisticated scheduler. This tends to cause task switches costing a thousand instructions or more. This is a high price to pay for a buffer pool "miss."

4.2. Critical Sections

Blasgen [BLAS79a] has pointed out that some DBMS processes have critical sections. If the buffer pool is a shared data segment, then portions of the buffer pool manager are necessarily critical sections. System R handles critical sections by setting and releasing locks which basically simulate semaphores. A problem occurs if the operating system scheduler deschedules a database process while it is holding such a lock. All other database processes cannot execute very long without accessing the buffer pool. Hence, they quickly queue up behind the locked resource. Although the probability of this occurring is low, the resulting convoy [BLAS79a] has a devastating effect on performance.

As a result of these two problems with the process-per-user model one might expect the server model to be especially attractive. The following section explores this point of view.

4.3. The Server Model

A server model becomes viable if the operating system provides a message facility where n processes can originate messages to a single destination process. However, such a server must do its own scheduling and multi-tasking. This involves a painful duplication of operating system facilities. In order to avoid such duplication, one must resort to the following tactics.

One can avoid multi-tasking and a scheduler by a first-come-first-served server with no internal parallelism. A work request would be read from the message system and executed to completion before the next one was started. This situation makes little sense if there is more than one physical disk. Each work request will tend to have one disk read outstanding at any instant. Hence, at most one disk will be active with a non-multi-tasking server. Even with a single disk, there is the issue that a long work request will be processed to completion while shorter requests must wait. The penalty on average response time may be considerable [SHAW74].

To achieve internal parallelism yet avoid multi-tasking, one could have user processes send work requests to one of perhaps several common servers. However, such servers would have to share a lock table and are only slightly different from the shared-code process per user model. Alternately, one could have a collection of servers, each of which would send low level requests to a group of disk processes which actually do the I/O and handle locking. A disk process would process requests in first-in-first-out order. Although this organization appears potentially desirable, it still may have the response time penalty mentioned above. Moreover, it results in one message per I/O request. In reality one has traded a task switch per I/O for a message per I/O, and the latter may be more expensive than the former.

4.4. Summary

There appears no way out of the scheduling dilemma; both the server model and the individual process model appear unattractive. The common solution for high performance DBMSs is multi-tasking in user space, thus duplicating operating system features.

One ultimate solution might be for an operating system to create a special scheduling class for the DBMS and other "favored" users. Processes in this class would never be forcibly descheduled but might voluntarily relinquish the CPU at appropriate intervals. This would solve the convoy problem mentioned in Section 4.2. Moreover, such special processes might also be provided with a fast path through the task switch/scheduler loop to pass control to one of their sibling processes. Hence, a DBMS process could pass control to another DBMS process at low overhead.

5.0. INTERPROCESS COMMUNICATION

It has been pointed out that an operating system message system often makes a server organization impossible. The only other point to be made concerns performance.

5.1. Performance

Although the author has never been offered a good explanation concerning why messages should be so expensive, the fact remains that in most operating systems the cost for a round trip message is several thousand instructions.

For example, in PDP-11/70 UNIX the number is about 5000. As a result care must be exercised in a DBMS to avoid overuse of a facility that is not cheap. Hence, otherwise viable DBMS organizations must sometimes be rejected because of excessive message overhead.

5.2. Summary

The problem in Section 4.0 and 5.0 is at least in part the overhead in some operating systems of task switches and messages. Either operating system designers must make these facilities cheaper or provide special "fast path" functions for DBMS consumers. If this does not happen, DBMS designers will presumably continue the present practice; implementing their own multi-tasking, scheduling and message systems entirely in user space. The result is a "mini" operating system running in user space in addition to a DBMS.

6.0. CONSISTENCY CONTROL

The services provided by an operating system in this area include the ability to lock objects for shared or exclusive access and support for crash recovery. Although most operating systems provide locking for files, there are a lesser number which support finer granularity locks, such as ones on pages or records. Such smaller locks are deemed essential in some database environments.

Moreover, many operating systems provide some cleanup after crashes. If they do not provide support for database transactions such as discussed in Section 2.4, then a DBMS must provide transaction crash recovery on top of whatever is provided.

It is sometimes proposed that both concurrency control and crash recovery for transactions be provided entirely inside the operating system (e.g., [LAMP76a]). At least conceptually, they should be at least as efficient as if provided in user space. The only problem with this approach is buffer management. If a DBMS provides buffer management in addition to whatever is done by the operating system, then transaction management by the operating system is impacted as discussed in the following sections.

6.1. Commit Point

When a database transaction commits, a user space buffer manager must ensure that all appropriate blocks are flushed and a commit delivered to the operating system. Hence, the buffer manager cannot be immune from knowledge of transactions, and operating system functions are duplicated.

6.2. Halloween Problem

Consider the following employee data:

NAME	SALARY	MANAGER
Smith	2000	Jones
Jones	1900	
Brown	900	Smith

and the update which gives a 20 percent pay cut to all employees who earn more than their managers. Presumably, Brown is the only employee who receives a decrease, although there are alternative semantic definitions.

Suppose the DBMS updates the data set as it finds "overpaid" employees, depending on the operating system to provide backout or recover-forward on crashes. If so, Brown might be updated before Smith was examined, and as a result, Smith might also get the pay cut. It is clearly undesirable to have the outcome of an update depend on the order of execution. (Hence, the name Halloween!)

If the operating system maintains the buffer pool and an intentions list for crash recovery, it can avoid this problem [STON76a]. However, if there is a buffer pool manager in user space, it must maintain its own intentions list in order to properly process this update. Again operating system facilities are being duplicated.

6.3. Summary

It is certainly possible to have buffering, concurrency control and crash recovery all provided by the operating system. However, to be successful the performance problems mentioned in Section 2.0 must be overcome. It is also reasonable to have all three services provided by the DBMS in user space. However, if buffering remains in user space and consistency control does not, then a lot of code duplication appears inevitable. Presumably, this will cause performance problems in addition to increased human effort.

7.0. PAGED VIRTUAL MEMORY

It is often claimed that the appropriate operating system tactic for database management support is to bind files into a user's paged virtual address space. We briefly discuss the problems inherent in this approach.

7.1. Files are Large

Any virtual memory scheme must handle files which are large objects. Popular paging hardware creates an overhead of 4 bytes per 4096 byte page. Consequently, a 100 Mbyte file will have an overhead of 100K bytes for the page table. Although main memory is decreasing in cost, it may not be reasonable to assume that a page table of this size is entirely resident in primary memory. Therefore, one has the possibility that an I/O operation will induce two page faults: one for the page containing the page table for the data in question and one on the data itself. To avoid the second fault one must "wire down" a large page table in main memory.

Conventional file systems include the information contained in the page table in a file control block. Especially in extent based file systems, a very compact representation of the information is possible. A run of 1000 consecutive blocks can be represented as a starting block and a length field. However, a page table for this information would store each of the 1000 addresses even though they differ by one from their predecessor. Consequently, a file control block is usually made main memory resident at the time the file is opened. As a result, the second I/O need never be paid.

The alternative is to bind "chunks" of a file into one's address space. Not only does this provide a multi-user DBMS with a substantial bookkeeping problem concerning whether needed data is currently addressable but also may require a number of bind-unbind pairs in a transaction. Since the overhead of a "bind" is likely to be comparable to that of a file open, this may slow performance substantially.

An open question concerns whether novel paging organizations can assist with the problems of this section.

7.2. Buffering

All of the problems discussed in Section 2.0 concerning buffering (e.g., prefetch, non LRU management and selected force out) exist in a paged virtual memory context. How they can be cleanly handled in this context is an open question.

8.0. CONCLUSIONS

The bottom line appears to be that operating system services in many existing systems are either too slow or inappropriate. Existing DBMSs usually provide their own and make little or no use of the ones provided by the operating system. Hopefully, future operating system designers will become more sensitive to DBMS needs.

A DBMS would prefer a small efficient operating system with only desired services provided. The closest thing currently available are so called "real time" operating systems which provide minimal facilities efficiently. On the other hand, most general purpose operating systems provide all things to all people at much higher overhead. Hopefully, future operating systems will be able to provide both sets of services in one environment.

3

Distributed Database Systems

In my opinion distributed database systems will be extremely important during the rest of this decade. I have several scenarios on how this may come about; some are described in this introduction.

First, economics forced most computing enterprises to centralize in the early 1960s. After all, most machines cost millions of dollars, and justifications were easier if such a machine could serve the needs of everybody. The result was that centralized corporate data processing centers were created to run such "big thumpers." Over time, central DP tended to become unresponsive to the needs of smaller groups in an organization, and frustration set in. As soon as it became economically feasible, many such groups purchased their own machines. The typical criteria was that the machine cost an amount small enough so it could be bought out of discretionary funds from the group itself or from the budget of the smallest enclosing organizational unit. Such "underground computers" have become omnipresent in organizations today.

Obviously, they are all networked together if for no other reason than to send electronic mail to other persons in the organization. Then, one has a situation where many groups have their own databases on their own machines, and central data processing presumably is still the custodian of "the corporate database" (i.e., financial information, inventory, etc.). Many arms of a company need access to this "sea" of data. Only a distributed database system allows this to happen without the necessity of a user knowing where his desired data is, knowing how to login to the appropriate machine, and how to use appropriate data accessing software. In fact, so-called micro-to-mainframe links are a first primitive step in this direction.

Another reason for distributed databases is purely economical. The following figure suggests a typical price curve for the cost of a MIP (million instructions per second). As the CPU increases in speed from a personal computer to the fastest machine available, the cost per MIP rises gradually and then dramatically as the limits of technology are pushed for additional speed. An organization can purchase a large fast machine (and thereby run toward the right-hand side of the curve), or it can purchase several (or even many) smaller machines and run further to the left. It is clearly more economical to make the latter decision. Moreover, with several CPUs, one has the possibility of designing a fault tolerant architecture. This line of reasoning has motivated many of the newer start-up computer companies, (e.g., Tandem Computers, Tolerant Systems, Sequoia, and ELXSI). All hope to make a big machine out of several smaller machines working together, and most propose using very low cost CPUs (typically Motorola 68000s) for their building block machines. The companies who propose architectures that do not support the ability of each processor to access each disk (e.g., Tandem) must offer distributed database access. Those that offer the above capability still must offer distributed access to data if they wish to attach two systems together. Whichever mechanism ultimately prevails (and this is hotly debated currently), I suspect such architectures will become much more important in the future and require distributed database systems in the process.

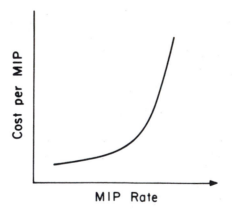

Cost Curves of Machines

A third reason is geographically distributed access. Most companies are geographically distributed (e.g., have divisions in Phoenix or Peoria). It is common practice for each division to run semi-autonomously (i.e., have their own "big thumper"). Any person in top management who requires a coherent picture of the corporate state requires access to data on multiple computer systems, in other words a distributed database system.

There are many technical problems to extending a relational database system to manage distributed data. These include:

1) extending query processing to select a plan which includes data transmission and the possibility of performing several pieces of the plan in parallel on different machines.

2) extending concurrency control mechanisms so a transaction can have resources locked at multiple sites. This requires some solution to the possibility that deadlocks can span multiple machines.

3) extending crash recovery to deal with the possibility that multiple machines can crash inopportunely and network failures are possible. Moreover, a transaction may have updates to data that physically resides on two different machines. A consistent database is only guaranteed if BOTH local updates are committed or NEITHER local update is committed.

4) extending the data dictionary to hold information on distributed objects.

We set about designing Distributed INGRES in 1977. Immediately we had to cope with all of these issues. Our guiding theme was to construct a system that would work well on a collection of machines connected by a high-speed network. The University of California already had 5 PDP-11s or VAXs installed or on order. Moreover, there was a lot of local interest in high-speed networking; hence, we thought an environment of several VAXs connected by an Ethernet (or equivalent technology) was just around the corner. Consequently, we were anxious to prove that INGRES could provide throughput in such an environment which was linear in the number of machines over which the data was distributed. This focus on a high-speed local network environment distinguished our project from SDD-1, which assumed a low-speed long-haul network. Hence, they attempted to minimize data transmissions and spent effort on query optimization tactics (such as semi-joins) appropriate to such an environment, while we attempted to exploit parallelism.

The first paper in this section discusses the design of Distributed INGRES and gives performance numbers and comments on our software development experience. The next two papers discuss query processing tactics. The first discusses the so-called fragment and replicate strategy that we implemented.

Later optimization studies tended to make the query optimization problem more and more complex, and we began to search for a simpler methodology. The second query-processing paper discusses a new approach to distributed query processing that may have considerable promise. Finally, I have included the paper by Dale Skeen on three-phase commit protocols because I think it presents a clear framework within which to consider the question, "how reliable does one want a crash recovery protocol to be?"

## CHAPTER NINE

The Design and Implementation of Distributed INGRES

Michael Stonebraker

ABSTRACT

In this paper we discuss the design of Distributed INGRES, an extension of conventional one-site INGRES to manage data on multiple computer systems. We also discuss the implementation of the system and present selected performance numbers.

1.0. INTRODUCTION

In 1978, we began the construction of a distributed database system. As noted in [STON80b], it was clear that the INGRES project had to expand its horizons, and this was an obvious direction. At the time, we had successfully made the one-site version of INGRES reasonably usable on a DEC PDP-11/70. As a result, bigger challenges did not particularly intimidate us.

The first issue was the choice of an environment to use. The only networking hardware and software available to us were:

1) a system called Berknet. This was UNIX software which multiplexed RS232 communications lines. Intermediate sites would forward messages to their ultimate destinations. Because of noise problems on the lines, bandwidth was limited to 1200 baud.

2) the Arpanet. At the time we had a very distant host connection to the IMP at Lawrence Berkeley Labs. This connection ran at 9600 baud. From LBL to other sites, bandwidth was 50K baud.

By this time, there were three PDP-11s in the EECS Department, and VAXs were on order. I was intrigued by the possibility of communicating over reasonable distances (say the 1500 feet between UC buildings) at much higher speed. It was clear that Ethernet technology could provide at least 1 megabit/sec. Moreover, I was enthusiastic that a reasonable database machine could be constructed by a collection of conventional computers (say VAXs or PDP-11s) communicating on a high speed local area net (LAN). Basically, [STON79] presents the architectural arguments in favor of this point of view. It should be noted that this architecture has become quite popular in 1984 for so-called transaction processing systems.

The choices were to accept low speed communication or to develop our own software and hardware to go faster. After much soul-searching, we elected to build our own networking. Although we failed to realize it at the time this amounted to a commitment to build a substantial amount of UNIX kernel code and to find prototype high speed hardware. Larry Rowe and Ken Birman set about the task of building networking software, and we contracted to buy prototype token-ring hardware being built at the University of California in Irvine.

After delivery of our VAX in 1978 and conversion of one-site INGRES to this environment, work began in earnest. From the beginning we designed the system so that fragments of relations could be distributed among sites in a network. Moreover, the location of a relation would be controlled by a distribution criteria which could be any qualification in QUEL which spanned only one relation (i.e., had only one tuple variable). Also, the fragment-and-replicate processing strategy was designed in 1978 and controlled our thinking about query processing.

A rudimentary version of Distributed INGRES worked in 1979 on a single VAX pretending that it was multiple VAXs. At this point, the networking software was still being constructed and the hardware was in the debug stage. Progress was difficult because debugging the network code required stand-alone time. This was difficult to schedule so as to balance the needs of the regular INGRES developers for reliable uptime and the network developers who didn't want to work the graveyard shift. Also, as debugging of the network hardware proceeded, we experienced the usual wave of hardware problems that occur to other components on the same bus to which the prototype hardware is connected. These were difficult to locate and correct. Basically, we were attempting to do production work (i.e., build Distributed INGRES), hardware debugging, and operating system debugging on a single machine.

Throughout 1980 and 1981 the network software and hardware stayed in a state of "almost working," and it became evident that reliable software and hardware was an elusive goal which was receding into the future. The death knell for this portion of the project occurred when Bill Joy announced that he was building competing networking software. Given his reputation for producing working code quickly, this was a demoralizing event. Also, he had set less aggressive goals than the software we were attempting; hence his chances for success were high.

Of course, the ultimate outcome was that we turned to waiting for Bill Joy's networking code and to debugging the Ethernet hardware which it ran on. The frustrating wait continued through multiple releases of UNIX. By this time the Distributed INGRES code had been patched, repatched, and converted between several versions of UNIX. It became hard to get anybody to work on it for very long, because it was extremely difficult to debug. Not only is any multiprocessor software extremely hard to debug because it is fundamentally asynchronous, but debugging had to be done with no sophisticated debugger. By this time, we had learned not to take on any other side projects, so a multiwindow debugger, which could monitor multiple processes, was not attempted. Rather we relied on multiple terminals logged in to different machines side by side as a debugger. Additional difficulties were the stress levels Distributed INGRES puts on any networking software. Our experience was that if anybody could break Berkeley networking software, Distributed INGRES could do it. The added difficulty was that errors were hard to isolate among buggy Ethernet interfaces, buggy networking code and buggy Distributed INGRES code. Progress was very slow and exceptionally demoralizing. Finally, in early 1983 we got enough bugs out of the system to do some performance testing. The system is currently in a state where it "more or less works." No release of the system to other users is planned.

The remainder of this paper indicates the design of the process structure, the design of the system catalogs and the transaction management subsystem and some of the performance experiments. Last, we indicate some lessons from this implementation experience.

2.0. DISTRIBUTED INGRES COMMANDS

A distributed database is created at a collection of sites, S1,...,Sk by a DCREATEDB command of the following form:

DCREATEDB DBNAME at site-list

For example, one could create an example database at Paris and Berkeley as follows:

DCREATEDB EXAMPLE at Berkeley, Paris

The creator automatically becomes the database administrator of the new database, and a collection of system catalogs is created for this database at each site in the site-list. This collection of system catalogs resembles those used in one-site INGRES with some extensions to be discussed later. Berkeley and Paris are logical names of machines which are mapped to machine identifiers by table look-up. Of course, the creator must be a valid user at each site.

At any time, the creator may expand the site-list with an EXPAND command, e.g.:

EXPAND EXAMPLE at Boston, Atlanta, Houston, Phoenix

This results in a set of system catalogs being created at each new site. To drop sites from a distributed database, one uses the DROP command, e.g.:

DROP EXAMPLE at Atlanta, Houston

One invokes Distributed INGRES from any site in the site-list as follows:

DINGRES EXAMPLE

This command can be executed either from the INGRES terminal monitor or from a host language EQUEL program written in C. Unfortunately, there is no name server implemented, so the above database cannot be accessed from sites other than those in the site-list.

Once Distributed INGRES is invoked, normal QUEL commands can be executed, and relations can be created and destroyed in the current database. The create command is the following:

DCREATE RELNAME (column-name = format, . . .,
                 column-name = format)
                 at site-list

For example:

DCREATE EMP (NAME = c20, AGE = i2, SALARY = i4,
             DEPT = c10, MANAGER = c20)
             at Berkeley, Paris, Boston

This command creates a relation at a collection of sites. These sites are some subset of the sites where the current database exists. The default site (if no site-list is given) is the current site only, and the keyword ALL allows one to create a relation at all available sites in the current database. The effect of a DCREATE command is to insert the relation definition in the system catalogs at each site in the site-list.

Distributed INGRES allows a user to partition a distributed relation among the sites where it exists. These "fragments" are specified as follows:

DISTRIBUTE EMP
        at Berkeley where EMP.DEPT = "shoe"
        at Paris   where EMP.DEPT = "toy"
        at Boston   where EMP.DEPT ≠ "toy" and
                    EMP.DEPT ≠ "shoe"

A single site relation is a special case of the distribute command, e.g.:

DISTRIBUTE ONE-SITE at Berkeley

The current implementation parses incoming QUEL commands by looking in the system catalogs at the site where the command originates. Hence, a relation can only be accessed from sites in the collection specified in the DCREATE command. However, Distributed INGRES allows relations to be extended to new sites as follows:

> EXTEND EMP to Phoenix

Lastly, they can be destroyed at one or more sites by:

> DESTROY EMP at Phoenix

When a relation is destroyed at its final site, all traces of it disappear. This approach to naming is simple to implement and does not require the parser to search other sites for formatting information on relations.

The system catalogs at each site contain information on each relation known at that site. This information includes formatting information in the RELATION and ATTRIBUTE relations much as indicated in the first paper in this book. Moreover, the distribution criteria for all relations is contained in two additional relations. The DISTRIB relation contains a tuple for each fragment of a distributed relation. For example, the EMP relation has three fragments respectively at Berkeley, Paris and Boston. The DISTRIB relation contains primarily the name of the fragmented relation and the site of each fragment. The actual qualification which specifies the logical partition is stored in a second TREE relation and a unique identifier is stored in DISTRIB to point to it. Hence, DISTRIB is of the form:

> DISTRIB (RELNAME, SITENAME, UNIQUE-ID)

The qualification may be a long field and INGRES currently only accommodates 512-byte fields; hence, the qualification may be split into several tuples each with a sequence number as follows:

> TREE (UNIQUE-ID, SEQUENCE#, QUALIFICATION)

The entries in TREE and DISTRIB for a given relation are identical for each site in the site-list. Whenever the distribution criteria is changed (via a DISTRIBUTE command), all copies of these tables are updated.

3.0. EXECUTION IN DISTRIBUTED INGRES

Distributed INGRES consists of a process called "master INGRES" which runs at the site where the user's application is run and where his terminal is located. In addition, there is a process called "slave INGRES" which runs at any site where data must be accessed. Last, there is a receptor process which is spawned to accept relations, which must be moved from one site to another. Figure 9.1 shows this structure graphically.

The master process parses the command, resolves any views, and creates an action plan to solve the command using the fragment and replicate technique. The slave process is essentially single-machine INGRES [STON76a, STON80b] with minor extensions and with the parser removed. The master and slaves communicate using the intermachine message system present in

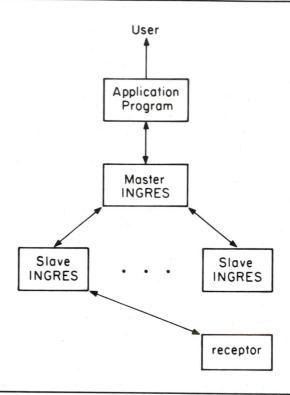

FIGURE 9.1. The Distributed INGRES Process Structure

the 4BSD version of UNIX.

Currently, all QUEL commands without aggregates are processed correctly for distributed data. Consider, for example, the following update:

RANGE OF E IS EMP
REPLACE E(DEPT = "toy") WHERE E.SALARY > 10000

This command is processed by all sites containing fragments of the EMP relation. All qualifying tuples are updated and their site location may be changed. For example, the tuple of an employee earning more than 10000 in the shoe department would be moved from Berkeley to Paris.

Distributed INGRES uses a two phase commit protocol [GRAY78, LAMP76a]. Slaves send a "ready" message to the master when they are prepared to commit an update. Tuples which change sites are included with this message. The master then redistributes the tuples by piggybacking them onto the commit message. A three-phase commit protocol can optionally be used [SKEE82] for added reliability. In this case, the above redistribution is handled in the second phase.

When a command spans data at multiple sites, a rudimentary version of the fragment-and-replicate query processing strategy is used. For example, suppose a second relation

DEPT (DNAME, FLOOR, BUDGET)

exists at two sites as follows:

DISTRIBUTE D
   at Berkeley where D.BUDGET > 5
   at Paris   where D.BUDGET ≤ 5

Consider the query submitted by a Boston user:

RANGE OF E IS EMP
RANGE OF D IS DEPT
RETRIEVE (E.NAME) WHERE E.DEPT = D.DNAME
             AND D.FLOOR = 1

First, the one variable clause "D.FLOOR = 1" is detached and run at both Berkeley and Paris, i.e.,

RANGE OF D IS DEPT
RETRIEVE INTO TEMP (D.DNAME) WHERE D.FLOOR = 1

The original query now becomes

RANGE OF E IS EMP
RANGE OF D IS TEMP
RETRIEVE (E.NAME) WHERE E.DEPT = D.DNAME

To satisfy the query, data movement must now take place. One relation (say TEMP) is replicated at each processing site. Hence, both Berkeley and Paris send their TEMP relations to each site which has a fragment of EMP. Therefore, the needed transmissions are:

TEMP(Paris) → Boston
TEMP(Paris) → Berkeley
TEMP(Berkeley) → Paris
TEMP(Berkeley) → Boston

Now, all three sites have a complete copy of TEMP and a fragment of the EMP relation. The above query is now performed at each site, and the resulting tuples are returned to the master site, where they are displayed to the user.

Since our Ethernet hardware has the capability to support broadcast, it is possible to perform the above four transfers by broadcasting each fragment of TEMP. However, the 4BSD operating system does not support multicast or broadcast transmissions. Consequently, the above four transmissions occur separately, and the strategy of replication may perform poorly [EPST78]. The network on which we planned to run [ROWE79a] supported broadcast, and we have not subsequently modified the query processing heuristics.

At the moment, the relation to be replicated is chosen arbitrarily, so TEMP and EMP are equally likely to be selected for movement. A more elegant strategy is being planned.

If a slave receives a command which requires moving data, it spawns a receptor process dynamically and sends blocked messages to this process. When the entire fragment is moved and installed in the recipient's database, the receptor is killed. Hence, the master sends commands to the slaves who in turn may send data to dynamically created receptors.

4.0. PERFORMANCE

First, it should be noted that Distributed INGRES is remarkably performance competitive. The following is a typical experiment. Consider that a database consists of 30,000 EMP tuples, each 38 bytes long and 1500 DEPT tuples each 18 bytes long. Consider the natural join of EMP and DEPT, with EMP hashed on the DEPT field and DEPT hashed on the DNAME field, i.e.:

        RANGE OF E IS EMP
        RANGE OF D IS DEPT
        RETRIEVE (E.ALL, D.ALL) WHERE E.DEPT = D.DNAME

This command was run using one-site INGRES, using Distributed INGRES but distributing the data so it is local to the site where the query originates, using Distributed INGRES but distributing the data so it is local to a single foreign machine, and using distributed INGRES with both relations evenly spread across two or three machines. In the 2- and 3-site cases DEPT was selected as the relation to be replicated in query processing. We measured CPU time spent in user space, CPU time spent inside the UNIX kernel and elapsed time. On the two and three machines cases, we used one or two additional 11/750s besides the INGRES 11/780. In these cases, we have presented the CPU time which we would expect if we could have run on multiple 11/780s by multiplying 11/750 CPU times by 0.629. This has been observed [HAGG83] to be the approximate performance difference between the two machines. Table 9.1 contains the measured results.

Notice that Distributed INGRES on a local database is about 20 percent slower than one-site INGRES. Moreover, Distributed INGRES on a remote database is another 20 percent slower yet. However, when processing can be spread across multiple machines, the CPU time spreads evenly, network costs are not significant, and elapsed time improves linearly as one adds machines. Note that an optimized version of Distributed INGRES should lower the 20 percent overhead somewhat. It is expected that judicious tuning could make

	user time	system time	elapsed time
Normal INGRES 11/780	8:41	0:38	9:37
Distributed INGRES - local database 11/780	8:57	0:47	10:34
Distributed INGRES - foreign database 11/750 11/780 02*780	0:05 9:01 9:04	0:03 0:42 0:44	14:32
Distributed INGRES - 2 sites 11/780 11/750 02*780	4:28 7:56 9:28	0:21 1:02 1:00	10:45
Distributed INGRES - three sites 11/780 11/750 11/750 03*780	3:11 5:27 5:14 9:54	0:13 0:43 0:40 1:05	7:41

TABLE 9.1. Performance of Joins

it competitive with single-site INGRES on local databases. On distributed data, the costs of moving data are not excessive and result in substantial parallelism.

5.0. CONCLUSIONS

It is suspected that a suitably optimized version of Distributed INGRES could achieve the objective of throughput increases linear with the number of machines. The only necessity would appear to be a database design which achieves two objectives:

1) ensure that the workload is evenly spread among the available machines and

2) ensure that the distribution criteria partition data so that most one relation commands can be processed on a single machine.

Whether such a database design can be achieved in practice is an open question.

From a software engineering point of view, one should note the difficulty we had in simultaneously making a leap in application code (i.e., Distributed INGRES), making a leap in operating system code (our networking software) and obtaining prototype hardware. Probably, one of these leaps could have been successfully made; however, all three provided extreme risk. The bottom line is that one should take much smaller steps to keep the probability of success high.

## CHAPTER TEN

Distributed Query Processing in a Relational Database System

Robert Epstein / Michael Stonebraker / Eugene Wong

ABSTRACT

In this paper we present a new algorithm for retrieving and updating data from a distributed relational database. Within such a database, any number of relations can be distributed over any number of sites. Moreover, a user supplied distribution criteria can optionally be used to specify what site a tuple belongs to.

The algorithm is an efficient way to process any query by "breaking" the qualification into separate "pieces" using a few simple heuristics. The cost criteria considered are minimum response time and minimum communications traffic. In addition, the algorithm can optimize separately for two models of a communication network representing respectively ARPANET- and ETHERNET-like networks. This algorithm is being implemented as part of the INGRES database system.

1.0. INTRODUCTION

In this paper we are concerned with algorithms for processing database commands that involve data from multiple machines in a distributed database environment. These algorithms are being implemented as part of our work in extending INGRES [HELD75b, STON76a] to manage a distributed database. As such, we are concerned with processing interactions in the data sublanguage, QUEL. The specific data model that we use is discussed in Section

---

R. Epstein, M. Stonebraker, and E. Wong, *ACM-SIGMOD Conference Proceedings*, ACM-SIGMOD International Conference on Management of Data, Austin, Texas, May 1978. Copyright 1978, Association for Computing Machinery, Inc.; reprinted by permission.

2.0. Some of our initial thoughts on these subjects have been presented elsewhere [STON77, WONG77].

We are not concerned here with control of concurrent updates or multiple copies [THOM75, LAMP76b, ROTH77, CHU76]. Rather we assume that these are handled by a separate mechanism or can be integrated into our algorithms.

This paper is organized as follows: In Section 2.0 we formalize the problem by indicating our view of a distributed database and the interactions to be solved. Then, in Section 3.0 we discuss our model for the computer network. In Section 4.0 a detailed algorithm is presented for handling the decomposition of queries in a distributed environment. There are a few complications concerning updates and aggregates in a distributed database which are covered in Sections 5.0 and 6.0. Lastly, in Section 7.0 we draw some conclusions.

2.0. THE DISTRIBUTED DATABASE MODEL

We adopt the relational model of data [CODD70, CHAM76a] and assume that users interact with data through the non-procedural query language, QUEL [HELD75b]. Algorithms for processing QUEL in a single machine environment (so called "decomposition") have been presented in [STON76a, WONG76]. New algorithms or extensions are needed in a distributed environment. Some familiarity with the notion of decomposition will be helpful in understanding this paper.

The database is assumed to consist of a collection of relations $R_1, R_2, \ldots,$ R_n. Each relation, R_i, may be at a unique site or may be spread over several sites in a computer network.

We shall refer to a relation as being "local" if it is stored entirely at one site, and "distributed" if portions of it are stored at different sites. By default relations will be assumed to be local unless explicitly stated to be otherwise. They can be explicitly created (or extended) to be distributed on all or a subcollection of the sites in the computer network. Call the sites $S_1, S_2, \ldots, S_n$. At a given site S_j there may be a portion (or fragment [ROTH77]) of R_i. Call the portion R_i^j.

We shall assume that each fragment is in fact a subrelation, i.e., a subset of the tuples, of a given relation. Hence there is no notion of fragments being projections of a given relation [ROTH77]. Supporting these more general fragments is infeasible given the current structure of INGRES.

A distribution criterion, which determines how tuples are to be allocated to fragments, may be optionally associated with each relation. If no distribution criterion exists, then tuples will be placed at the site where they happen to be processed. Figure 10.1 indicates one collection of relations, the fragments that are actually stored and their distribution criteria. An example

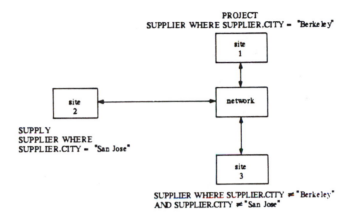

The user view: SUPPLIER (S#, SNAME, CITY)
PROJECT (J#, JNAME, CITY)
SUPPLY (S#, J#, AMOUNT)

The distribution of Fragments:

PROJECT
SUPPLIER WHERE SUPPLIER.CITY = "Berkeley"

site 1

network

site 2

SUPPLY
SUPPLIER WHERE
SUPPLIER.CITY = "San Jose"

site 3

SUPPLIER WHERE SUPPLIER.CITY ≠ "Berkeley"
AND SUPPLIER.CITY ≠ "San Jose"

FIGURE 10.1. A Sample Distributed Database

query for such a database is to find the job numbers supplied by the supplier named XYZ. In QUEL this is expressed as:

RANGE OF S IS SUPPLIER
RANGE OF Y IS SUPPLY
RETRIEVE INTO W(Y.J#)
    WHERE Y.S# = S.S#
    AND S.SNAME = "XYZ"

Note that this query involves fragments at all three sites.

3.0. COMMUNICATIONS NETWORK MODEL

We are primarily concerned with two types of communication networks, namely site-to-site and broadcast networks. In a site-to-site network we assume that there is a fixed cost to send one byte of data from any site to any other site. In a broadcast network we assume that the cost of sending data from one site to all sites is the same as that of sending the same data from one site to a single other site.

Our site-to-site model of a network is motivated by the ARPANET

[ROBE70] in which communication between two arbitrary sites will depend on what route the data must travel, i.e., on the topology of the network.

Our broadcast model is similar to the Ethernet [METC76] with two important simplifications. We assume that every site is always free to accept new messages. Thus a message will never have to be retransmitted because a site was too busy to accept the message. The Ethernet restricts the recipient of a message to be either one site or every site. We assume a more general addressing scheme where anywhere from one to all sites can be addressed in a message.

Regardless of which network model is used, we shall assume that it is desirable to present large blocks of data to the network for transmission. In other words, bulk transmission is more efficient.

It will be shown that a broadcast (or ether) network is particularly well suited to a relational database environment. The query processing algorithm can take explicit advantage of the broadcast capability of such a network. However, it is our intention to have INGRES support a database on either type of network.

4.0. QUERY DECOMPOSITION

INGRES supports four different data manipulation commands: RETRIEVE, APPEND, DELETE, and REPLACE. As mentioned in [STON76a], all update commands are actually processed by converting them to retrieve commands (to discover what to do) followed by low level file manipulation operations. Thus, the algorithm to decompose queries on a distributed system can be independent of whether it is an update or retrieval until the very end. For this reason, we shall restrict our discussion here to RETRIEVE and cover the relevant problems of updates in the next section.

4.1. Optimization Criteria

Minimizing response time and minimizing network traffic will be taken to be the two main optimization criteria in a distributed database environment. Minimizing response time involves minimizing the amount of processing needed to solve a query and using as much parallelism as possible from the various computer sites. Minimizing network traffic involves transmitting only the minimum data needed to solve the query. These two criteria are not unrelated. An increase in network traffic will improve response time if it results in greater parallel processing.

4.2. Network Decomposition Algorithm

We first present the skeleton of the basis algorithm. We subsequently discuss the detailed optimization tactic involved.

The algorithm to decompose a query has the following inputs:

1) the conjunctive normal form of the query (i.e., the qualification is a collection of clauses separated by AND's; each clause containing only OR and NOT).

2) the location of each fragment and its cardinality.

3) the network type (site-to-site or broadcast).

The algorithm is presented within the flowchart in Figure 10.2. The particular site where the query originates is called the "master" INGRES site. The master INGRES communicates with one "slave" INGRES at each site that is involved in processing the query. These "slaves" can be created by the "master" when appropriate. There are two types of commands that a master INGRES can give to a slave INGRES.

1) run the (local) query Q.

2) move the (local) fragment R_i of relation R to a subset of the sites in the network, $S_1, S_2, \ldots, S_m$.

The algorithm proceeds as follows:

1) Do all one-variable sub-queries. This has been shown in [YOUS78] to be almost always a good idea for non-distributed databases. It should be equally true for distributed databases.

    Note that in the example query from Section 2.0, we have a one-variable sub-query:

    RANGE OF S IS SUPPLIER
    RETRIEVE INTO TEMP(S.S#) WHERE S.NAME = "XYZ"

In step (1) the master INGRES at the site where the query originated instructs a slave at each of the three sites to run the above sub-query. The result is a fragment of TEMP at each site. The original query now becomes:

    RANGE OF T IS TEMP
    RANGE OF Y IS SUPPLY
    RETRIEVE INTO W(Y.J#) WHERE Y.S# = T.S#

Before actually running such a sub-query, if the relation has a distribution criterion, check to see if a clause in the distribution criterion at site i contradicts a clause in the sub-query. In general this requires a propositional calculus theorem prover. However, there are some simple cases for which contradiction is easily determined. For example, if the user's query includes a clause such as

    . . . AND SUPPLIER.CITY = "San Francisco"

examining the distribution criterion for site i might show

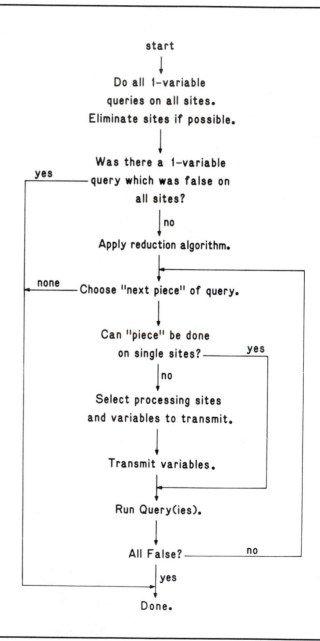

FIGURE 10.2. The Processing Algorithm

SUPPLIER WHERE SUPPLIER.CITY = "Berkeley"

Thus without actually running the sub-query on site i, the portion of SUPPLIER on site i can be eliminated from the query.

2) If there is a sub-query that was not satisfied on any site in (1), the entire query is false and we are done. This would happen in our example if TEMP had no tuples at all sites.

3) Apply the reduction algorithm [WONG76] to the query. This will recast the original query into a sequence of component queries, each of which is processed in order, independently.

Consider a query $Q(x_1, x_2, \ldots, x_n)$ in QUEL where each variable x_i references a relation R_i. Q is said to be *reducible* if it can be replaced by a sequence of two queries (Q', Q'') that overlap on only one variable, i.e.,

$$Q(x_1, x_2, \ldots, x_n) \rightarrow Q'(x_m, x_{m+1}, \ldots, x_n)$$

followed by

$$Q''(x_1, x_2, \ldots, x'_m)$$

where the range of x'_m is the result relation of Q'. For example the query:

RANGE OF S IS SUPPLIER
RANGE OF Y IS SUPPLY
RANGE OF J IS PROJECT
RETRIEVE (S.NAME) WHERE S.S# = Y.S#
            AND Y.J# = J.J#

can be reduced to two components, namely:

RETRIEVE INTO TEMP (Y.S#) WHERE Y.J# = J.J#

followed by

RANGE OF T IS TEMP
RETRIEVE (S.SNAME) WHERE S.S# = T.S#

It is shown in [WONG76] that the irreducible components of query are unique, and an intuitive argument is presented which indicates that these components form an advantageous sequence of sub-queries. To test this hypothesis, experimentation with actual data was recently undertaken by [YOUS78] and the results were convincingly affirmative. It should be equally advantageous in a distributed system.

This step will perform the reduction algorithm and arrange the irreducible components of the query in their unique sequence. We can then consider the sub-queries independently.

The example query from Section 2.0 is not reducible so this step has no effect.

4) Choose the "next piece" of the query to process. A query consists of a target list and a qualification (which is in conjunctive normal form). We define a "piece" as one or more clauses and their associated target lists.

Based on the query structure and the size and location of the fragments, the next "piece" of the query to be processed is selected. The algorithm to do this will be explained shortly. In our example there is only one remaining clause, which therefore must be the next piece.

5) If the piece to be run can be done on individual sites without moving portions of the relations, then we proceed to step (9). In our example TEMP is at three sites and SUPPLY is at one. Hence, data must be moved in order to proceed.

6) Select the site(s) that will process the next piece of the query. Depending on the number of sites, and whether it is a site-to-site or broadcast network, anywhere from one to all possible sites may be chosen. Suppose for our example that all three sites are chosen.

7) The sub-query must be two variable or more in order to reach this step. In order to process an n variable sub-query, fragments from $n-1$ relations must be moved, and the remaining relation will remain fragmented. Each site that does processing must have a complete copy of the $n-1$ relations. If processing is done on a single site, it must have copies of all n relations.

For our example we can broadcast supply to all sites. Each site will then have all of SUPPLY and a fragment of TEMP and will process the query producing a local fragment W. The answer to the query is the distributed relation W.

Alternatively, we can choose to broadcast TEMP to all sites involved in the query. Here we can view SUPPLY as distributed but with zero tuples on two of the three sites. Hence, fragments of TEMP will be sent to site 2. Site 2 then processes the same local query as above to produce a W, while sites 1 and 3 have no work to do.

Lastly, we can choose to equalize the distribution of the tuples in the relation that remains fragmented so as to guarantee that all processing sites have the same amount of work to do. This requires sending each site a complete copy of TEMP and moving one-third of the SUPPLIER tuples to each of the other two sites before proceeding as above.

8) Move the selected relation fragments to the selected sites. Each site will be directed, in turn, to send a copy of its selected fragments to the sites selected in step (6).

An optimization here is to have each site send only the domains needed in the query. Thus a fragment can be projected and duplicates removed.

   This step can take full advantage of a broadcast network since we are often broadcasting from one site to many sites.

9) The master INGRES now broadcasts the query to the selected sites and waits for all sites to finish. Once the query has been transmitted, this step involves only local processing.

   If no site finds the qualification to be true, then we know the query is false and no further processing need be done. Otherwise the clauses just run are removed from the query and the new range of the remaining variables is changed if necessary.

10) Go to step (4).

4.3. The Optimization Problem

As outlined in the flowchart, the processing algorithm that we have chosen involves several decisions: (1) What is the "next piece" of the query that should be processed? (2) Which sites should take part in the processing of that piece? (3) If the number of participating sites is greater than one, which of the relations should be left fragmented? (4) Should the fragmented relation be equalized in size among the processing sites?

4.4. Choosing the "Next Piece"

We have chosen to solve a query by "divide and conquer." That is, a query will be broken into one or more parts and each part will be processed in turn. The algorithm we pursue can justifiably be called a "greedy" algorithm. We will try to optimize each step, individually, without explicitly looking ahead to examine the global consequences. A possible refinement is to consider the structure of the residual query when deciding what should be done. The trade-off between cost and benefit remains to be studied.

   Results from decomposition on a single site have shown that reducing a query into its irreducible components is a good heuristic. Thus, after all one-variable sub-queries have been removed, the reduction algorithm will be used to transform the original query into its irreducible components which overlap on none, or one variable.

$$Q \rightarrow K_1, K_2, ..., K_i$$

We could stop at this point and simply execute each component in order, which is what we do on a single site. However, since any one component may span multiple sites, it may be desirable to subdivide further. Every component contains one or more clauses:

$$K_i = C_1, C_2, ..., C_j$$

The question is whether we should process the entire component at once or subdivide it? The answer is to subdivide only if the size of the result relation from subdividing is smaller than the communication cost of transmitting the source relations needed to process it. Here is an example to intuitively illustrate what can be achieved.

Consider the database from Section 2.0 with relations:

SUPPLIER (S#, SNAME, CITY)
PROJECT (J#, JNAME, CITY)
SUPPLY (S#, J#, AMOUNT)

and the query: "Find the names of supplier-project pairs such that the supplier supplies the project and the two are in the same city." In QUEL this can be stated as:

RANGE OF S IS SUPPLIER
RANGE OF J IS PROJECT
RANGE OF Y IS SUPPLY

RETRIEVE (S.NAME, J.JNAME)
        WHERE S.CITY = J.CITY
        AND   S.S# = Y.S#
        AND   J.J# = Y.J#

This query is irreducible and involves three variables. There is only one irreducible component (namely the entire query) and it involves three clauses. To keep the example simple we shall ignore site 3 from Figure 10.1 and pretend there are only two sites, which have:

site 1	site 2
PROJECT (200 tuples)	SUPPLY (400 tuples)
SUPPLIER (50 tuples)	SUPPLIER (50 tuples)

Assume that the tuples of the three relations have the same width. Now consider the costs and benefits of subdividing the component.

We need to examine the four possible choices:

(Q1) RETRIEVE INTO TEMP(S.SNAME, S.CITY, Y.J#)
        WHERE S.S# = Y.S#

(Q2) RETRIEVE INTO TEMP(S.SNAME, S.S#, J.JNAME, J.J#)
        WHERE S.CITY = J.CITY

(Q3) RETRIEVE INTO TEMP(J.JNAME, J.CITY, Y.S#)
        WHERE J.J# = Y.J#

(Q4) RETRIEVE (S.SNAME, J.JNAME)
          WHERE S.CITY = J.CITY
          AND S.S# = Y.S#
          AND J.J# = Y.J#

These are the only possible alternatives. Choosing any two clauses would be tantamount to Q4 since any two clauses involve all three relations.

Q4 would require moving 200 project tuples and 50 supplier tuples. The result relation would have to be moved in order to process the remaining query:

RANGE OF T IS TEMP
RANGE OF J IS PROJECT
RETRIEVE (T.SNAME, J.JNAME)
          WHERE T.CITY = J.CITY
          AND   J.J# = T.J#

If S.S# were a unique identifier for supplier and each supplier supplied only one job, then the result from Q1 would be at most 50 tuples. Thus the total network cost would be moving 50 supplier tuples followed by at most 50 tuples of TEMP.

But also consider the worst case. Suppose that S# is not unique and the entire cross-product of supplier and supply is formed. It would have 50 * 400 = 20,000 tuples! The decision whether to subdivide a component must be based on the expected size of the result relation. Some method for estimating the result size is needed.

But suppose the worst happens and the result size explodes geometrically. We can throw the result away and simply revert to running the whole component. In that case we would lose the time spent processing the abandoned query.

The accuracy of estimating the result size depends on a careful examination of the semantic content of the query (e.g., whether a clause involves an equality), on information concerning the distribution of values of the domains, (e.g., S# may be a primary key for the SUPPLIER relation with no more than one tuple for each possible value), and on the number of variables in the target list and their sizes. While compiling and keeping extensive statistics is impractical, a value indicating whether a domain is nearly a primary key or not may be both useful and easy to keep.

4.5. Determining How to Process the "Next Piece"

The second part of the optimization problem is how to process a given subquery (that is, which sites should be used as processing sites and which relation fragments should be moved). The more sites involved, the greater the parallelism. However, using more sites may involve greater communication costs and delays.

Presumably we will want to make decisions which minimize some application-dependent cost function which might look something like:

F(C1 * network-communication + C2 * processing-time)

To do this we will need to know how to calculate the amount of network traffic involved, the relative processing time, and the cost/benefits of equalizing the fragmented relation. We will now proceed to explain how to determine each of these. Notationally, we know there are:

N total sites in the network
n relations referenced in the "next piece"

We need to choose:

K sites to be processing sites
R_p as the relation to be left fragmented.

Let's number the processing sites so that $1 \leq j \leq K$. Furthermore, let's define M_i as the number of sites where R_i has data stored. At each processing site j we have a query involving

$$Q_j = Q(R_1, R_2, \ldots, R_p, \ldots, R_n)$$

4.6. Determining Network Cost Given R_p and K

Assuming that one relation R_p is left fragmented, and K sites (out of N) participate in processing, then the fragments of R_i have to be moved as follows:

for a processing site j, R_i is moved to K − 1 other sites.

for a non-processing site j, R_i is moved to K other sites and any fragments of R_p are moved to any one processing site.

The total communication cost is given by

$$\text{comm} = \sum_{j=1}^{K} C_{K-1}\left[\sum_{i \neq p} |R_i^j|\right] + \sum_{j=K+1}^{N}\left[C_K\left[\sum_{i \neq p} |R_i^j|\right] + C_1\left[|R_p^j|\right]\right]$$

where $C_K(x)$ denotes the cost of sending x bytes of data to K sites, a cost that depends on the network that is used.

4.7. Estimating Relative Processing Time

Define proc(Q) to be the time required to process the query Q if it were done on a single site. If K is greater than one then the processing time of a query, Q, can be improved from proc(Q) to $\max_j \text{proc}(Q_j)$. In other words, the processing time for the whole query is equal to the processing time of the site j with the most processing to be done. It is reasonable to assume that the processing time at each site is given by

$$\text{proc}\left[Q_j\right] = \frac{|R_p^j|}{|R_p|}\,\text{proc}\left[Q\right]$$

so that the overall processing time is

$$\max_j \text{proc}\left[Q_j\right] = \max_j \frac{|R_p^j|}{|R_p|}\,\text{proc}\left[Q\right]$$

assuming that all sites are of approximately equal processing speed.

4.8. Cost for Equalization

If each fragment of R_p was the same size, then the overall processing time would be given by $(1/K)\,\text{proc}(Q)$, since each fragment would have $(1/K)$ of the data. (This assumes, again, that all computer sites are of approximately equal speed.) This is the motivation for equalization.

To determine the cost of equalizing, let us define the function $\text{pos}(x)$ to be:

if $x > 0$ then $\text{pos}(x) = 0$
if $x \leq 0$ then $\text{pos}(x) = 0$

The amount of data to be moved in equalizing the fragments of R_p is given by

$$\sum_{j=1}^{N} \text{pos}\left[|R_p^j| - \frac{1}{N}|R_p| \right]$$

This added network cost would result in a processing improvement from $|R_p^j| / |R_p|$ to $1/K$. Thus it may be desirable to trade some network cost for an improvement in overall processing time.

We now know how to compute network communication cost, relative processing time, and the cost and benefit of equalizing R_p. We will now use this knowledge to minimize some example cost functions.

4.9. Minimizing Communication Costs

For the moment let's assume that the overall optimization criteria is to minimize communication costs. It is important to treat site-to-site and broadcast networks separately. We will first consider using a broadcast network and solving for K and R_p.

For a broadcast network $C_K(x) = C_1(x)$ for all $K \geq 1$. By examination of the communication cost function given in Section 4.5 it can be seen that the communication cost function is always minimized by $K = 1$ or $K > M_p$.

To see this observe that the cost function has three terms. The first term will be zero if K = 1. The third term will be zero if every site which has part of R_p is a processing site. Thus K must be $\geq M_p$, where M_p is the number of sites where R_p is present.

If we assume that $C_1(x)$ is linear in x and rearrange some terms then

$$\left[\text{COMM}\right]_{\text{broadcast}} = C_1\left[\sum_i |R_i| - \sum_i |R_i^1|\right] \quad \text{for} \quad K = 1$$

$$\left[\text{COMM}\right]_{\text{broadcast}} = C_1\left[\sum_i |R_i| - |R_p|\right] \quad \text{for} \quad K = N$$

Hence, the decision rule for minimizing communication in the broadcast network case is given by

If

$$\max_j \sum_i |R_i^j| > \max_i |R_i|,$$

choose K = 1 and choose the processing site (site 1) to be the one containing the most data. In this case there is no R_p. In other words, if one site has more data than the largest relation, then K = 1 and choose that site.

If

$$\max_j \sum_i |R_i^j| \leq \max_i |R_i|,$$

choose R_p to be the relation containing the most data and choose $K = M_p$.

The situation for site-to-site networks is quite different. For that case we shall assume $C_K(x) = K C_1(x)$ and that $C_1(x)$ is again linear in x. We note that, independent of K the choice of R_p that minimizes communications is the relation with the most data, i.e., $\max | R_i |$. Once R_p is chosen, the value of K that minimizes communications is determined as follows:

Let the sites be arranged in decreasing order of $\sum_i | R_i^j |$. Then, choose K to be 1 if

$$\sum_{i \neq p}\left[|R_i| - |R_i^1|\right] > |R_p^1|$$

otherwise choose K to be the largest j such that

$$\sum_{i \neq p}\left[|R_i| - |R_i^j|\right] \leq |R_p^j|$$

The interpretation of this decision rule is as follows. A site should be chosen as a processing site if and only if the data that is to receive as a processing site is less than the *additional* data that it would have to send as a nonprocessing site.

If minimization of communication cost is the sole criterion of optimization, then the best choices for both K and R_p have been completely determined for both broadcast and site-to-site networks. We expect the following exceedingly simple rule to be reasonable for choosing the number of processing sites:

Choose R_p to be the largest relation.

if N = 2 and n = 2 then K = 2

if N ≠ 2 then K = M_p for broadcast network

K = 1 for site-to-site network

4.10. Minimizing Processing Time

Suppose for the moment that our goal was only to minimize processing time and we were willing to ignore any network costs or delays. In this case we would want K = N so that we could distribute the work among all sites. We would still need to choose one relation to remain fragmented. The actual processing time will be independent of whatever relation we choose. To see this, notice that when we equalize the fragmented relation the processing time goes from

$$\max_j \frac{|R_p^j|}{|R_p|} \text{ proc } (Q) \ to \ \frac{1}{K} \text{ proc } (Q),$$

which is independent of R_p.

Since we can choose any R_p our choice for R_p should be the relation which minimizes network traffic. Thus we are looking for R_p which minimizes:

$$\sum_{j=1}^{N} C_{N-1} \left[\sum_{i \neq p} |R_i^j| \right] + \sum_{j=1}^{N} \text{pos} \left[|R_p^j| - \frac{1}{N} |R_p| \right]$$

4.11. Summary

The true optimal solution cannot be determined without knowing the precise relationships between processing time and communication costs, the distribution of data among the N sites, and the true processing time for each site. Any optimal solution would have to consider the possibility of using any value of K from 1 to N.

Exactly how to choose R_p and K is an open-ended question until the cost criteria have been specified. We have shown solutions at two extremes (minimum network traffic and minimum processing time).

Note the similarity between the "next piece" decision and the next tuple variable to be chosen for substitution in single site decomposition. The same inability to achieve a true optimum is present in both cases.

Just as refinement of the decision-making process was presented in [YOUS78] for decomposition, we plan to do experimentation concerning cases where each possible algorithm is best.

5.0. UPDATES

INGRES will be expanded to allow distributed relations with optional distribution criteria. When inserts occur they can cause tuples to be placed on specific sites. In the case of a replace command, they can cause tuples to be moved from one site to another.

We will assume that a distribution criterion maps a tuple to a unique site or to no site at all. It is possible that a criterion disallows certain values. Since the distribution criterion is related to an integrity constraint [STON75], tuples which cannot belong to any site could be treated as a violation of an integrity constraint.

With a distribution criterion we will guarantee that the collection of all the fragments of a relation contains no duplicates. Without a distribution criterion, any one fragment will contain no duplicates, but the collection of all sites can contain duplicates. To support any other rule seems too costly.

The processing of an update will proceed as follows:

1)   At the end of the query decomposition, one or more sites will have a portion of a temporary relation that holds the changes to be made to the result relation.

2)   Each site performs the updates specifically designated for it.

3)   The remaining updates (if any) are sent directly to their correct sites.

4)   Each site completes any new updates received.

The decomposition algorithm can help the update processing by never moving the result relation. For example, in the query:

    RANGE OF P IS PROJECT
    RANGE OF S IS SUPPLIER
    DELETE P WHERE P.CITY = S.CITY

decomposition has the choice of moving either P or S. By always choosing NOT to move P (the result relation variable), we optimize the update processing. This is because step (3) above will then have no tuples for other sites. However, choosing not to move the result relation may be a poor tactic during decomposition. The trade-off cannot readily be determined without advance knowledge of how many tuples of the result relation satisfy the qualification.

We will now identify what must be done for each update command, with or without a distribution criterion.

For an *APPEND* command, each tuple to be appended is put into a temporary relation and then split according to steps (1) and (4) above. If there is no distribution criterion, the tuples can be appended directly instead of going through a temporary relation.

For a *DELETE* command, the temporary relation consists of a tuple identifier (TID) and machine identifier (MID). The algorithm is the same regardless of the distribution criterion. Note that if we guarantee that the result relation is not moved during decomposition, we do not need the MID. The set of TIDs is only for the machine in which they reside. In fact, if the result relation is not moved during decomposition, the temporary relation is not needed. The deletes can be done directly.

For a *REPLACE* command, the TID, MID, and the new tuple must be saved. If the relation does not have a distribution criterion the replace command is processed in the same manner as a DELETE. With a distribution criterion, it is possible that a tuple will have to be moved from its current site to another. If this happens, it must be deleted at the current site and marked to be appended at its new site. If decomposition moves the result relation and a tuple has to change sites because of a REPLACE, steps (3) and (4) must be repeated twice.

In order to provide for recovery from a system crash during an update, updates are not done directly, instead we use a "deferred update" file [STON76a]. The deferred update file will contain a full image of all changes that must occur before any actual updates take place. The deferred update mechanism is hidden below the mechanism we have been discussing.

All update processing is controlled by the master INGRES. The individual sites can all perform the updates in parallel. If the result relation is never moved during decomposition, additional network costs can only occur in APPEND, and REPLACE commands where the distribution criterion forces the tuples to be moved to a new site.

6.0. PROCESSING OF AGGREGATES

The current implementation of INGRES processes aggregates (min, max, avg, sum, and count) first and then decomposes the remaining aggregate-free query. Although this is not always optimal, it typically is and it is a simple query processing strategy.

For Distributed INGRES we also plan to process all aggregates first. Some optimization specific to aggregates can be done. For example, aggregates that range over only one relation and are done without removing duplicates can be processed on individual sites, and the aggregated results are transmitted back to the master site where they are combined to produce the final result.

Aggregates which involve more than one relation or which require duplicates to be removed are processed by first retrieving the values to be aggregated into a distributed temporary relation, and then aggregating on that temporary relation. If the aggregate requires duplicates to be removed, then the temporary relation will have to be collected onto a single site in order to remove duplicates.

Other optimization techniques such as processing as many aggregates as possible in the same pass through the relation, and optimizing the by-domains references in aggregate functions, will continue to be performed.

7.0. CONCLUSIONS

The model we propose for a distributed database is very flexible. Portions of a relation can exist at any number of sites and an optional distribution criteria can be used to assign tuples to specific sites.

The algorithm for decomposing a query involves examining the structure of a query's qualification. The query is processed by choosing for processing one or more clauses of the qualification at a time. It is inevitable that some data will have to be moved from site to site in order to process a query. The algorithm tries to move only the smallest amount of data, and tries to get the maximum amount of parallel processing possible. In addition, by trying to avoid moving the result relation, we help to optimize the update processing. During query processing it is frequently desirable to broadcast data from one site to several other processing sites, which makes a broadcast network extremely desirable.

## CHAPTER ELEVEN

Dynamic Rematerialization: Processing Distributed Queries Using Redundant Data

Eugene Wong

ABSTRACT

In this paper an approach to processing distributed queries that makes explicit use of redundant data is proposed. The basic idea is to focus on the dynamics of materialization, defined as the collection of data and partial results available for processing at any given time, as query processing proceeds. In this framework the role of data redundancy in maximizing parallelism and minimizing data movement is clarified. What results is not only the discovery of new algorithms but an improved framework for their evaluation.

1.0. INTRODUCTION

In this paper we propose a new formulation for the problem of processing queries in a distributed database system. By such a system we mean a collection of autonomous processors, communicating via a general communication medium, and accessing separate and possibly overlapping fragments of a database. The user's view of data is to be an integrated whole, both fragmentation and redundancy being invisible. Geographical dispersion, although sometimes present, is not an essential ingredient of such a system, and the range of systems so encompassed includes not only the classical geographically distributed databases but also configurations that are in effect database machines. The problem of distributed execution of queries is common to all these systems.

In the query-processing algorithm designed for the SDD-1 distributed database management system [WONG77], an irredundant subset of the database is used during the execution of any single query. No effort was made to exploit the possible existence of multiple copies either to maximize parallel operations or to minimize data moves. A related and somewhat hidden characteristic inherent in the SDD-1 algorithm is that parallel processing is opportunistic rather than deliberate.

These characteristics were recognized in [EPST78] where the emphasis fell heavily on maximizing parallelism. The algorithm proposed there, and implemented for the distributed version of INGRES, achieves a high degree of parallelism by partitioning one relation among the processing sites and replicating all other needed relations at every site. We shall call this the FR (fragment and replicate) algorithm. For a query referencing many relations, the degree of data replication and the resulting communication cost to achieve this replication may be prohibitive. Thus, the FR algorithm is best applied to pieces of a many-variable query, one at a time, each with only two or three variables. Experience of using the FR algorithm in the distributed version of INGRES [EPST80a] indicates that the procedure of splitting a query before applying the FR algorithm is not an easy one to optimize.

It is time then, to seek a new formulation of the problem of distributed query processing that puts the issue of redundancy and parallelism into better focus. One such formulation was suggested by some recent work on database partitioning in a distributed system [WONG84].

2.0. PARTITIONING A DATABASE

Let D denote the database as viewed by a user. Let M_i denote the data residing at processing site i. We assume that $\bigcup_i M_i = D$ and call $M = \{M_i\}$ a *materialization* of D. Suppose that the database designer is free to choose M. How should he choose?

Among the major issues to be resolved is that of redundancy. Intuitively, the cost of redundancy is paid on updates and benefit accrued on retrieval. What we need is a conceptual framework to make this precise. Let Q denote a collection of queries on a database D. We shall say that a materialization M of D is *locally sufficient* (relative to Q) if for every q in Q and for every i there exists a local query q_i on M_i such that

$$\text{result } (q, D) = \bigcup_i \text{result } (q_i, M_i).$$

Local-sufficiency means that no intercommunication is necessary to process q. The only data movement needed is a final one to collect the results.

For two materializations M and M' denote $M > M'$ if $M_i \supseteq\; = M'_i$ for every i. A locally sufficient M is said to be *minimally redundant* if there exists no $M' < M$ (other than M itself) that is locally sufficient. Minimum redundancy means that data reduction at local sites cannot preserve local sufficiency.

Suppose we assume that it always takes longer to process a query when there are more data. Then, in terms of both retrieval and update, it is better to have minimal redundancy than not. Thus, minimally redundant materializations represent a desirable class of partitions for the database.

3.0. QUERY PROCESSING BY DYNAMIC REMATERIALIZATION

In terms of the concepts that we have introduced for database partitioning, query processing can be viewed as a dynamic process of changing materializations. Let q be a single query. Let $M_i^{(t)}$ denote the data at i available and selected for processing q at any stage t of processing. $M^{(t)} = \{M_i^{(t)}\}$ will be called the materialization at t. Any algorithm for distributed query processing can be represented as a sequence of *states*: $(q^{(t)}, M^{(t)})$, $t = 0, 1, 2, \ldots, N$. The terminal state $(q^{(N)}, M^{(N)})$ is required to be locally sufficient and to satisfy the condition

$$\bigcup_i \text{result } (q_i^{(N)}, M_i^{(N)}) = \text{result } (q, \bigcup_i M_i^{(0)}).$$

In other words, from the terminal state only local processing and gathering up of results are needed to complete processing. Transition between two successive states $(q^{(t)}, M^{(t)})$ and $(q^{(t+1)}, M^{(t+1)})$ occurs as a result of data movement and/or local processing. A transition will be called a *redistribution* if only data movement is involved, and a *local derivation* if:

1) $(q^{(t+1)}, M^{(t+1)})$ is derived from $(q^{(t)}, M^{(t)})$ by local processing, and

2) result $(q^{(t+1)}, M^{(t+1)})$ = result $(q^{(t)}, M^{(N)})$.

For any terminal state $(q^{(N)}, M^{(N)})$, a measure of the parallelism that it affords is given by

$$\tau(q^{(N)}, M^{(N)}) = \max_i (\text{time to process } q_i^{(N)} \text{on } M_i^{(N)}).$$

The cost to reach $(q^{(N)}, M^{(N)})$ can be expressed as

$$C(q^{(N)}, M^{(N)}) = C_0(N) + \sum_{t=1}^{N} T_t((q^{(t-1)}, M^{(t-1)}), (q^{(t)}, M^{(t)}))$$

where $C_0(N)$ is the cost of resynchronization between transitions and T_t is the cost of making the t-th transition.

If a compatible scale for τ and C is known, the problem can then be stated as one of optimal control. Even though the optimization problem is unlikely to be solved in any general sense, it provides a framework that allows algorithms proposed on heuristic grounds to be evaluated.

4.0. STRATEGIES BASED ON AN INITIALLY FEASIBLE SOLUTION

Let $q^{(0)} = q$ be the query to be processed and $M^{(0)}$ the data initially available for processing q. We say (q, M) is an *initially feasible solution* if it is a "locally sufficient redistribution" of $(q^{(0)}, M^{(0)})$, i.e., M is locally sufficient and derivable from $M^{(0)}$ by moving data. The cost of using such a strategy consists of several components, of which we assume the following to be dominant:

1) $C(M^{(0)}, M)$ = cost of moves,

2) $\tau (q, M)$ = cost of terminal parallel processing.

We shall say a strategy is of the *IFS type* if it consists of the following steps:

1) One seeks a $(q^{(1)}, M^{(1)})$ that is a "local derivation" of $(q^{(0)}, M^{(0)})$.

2) If no such local derivation can be found, one seeks an initially feasible solution (q, M).

3) One seeks to improve (q, M) by replacing the one-transition strategy $(q, M^{(0)}) \rightarrow (q, M)$ by a "short" sequence of transitions. Perform the first transition $(q, M^{(0)}) \rightarrow (q^{(1)}, M^{(1)})$ in the sequence.

4) Iterate, with $(q^{(1)}, M^{(1)})$ replacing $(q^{(0)}, M^{(0)})$.

Both the SDD-1 and FR algorithms are variations of IFS algorithms. In the SDD-1 case, the initially feasible solution (q, M) is restricted to be not merely locally sufficient but single-site sufficient. That is, there exists a site j such that q can be processed entirely on M_j. The choice for M in the FR algorithm is to replicate every relation but one, which is locally sufficient for almost all q. It seems clear that to qualify for selection as the initial choice as a feasible solution, (q, M) should be at least "noninferior" with respect to the pair of costs $(C (M^{(0)}, M), \tau (q, M))$. That is, there exists no initially feasible solution that is equal or better in both (C, τ) and strictly better in at least one. Neither the SDD-1 nor the FR algorithm guarantees this in general.

Example 4.1: Consider a conceptual schema given by

PERSON (SOCSEC, NAME, STATE-OF-RES)
CORP (CID, CNAME, STATE-OF-INC)
EMP (SOCSEC, CID, POSITION, SALARY)

Suppose that there are two sites with their local schemas given by the following view definition statements:

RANGE OF P IS PERSON
RANGE OF C IS CORP
RANGE OF E IS EMP
DEFINE PERSON-1 (P.ALL) WHERE P.STATE-OF-RES = "N.Y."
DEFINE CORP-1 (C.ALL) WHERE P.STATE-OF-INC = "N.Y."
DEFINE EMP-1 (E.ALL) WHERE E.SALARY $\leq$ 25000
DEFINE PERSON-2 (P.ALL) WHERE P.STATE-OF-RES $\neq$ "N.Y."
DEFINE CORP-2 (C.ALL) WHERE C.STATE-OF-INC $\neq$ "N.Y."
DEFINE EMP-2 (E.ALL) WHERE E.SALARY > 25000

Now consider a query

RETRIEVE (P.NAME) WHERE P.SOCSEC = E.SOCSEC
          AND C.CID = E.CID
          AND C.NAME = "IBM"

We begin with the materialization.

$M_1^{(0)}$ = (PERSON-1, CORP-1, EMP-1)
$M_2^{(0)}$ = (PERSON-2, CORP-2, EMP-2)

Processing the clauses that involve only local operations, we get

$M_1^{(1)}$ = (P 1, C 1, E 1)
$M_2^{(1)}$ = (P 2, C 2, E 2)

where

Pk = PERSON-k projected on (SOCSEC, NAME)

Ck = CORP-k restricted to (NAME = "IBM") and
        projected on (CID)

Ek = EMP-k projected on (SOCSEC, CID)

Now assume the following statistics for these relations:

Relation	#Tuples	Tuple Width in Bytes
$P1$	1000	29 (9,20)
$P2$	1000	29 (9,20)
$C1$	1	5
$C2$	0	5
$E1$	1000	14
$E2$	1000	14
$C1$ (cid) $E2$	100	14
$C1$ (cid) $E1$	1000	14

The initial feasible solution in the SDD-1 algorithm would consist of site 1 as the final processing site and

$$\mathbf{M} = \{\text{move } P\,2 \text{ and } E\,2 \text{ to site } 1\}$$

which entails moving 43 kbytes of data. On the other hand, the FR algorithm would yield a materialization

$$M_1 = (P\,1,\,C\,1,\,E\,1,\,E\,2)$$
$$M_2 = (P\,2,\,C\,1,\,E\,1,\,E\,2)$$

with

$$\mathbf{M}_1 = \{\text{move } E\,2 \text{ to site } 1\}$$
$$\mathbf{M}_2 = \{\text{move } C\,1 \text{ and } E\,1 \text{ to site } 2\}$$

which in this example corresponds to the $M^{(2)}$ that minimizes communication cost $C(M)$ and entails moving 28 kbytes of data. $\mathbf{M}_2$ can be reduced by joining $C\,1$ to $E\,1$ and moving the join instead of $E\,1$ (1405 bytes). $\mathbf{M}_1$ can be reduced by moving $C\,1$ to site 2, joining $C\,1$ with $E\,2$, and moving the join. The resulting sequence of materialization would appear as follows, where ∞ denotes join:

$$M^{(1)} = \{(P\,1,\,C\,1,\,E\,1),\,(P\,2,\,E\,2)\}$$
$$M^{(2)} = \{(P\,1,\,C\,1,\,E\,1),\,(P\,2,\,C\,1,\,E\,2)\}$$
$$M^{(3)} = \{(P\,1,\,E\,1 \infty C\,1),\,(P\,2,\,E\,2 \infty C\,1)\}$$
$$M^{(4)} = \{(P\,1,\,E\,1 \infty C\,1,\,E\,2 \infty C\,1),\,(P\,2,\,E\,1 \infty C\,1,\,E\,2 \infty C\,1)\}$$

and $M^{(4)}$ is now locally sufficient. The total amount of data moved is 2805 bytes, and no more processing is involved than either the FR or the SDD-1 algorithm. For our example, the strategy that we have found is just about the best possible over a wise range of relative costs for communication and local processing.

5.0. REPEATED-JOIN STRATEGIES

The database-partition problem suggests the following class of query processing strategies: Consider a relational database $D = \{R_1,\,R_2,\dots,\,R_m\}$ where R_k are relations. We shall say a query q is *admissible* if it is a finite repetition of "restriction," "projection," and "join" on the relations in D. We shall say an admissible q is *elementary* if it involves at most one join. Now, suppose that for any D we know how to find a "good" materialization $M(D)$ that is locally sufficient for all elementary queries. Then, we can construct a query processing algorithm as follows: construct a sequence

$$D = D^{(0)}, D^{(1)}, \ldots, D^{(N)}$$
$$q^{(0)}, q^{(0)}, \ldots, q^{(N)}$$

such that $q^{(N)} = q$, and for each t $q^{(t)}$ is an elementary query on $D^{(t)}$ and $D^{(t+1)} \subset \{D^{(t)}, \text{result } (q^{(t)}, D^{(t)})\}$. Since for each $D^{(t)}$ we know how to find a materialization $M(D^{(t)})$ that is locally sufficient for all elementary queries, $M(D^{(t)})$ is *a fortiori* locally sufficient for $q^{(t)}$. The *repeated-join* algorithm consists of repeating for each t the following steps.

1) Execute $q^{(t)}$ on $M(D^{(t)})$.

2) To obtain $D^{(t+1)}$, add result $(q^{(t)}, D^{(t)})$ to $D^{(t)}$ and eliminate the relations no longer needed in processing q.

3) Construct $M(D^{(t+1)})$.

How good this algorithm is depends on:

1) whether we can construct $M(I^{(t)})$ as claimed, and

2) the cost in resynchronization and data movement in making the transition $M(D^{(t)}) \rightarrow M(D^{(t+1)})$.

Our preliminary study suggests that the efficacy of this class of algorithms is enhanced if we augment the semantics of the relational model and use the semantics to restrict the class of admissible queries.

Roughly speaking, the semantic augmentation that we undertake corresponds to distinguishing between entities and relationships [CHEN76], [WONG79], but we shall define the semantics strictly in terms of the constructs of the relational model.

First, we classify the sets that serve as domains of the relations in the database into *identifier* and *value*. D is an identifier domain if and only if there is a unique relation E_D such that the elements of D are in one-to-one correspondence with the tuples of E_D. We shall say D is the *key* of E_D.

Every relation must have at least one identifier domain. A relation will be called an e-relation (entity) if it has a key, and an r-relation (relationship) otherwise.

Example 5.1:

> PERSON (* *SOCSEC*, NAME, STATE-OF-RES)
> CORP (* *CID*, CNAME, STATE-OF-INC)
> EMP (*SOCSEC, CID*, POSITION, SALARY)

where italics indicate an identifier domain and * indicates a key. Clearly, PERSON and CORP are e-relations and EMP is an r-relation.

Now suppose that we limit the admissible data manipulation operations to the following:

1)　restriction-Boolean condition on values,
2)　projection,
3)　join on an identifier domain D,
4)　closure.

Note that admissible joins are limited. For example, the join

$$\text{PERSON (STATE-OF-RES = STATE-OF-INC) CORP}$$

would be an inadmissible operation because the join is on a nonidentifier domain, but the following operation is admissible:

$$(\text{PERSON} (\overset{\text{SOCSEC}}{\infty}) \text{EMP} (\overset{\text{CID}}{\infty}) \text{CORP}) \left[\text{STATE-OF-RES} = \text{STATE-OF-INC}\right]$$

Let $\overset{D}{\alpha}$ denote the semijoin operator defined in [BERN79]. That is, $A \overset{D}{\alpha} B$ is the projection on A of the join $A \overset{D}{\infty} B$. The following proposition gives a condition for local sufficiency in terms of the semijoin.

Proposition 5.1: Let D be a collection of relations. Let M be a materialization of D such that to each e-relation E corresponds a unique $E(k)$ in M_k such that

$$E = \bigcup_k E(k).$$

Then, M is locally sufficient for all elementary queries if for every $R \in D$ and every identifier domain D in R

(5.1)

$$R \overset{D}{\alpha} E_D(k) \in \text{closure} (M_k) \text{ for every } k.$$

Proof: For R and S in D, we can write

$$R \overset{D}{\alpha} S = \bigcup_k (R \overset{D}{\alpha} E_D(k)) \overset{D}{\infty} (S \overset{D}{\alpha} E_D(k)).$$

Since projection and restriction commute with union, the proposition is proved.

Condition (5.1) provides a simple means for testing the local sufficiency of a materialization M for elementary queries. Further, if M fails the test, (5.1) provides a means for augmenting M to make it locally sufficient. As such, (5.1) makes the repeated-join algorithm work. At each step t in the algorithm, to construct $M(D^{(t+1)})$, we only need to distribute enough of the result $(q^{(t)}, D^{(t)})$ so that

(5.2)

$$\text{result } (q^{(t)}, D^{(t)}) \overset{D}{\alpha} E_D(k) \in \text{closure} (M_k(D^{(t+1)}))$$

for every k and every D.

Example 5.2: Take the schema in Example 5.1, and consider the same query as in Example 4.1. We have

$$D = \{\text{PERSON, CORP, EMP}\}$$

$$q = \text{PERSON} \overset{\text{SOCSEC}}{\underset{\alpha}{}} (\text{EMP} \overset{\text{CID}}{\underset{\alpha}{}} (\text{CORP (NAME = ``IBM''})))[\text{NAME}].$$

Define PERSON-k and CORP-k as in Example 4.1, but define

$$\text{EMP} - k = (\text{EMP} \overset{\text{SOCSEC}}{\underset{\alpha}{}} \text{PERSON} - k) \cup (\text{EMP} \overset{\text{CID}}{\underset{\alpha}{}} \text{CORP} - k)$$

Take the initial materialization to be

$$M^{(0)} = \{(\text{PERSON} - k, \text{CORP} - k, \text{EMP} - k), k = 1, 2\}.$$

Then $M^{(0)}$ is locally sufficient for all elementary queries on D. Now, take

$$D^{(0)} = D = \{\text{PERSON, CORP, EMP}\}$$

$$q^{(0)} = (\text{EMP} \overset{\text{CID}}{\underset{\alpha}{}} (\text{CORP (NAME = ``IBM''})))[\text{SOCSEC}]$$

Here, we have no need to distinguish $q^{(0)}$ from its result. Hence, we can write

$$D^{(1)} = \{\text{PERSON}, q^{(0)}\}$$

$$q = q^1 = (\text{EMP} \overset{\text{CID}}{\underset{\alpha}{}} q^{(0)})[\text{NAME}]$$

As in Example 4.1, assume that

$$\text{CORP-2 (NAME = ``IBM'')} = \Phi$$

Hence, $q_2^{(0)} = \Phi$ and $q^{(0)} = q_1^{(0)}$.

To satisfy (5.1), we can take

$$M_1^{(1)} = (\text{PERSON} - 1, q_1^{(0)})$$
$$M_2^{(1)} = (\text{PERSON} - 2, q_1^{(0)})$$

which requires moving $q_1^{(0)}$ to site 2. Alternatively, we can take

$$M_2^{(1)} = (\text{PERSON} - 2, q_1^{(0)} \overset{\text{SOCSEC}}{\underset{\alpha}{}} \text{PERSON} - 2)$$

which would entail first moving (PERSON-2) [SOCSEC] to site 1 and then moving $q_1^{(0)} \overset{\text{SOCSEC}}{\underset{\alpha}{}}$ PERSON-2 to site 2. However, the double move would be obviated by storing at each site an index for the distribution of identifiers.

For a given q, the sequence $q^{(n)}$ is by no means unique, and the optimization problem is to choose $q^{(n)}$ so as to minimize cost, however cost is defined.

6.0. CONCLUSION

In this paper we propose a new approach to distributed query processing. This approach focuses on how the data available at each site change as processing proceeds. We believe that issues of parallelism and redundancy are rendered cleaner by this approach. Our immediate goal is not so much to find better algorithms, but to provide a conceptual framework in which new classes of algorithms can be formulated in a natural way.

## CHAPTER TWELVE

Nonblocking Commit Protocols

Dale Skeen

ABSTRACT

Protocols that allow operational sites to continue transaction processing even though site failures have occurred are called "nonblocking." Many applications require nonblocking protocols. This paper investigates the properties of nonblocking protocols. Necessary and sufficient conditions for a protocol to be nonblocking are presented and from these conditions a method for designing them is derived. Both a central site nonblocking protocol and a decentralized nonblocking protocol are presented.

1.0. INTRODUCTION

Recently, considerable research interest has been focused on distributed database systems [LORI77, ROTH77a, SCHA78, SVOB79]. Several systems have been proposed and are in various stages of implementation, including SDD-1 [HAMM79], SYSTEM-R [LIND79], and INGRES [STON79a]. It is widely recognized that distributed crash recovery is vital to the usefulness of these systems. However, resilient protocols are hard to design and they are expensive. Crash recovery algorithms are based on the notion that certain basic operations on the data are logically indivisible. These operations are called "transactions."

1.1. Transaction Management

By definition, a transaction on a distributed database system is an atomic operation: either it executes to completion or it appears never to have executed at all. However, a transaction is rarely a physically atomic operation, rather, during execution it must be decomposed into a sequence of physical operations. This discrepancy between logical atomicity (as seen by the

D. Skeen, *ACM-SIGMOD Conference Proceedings*, ACM-SIGMOD International Conference on Management of Data, Ann Arbor, Michigan, June 1981. Copyright 1981, Association for Computing Machinery, Inc.; reprinted by permission.

application) and physical atomicity poses a significant problem in the implementation of distributed systems. This problem is amplified when transaction atomicity must be preserved across multiple failures. Nonetheless, most applications require that a notion of transaction atomicity (above the level of physical atomicity) be supported and made resilient to failures.

Preserving transaction atomicity in the single site case is a well understood problem [LIND79, GRAY78]. The processing of a single transaction is viewed as follows. At some time during its execution, a "commit point" is reached where the site decides to "commit" or to "abort" the transaction. A "commit" is an unconditional guarantee to execute the transaction to completion, even in the event of multiple failures. Similarly, an "abort" is an unconditional guarantee to "back out" the transaction so that none of its results persist. If a failure occurs before the commit point is reached, then immediately upon recovering the site will abort the transaction. Commit and abort are irreversible. See [LIND79] for a discussion on implementing this abstraction of transaction management.

The problem of guaranteeing transaction atomicity is compounded when more than one site is involved. Given that each site has a local recovery strategy that provides atomicity at the local level, the problem becomes one of ensuring that the sites either unanimously abort or unanimously commit. A mixed decision results in an inconsistent database.

Protocols for preserving transaction atomicity are called "commit protocols." Several commit protocols have been proposed [ALSB76, HAMM79, LAMP76a, LIND79, STON79a]. The simplest commit protocol that allows unilateral abort is the two phase commit protocol illustrated in Figure 12.1 [GRAY78, LAMP76a]. This protocol uses a designated site (Site 1 in the figure) to coordinate the execution of the transaction at the other sites. In the first phase of the protocol the coordinator distributes the transaction to all sites, and then each site individually votes on whether to commit (yes) or abort (no) it. In the second phase, the coordinator collects all the votes and informs each site of the outcome. In the absence of failures, this protocol preserves atomicity.

1.2. Nonblocking Commit Protocols

Consider what happens in the two phase protocol if both the coordinator and the second site crash after the third site has voted on the transaction, but before the third has received a commit message. There are several possible execution states of the transaction; two are of interest.

First, either of the failed sites may have aborted the transaction. Secondly, all sites may have decided to commit the protocol. In the latter situation, if the coordinator failed between sending commit messages and if the second site failed after receiving a commit message, then the transaction has been committed at the second site. Since site 3 has no way of determining the status of the transaction at the second site, it cannot safely proceed. Instead, execution of the transaction must be "blocked" at site 3 until one of

	SITE 1	SITE 2
(1)	Transaction is received. "start xact" is sent.	
		"start xact" is received. Site 2 votes: "yes" to commit, "no" to abort. The vote is sent to Site 1.
(2)	The vote is received. If vote = yes and Site 1 agrees, then "commit" is sent; else, "abort" is sent.	
		Either "commit" or "abort" is received and processed.

FIGURE 12.1. The Two Phase Commit Protocol (2 sites)

the failed sites has recovered.

The two phase commit protocol is an example of a "blocking" protocol: operational sites sometimes wait on the recovery of a failed site. Locks must be held on the database while the transaction is blocked.

A protocol that does not require operational sites to block until a failed site has recovered is called a "nonblocking protocol."

1.3. Termination and Recovery Protocols

When the occurrence of site failures render the continued execution of the commit protocol impossible, then a "termination protocol" is invoked. The purpose of a termination protocol is to terminate transaction execution as quickly as possible at the operational sites. The protocol, of course, must guarantee transaction atomicity. Clearly, a termination protocol can accomplish its task only if a nonblocking commit protocol is used. In Section 6.0, we derive a centralized termination protocol.

The final class of protocols required to handle site failures is called "recovery protocols." These protocols are invoked by failed sites to resume transaction processing. Recovery protocols are not discussed in this paper; interested readers are referred to LIND79, HAMM79, SKEE81a.

In the next section we present the formalisms required in the remainder of the paper. Commit protocols are modeled by finite state automata. The local state and the global state of a transaction are defined.

In the third section two prevalent commit paradigms are presented: the central site model and the decentralized model. It is shown that protocols in both models have synchronization points. This property will be used in designing nonblocking protocols.

In the fourth section the major results of the paper are presented. First, necessary and sufficient conditions for a protocol to be nonblocking are derived. Next, we demonstrate that "buffer states" can be added to a protocol to make it nonblocking. For most practical protocols, a single buffer state is sufficient.

In the fifth section we present a protocol invoked to terminate the transaction at the operational sites after the occurrence of (multiple) site failures.

Throughout the paper two assumptions about the underlying communications network are made:

1) point-to-point communication is possible between two operational sites (i.e., the network never fails),

2) the network can detect the failure of a site (e.g., by a "timeout") and can reliably report this to an operational site.

2.0. FORMAL MODEL SUMMARIZED

In this section, we use a generalization of the formal model introduced in [SKEE81a] to describe commit protocols. Transaction execution at each site is modeled as a finite state automaton (FSA), with the network serving as a common input/output tape to all sites. The states of the FSA for Site i are called the "local states" of Site i.

A state transition involves the site reading a (nonempty) string of messages addressed to it, writing a string of messages, and moving to the next local state. The change of local state is an instantaneous event, marking the end of the transition (and all associated activity). In the absence of a site failure, a state transition is an atomic event. State transitions at one site are asynchronous with respect to transitions at other sites.

In Figure 12.2, this model is illustrated for the two phase commit protocol of Figure 12.1. One FSA describes the protocol executed by the coordinator, while the other describes the protocol executed by each slave. Each FSA has four (local) states: an "initial state" (q_i), a "wait state" (w_i), an "abort state" (a_i), and a "commit state" (c_i). Abort and commit are "final states," indicating that the transaction has been either aborted or committed, respectively.

Figure 12.2 also illustrates the conventions used in the remainder of the paper. Local states for Site i are subscripted with i. Messages sent or received by a slave are subscripted with that slave's site number.

The finite state automata describing a commit protocol exhibit the following four properties:

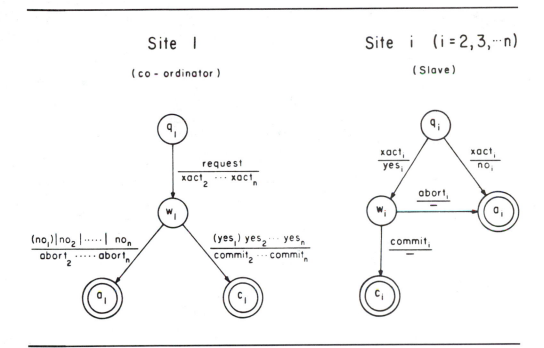

FIGURE 12.2. The FSAs for the Two Phase Commit (n sites)

1) The FSAs are nondeterministic. The behavior of each FSA is not known *apriori* because of the possibility of deadlocks, failures, and user aborts. Moreover, when multiple messages are addressed to a site, the order of receiving the messages is arbitrary.

2) The final states of the FSAs are partitioned into two sets: the "abort" states, and the "commit" states.

3) Once a site has made a transition to an abort state, then transitions to nonabort states are not allowed. A similar constraint holds for commit states. Consequently, the act of "committing" or "aborting" is irreversible.

4) The state diagram describing a FSA is acyclic. This guarantees that the protocol executing at every site will eventually terminate.

Protocols are often characterized by the number of "phases" required to commit the transaction. Intuitively, a phase occurs when all sites executing the protocol make a state transition. The number of phases in a protocol is a rough measure of its complexity and cost (in messages). Distributed protocols generally require at least two phases.

2.1. Global Transaction State

The "global state" of a distributed transaction is defined to consist of:

1)   a global state vector containing the local states of the participating FSAs and

2)   the outstanding messages in the network.

The global state defines the complete processing state of a transaction.

The graph of all global states reachable from the initial global state is instrumental in specifying and analyzing protocols. For example, a global state is said to be "inconsistent" if it contains both a local commit state and a local abort state. Protocols which maintain transaction atomicity can have no inconsistent global states. Figure 12.3 gives the reachable state graph for the two phase protocol discussed earlier.

A global state is said to be a "final state" if all local states contained in the state vector are final states. A global state is a "terminal state" if from it there are no immediately reachable successors. A terminal state that is not a final state is a deadlocked state: the transaction will never be successfully completed.

Given that the state of Site i is known to be s_i, then it is possible to derive from the global state graph the local states that may be concurrently occupied by other sites. This set of states is called the "concurrency set" for state s_i.[1]

Although the reachable global state graph grows exponentially with the number of sites, in practice we seldom need to actually construct the graph. In subsequent sections, we will be able to infer most properties of the graph by examining properties of the local states.

2.2. Committable States

A local state is called "committable" if occupancy of that state by any site implies that all sites have voted "yes" on committing the transaction. A state that is not committable is called "noncommittable."[2] Intuitively, a site in a "noncommittable" state does not know whether all the other sites have voted to commit.

In the two phase protocol of Figure 12.2, the only "committable" state is the commit state (c_i); all other states are "noncommittable." Recall, that this protocol is a blocking protocol, and it is common for blocking protocols to have only one "committable" state. We will assert (without proof) that

---

[1]Formally, the "concurrency set" of state s_i is the set of all local states s_j, where $i \neq j$, such that s_i and s_j are contained in the same (reachable) global state.

[2]To call "noncommittable" states "abortable" would be misleading, since a transaction that is not in a final commit state at any site can still be aborted. In fact, sometimes transactions in "committable" (but not commit) states will be aborted because of failures.

(initiol stote)

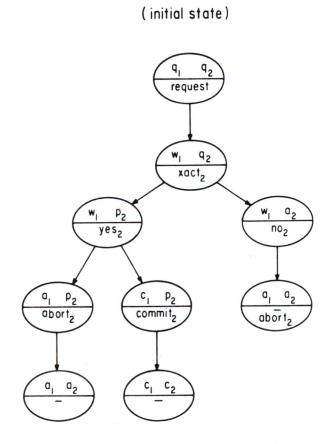

FIGURE 12.3. Reachable State Graph for the Two Phase Commit Protocol

nonblocking protocols always have more than one "committable" state.

2.3. Site Failures

Since the sending of more than one message is not a physically atomic operation, it cannot be assumed that local state transitions are atomic under site
failures. A site may only partially complete a transition before failing. In
particular, only part of the messages that were to be sent during a transition
may, in fact, be transmitted.

Failures cause an exponential growth in the number of reachable global
states. Fortunately, it will never be necessary to construct the (reachable)

global state graph with failures. In the subsequent sections, any reference to global state graphs will be to graphs in the absence of failures.

3.0. THE TWO PARADIGMS FOR COMMIT PROTOCOLS

Almost every commit protocol can be classified into either one of two generic classes of commit protocols: the "central site" class or the (completely) "decentralized" class. These classes represent two very distinct philosophies in commit protocols. In this section, we characterize and give an example of each class. The examples were chosen because they are the simplest and most renowned protocols in these classes. However, neither example is a nonblocking protocol. In the next section we will show how to extend both of them to nonblocking protocols.

3.1. The Central Site Model

This model uses one site, the "coordinator," to direct transaction processing at all the participating sites, which we will denote as "slaves."

The properties of protocols in this class are:

1)   There is a single coordinator, executing the "coordinator protocol."

2)   All other participants (slaves) execute the "slave protocol."

3)   A slave can communicate only with the coordinator.

4)   During each "phase" of the protocol the coordinator sends the same message to each slave and waits for a response from each one.

The two phase protocol presented in Figures 12.1 and 12.2 is the simplest example of a central site protocol. Other examples can be found in [LAMP76a, HAMM79, SKEE81a]. Central site protocols are popular in literature because they are relatively cheap, conceptually simple, and robust to most single site failures. Their major weakness is their vulnerability to a coordinator failure.

Property (4) assures that the sites progress through the protocol at approximately the same rate. Let us define this property as follows:

> Definition: A protocol is said to be "synchronous within one state transition" if one site never leads another site by more than one state transition during the execution of the protocol.

The central site protocol (including both the coordinator protocol and the slave protocol) is "synchronous within one state transition." This property will be used in constructing nonblocking central site commit protocols.

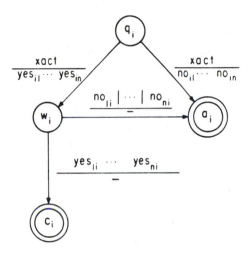

FIGURE 12.4. The Decentralized Two Phase Commit Protocol (n sites)

3.2. The Decentralized Model

In a fully decentralized approach, each site participates as an equal in the protocol and executes the same protocol. Every site communicates with every other site.

Decentralized protocols are characterized by successive rounds of message interchanges. We are interested in a rather stylized approach to decentralized protocols: during a round of message interchange, each site will send the identical message to every other site. A site then waits until it has received messages from all its cohorts before beginning the next round of message interchange. To simplify the subsequent discussion, during a message interchange we will speak as if sites send messages to themselves.

The simplest decentralized commit protocol is the "decentralized two phase commit" illustrated in Figure 12.4. All participating sites run this protocol. (Messages are doubly subscripted: the first subscript refers to the sending site, the second refers to the receiving site.)

In the first phase each site receives the "start xact" message,[3] decides whether to unilaterally abort, and sends that decision to each of its cohorts. In the second phase, each site accumulates all the abort decisions and moves to a final state.

Like the central site two phase protocol, the decentralized two phase protocol is "synchronous within one state transition." Sites progress through the protocol at approximately the same rate.

4.0. NONBLOCKING COMMIT PROTOCOLS

In this section we present the major result of this paper: necessary and sufficient conditions for a protocol to be "nonblocking." We then augment the protocols presented in the last section to construct nonblocking protocols.

4.1. The Fundamental Nonblocking Theorem

When a site failure occurs, the operational sites must reach a consensus on committing the transaction by examining their local states.

Let us consider the simplest case, where only a single site remains operational. This site must be able to infer the progress of the other sites solely from its local state. Clearly, the site will be able to safely abort the transaction if and only if the concurrency set for its local state does not contain a commit state. On the other hand, for the site to be able to safely commit, its local state must be "committable" and the concurrency set for its state must not contain an abort state.

A blocking situation arises whenever the concurrency set for the local state contains both a commit and an abort state. A blocking situation also arises whenever the site is in a "noncommittable" state and the concurrency set for that state contains a commit state – the site cannot commit because it cannot infer that all sites have voted yes on committing, and it cannot abort because another site may have committed the transaction before crashing. Notice that both two phase commit protocols can block for either reason.

These observations imply the following simple but powerful result.

> Theorem 1: (the fundamental nonblocking theorem). A protocol is "nonblocking" if and only if it satisfies both of the following conditions (for every participating site):
>
> 1) there exists no local state such that its concurrency set contains both an abort and a commit state,
>
> 2) there exist no "noncommittable" state whose concurrency set contains a commit state.

Again, the single operational site case demonstrated the necessity of the

---

[3]We do not model the mechanism by which the transaction is distributed to the sites. This is most likely performed by the site receiving the transaction request from the application.

conditions stated in the theorem. To prove sufficiency, we must show that it is always possible to terminate the protocol, in a consistent state, at all operational sites. In Section 5.0 we present two "termination protocols" that always successfully terminate the transaction executed by a commit protocol obeying both conditions of the fundamental nonblocking theorem.

A useful implication of this theorem is the following corollary.

> Corollary: A commit protocol is nonblocking with respect to k-1 site failures $(2 < k \leq$ the number of participating sites) if and only if there is a subset of k sites that obeys both conditions of the fundamental nonblocking theorem.

It is obvious that a protocol with k sites obeying the fundamental theorem will be nonblocking as long as one of those k sites remains operational. (The case where k=2 is a special case that has been examined in [SKEE81b].)

The fundamental nonblocking theorem provides a way to check whether a protocol is nonblocking; however, it does not provide a methodology for constructing nonblocking protocols. In the next section we develop a set of design rules that yield nonblocking protocols. These rules take the form of structural constraints.

4.2. Buffer States

The two phase central site (slave) protocol and the two phase decentralized protocol are very similar: they are structurally equivalent, and they are both synchronous within one state transition. These similarities, especially the latter, suggests that a common solution to the blocking problem may exist. Their common structure, which is illustrated in Figure 12.5 for reference, constitutes the "canonical two phase commit protocol."

Consider a protocol that is synchronous within one state transition. The concurrency set for a given state in the protocol can contain only the states that are adjacent to the given state and the given state, because the states of the participating sites never differ by more than a single state transition. In the canonical two phase commit protocol, the concurrency set of state q contains q, w and a. The concurrency set for state w contains all of the local states of the protocol.

This observation together with the fundamental nonblocking theorem yields:

> Lemma: A protocol that is synchronous within one state transition is "non-blocking" if and only if:
>
> 1) it contains no local state adjacent to both a commit and an abort state, and
>
> 2) it contains no "noncommittable" state that is adjacent to a commit state.

State w violates both constraints of the lemma. To satisfy the lemma we can introduce a "buffer" state between the wait state (w) and the commit state (c). This new protocol is illustrated in Figure 12.6. Since the new state is a "committable" state, both conditions of the lemma are satisfied. The

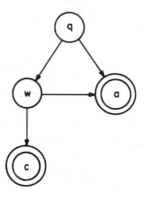

FIGURE 12.5. The Canonical Two Phase Commit Protocol

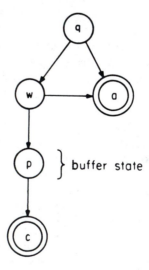

FIGURE 12.6. The Canonical Nonblocking Commit Protocol

buffer state can be thought of as a "prepare to commit" state, and, therefore, is labeled p in the illustration.

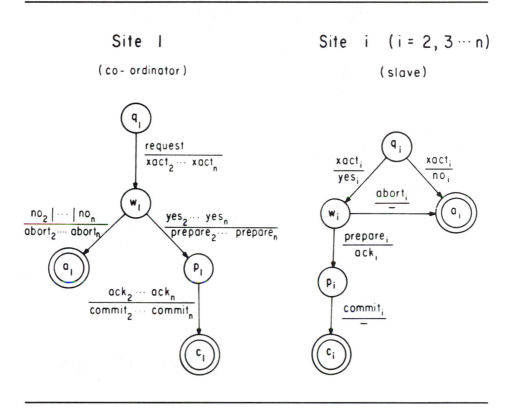

FIGURE 12.7. A (Three Phase) Nonblocking Central Site Commit Protocol

We will refer to this protocol as the "canonical nonblocking protocol." It is a three phase protocol.

The above lemma is a very strong result. Since all proposed commit protocols are "synchronous within one state transition," the lemma can be applied directly. In [SKEE81b] the lemma is generalized to apply to less "synchronous" protocols.

The lemma imposes constraints on the local structure of a protocol. This is convenient since it is much easier to design protocols using local constraints than using global constraints. As an example, the "canonical three phase" protocol was designed using the constraints given in the lemma.

The significance of the canonical three phase commit protocol is that it can be specialized to yield practical nonblocking protocols. In the next sections, two nonblocking protocols are presented − a central site protocol and a decentralized protocol. Both protocols were derived directly from the canonical three phase protocol.

4.3. A Nonblocking Central Site Protocol

A nonblocking central site protocol is illustrated in Figure 12.7. The slave protocol is the canonical three phase protocol (with appropriate messages added). The coordinator protocol is also a three phase protocol that is a straightforward extension of the two phase coordinator protocol. The "prepare" (p) state in the coordinator directs the slaves into their corresponding prepare state.

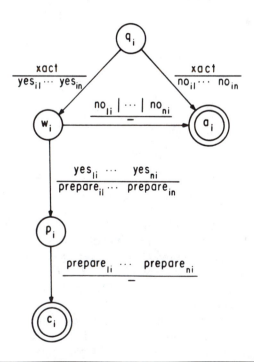

FIGURE 12.8. A (Three Phase) Nonblocking Decentralized Commit Protocol

4.4. A Nonblocking Decentralized Protocol

A nonblocking decentralized protocol is illustrated in Figure 12.8. Again, the protocol is the canonical nonblocking protocol. The addition of the prepare state translates to another round of messages in the decentralized class.

5.0. TERMINATION PROTOCOLS

Termination protocols are invoked when the occurrence of site failures renders the continued execution of the commit protocol impossible. This occurs when the coordinator fails in a central site protocol, or when any site fails during a decentralized protocol. The purpose of the termination protocol is to terminate the transaction at all operational sites in a consistent manner.

Clearly, a termination protocol can accomplish its task only if the current state of at least one operational site obeys the conditions given in the fundamental nonblocking theorem. However, since subsequent site failures may occur during the termination protocol, in the worst case it will be able to terminate correctly only if all of the operational sites obey the fundamental nonblocking theorem.

We now present a central site termination protocol. It will successfully terminate the transaction as long as one site executing a nonblocking commit protocol remains operational.

A decentralized termination protocol is presented in [SKEE81b].

5.1. Central Site Termination Protocol

The basic idea of this scheme is to choose a coordinator, which we will call a "backup coordinator," from the set of operational sites. The "backup coordinator" will complete the transaction by directing all the remaining sites toward a commit or an abort. Since the "backup" can fail before terminating the transaction, the protocol must be reentrant.

"Backup coordinators" were introduced in SDD-1 [HAMM79]. The scheme presented is a modification of that scheme.

When the termination protocol is invoked, a backup must be chosen. The method used is not important. The sites could vote, or, alternatively, the choice could be based on a preassigned ranking.

Once the backup has been chosen, it will base the commit decision only on its local state. The rule for deciding is:

> Decision Rule For Backup Coordinators: If the concurrency set for the current state of the backup contains a commit state, then the transaction is committed. Otherwise, it is aborted.

The backup executes the following two phase protocol:

Phase 1: The backup issues a message to all sites to make a transition to its local state. The backup then waits for an acknowledgment from each site.

Phase 2: The backup issues a commit or abort message to each site. (By applying the decision rule given above.)

If the backup is initially in a commit or an abort state, then the first phase can be omitted.

Phase 1 of the backup protocol is necessary because the backup may fail. By insuring that all sites are in the same state before committing (aborting), the backup insures that subsequent backup coordinators will make the same commit decision. A proof of correctness for this protocol can be found in [SKEE81b].

Let us consider an invocation of the protocol by the "canonical" three phase commit protocol. The backup will chose to abort on states q, w, and a, and to commit on states p and c. If the chosen backup was in state p initially, then the messages sent to all sites are:

1)   "move to state p," and

2)   "commit."

6.0. CONCLUSION

In this paper we formally introduced the "nonblocking" problem and the associated terminology. Although this problem is widely recognized by practitioners in distributed crash recovery, it is the author's belief that this is the first time that the problem has been treated formally in the literature.

Also, the two most popular commit classes − central site and decentralized − were characterized. Every published commit protocol is a member of one of the classes. These classes are likely to prevail in the future.

We illustrated each commit class with a two phase protocol. Two phase protocols are popular because they are the simplest and the cheapest (in the number of messages) protocols that allow unilateral abort by an arbitrary site. Unfortunately, two phase protocols can block on site failures.

The major contributions of this paper are the "fundamental nonblocking theorem" and, from it, necessary and sufficient conditions for designing both central site and distributed nonblocking protocols.

We presented two such nonblocking protocols: the three phase central site and the three phase distributed commit protocols. The three phase protocols were derived from the two phase protocols by adding a "prepare to commit" state. This addition is the least modification that can be made to a two phase protocol in order for it to satisfy the fundamental nonblocking theorem. Therefore, such three phase protocols are the simplest (and cheapest) nonblocking protocols.

Nonetheless, an additional phase imposes a substantial overhead (in the number of messages). This overhead can be reduced by having only a few sites execute the three phase protocol; the remaining can execute the cheaper two phase protocol. The transaction will not block as long as one of the sites executing the three phase protocol remains operational. Since two site failures are always necessary to block a transaction ([SKEE81b]), the number of sites executing the three phase protocol should be greater than two.

Lastly, we presented a termination protocol to be invoked when a coordinator fails in a central site commit protocol or when any site fails in a decentralized commit protocol.

It is not necessary that the commit protocol and the termination protocol belong to the same class. In some environments, it may be reasonable to run a central site commit protocol and a decentralized termination protocol.

4

User Interfaces for Database Systems

This section includes four papers on user interfaces originating in the INGRES project. The first paper describes the design of EQUEL, a preprocessor that allows QUEL commands to be executed from within a C program. It was written after we realized that INGRES needed to be called from a host language. One has the choice of writing a subroutine call interface (such as is done for IMS), modifying the compiler for one's favorite programming language to extend it with database calls, or writing a preprocessor. We never considered writing a subroutine call interface, since we knew it was a Sisyphusian undertaking. One has only to look at any code fragment for a subroutine call interface to realize the futility of the approach. It makes little sense to design a "new technology" database system, which is supposed to be easy to use, and simultaneously, design a subroutine call user interface. On the other hand, extending the compiler would clearly be a major undertaking. Hence, we settled easily on a preprocessor and designed EQUEL in late 1975. It survives to this day almost unchanged.

When reading about EQUEL, one should keep in mind two points. First, EQUEL has implicit control flow, in that it automatically iterates over a collection of specified tuples. On the other hand, so-called cursor-oriented interfaces (e.g., [ASTR76] and current SQL/DS) force a user to bind a command to a cursor and then, explicitly, fetch qualifying tuples one at a time. In this way, the user must program his own control flow. In my opinion, implicit control flow has the advantage that one need never check for errors in commands as they are automatically handled, and the run-time support system can cleverly buffer tuples in the user program before it asks for them. In this way, the number of calls to the data manager is reduced. On the other hand, a cursor-oriented system allows multiple commands to be active at one time, and a user can intermix requests from two different tuple collections.

The second point to remember is the degree of flexibility in substituting programming language variables at run time into a database command. Many systems (including SQL/DS) only allow a programmer to substitute run-time values where a constant would normally be expected in the command. This makes parsing and query planning at compile-time feasible, but seriously limits the generality of the interface. In contrast, EQUEL allows larger portions of the command to remain unspecified until run time. However, the penalty for this "late binding" is to delay parsing and query planning until run time.

Current programming language interfaces to database systems allow a programmer to specify a set of records and then iterate FORWARD over the collection. In applications, such as browsers, where one wishes to move both forward and backward through a collection of records, current interfaces fail to provide the needed facilities. Hence, we have included as our second paper a proposal for a new programming language interface (called portals), which appears to have many advantages over current interfaces.

One thing we learned from our design of EQUEL was how difficult it is to attach a database system cleanly to a programming language. A basic problem is that the two environments do not have the same underlying type system. For example, the database has a type "relation" that is not supported in the programming language environment. Moreover, one would like to pass references to tuples as arguments to programming language procedures. Such a feature is impossible because the programming language does not know the structure of a tuple returned at run time from the database. The obvious solution to such problems is to build a new programming language, which could do both general purpose computation and database access in one environment. Alternatively, one could extend a modern programming language (e.g., Pascal) with desired features.

Larry Rowe joined the INGRES project in 1976 and began work on such a database programming language. The objective was to produce something much cleaner than EQUEL (which I describe sometimes as an attempt to glue an apple onto a pancake). The resulting language, RIGEL, became operational in 1979, and has been used at several universities. The third paper discusses the RIGEL programming language.

Unfortunately, RIGEL has the same sort of performance problems discussed in the 1980 retrospection article because it is built partly on top of INGRES. It also has the additional problem faced by all new programming languages, that of user acceptance. My personal belief is that most programmers are fervently committed to whatever programming language they learned first or use most often. Moreover, one quickly sinks into theological disputes when attempting to discuss the merits and demerits of any given programming language. Hence, new general purpose languages have a difficult time gaining acceptance, unless they have the Department of Defense insisting on their use.

By 1979, it was evident that any database-oriented program was at least 60% composed of code to manipulate the screen. Typical numbers for user programs are:

    screen manipulation   – 60%
    computation and control   – 15%
    database access   – 25%

Obviously, one should attack the 60% if one wants to create a programming environment that allows applications to be constructed rapidly. Moreover, the best interface between the application program and the screen is through forms. The general control flow for most business data processing applications is:

    put a form on the screen
    data entry by operator into the form
    edit checking of input data
    database command(s) as a result of data entry
    put a new form on the screen with the result of the transaction

Languages are becoming available commercially which attempt to support the programming of such applications quickly and have been termed "4th generation languages." One of the most advanced languages of this flavor is FADS, also constructed by Larry Rowe and discussed in the fourth paper in this section.

I find it amusing that the programming language research community has totally ignored the design of forms-oriented data access languages. Such languages promise to be of extreme practical significance during this decade and will be constructed with negligible input from the experts on programming languages. It is reminiscent of report writers (e.g., RPG), which were also ignored by the mainstream programming language community. There have been modest efforts to build a bridge between the database community and the programming language community (e.g., [BROD80, BROD84]). However, at the moment, they are still very far apart.

All interfaces described in this section are operational, except for portals, for which a paper design has been completed.

## CHAPTER THIRTEEN

Embedding a Relational Data Sublanguage in a General Purpose Programming Language

Eric Allman / Michael Stonebraker / Gerald Held

ABSTRACT

This paper describes an operational precompiler which embeds the relational data sublanguage QUEL into the general purpose programming language C. Also briefly described are two operational subsystems written in this combined language. Lastly some of the language oriented shortcomings that have been observed in QUEL and QUEL augmented by C are discussed.

1.0. INTRODUCTION

INGRES (Interactive Graphics and Retrieval System) is a relational database system which is implemented on a PDP-ll/40 based hardware configuration at Berkeley. INGRES runs as a normal user job on top of the UNIX operating system developed at Bell Telephone Laboratories [RITC74b]. The only significant modification to UNIX that INGRES required was a substantial increase in the maximum file size allowed. This change was implemented by the UNIX designers. The implementation of INGRES is primarily programmed in C, a

E. Allman, M. Stonebraker, and G. Held, *ACM-SIGMOD Conference Proceedings*, ACM-SIGMOD International Conference on Management of Data, Salt Lake City, Utah, March 1976. Copyright 1976, Association for Computing Machinery, Inc.; reprinted by permission.

high level language in which UNIX itself is written. Parsing is done with the assistance of YACC, a compiler-compiler available on UNIX [JOHN74].

The advantages of a relational model for database management systems have been eloquently detailed in the literature, [CODD70, CODD74, DATE74] and hardly require further elaboration. In choosing the relational model, we were particularly motivated by (a) the high degree of data independence that such a model affords, and (b) the possibility of providing a high level and entirely procedure-free facility for data definition, retrieval, update, access control, support of views, and integrity verification.

INGRES runs as three processes which communicate via the UNIX interprocess communication facility, together with a fourth "front end" process. One of these front ends is an interactive terminal monitor which allows the user to formulate, edit, print and execute interactions in the data sublanguage QUEL. As will be seen, the precompiler allows (among other things) a fourth process of a user's choosing to be substituted for the terminal monitor.

INGRES is currently operational and most performance oriented access paths are implemented [HELD75a]. Support for 1, 2 and 4 byte integers, 4 and 8 byte floating point numbers and fixed length character strings of 255 bytes or less is provided. The INGRES system contains about 250,000 bytes of code, some of which is overlaid into one of the three processes.

In this paper we indicate the design of an operational precompiler which embeds the data sublanguage QUEL supported by INGRES into the general purpose programming language C [RITC74a]. To this end we describe QUEL in Section 2.0. Then in Section 3.0 we briefly indicate the form of the precompiler and decisions made concerning its construction. We also indicate the nature of two applications written using this precompiler. Lastly in Section 4.0 we indicate some language problems associated with QUEL and QUEL embedded in C. These include:

1)   dynamic schemas,
2)   no recursion,
3)   types and type checking,
4)   syntax, especially in nested aggregation.

2.0. QUEL

QUEL (QUEry Language) has points in common with Data Language/ALPHA [CODD71], SQUARE [BOYC73] and SEQUEL [BOYC74] in that it is a complete [CODD72] query language which frees the programmer from concern for how data structures are implemented and what algorithms are operating on stored data. As such, it facilitates a considerable degree of data independence [STON74a].

EMP	NAME	DEPT	SALARY	MANAGER	AGE
	Smith	toy	10000	Jones	25
	Jones	toy	15000	Johnson	32
	Johnson	toy	14000	Harding	29
	Baker	admin	20000	Harding	47
	Harding	admin	40000	none	58

Indicated here is an EMP relation with domains NAME, DEPT, SALARY, MANAGER and AGE. Each employee has a manager (except for Harding, who is presumably the company president), a salary, an age, and is in a department.

A QUEL interaction includes at least one RANGE statement of the form:

RANGE OF variable-list IS relation-name

The symbols declared in the range statement are variables which will be used as arguments for tuples. These are called TUPLE VARIABLES. The purpose of this statement is to specify the relation over which each variable ranges.

Moreover, an interaction includes one or more statements of the form:

Command Result-name (Target-list)
    [WHERE Qualification]

Here, Command is either RETRIEVE, APPEND, REPLACE, or DELETE. For RETRIEVE and APPEND, Result-name is the name of the relation which qualifying tuples will be retrieved into or appended to. For REPLACE and DELETE, Result-name is the name of a tuple variable which, through the qualification, identifies tuples to be modified or deleted. The Target-list is a list of the form

Result-domain = Function . . .

Here, the Result-domains are domain names in the result relation which are to be assigned the value of the corresponding function.

The following suggest valid QUEL interactions. A complete description of the language is presented in [HELD75b].

Example: Find the birth date of employee Jones.

RANGE OF E IS EMP
RETRIEVE INTO W (BDATE = 1975 − E.AGE)
      WHERE E.NAME = "JONES"

Here, E is a tuple variable which ranges over the EMP relation and all tuples in that relation are found which satisfy the qualification E.NAME = "Jones". The result of the query is a new relation, W, which has a single domain, BDATE, that has been calculated for each qualifying tuple. If the result relation is omitted, qualifying tuples are returned to the calling process. If this process is the terminal monitor, it in turn prints them on the user's terminal.

Other front end processes may do what they please with such tuples. Also, in the Target-list, the "Result-domain =" may be omitted if Function is of the form Variable.Attribute (e.g., NAME = E.NAME may be written as E.NAME − see the final example in this section).

Example: Delete the information about employee Jackson.

        RANGE OF E IS EMP
        DELETE E WHERE E.NAME = "Jackson"

Here, the tuples corresponding to all employees named Jackson are deleted from EMP.

Example: Give a 10 percent raise to Jones

        RANGE OF E IS EMP
        REPLACE E(SALARY BY 1.1 * E.SALARY)
                WHERE E.NAME = "Jones"

Here, E.SALARY is to be replaced by 1.1 * E.SALARY for those tuples in EMP where E.NAME = "Jones". (Note that the keywords IS and BY may be used interchangeably with "=" in any QUEL statement.) Also, QUEL contains aggregation operators including COUNT, SUM, MAX, MIN, and AVG. Two examples of the use of aggregation follow.

Example: Replace the salary of all toy department employees by the average toy department salary.

        RANGE OF E IS EMP
        REPLACE E(SALARY BY AVG (E.SALARY WHERE E.DEPT = "toy"))
                WHERE E.DEPT = "toy"

Here, AVG is to be taken of the salary attribute for those tuples satisfying the qualifications E.DEPT = "toy". Note that AVG(E.SALARY WHERE E.DEPT = "toy") is scalar valued and consequently will be called an *aggregate*. More general aggregations are possible as suggested by the following example.

Example: Find those departments whose average salary exceeds the company-wide average salary, both averages to be taken only for those employees whose salary exceeds 10000.

        RANGE OF E IS EMP
        RETRIEVE INTO HIGHPAY (E.DEPT)
        WHERE   AVG(E.SALARY BY E.DEPT WHERE E.SALARY > 10000)
                >
                AVG (E.SALARY WHERE E.SALARY > 10000)

Here, AVG(E.SALARY BY E.DEPT WHERE E.SALARY > 10000) is an *aggregate function* and takes a value for each value of E.DEPT. This value is the aggregate AVG (E.SALARY WHERE E.SALARY>10000 and E.DEPT = value).

The qualification expression for the statement is then true for departments for which this aggregate function exceeds the aggregate AVG(E.SALARY WHERE E.SALARY>10000).

In addition to the above QUEL commands to manipulate relations, INGRES also supports a variety of utility commands including ones to:

1) bulk copy data into and out of INGRES relations from or to UNIX files,

2) create and destroy relations,

3) add and delete integrity constraints [STON75],

4) add and delete secondary indices [HELD75a],

5) change the access method used to store a given relation.

For a complete description of the currently operational INGRES commands the reader is referred to [ZOOK75].

3.0. THE C PRECOMPILER

A precompiler has been constructed which embeds QUEL and all other INGRES commands in the programming language C. This precompiler performs the following functions:

1) Inserts code in the user program to spawn at run time the process structure shown in Figure 13.1. (Actually pipe B is two interprocesses communication pipes, one for data and one for termination conditions. However, for simplicity of exposition they will not be distinguished.)

2) Looks for lines in the C program which do not begin with "**##.**" These are assumed to be valid C language statements and are copied without modification to the output file.

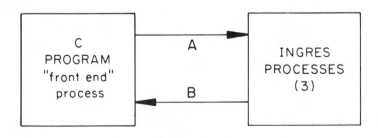

FIGURE 13.1. The Forked Process Structure

3) Looks for lines in the C program prefaced by a "**##**." These lines are processed by the precompiler and must be either a variable declaration or begin an INGRES command with an INGRES keyword. The choice of "**##**" was motivated by the use of "**#**" as a compiler directive in C.

If a variable declaration is found, the variables defined are noted as legal for inclusion in INGRES statements.

For a line containing an INGRES command a version of the INGRES parser is invoked to parse the command looking for C-variables. If none appear code is inserted to write the line unmodified down pipe A. If a variable appears, code is inserted to write its value down the pipe in its proper form prefaced by a type designator so the lexical analyzer in INGRES can appropriately deal with the variable. The remainder of the line is passed in unmodified form as above. The rationale for not completely parsing an INGRES line is given in Section 4.0.

The precompiler also inserts code to read pipe B for completion information and calls the procedure IIerror. The user may define IIerror himself or have the precompiler include a standard version of IIerror which prints the error message and continues.

The precompiler also notes the end of a command for allowed multiline INGRES statements and whether the command will return data through pipe B (that is, the command is a RETRIEVE with no result relation name given). In this case the target list must be of the form:

C-variable = QUEL function . . .

If data is to be returned, the precompiler, in addition to performing all the above steps, outputs code to do the following:

1) Read pipe B for a tuple formated as type/value pairs, inserting values for the C-variables declared in the target list. If necessary, values are converted to the correct type of the declared C-variable.

2) Pass control to the block following the RETRIEVE. Following the block it inserts code to go back to step (1) if there are more tuples. In this way "piped" return [CODD71] is supported and a precompiler recognizes the delimiters of a C-block by "**##{**" and "**##}**" respectively.

Two short examples illustrate the precompiler syntax.

Example: The following section of code implements a small front end to INGRES which performs only one query. It reads in the name of an employee and prints out the employee's salary in a suitable format. It continues to do this as long as there are more names to be read in. The functions READ and PRINT are assumed to have the obvious meaning.

```
main ( )
{
## char NAME[20];
## int SAL;
while (READ(NAME))
        {
##       RANGE OF E IS EMP
##       RETRIEVE (SAL = E.SALARY)
##       WHERE E.NAME = NAME
##           {
                PRINT("The salary of ",NAME," is ",SAL);
##           }
        }
}
```

Example: Read in a relation name and two domain names. Then for each of a collection of values which the second domain is to assume, do some processing on all values which the first domain assumes. (We assume the functions READ and PROCESS exist and have the obvious meaning.)

```
## int VALUE;
## char RELNAME[13], DOMNAME[13], QUAL[80];
## char DOMNAME2[13];
READ(RELNAME);
READ(DOMNAME);
READ(DOMNAME2)
## RANGE OF X IS RELNAME
while (READ(QUAL))
        {
##    RETRIEVE (VALUE = X.DOMNAME)
##      WHERE X. DOMNAME2 = QUAL
##          {
                PROCESS (VALUE);
##          }
        }
```

There are currently two applications written using the precompiler. One is a geo-data system called GEO-QUEL described in [GO75]. Basically it augments QUEL with display oriented features. The designers estimated a factor of 50 code reduction was achieved using the precompiler over what would be required in C alone. Such factors should be realized in a wide variety of applications that are largely data management (e.g., computer aided design, computer aided instruction, etc.). The second application was a C program to give a user interface appropriate to an inventory control application. Both interfaces required less than 3 man months of programming effort and it is envisioned that a wide variety of user tailored "front ends" will eventually be implemented in this fashion.

4.0. PROBLEMS WITH SUBLANGUAGES AND EMBEDDED SUBLANGUAGES

We note that QUEL (along with associated utility commands) embedded in C bears some resemblance in features to other very high level languages, e.g., VERS and SETL. However, it is implemented primarily as a database management system which involved the following decisions.

1) Relations are implemented in the file system via a variety of access methods and not as core arrays.

2) Protection is being handled at the user language level [STON74c] and in no way involves the UNIX protection system for files.

3) Integrity control schemes [STON75] are supported.

4) For protection reasons as well as because of address space limitations, the system runs as multiple processes.

The following problems are present in QUEL or in QUEL embedded in C. Some result from the above considerations.

4.1. Dynamic Schemas

The CODASYL DBTG report proposes a schema (in essence a description of the database) which is static and does not vary with time. In INGRES a user is allowed to execute a RETRIEVE INTO statement which creates a new relation, and hence alters the relational schema. This is analogous in general purpose programming languages to allowing a user to create space for variables at run time (such as is done in SIMULA). However, in programming languages such variables are local to an invocation of the program and space disappears when the program terminates.

In INGRES, relations created during execution do not disappear when the program terminates (since the programmer may wish to use such a relation again). In fact, INGRES keeps relations for a period of time specified by a database administrator and provides a SAVE command should the user wish that they be kept longer.

This causes several problems. If the relational schema is altered at precompile time at least four dilemmas occur:

1) It may be impossible to do the alteration because the relation to be created at run time may depend on other relations (created by other programs) which do not yet exist in the schema (because the other programs have not yet been precompiled).

2) There may be name conflicts; i.e., a user may be required not to use the same name for a relation in different programs.

3) DESTROY relname is a legal command, and in this case the schema cannot be altered until runtime.

4) It may be impossible to alter the schema because changes could easily depend on run-time values.

For instance, the precompiler supports the statements

```
READ(A);
## RETRIEVE INTO A (  )
```

If the schema is not altered until run time, the following problem is evident: INGRES statements cannot be parsed until run time since the legality of a command cannot be determined until then (e.g., RANGE of E is W gives a run time error if W does not exist; this cannot be known at precompile time).

Moreover, one can write programs such that the legality of an INGRES command cannot even be determined at the start of program execution. For example, in the program

```
READ(A);
if (A > 5)
    {
##  CREATE W (  )
    }
    .
    .
    .
##  RANGE OF E IS W
    .
    .
```

the legality of the RANGE command cannot be determined until it is executed.

Parsing during execution (as is done in INGRES) has an obvious run time cost. For example, the following program will result in parsing the RE-TRIEVE statement 1000 times:

```
for (i = 1; i < 1000; i = i + 1)
    {
##  RETRIEVE . . .
    }
```

One approach to avoiding multiple parsing could be to name the retrieve command in a definition and then call it with parameters in a manner similar to the definition and invocation of MACROs. The following syntax could, for example, be supported.

```
## DEFINE MYSTATEMENT(RELATION, DOMAIN, QUAL)
## char RELATION [20], DOMAIN[20], QUAL[20]
## int SAL
## RANGE OF E IS RELATION
## RETRIEVE (SAL = E.SALARY)
## WHERE E.DOMAIN = QUAL
## END MYSTATEMENT
```

.

.

```
## MYSTATEMENT(MYRELATION, MYDOMAIN, MYQUAL)
```

In certain situations this might save multiple parsing. This could happen if the definition was sent down pipe a, parsed, and stored by INGRES in parsed form. Invocation would then simply involve parameter validation. However, when the parameter list contains a relation name (as above), reparsing the statement at each call is unavoidable. The added complexity of distinguishing the above cases was judged not worth the effort by the authors. Restricting the allowable definitions to ensure no multiple parsing was considered unacceptable by the authors. Also, if definitions are not local to the invocation of a program (as might be desirable), some of the problems mentioned earlier reappear. As a result, this approach was not followed.

The relational schema in INGRES can also be considered to include

1)   integrity constraints on relations,

2)   access control statements for relations,

3)   view definitions.

Algorithms to support (1)-(3) are given in [STON74c, STON75] and basically involve making modifications to a QUEL statement at the source language level. If the precompiler makes these modifications, the same sorts of problems discussed earlier in this section appear. (For example, an integrity constraint can be changed between precompile time and execution time. Also dilemma (4) above indicates that one cannot necessarily know at precompile time what integrity constraints to enforce.) Again, if modifications are done at execution time (as in INGRES), the run time overhead must be tolerated.

Other than substantially restricting the allowable operations, (and as a result restricting the generality of the "front ends" which are possible) the authors see no solution to this parse-at-execution problem. One attempt at restriction to support precompile-time-parsing is to forbid all commands which can change the database schema. These include RETRIEVE INTO, CREATE, and DESTROY. Even this is not foolproof unless one forbids these same commands when the interactive terminal monitor is the front end process.

4.2. Recursion

There is no recursion in INGRES itself (i.e., no INGRES commands are implemented by invoking other INGRES commands). Secondary indices could easily be treated this way if this feature existed. Also, no recursion is allowed by the precompiler (i.e., the C-block executed for each tuple cannot contain an INGRES command.) There are, however, many database applications in which recursive algorithms for data access are very natural. A common example is the bill of materials (or parts explosion) problem. Here, the database contains tuples describing every sub-assembly and part in a product. The problem is to create a list of all parts which are components of the major assembly, a sub-assembly, a sub-sub-assembly and so on to an unknown depth. An equivalent example in the employee relation would be to "find all employees who work directly or indirectly for Harding."

Although recursion is allowed in C and many other programming languages, it appears difficult to implement in programming systems which span more than one process. Tuples are returned to a C program through a pipe. Allowing a second QUEL command to be executed before tuples from the first command are cleared from the pipe will result in additional information at the end of the pipe which is not available until all tuples from the first command are read from the pipe.

One solution would appear to be to fork a second collection of INGRES processes with their own pipes (i.e., call INGRES recursively). Since recursion could be fairly deep, the available pipes could be soon exhausted. Moreover, pipes are much more expensive to create than the execution of a subroutine call.

Since recursive calls to the database system do not seem feasible, what is necessary is to include within INGRES the capability for recursive data access. The data sublanguage must be extended to have a primitive operation such as RETRIEVE* in the following query:

```
/*find all employees who work for Harding
   (directly or indirectly) */
RANGE OF E IS EMP
RANGE OF A IS ANSWER
RETRIEVE* INTO ANSWER (NAME = E.NAME)
      WHERE E.MANAGER = "Harding"
      OR    E.MANAGER = A.NAME
```

Here, RETRIEVE* must be defined so as to re-process the query until the size of the result relation stops growing. No current system has this between capability and it is suggested as an important problem for relational language designers to cope with.

4.3. Types and Type Checking

Conversion of types between the database system and the C program acting as the front end presents a number of problems. Since the precompiler cannot know what types various domains will be at run time (for the same reasons as outlined in Section 4.1), one of two approaches must be used.

The first approach is to insist that the type of a variable that is used in the C program match the type of the value that is returned from INGRES. Otherwise, an error could be generated. This is clearly unacceptable, as it removes desirable data independence. For example, it should make no difference to the C program if INGRES stores a domain as a one or a two byte integer even though the C program prefers to consider it as a two byte integer.

The second approach (which is followed by the precompiler) is to perform run time type conversion between all types of C variables and all INGRES domain types.

In the current implementation the collection of types is not extensible in INGRES. Similarly, C does not support extensible types. Hence, the precompiler can include all necessary conversion routines. However, languages with extensible types have obvious appeal and the same statement holds for database systems. Should such systems appear, they would be required to cope with the dilemma illustrated by the following example.

Suppose the database system supported the domain type COLOR = {RED, BLUE, GREEN, YELLOW}. Suppose further that a user of the host language defined a type COLOR1 = {BLUE, VIOLET, GREEN, RED, BLACK}. Obviously the conversion from one to the other is complex and requires a complete description of both COLOR and COLOR1. It is not clear how the precompiler can easily be made aware of both descriptions.

Moreover, consider the case where the database system requires user supplied conversion routines (for example for the domain types DOLLARS and PESOS). This routine must be available to the precompiler if it is required to convert one to the other (or something else to either one). Moreover, if the user wishes to define a new data type (say FRANCS), he must know the type of the stored domain which he will be converting from in order to supply the appropriate routine. Data independence is unavoidably sacrificed or the user must supply a complete collection of conversion routines.

4.4. Syntax

There are various syntactical problems in QUEL. One concerns aggregation in the language and involves the scope of tuple variables. It will be illustrated by the examples to follow.

Example: Find the average salary of those employees who make more than the average company salary.

```
RANGE OF E IS EMP
RANGE OF F IS EMP
RETRIEVE (COMP=AVG(E.SALARY WHERE E.SALARY >
          AVG(F.SALARY)))
```

It should be noted that the scope of each tuple variable is local to the aggregate involved. However, when a BY clause is present the scope of the variable used must be global as the following example suggests.

Example: For each department find the average salary of those employees who make more than the average salary of their department.

```
RANGE OF E IS EMP
RANGE OF F IS EMP
RETRIEVE (COMP = AVG(E.SALARY BY E.DEPT
                WHERE E.SALARY
                  >
                AVG(F.SALARY WHERE F.DEPT = E.DEPT)),
      DEPT = E.DEPT)
```

This command has several objectionable features.

1) It is difficult to understand even if the semantics of aggregation are known.

2) In the first AVG, E is a local variable when used anywhere but in the BY clause. Hence, the first E.DEPT is global to the interaction, and is the same variable as the third E.DEPT. On the other hand, E.SALARY is local to the aggregation. This mixing of scopes is objectionable; however, it cannot be solved simply by introducing a new dummy variable. The following two statements are not semantically equivalent:

```
RANGE OF E IS EMP
RETRIEVE (COMP = AVG(E.SALARY BY E.DEPT),
    DEPT = E.DEPT)
```

```
RANGE OF E IS EMP
RANGE OF E1 IS EMP
RETRIEVE (COMP = AVG(E1.SALARY BY E.DEPT),
    DEPT = E.DEPT)
```

For the example relation considered the first answer is:

COMP	DEPT
13000	toy
12000	candy
30000	admin

while the second answer is:

COMP	DEPT
18500	toy
18500	candy
18500	admin

This result is caused by the second expression being evaluated on the cross product of E and E1.

Several fixes have been considered but rejected for one reason or another.

3) The second E.DEPT which appears is not local to the second aggregate because it appears in an outer aggregation.

A clean resolution of these objectionable features is clearly desirable. The option of restricting aggregates to be simple enough so the problem can go away is not very attractive. (For example no nesting, no multivariate aggregations, and delete the tuple variable everywhere but in the BY clause is one solution.)

5.0. SUMMARY

In this paper we have described how the relational language QUEL has been embedded in the programming language C and have discussed problems with data sublanguages and embedded data sublanguages. Most of these problems are inherent to a database environment and are suggested as important topics for research.

## CHAPTER FOURTEEN

Database Portals:
A New Application
Program Interface

Michael Stonebraker / Lawrence A. Rowe

ABSTRACT

This paper describes the design and proposes an implementation for a new application program interface to a database management system. Programs which browse through a database making ad-hoc updates are not well served by conventional embeddings of DBMS commands in programming languages. A new embedding is suggested which overcomes all deficiencies. This construct, called a "portal," allows a program to request a collection of tuples at once and supports novel concurrency control schemes.

1.0. INTRODUCTION

There have been several recent proposals for user interfaces that allow a user to "browse" through a database [CATT80, HERO80, MARY80, ROWE82, STON82b, ZLOO82]. Such interfaces allow one to select data of interest (e.g., "all employees over 40") and then navigate through this data making ad-hoc changes.

A simple illustration of a browsing program is described with the aid of Figure 14.1. This program allows a user to "edit" a relation. It is similar to a full screen, visual text editor (e.g., VI [JOY79b] or Emacs [STAL81]) except that a relation rather than a text file is edited. This example browser will be used to motivate the need for a new programming language interface to a database management system.

In Figure 14.1 data from the EMP relation is displayed. Since only a few rows of the relation can fit on the screen at one time, cursor commands are provided to scroll forward and backward. In other words, the screen provides

M. Stonebraker, L. A. Rowe, *Proceedings of the Tenth Very Large Data Base Conference*, Singapore, August 1984. Reprinted with permission of the VLDB Endowment; copyright © 1984.

```
┌─────────────────────────────────────────────────────┐
│                    EMP relation                       │
│                                                       │
│     NAME        │ AGE │ SALARY  │  DEPT               │
│   Ken Johnson   │ 43  │ 25000   │ sales               │
│   Sue Keller    │ 40  │ 28000   │ accounting          │
│   Dave Smith    │ 52  │ 30000   │ purchasing          │
│   Kathy Able    │ 28  │ 22000   │ accounting          │
│   George Toms   │ 26  │ 18000   │ shipping            │
│   Mike Baker    │ 34  │ 27000   │ sales               │
│                                                       │
│    FIND    INSERT    DELETE    UPDATE    QUIT         │
└─────────────────────────────────────────────────────┘
```

FIGURE 14.1. Relation Editor Interface

a "portal" onto the employee relation which the user can reposition. Commands are also provided so a user can edit the data on the screen. For example, Dave Smith's salary can be changed by repositioning the cursor to the field containing 30,000 and entering a new value.

Other operations are listed at the bottom of Figure 14.1. The FIND operation scans forward or backward through the data from the current row until the first row satisfying a user specified predicate is found. The INSERT and DELETE operations allow the user to enter or remove rows from the table. The UPDATE operation commits changes to the database so they become visible to other users. Lastly, the QUIT operation exits the editor.

The data manipulation facilities supported by conventional programming language interfaces [ALLM76, ASTR76, SCHM77, ROWE79b, WASS79] allow a program to bind a query to a database cursor,[1] open it, and fetch the qualifying tuples sequentially. Moreover, one can specify that a query or collection of queries is to be a transaction [ESWA76, GRAY78]. The DBMS provides serializability and an atomic commit for such transactions.

There are several drawbacks when such an interface is used to implement a browser such as the one discussed above. First, the relation editor can scroll backwards, thereby requiring that the cursor be repositioned to a previously fetched tuple. This feature is not supported by a conventional programming language interface (PLI). Secondly, current PLI's return one record

---

[1] A database cursor is an embedded query language concept and not the cursor displayed on a CRT.

at a time. When the user scrolls forward or backward, a browsing program would prefer that the DBMS return as many records as will fit on the screen. This protocol would simplify the browsing program code.

Next, to implement the FIND operation the browser must scan forward or backward to the first tuple that satisfies a given predicate. Of course, the predicate could be tested in the application program. However, this would duplicate functions already present in the DBMS. A cleaner and more efficient solution would be to use the DBMS search logic through a new programming language interface.

Lastly, to implement the UPDATE operation the relation editor must be able to commit updates incrementally during the execution of a single query. Conventional transaction management facilities do not support this kind of update.

This paper describes programming language constructs that provide the data manipulation and transaction management facilities required to implement database browsers. The basic idea is to have the database management system support an object, called a PORTAL,[2] that corresponds to the data returned by a single query and allow a program to retrieve data from it. Figure 14.2 shows a general model for the proposed system. The DBMS allows a program to selectively retrieve or update data from the portal with a new collection of DBMS commands.

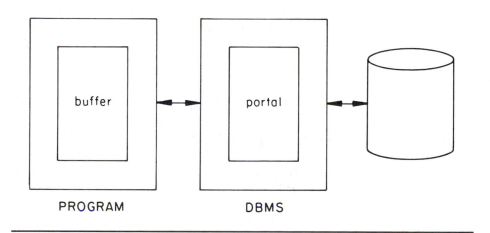

FIGURE 14.2. General Model for Portals

---

[2] We chose this term rather than window to avoid confusion with window managers through which a browser might display its output.

A portal can be thought of as a relational "view" that is "ordered." The query that defines the portal retrieves the data in some particular sequence which establishes the ordering of tuples in the portal. Each tuple will have an extra field that contains a unique sequence number, called a "line identifier" (LID) [STON83b] which represents the current position of the tuple in the portal. Line identifiers are automatically updated when tuples are inserted into or deleted from the portal so the position of each tuple is always represented by the line identifier.

Commands are provided which return collections of portal tuples to the application program. For example, a program can request tuples which:

1) match a predicate (e.g., "all employees over 40"),

2) match a given range of LID values (e.g., have an LID between 509 and 522),

3) are within a given distance from an indicated tuple (e.g., the tuples less than 12 away from the tuple corresponding to Jones).

Changes made to the data in a portal are propagated to the relations that define it when the update is committed. Six commit modes are supported so that different forms of concurrency control can be implemented by an application program. In addition to modes that allow one or more queries to be treated as an atomic transaction, a mode is provided that allows a transaction to be committed incrementally.

This paper describes the design and a proposed implementation of this new application program interface. Section 2.0 presents the design of the portal abstraction. Section 3.0 describes a proposed implementation of portals and two performance oriented variations. Then, Section 4.0 indicates the suggested concurrency control alternatives. Lastly, Section 5.0 discusses some issues in designing versions of the language constructs for different programming languages and compares portals to other application program interfaces.

2.0. APPLICATION PROGRAM INTERFACE

The application program interface includes language constructs to define a portal, to open and close a portal, to fetch tuples from a portal, to update tuples in a portal, and to further restrict a portal. A portal is defined by specifying a query that selects the tuples that are in it. The general format of a portal definition is similar to the definition of a cursor [ASTR76] and is[3]

LET PORTAL BE (Target-list) [WHERE qualification]

where PORTAL is the name of the portal, Target-list is a comma-separated list of expressions that define the columns or attributes in the portal, and

---

[3] [x] indicates that x is optional.

qualification is a predicate that determines which tuples are in the portal. For example, given an employee relation with the following attributes

EMP (NAME, ADDRESS, AGE, SALARY, YEARS-SERVICE, DEPT)

the command

LET P BE (EMP.NAME, EMP.SALARY,
      BIRTHYEAR = 1982 − EMP.AGE)
WHERE EMP.SALARY > 25000

defines a portal, P that contains the NAME, SALARY, and BIRTHYEAR of employees whose salary is greater than 25,000.

The portal definition can be a multiple variable query. For example, given a department relation

DEPT (DNAME, MGR, FLOOR, BUDGET)

a portal that contains employee and department information can be defined by

LET P1 BE (EMP.NAME, EMP.DEPT, DEPT.FLOOR)
WHERE EMP.DEPT = DEPT.DNAME

This portal contains the name, department, and department floor for all employees. The portal definition can also include programming language variables. For example, the following declaration

LET P2 BE (EMP.NAME)
WHERE EMP.SALARY > X AND Q

includes two program variables, X and Q, that allow the employee's salary and some other predicate (e.g., "EMP.AGE < 20") to be substituted at runtime.

The definition of a portal causes the query to be parsed and stored by the DBMS. Then, opening a portal causes the values of run-time variables in the portal query to be passed to the DBMS. The open command also specifies the program buffer into which data will be fetched and an optional lock mode for the portal. The general format of the open command is

OPEN PORTAL INTO VARIABLE [WITH LOCK-MODE = N]

where PORTAL is the name of the portal, VARIABLE is a program buffer, and N is an integer that identifies a LOCK-MODE. The program buffer is an array of records declared in the application program which determines the maximum number of tuples that can be retrieved from the portal by one command. Lock modes and transaction management are discussed in Section 4.0.

A portal remains open until it is explicitly closed by a close command. The format of a close command is

CLOSE PORTAL

Figure 14.3 shows a PASCAL program fragment that declares a buffer, defines a portal named P and opens it. The buffer, named BUF, has a field for each user-defined attribute in the portal. A portal also has an implicitly defined LID field which must be included in the buffer record.

Data can be retrieved from the portal and stored in the program buffer by the FETCH command. For example, the command

FETCH BUF

fetches data from P and stores it into BUF. When the program run-time environment passes this command to the DBMS, it also passes the number of records that can be stored in the buffer. The DBMS returns to the program the number of requested tuples. The data values returned from the portal are automatically converted to the appropriate data types and stored in the buffer.

A built-in function is provided that indicates how many records were actually stored in the buffer by the last FETCH command. For example, if the portal in Figure 14.3 contained only 5 records, the FETCH command above would not fill the buffer. On the other hand, if the portal contained

---

```
{ declare buffer }
var  BUF: array [1..10] of
              record
                    LID: integer;
                    NAME: array [1..20] of char;
                    SALARY: real;
                    AGE: integer
              end
     begin
        . . .
     LET P BE (EMP.NAME, EMP.SALARY, EMP.AGE)
        WHERE EMP.SALARY > 25000
     OPEN P INTO BUF
        . . .
     end
```

FIGURE 14.3. PASCAL Program Fragment That Declares a Portal

50 tuples, the command would fetch only the first 10 tuples because only that number can fit in the buffer. The program can retrieve the next 10 tuples by executing a FETCH command with a WHERE-clause as follows:

FETCH BUF WHERE P.LID > 10

This command fetches 10 tuples beginning with tuple number 11. Notice that the portal name, in this case P, is used to reference tuples in the portal.

A FETCH command can have an arbitrary qualification that will restrict the tuples retrieved to those that satisfy a predicate. For example, the program might want to retrieve employees under 20 who make more than 40,000. The command to retrieve these records is

FETCH BUF WHERE P.AGE < 20 AND P.SALARY > 40000

The FETCH command can also be used to retrieve data by position and to search forwards or backwards. The general format of the fetch command is:[4]

FETCH [PREVIOUS] BUFFER
[{WHERE | AFTER | BEFORE | AROUND} qualification]

A position fetch uses the keyword AFTER, BEFORE, or AROUND rather than WHERE. A fetch with an AFTER-clause indicates that the first tuple that satisfies the qualification and the tuples immediately after it in the portal ordering are to be retrieved. For example, if the following command was executed on the portal defined in Figure 14.3, it would retrieve 10 tuples beginning with tuple number 40:

FETCH BUF AFTER P.LID = 40

Tuples 40 to 49, if they exist, would be stored in BUF. The tuple that satisfies the qualification (i.e., tuple number 40) is stored in BUF [i]. Subsequent returned tuples follow the selected one in LID order and do not necessarily satisfy the qualification in the FETCH command (e.g., "P.LID = 40"). In contrast, all tuples returned by a restriction FETCH (i.e., one that includes a WHERE-clause) must satisfy the qualification.

The keyword BEFORE indicates that the first tuple that satisfies the qualification should be stored at the end of the buffer. Consequently, the buffer will contain the qualifying tuple and the tuples that immediately precede it. The keyword AROUND indicates that the qualifying tuple should be stored in the middle of the buffer. The qualification in a position FETCH can be an arbitrary predicate such as

. . . AFTER P.LID > 10 AND P.AGE < 25

which retrieves tuples beginning with the first one found after tuple number

---

[4] {x | y} indicates that x or y must appear.

10 that satisfies the qualification on age.

Most browsers also allow users to search backwards. The FETCH PRE-VIOUS command can be used to implement this function. It scans backward through the portal rather than forward. For example, the command

FETCH PREVIOUS BUF BEFORE P.LID < N AND Q

searches for the first record before the current one that satisfies a search predicate.

The qualification in a fetch command can be any boolean combination of terms involving portal variables (e.g., P.AGE = 40) and application program variables (e.g., Q from the example above). It is also possible to support qualifications involving join terms to other database relations.

A command is provided which allows a programmer to restrict the portal to a smaller subset of the data that it currently contains. The format of the restrict command is:

RESTRICT PORTAL WHERE qualification

This command removes from the portal all tuples which do not satisfy the qualification. For example,

RESTRICT P WHERE P.AGE > 25

removes all employees 25 and under from the portal. A restrict command is equivalent to defining a new portal with a qualification obtained by AND'ing the new qualification to the one that defined the portal. The restrict command functions in much the same way as a marking [RIET81] of a relation, although our other commands and suggested implementation are quite different.

The portal abstraction also includes commands to insert, delete, and replace tuples in the buffer. The general format of the REPLACE command is

REPLACE BUFFER-REFERENCE (target-list)

where BUFFER-REFERENCE is a program reference to a record in the buffer (e.g., BUF [i]). For example, the following command changes the age of the tuple stored at BUF [4]:

REPLACE BUF[4] (AGE = 25)

The INSERT command appends a tuple to the portal. The general format of this command is:

INSERT (Target-list) BEFORE BUFFER-REFERENCE

This command inserts the tuple before the buffer array element referenced. The elements in the buffer are moved down to make room for the new data. Since the buffer is fixed size, the last record must be removed from the buffer. The new record is assigned the LID of the element it is being inserted before, and the LIDs of all records following the new element are incremented. The new tuple and its LID are passed to the DBMS which updates the portal.

The last update command allows tuples to be deleted. The format of this command is:

DELETE BUFFER-REFERENCE

The LID of the buffer element referenced is set to zero to indicate that it has been deleted. The LIDs of all records that follow it in the buffer are decremented. Then, the deleted record and its original LID are passed to the DBMS which updates the portal. Update commands are passed to the DBMS which records the changes so that subsequent FETCHs will return the new data. The lock mode selected when the portal is opened will determine when the update is committed to the database. Lock modes will be discussed in Section 4.0.

3.0. IMPLEMENTATION STRATEGY

This section describes a basic strategy for implementing the portal abstraction and two improvements on this theme for augmented performance. The basic strategy is to create an ordered temporary relation that contains the portal data. Portal commands would then be translated into conventional queries on this temporary relation. A tuple in the temporary relation must contain a column for each attribute in the portal and a TID[5] to each tuple used to construct it. For example, given the portal defined in Section 2.0,

LET P BE (EMP.NAME, EMP.AGE, EMP.DEPT,
      DEPT.FLOOR)
WHERE EMP.DEPT = DEPT.DNAME

a temporary relation is created by executing the following query:

RETRIEVE INTO TEMP(EMP.NAME, EMP.AGE, EMP.DEPT,
      DEPT.MGR, EMP-TID = EMP.TID, DEPT-TID = DEPT.TID)
WHERE EMP.DEPT = DEPT.DNAME

TEMP is organized as an ordered relation [STON83b], and the DBMS will automatically create and maintain the LID attribute using an auxiliary storage structure called an "ordered B-tree" (OB-tree). An OB-tree is similar to a B+-tree (i.e., data is stored in the leaves of the tree and a multi-level index is provided to access the data as indicated in Figure 14.4). The leaf pages in the tree contain TIDs for tuples in the relation. The LID ordering of the tuples is represented by the order of the TIDs in the leaf pages. Hence, traversing the leaf pages from left to right scans the tuples in LID order (i.e., the first TID in the leftmost page is the tuple with LID 1). Non-leaf pages contain

---

[5] In a relational DBMS, a pointer to a tuple in a relation is called a "tuple identifier" (TID).

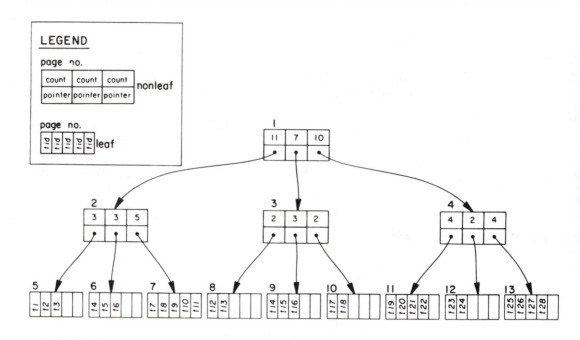

FIGURE 14.4. An OB-tree

pointers to the next level of the index or a leaf page and counts of the number of tuples in that subtree.

The tree structure and the tuple counts can be used by the DBMS to retrieve or update tuples based on their LID. For example, to find the l-th tuple, the DBMS begins at the root page and selects the subtree that contains the tuple by performing a simple calculation. Assuming that s_i is the number of tuples in the first i subtrees, which is defined by the following formula

$$s_i = \sum_{j=1}^{i} count_j$$

the subtree that contains the l-th tuple is pointed to by the entry at

$$\min_i \{s_{i-1} < l \le s_i\}$$

This process is performed iteratively until the algorithm reaches a leaf page which is guaranteed to contain the tuple. The calculation at intermediate levels of the tree to select a subtree must take into account the number of tuples that precede the first tuple in the subtree. Assuming that this number is x, the calculation to select the correct subtree for intermediate levels is

$$\min_{i} \{x + s_{i-1} < l \leq x + s_i\}$$

The value for x is s_{i-1} at the next outer level. The TID for the l-th tuple is stored in the leaf page at entry $l - x$.

For example, in Figure 14.4 to find the tuple with LID 17, the algorithm will examine page 1 and select the second subtree because 17 is between 11 (s_1) and 18 (s_2). Examining page 3 with x equal to 11, the algorithm selects page 10 because 17 is between 16 ($x + s_2$) and 18 ($x + s_3$). Page 10 is a leaf and the TID for tuple 17 is stored in the first entry ($l - x$).

Insertions into an OB-tree are implemented by inserting a TID for a new tuple into the appropriate leaf page and updating the counts. A standard B-tree split algorithm is used if the leaf page is full [KNUT78]. Deletions and replaces are implemented in a similar way. A complete description of these operations and a prototype implementation of OB-trees are described in [LYNN82].

The DBMS executes portal commands by transforming them into queries on the temporary relation. For example, the fetch command

FETCH BUF WHERE P.AGE < 25

is implemented by executing the query

RETRIEVE (TEMP.LID, TEMP.ALL)
    WHERE TEMP.AGE < 25

Recall that the number of records that can fit in the program buffer is passed to the DBMS along with the command so that only the requested number of tuples is returned.

A position fetch is implemented by executing two retrievals. Suppose the position fetch was

FETCH BUF AFTER P.LID > 10 AND P.AGE < 25

and that the buffer named BUF in the program can hold N records. First, the LID of the first qualifying tuple is found

RETRIEVE (L = min(TEMP.LID))
WHERE TEMP.LID > 10 AND TEMP.AGE < 25

Then the query

RETRIEVE (TEMP.LID, TEMP.ALL)
    WHERE L ≤ TEMP.LID AND TEMP.LID ≤ L+N−1

returns N tuples beginning with the l-th tuple. AFTER and AROUND position fetches can be implemented using a similar technique.

FETCH PREVIOUS commands can be implemented by scanning the OB-tree backwards. Moreover, the execution of FETCH commands that include joins with other relations is easy because the portal is stored as a relation. Update commands on the portal are implemented by executing queries to update the temporary relation and writing an intentions list that will be used by the transaction manager to update the affected relation(s). Finally, restriction commands are implemented by creating a new temporary relation.

The first improvement on this strategy is to create the temporary relation incrementally. At any time the temporary relation contains all tuples with LIDs less than the maximum LID that has been fetched thus far. If the data required by a fetch command is in the temporary relation, a retrieval is executed to fetch it. Otherwise, the portal query is resumed to retrieve more data into the temporary relation before the retrieval can be executed. An update command can only modify data that has already been fetched so the data to be changed must be in the temporary relation.

A second improvement is to materialize the portal dynamically and to buffer only a fixed amount of data, say B tuples. For example, one might buffer the tuple with the highest LID requested by the last fetch command and the previous B-1 tuples. However, it is not unreasonable for the DBMS to fetch tuples ahead of the current fetch command. Whenever a fetch command cannot be satisfied by data in the buffer, the portal query is resumed to retrieve tuples with higher LIDs. On the other hand, if the fetch requires data with lower LIDs than any tuples in the buffer, then the portal query must be restarted at the beginning. An OB-tree can still be used to support this implementation of a portal. The LID of the first tuple in the buffer must be maintained by the DBMS as tuples are scrolled out of the buffer. This number must be subtracted from the LID used in all portal commands to yield correct responses from the OB-tree.

It is expected that B can be optimized to provide good response time for most portal users. A user who browses many records without locality of reference could obtain good response time with a large B. On the other hand, a user performing sequential processing would be satisfied with a small value. Lastly, note that a sufficiently large value of B approximates the first improvement described above.

The techniques noted above involve creating a temporary relation corresponding to a portal. An alternate implementation would store pointers to the tuples in the primary relations in the temporary relation, using the temporary relation as a kind of secondary index. For example, given the portal definition

LET P BE (EMP.ALL) WHERE EMP.SALARY > 20000

the DBMS does not have to make a copy of the data in the EMP relation. The ordered temporary relation could be defined by

RETRIEVE INTO TEMP(EMP.TID)
WHERE EMP.SALARY > 20000

Fetch commands that involve only the LID attribute can be implemented by restricting TEMP to the qualifying entries and using the TIDs to access the EMP tuples. This is the suggested implementation of markings [RIET81]; however it requires an extra disk read to fetch the data so portal commands would perform more slowly.

In the next sections we assume that portals are implemented by a dynamic buffering scheme with B tuples in the buffer supported by an OB-tree.

4.0. CONCURRENCY CONTROL

This section proposes concurrency control facilities for portals. Several lock modes are presented so that a portal user can select an option with appropriate consistency and performance characteristics. These alternatives are now enumerated.

1) The tuples which currently reside in the buffer have a write lock. When a tuple scrolls out of the buffer, its lock is released. Updates are committed as they are received. This is expected to be the normal lock mode for portals.

2) This option is the same as number 1 except that an update is not committed until it scrolls out of the buffer. This mode is appropriate when a user makes several changes that will be scrolled out of the buffer at the same time. Consequently, they would be made visible to other users together.

3) This option is a variant on optimistic concurrency control [BHAR80, KUNG81]. The browsing program does not lock a tuple until it is deleted or replaced. When a tuple in a portal is modified, the tuple(s) from the relation(s) that define the portal are locked and the portal tuple is recreated from the real relations. If the portal tuple to be modified is the same as the recreated tuple, the update is allowed. Otherwise, the modification must be rejected. Updates are committed immediately; hence a browsing application holds locks only for the time required to read, validate and then write desired data. Like other optimistic concurrency control algorithms, a user must restart when an update is rejected. Unfortunately, this requires restarting the portal query and repositioning to desired data. The expense of this restart will make option 3 unattractive except in situations where the probability of conflict is very low.

4) This option is the same as number 3 except that all tuples returned by the last fetch command are locked, refetched, and compared with the recreated values when an update is attempted. This update is committed only if they all are the same. This mode is appropriate if an update is determined by data elsewhere in the scope of the current fetch command.

5) Transactions are defined explicitly by the program. A begin and end transaction command are executed to delimit the beginning and end of the transaction. Consequently, a transaction can be an arbitrary collection of FETCH, INSERT, DELETE, and REPLACE commands.

6) All commands between opening and closing a portal are considered one transaction.

The motivation for these lock modes is as follows. Modes 1 and 2 lock data that is being browsed only while the user can see it (i.e., when it has been fetched). Otherwise, the data can be changed by others. Modes 3 and 4 are similar to modes 1 and 2 except for the use of optimistic concurrency control which may be more efficient. Mode 5 gives control to the application programmer and mode 6 makes the entire browsing session a transaction. Modes 5 and 6 provide the most and least flexibility, respectively.

The conventional definition of a transaction is that it is a collection of reads and writes which are atomically committed and serializable [GRAY78, ESWA76]. Lock modes 3-6 obey this model. For example, lock mode 4 can be implemented as follows:

```
BEGIN TRANSACTION
        recreate the most recently fetched tuples
        IF tuples changed
                THEN abort the REPLACE or DELETE
                ELSE update relation(s)
END TRANSACTION
```

Lock modes 1 and 2, on the other hand, do not correspond to any atomically committed and serializable collection of reads and writes. They both require that locks be held after the end of an atomically committed action. The properties of such locking schemes are an interesting topic for investigation.

The implementation of the lock modes 3 through 6 for portals can use a conventional transaction manager that locks physical entities and supports operations to begin, commit, and abort transactions. The general strategy is to update the temporary relation when the update command is executed. In addition, updates for the primary relation(s) are generated and written to a log. These updates are committed at the appropriate time and all locks are released.

Lock modes 1 and 2 require slight changes to a transaction manager in that locks cannot be released at the time that a transaction is committed. Rather locks are candidates for release when the tuple scrolls out of the buffer. If a portal is defined on a single primary relation, they can be released at this time. However, if a portal is defined by a join, a lock can be released only if the tuple is not used to construct another portal tuple which is currently locked. For example, suppose the portal definition was

LET P BE (EMP.NAME, EMP.DEPT, DEPT.FLOOR, DEPT.MGR)
WHERE EMP.DEPT = DEPT.DNAME

and two employees, say Smith and Jones from the toy department, are in the DBMS buffer. Consequently, the two EMP relation tuples and the DEPT relation tuple would be locked. If Smith's tuple was removed from the portal, the lock on his tuple in the EMP relation can be released. However, the lock on the toy department tuple could not be released because it is used to construct Jones' tuple in the portal. In other words, the buffer must be searched to see if the department tuple is used elsewhere before that lock can be released. Hence, deciding if a lock is releasable may be an expensive operation.

However, lock reclamation does not have to be performed each time a tuple is removed from the buffer, and it may be advantageous to perform lock releases periodically. Such a mechanism is analogous to garbage collection of free space by a programming language run-time system.

5.0. DISCUSSION

This section discusses several issues concerning the design and implementation of the portal abstraction. Then, it discusses the advantages of portals compared to conventional programming language interfaces.

5.1. Design Issues

First, the language constructs presented in Section 2.0 map a portal into a buffer which is a static 1-dimensional array. The constructs can be generalized to dynamic and n-dimensional arrays. If the programming language into which the constructs are embedded has dynamic arrays, the size of the program buffer can be redefined at runtime. The DBMS can pass a count of the number of records that will be returned by a fetch command before the records are returned. Using this information the run-time support routines in the user program can dynamically allocate an array to hold the returned records. This would relieve the program of executing multiple fetch commands when the number of returned tuples exceeds a static buffer size.

Ordered relations can also be generalized to n dimensions [STON83b]. In this case a relation can have several LIDs, one for each dimension. The language constructs discussed in Section 2.0 can be easily generalized to support a portal with multiple LIDs which is mapped to an n-dimensional buffer. This feature would be especially valuable to browsers such as SDMS [HERO80] which implement 2 dimensional scrolling.

Lastly, a database system that implements portals must be able to save and restore the currently executing query. This is necessary because programs can open multiple portals and because the implementation strategy discussed in Section 3.0 sometimes requires restarting the portal query.

5.2. Advantages of Portals

There are several advantages of portals compared to normal programming language interfaces. We enumerate several.

1) All buffering is performed in the portal.
   The application program is freed from the responsibility of this task.

2) More flexible concurrency control is possible.
   It is certainly possible to support traditional transaction processing with a portal. However, novel locking policies are also possible which can lead to more parallelism in some situations.

3) Code duplication is not required.
   A portal can easily implement the RESTRICT command and the FETCH WHERE command by translating them into appropriate DBMS commands. A conventional application program interface does not support this function, and providing it in application level code is redundant.

4) Traditional transaction management can be efficiently supported.
   A small value for the size of the buffer, B, may be chosen for such applications. It is even possible to choose B=1 and effectively obtain a programming language interface similar to that of a conventional cursor-oriented one. In this case portals should be optimizable to provide efficiency nearly equal to a traditional application program interface. As such, portals can be considered to be a generalization of a traditional application program interface.

5) Greater efficiency may be provided in some situations.
   The application program must pass control to the DBMS once per FETCH command for a portal implementation. On the other hand, control may change hands as often as once per tuple in a cursor oriented application program interface. A browsing application which sequentially scans a relation calls the DBMS once per screen (say each 24 tuples) using a portal whereas it might make a call once per tuple otherwise. Consequently, a portal might outperform a conventional interface for this situation.

6) View management is easily accomplished.
   Because portals are defined by queries which may span multiple relations, updating a portal is semantically identical to updating relational views [DAYA78, STON75]. The general problem of updating views is impossible; however, portal updates affect only a single tuple at one time. In this case, the affected tuple has a TID for every tuple in every relation which was used to compose it. One can simply make the obvious update to the specified underlying tuple(s). Although this algorithm is not free from semantic difficulties, it is the only practical candidate in this environment.

6.0. CONCLUSIONS

A new application program interface to a relational database system has been described which makes it easier to implement database browsers. The interface is based on the concept of a portal that supports querying and updating an ordered view. Several lock modes were suggested that can be used to implement browsing transactions with varying consistency and parallelism requirements.

At the current time OB-trees are operational [LYNN82]. Moreover, performance experiments [STON83b] suggest that they perform comparably to normal secondary indexes. Space requirements are also comparable to a normal secondary index. Work is proceeding on implementing the support code for portals using OB-trees so that their performance can be compared to traditional interfaces.

ACKNOWLEDGEMENTS

Several people have contributed ideas that have been incorporated into this proposal. We want to thank Paul Butterworth, Joe Kalash, Richard Probst, Beth Rabb, and Kurt Shoens for their contributions.

## CHAPTER FIFTEEN

Data Abstraction, Views and Updates in RIGEL

Lawrence A. Rowe / Kurt A. Shoens

ABSTRACT

Language constructs to support the development of database applications provided in the programming language RIGEL are described. First, the language type system includes relations, views, and tuples as built-in types. Tuple-values are introduced to provide more flexibility in writing procedures that update relations and views. Second, an expression that produces sequences of values, called a "generator," is defined which integrates relational query expressions with other iteration constructs found in general-purpose programming languages. As a result, relational expressions can be used in new contexts (e.g., as parameters to procedures) to provide new capabilities (e.g., programmer-defined aggregate functions).

Lastly, a data abstraction facility, unlike those proposed for other database programming languages, is described. It provides a better notation to specify the interface between a program and a database and to support the disciplined use of views.

All of these constructs are integrated into a sophisticated programming environment to enhance the development of well-structured programs.

1.0. INTRODUCTION

Previous attempts at providing database access in a programming language were based on embedding database constructs into an existing language [ALLM76, CHAM76b, DATE76, BRAT77, MERR77, and SCHM77]. This embedding was accomplished by calling subroutines to execute database

L. A. Rowe, K. A. Shoens, *ACM-SIGMOD Conference Proceedings*, ACM-SIGMOD International Conference on Management of Data, Boston, Massachusetts, June 1979. Copyright 1979, Association for Computing Machinery, Inc.; reprinted by permission.

functions directly, by using a preprocessor to translate queries into subroutine calls, or by modifying an existing compiler. Although each of these attempts succeeded in providing access to the database, the resulting programming environment was less than satisfactory. The database constructs are not integrated into the language because the designers were constrained by the existing languages [PREN78].

RIGEL[1] is an experimental general-purpose programming language designed for the development of database applications. It offers a better programming environment because it was designed from the start with an emphasis on the language mechanisms needed to develop database applications. These include relations, views, and tuples as built-in data types, a flexible notation for expressing relational queries which is integrated with the iteration constructs in the language, and a data abstraction facility which handles the interface between a program and a database well. RIGEL is the language component of a sophisticated programming environment which provides interactive program development, intermixed interpretive and compiled execution of program components, and interactive debugging. Such an interactive programming environment gives a programmer powerful tools to support the rapid development of programs [WEGB71]. By the time this paper appears, the first version of the system will be implemented.

Other new languages designed expressly for database applications are TAXIS [MYLO78] and PLAIN [WASS78]. TAXIS seeks to make the development of applications easier by limiting the kinds of applications which can be written in the language and by supporting a rigidly structured programming environment. The alternative is to code applications in a good general-purpose programming language using a library of predefined abstractions designed specifically for the class of applications (e.g., procedures to display menus on a video terminal and to process user requests). As with many application-specific languages, it is not certain that TAXIS offers a clear advantage in program development time. In addition, the general-purpose language can be used to program a wider range of database applications.

PLAIN, on the other hand, is a general-purpose programming language which takes a different approach to both the expression of queries and data abstraction than the approach taken in RIGEL. In PLAIN, the programmer specifies how a high-level query is to be processed which means that programs may have to be recoded to take advantage of execution efficiencies resulting from a change to the database storage structure. A more important difference is that, as will be shown, the data abstraction facility provided in RIGEL is better suited to defining the interface between a program and a database than that provided in PLAIN.

This paper presents the design of language constructs provided in RIGEL to express database queries, to specify the interface between a program and a

---

[1] RIGEL (ri jel) is a bright bluish star — the most luminous in the constellation Orion. We have followed a tradition of naming languages after mathematicians and astronomical bodies. Besides, it seemed like a nice name. . . .

```
nameType: type = array 1...NAMESIZE of char;
idNumType: type = integer;
titleType: type = array 1...TITLESIZE of char;
gradeType: type = (A, B, C, D, F, I);
COURSE: relation
        C#: idNumType;                /*Course number */
        TITLE: titleType;            /*Course title */
        P#: idNumType;               /*Teaches course */
        key C#;                      /*Unique courses */
end;
PROFESSOR:relation
        P#: idNumType;               /*Prof's employee # */
        NAME:nameType;
        SALARY:real;
        RANK: (lec, asst, assoc, full, special);
        YEARSSERVICE: integer;
        key P#;
end;
STUDENT: relation
        S#: idNumType;               /*Student number */
        NAME: nameType;
        MAJOR: nameType;
        LEVEL: (frosh, soph, jr, sr, grad, other);
        key S#;
end;
ENROLLMENT: relation
        S#: idNumType;
        C#: idNumType;
        GRADE: gradType;
        key S#, C#;
end;
```

FIGURE 15.1. Example Database

database, and to use views.

The notation for expressing queries is based on expressions which produce a sequence of values similar to that used in Relational PASCAL [SCHM77] and discovered independently by [PREN77]. The use of these expressions has been generalized to allow sequences of values other than tuples (e.g., reals) to be specified and to allow their use in contexts other than relation constructors (e.g., as parameters to procedures). This generalization results in a convenient, well-integrated notation for expressing queries which, for example, leads naturally to programmer-defined aggregate functions (e.g., standard deviation).

The virtues of data abstractions as notations to describe interfaces to databases have been extolled by researchers in programming languages and database systems [HAMM76a, PREN77, TSIC77a, BROD78]. Several language proposals exist with a data abstraction facility based on the concept of abstract data types [FURT78, SCHM78, WASS78, WEBE78]. RIGEL has a data abstraction facility, based on a program structuring concept developed by Wirth [WIRT77] which provides a better notation for specifying a database interface that consists of several relations, views, and high-level abstract operations.

Finally, the language supports views as a built-in data type. Both retrieval and update operations are provided on views. The view and data abstraction mechanisms were designed together so that views can be specified in an abstraction in such a way as to separate the view representation as seen by a user of the view from its implementation and to allow updates on views to be specified as high-level abstract operations. This approach enhances data independence because the implementation of view updates is isolated from the program. Moreover, view updates are specified explicitly so that a programmer knows precisely what set of updates is allowed, eliminating the uncertainty present in approaches based on automatically translating view updates [STON75, ASTR76, DAYA78].

These simple, yet powerful, language constructs can be used together to develop a wide range of database applications. The remainder of this paper presents the details of the language constructs. Section 2.0 presents the notation for expressing queries. Section 3.0 describes the update constructs. Section 4.0 discusses data abstraction and presents an example of an external schema. Finally, Section 5.0 illustrates the use of views in a data abstraction.

Figure 15.1 shows the declarations for a college database which is used in all of the succeeding examples. There is a student relation, course relation, professor relation, and a relation expressing the association of a student enrolled in a course. Each relation has a primary key as specified in the "key-clause." To simplify the presentation, each course is assumed to be offered only once each term and taught by one professor.

2.0. GENERATORS

The FOR-statement found in conventional programming languages is extended in RIGEL to express relational queries by what is called a "generator" expression which produces a sequence of values. This section illustrates the use of generators to express queries, to define aggregate functions, and to construct new relations.

A FOR-statement to sum the elements of an array is written:

```
sum := 0;
FOR i IN 1..10 DO
    sum := sum+A[i];
END;
```

The body of the for-statement is executed once for each value of i, in this example, 1, 2, . ., 10. The variable i is called an "iteration-variable" and the expression 1..10 is called a "generator" because it produces or generates the sequence of values that is to be assigned to the iteration-variable. The expression "i IN 1..10" between the FOR and DO is called a "bind" expression because it specifies a sequence of bindings for the iteration-variable.

The FOR-statement and bind expressions can be used to specify retrievals from relations. For example,

```
FOR S IN STUDENT WHERE S.LEVEL="soph" DO
    print(S.NAME, S.MAJOR);
END;
```

prints the name and major of all sophomore students. The iteration-variable S is bound in turn to tuples in the STUDENT relation that satisfy the predicate specified in the WHERE-clause. Other data manipulation languages refer to S as a range variable (QUEL[HELD75b]) or cursor (SEQUEL [CHAM76b]), but in programming languages it is just another iteration-variable. By recognizing this fact, queries can be integrated with other iteration constructs. Notice that this notation for queries implies that each relation has an implicitly defined generator that produces each tuple in the relation.[2] Although this may seem to imply that retrievals are implemented by scanning the entire relation, query optimizations used to implement high-level query languages can be used to improve execution performance [ASTR76, WONG76].

To specify more complex queries, bind expressions can be generalized to several iteration-variables. For example, to print the name, level, and grade of students in an Economics course, one writes

```
FOR S IN STUDENT, C IN COURSE, E IN ENROLLMENT
    WHERE C.TITLE="ECON1" AND C.C#=E.C# AND E.S#=S.S# DO
    print(S.NAME, S.MAJOR, E.GRADE);
END;
```

In these examples, both the binding of iteration-variables and the computation to be performed are specified. Some queries involve passing a sequence of values to a procedure, for example, professor salaries to an averaging function to calculate average salary. The sequence of values can be specified in the following way

---

[2] A tuple refers to a "record in a relation." The importance of this distinction is illustrated in the next section.

> P.SALARY : P IN PROFESSOR

The colon-operator produces a value (specified by the left operand) for each binding of iteration-variables (specified by the right operand). The left operand is an expression; the right operand is a bind expression. The entire expression is a generator. To calculate average salaries, one writes:

> AVG(P.SALARY : P IN PROFESSOR)

This example illustrates how bind expressions can be used to define generators and how generators can be passed to procedures. Because these are general mechanisms in the language, a programmer has considerable freedom to define arbitrary procedures which take generator arguments and to call those procedures with different sequences of values specified by generator expressions. For instance, programmers can define new aggregate functions as illustrated in a later section.

Generator expressions can also be used to produce a sequence of records by use of a "record-constructor." When combined with a "relation-constructor," a temporary relation can be created. For example, to create a temporary relation with a tuple for each student in an Economics course one writes

> TEMP:=
> {<S#:S.S#, NAME:S.NAME,LEVEL:S.LEVEL, GRADE:E.GRADE>:
>   S IN STUDENT, C IN COURSE, E IN ENROLLMENT
>   WHERE C.TITLE="ECON1" AND C.C#=E.C# AND E.S#=S.S#};

The expression "{ . . .}" constructs a relation which in this example is assigned to the variable TEMP.[3] The expression "<. . .>" constructs a record with record-field names that are explicitly specified and expressions that specify the values which are to be assigned to the fields. Record-constructors are like target-lists in QUEL [HELD75b].

In these examples, the use of generator expressions to specify sequences of values has been illustrated. Generators can also be specified by a procedure-like routine called a generator. Generator routines are similar to CLU iterators (for details see [LISK77] or [ROWE78]). Regardless of how a generator is specified, they can be used in all of the contexts illustrated here (e.g., in bind expressions or as arguments to procedures).

We have shown that bind expressions and generators are fundamental unifying concepts that provide a good notation for expressing queries. They extend previous work [PREN77, SCHM77] by allowing relational expressions (i.e., generators) to be passed to procedures as arguments and by allowing generators to be specified procedurally.

---

[3] RIGEL is a strongly-typed language; thus, all variables must be declared. The declaration constructs have been omitted to simplify the presentation.

3.0. UPDATES

In this section language constructs to specify updates (REPLACES, DELETES, and APPENDS) and database transactions are presented. REPLACES and DELETES are specified using an extension to the FOR-statement which identifies relations to be modified, called an UPDATE-statement. Simple statements, used inside the UPDATE-statement, are provided to carry out REPLACES and DELETES. An additional statement, which may be used anywhere, is available to append tuples to relations. A language construct is also provided to define database transactions, a sequence of updates that appear to concurrent database users as an atomic operation. At the end of this section, an extension to the language type system is described which allows updates to be performed in procedures called from the body of an UPDATE-statement.

The REPLACE- and DELETE-statements, when used inside an UPDATE-statement, cause the corresponding action to take place. For example, suppose all professors are to be given raises but that the amount of raise is dependent on current salary, rank, and years of service. Assume that a function, called newSalary, is provided that calculates the professor's new salary. To update salaries one writes

```
UPDATE P IN PROFESSOR DO
  REPLACE P BY P<SALARY:newSalary(P.SALARY,P.RANK,
                                   P.YEARSSERVICE)>;
END;
```

The semantics of this statement are to read through the PROFESSOR relation, saving the changed tuples in a batch update file. After all iterations have been completed, the batched updates are performed on the relation. Therefore, the changes to the relation are not visible until after the execution of the UPDATE-statement. "P<. . .>" constructs a new record by making a copy of P and then simultaneously changing the specified fields. This simultaneous change is needed to avoid integrity violations that might arise from constraints that relate two record fields.

To delete tuples, a DELETE-statement rather than a REPLACE-statement is used in the body of the UPDATE-statement. For example, to delete all courses taught by A. Johnson, one writes

```
UPDATE C IN COURSE FOR P IN PROFESSOR
  WHERE P.NAME="Johnson, A." AND P.P#=C.P# DO
   DELETE C;
END;
```

In this example, the COURSE relation can be updated but not the PROFESSOR relation. DELETES and REPLACES to different relations can be intermixed in the body of the UPDATE-statement. However, a relation can only have one updatable iteration-variable active at a time. This restriction is enforced by a run-time check. The UPDATE constructs described here do not solve the problem of non-functional updates, that is, replacing one value by many [STON76a].

Records are inserted into a relation by using an APPEND-statement. For example,

    APPEND <S#:1024,NAME:"Smith, K.",MAJOR:"EECS",LEVEL:jr>
      TO STUDENT;

inserts a new student into the STUDENT relation. In contrast to the DELETE- and REPLACE-statements, the APPEND-statement is not used in the body of an UPDATE-statement.

A database transaction is expressed by using a "transaction-block," e.g.,

    TRANSACTION
      UPDATES COURSE,PROFESSOR;
    BEGIN
      UPDATE P IN PROFESSOR WHERE P.NAME = "Johnson, A." DO
        UPDATE C IN COURSE WHERE C.P#=P.P# DO
          DELETE C;
        END;
        DELETE P;
      END;
    END;

This example deletes Professor Johnson and all courses he teaches. The updates list is required because UPDATE-statements may occur in called procedures; without it, interprocedural data-flow analysis would be required to determine which relations might be changed. The ability to group together updates in order to maintain database integrity is a necessary language feature for the development of database applications.

A major problem in designing the UPDATE constructs is to allow a procedure, called in the body of an UPDATE-statement, to replace or delete a tuple. For instance, in the salary increase example at the beginning of this section, a procedure updateSalary that takes a PROFESSOR tuple and replaces the salary could have been provided rather than newSalary. The updates would then be coded

    UPDATE P IN PROFESSOR DO
      updateSalary(P);
    END;

The problem is what type is the formal argument to updateSalary? Up to this point, an iteration-variable bound to a tuple in a relation has been treated as a record-value. That is, the iteration-variable is actually bound to a copy of the tuple. However, to do updates, a reference to the tuple is needed rather than to a copy. The solution is to introduce a type that denotes "a reference to a tuple in a relation." UpdateSalary can then be coded as follows

```
updateSalary:PROCEDURE(A:TUPLE PROFESSOR'type)=
BEGIN
   . . .
   REPLACE A BY A< . . .>;
   . . .
END;
```

The tuple-type specifies the type of relation of which the tuple is a member. In this case, PROFESSOR'type specifies the type of the variable PROFESSOR. The suffix 'type is an example of an "attribute function."

There is a problem with introducing values of type tuple into the language. In actuality, tuple-values are addresses on secondary memory. Consider the following program fragment:

```
FOR S IN STUDENT WHERE S.NAME="Smith, K." DO
   X:=S;
END;
```

After executing this code, X would reference Smith's tuple in the STUDENT relation. Somewhere later in the program one might try to reference Smith's tuple through X. This cannot be allowed because the tuple might have been moved by a later update from this program or from a concurrent user or by a change in the storage structure used to store the STUDENT relation. This restriction is achieved by not allowing tuple-values to be assigned. In this example, the assignment "X:=S" is flagged as a compile-time error.

This section has presented a complete set of update constructs which have been carefully integrated into the retrieval mechanisms presented in the previous section. The introduction of tuple-values allows REPLACES and DELETES to be executed in procedures called from the body of an UPDATE-statement, which enhances the power of procedures in the language. This feature is exploited in the view update mechanism discussed below. Before discussing the view mechanisms though, the data abstraction constructs must be presented.

4.0. DATA ABSTRACTION

In this section the data abstraction facility provided in RIGEL is described. Data abstractions are used to define the interface between a program and a database, as well as the interfaces between parts of a large program. The abstraction facility is also used to separate the representation of a view from the code which implements it. Thus, the data abstraction facility is extremely important for the development of well-structured database applications.

Data abstraction mechanisms can be provided in a language by "abstract data types" (ADT) or by "modules." An ADT mechanism allows a programmer to associate primitive operations with one data structure type (e.g., a stack with "pop," "push," "isEmpty," and "top" operations). The declaration of an ADT adds a new type to the language which can be used, for example, to declare variables of that type (e.g., stack). Thus, an ADT mechanism is designed to define one type which can be used to create several instances of the object. For example, ADTs are provided in SIMULA [BIRT73] because simulation programs are concerned with the movement of multiple instances of various types of entities through a system.

The differences between ADTs and modules is that modules do not define a single type. A module mechanism is designed to allow several types, variables, and procedures to be declared together and to be used in an application program as a unit. A simple example would be an I/O subroutine library which defines types (buffer and file descriptor types), variables (status variables), and procedures ("openFile," "read," etc.). A program that uses the I/O module creates only one instance of the objects it defines, called "importing" the module. Modules are provided in MODULA [WIRT77] because system programs are primarily concerned with interfaces between pieces of hardware and software. These interfaces are comprised of more than one type and are only instantiated once in a program.

ADTs can be used like modules and modules can be used to define ADTs, but each is more convenient for the use for which it was defined. More extensive comparisons of these two abstraction mechanisms are available elsewhere ([GOOS78, WIRT77]). Nevertheless, ADTs are best suited to problems which require multiple instantiations of one type while modules are best suited to problems which require one instantiation of a collection of types, variables and procedures.

The predominant use of data abstraction in database applications is to define the interface between a program and a database, called an "external schema" by some database practitioners. This interface is often quite complex and only one instance is needed. Clearly, modules are the most natural notation for their specification.

A module in RIGEL has three sections: public, private, and initialization. The public section defines the objects that can be accessed by the user of the module, called its "client." The private section implements the objects defined in the public section. Objects local to the private section cannot be directly accessed by the client. The initialization section is executed when the module is defined so that necessary initialization can be completed.

The public section specifies the abstract semantics and the private section specifies the implementation. Used correctly, modules provide a means for isolating a client program from the representational details of the

```
scheduleSchema: module =
public
        COURSE: relation
                C#: idNumType;
                TITLE:titleType;
                P#:idNumType;
                key C#;
        end
        PROFESSOR: relation
                P#: idNumType;
                NAME:nameType;
                SALARY:real;
                RANK: (lec, asst, assoc, full, special);
                YEARSSERVICE: integer;
                key P#;
        end;
        assignProf: procedure(prof:nameType, class:titleType);
        scheduleReport:procedure;
        . . .
private
        assignProf: procedure=
        begin
          UPDATE C IN COURSE FOR P IN PROFESSOR
            WHERE C.TITLE = class AND P.NAME = prof DO
              REPLACE C BY C<P#: P.P#>;
          end;
        end;
    . . .
end;
```

FIGURE 15.2. Example Module Declaration

abstraction. Figure 15.2 shows a module definition for an interface to the college database that might be used by a program that is scheduling professors and classes.[4] The public section includes all declarations that must be

---

[4] The binding of program variables COURSE and PROFESSOR to relations stored in a database is not shown. Language mechanisms to control this binding were discussed in a previous paper [PREN78]; details are also given in the language specification [ROWE78].

seen by an application programmer to use the relations and procedures. After importing the module, the relations and procedures are accessed in the usual way. For example, to assign Professor R. Burns to teach PHYSICS 1, one writes

> assignProf("Burns, R.", "PHYSICS1");

Notice that the number of arguments and their types are given in the public section because a client must know this information to use the procedure. They are not repeated in the private section where the procedure body is specified to avoid needless inconsistency errors and to insure that if the argument declarations are changed only one change to the program text is necessary.

Modules provide a better notation than ADTs for specifying a program interface to a database. For example, only those relations and views which a program may access are declared in the public section. Moreover, high-level abstract operations can be associated with the data by declaring them in the module, thus providing a complete specification of the database interface.

5.0. VIEWS

This section illustrates the use of updatable views in RIGEL. A view is an abstract relation which can be used to simplify the access to a database, to protect parts of a database, and to enhance data independence [CHAM75]. The definition of a view is comprised of the declaration of the abstract relation which the view simulates and the specification of how a view tuple is constructed from the tuples in the underlying relations, called the "base relations." These parts are called, respectively, the "abstract relation declaration" and the "mapping specification." The user of a view should only see the abstract relation declaration because the mapping specification is part of the view implementation. This separation and information hiding can be achieved by putting the abstract relation declaration in the public section of a module and the mapping specification in the private section of a module. In this way, the use of modules complements the use of views.

For performance and consistency reasons, queries on a view are translated into queries on the base relations rather than being executed directly on a materialization of the view [STON75]. This translation is possible for all retrievals but not for all updates. Views and updates exist for which no sequence of operations on the base relations will produce a correct update when the data is accessed through the view (i.e., undefined updates). Other examples exist for which more than one sequence of operations will produce a correct view update but each produces a very different meaning on the underlying data (i.e., ambiguous updates) [DAYA78]. The problem is to decide how view update facilities should be provided in a language. There are four possibilities:

1) Views may not be updated.

2) Views may be updated but the programmer must specify what base relation updates are to be executed, i.e., for those updates that are to be allowed, the programmer must specify the translation of the high-level operation.

3) Views may be updated only by updates that can be unambiguously translated to base relation updates by some update translation algorithm.

4) Views may be updated and language constructs are provided to allow a programmer to specify the translation of ambiguous and undefined updates that are not handled by the translation algorithm, i.e., all updates are allowed.

The first alternative was rejected because it seriously restricts the utility of views.

Several attempts were made to formulate language constructs to allow programmer-defined augmentations to an update translation algorithm, i.e., the fourth alternative. Each attempt introduced significant language complexity and, in most cases, resulted in programs that would be impractical to execute.

The third alternative attempts to support arbitrary view updates by using the standard update constructs defined for relations. However, should one desire an ambiguous update no convenient notation is supplied for the programmer to express that update. Another consequence of adopting this alternative is that a programmer would not know whether a particular view update was legal until it was translated, or in some cases, executed [STON75, ASTR76, DAYA78]. Moreover, the update translation algorithms depend on the view mapping specification which the programmer presumably cannot access. The second alternative, on the other hand, acknowledges that only a limited set of view updates are possible and provides a way to associate the appropriate semantics with the view update expressed as a high-level abstract operation. In most applications, because few distinct view updates are required, the burden on the programmer to specify the translation would be insignificant. Moreover, data independence would be enhanced by the discipline of explicitly coding the view updates as high-level operations. Consequently, the second alternative was judged superior to the third alternative.

The remainder of this section presents the language constructs provided in RIGEL to define and use views. The presentation is based on a module that might be used by the professor of a class. The module is comprised of a view of the students enrolled in the class and operations that he might access to handle some typical actions: adding and dropping students, counting the number of classes a student is taking, assigning grades, and calculating the grade point average of various groups of students.

Figure 15.3 shows the public section of the courseView module. It includes the view for ECON1 and the abstract operations. Assuming that the

```
courseView: module=
public
ECON1: view
        S#:idNumType;
        NAME:nameType;
        GRADE:gradeType;
end;
addStudent:procedure(student:nameType);
dropStudent:procedure(student:tuple ECON1'type);
assignGrade:procedure(student:tuple ECON1'type,
                            courseGrade:gradeType);
countClasses:procedure(student:tuple ECON1'type):integer;
avgGPA:procedure(grades:generator:gradeType): real;
private
end; /*courseView */
```

FIGURE 15.3. Public Section of CourseView Module

module has been imported into the current scope, a query to list students with incompletes is written:

```
FOR S IN ECON1 WHERE S.GRADE = I DO
    print(S.NAME);
END;
```

To add a student to the course, the addStudent procedure is invoked, e.g.,

```
addStudent ("Smith, K.")
```

To assign a grade to each student the following is executed

```
UPDATE S IN ECON1 DO
    assignGrade(S.getGrade(S.NAME));
END;
```

where getGrade is a function that returns a grade for each student (e.g., it might be read from a terminal). Notice that the type of the first argument to assignGrade is a tuple in the view. AssignGrade will perform an update on the student's tuple in the ENROLLMENT base relation.

Other examples to illustrate view use are

```
/*calculate class grade point average*/
avgGPA(S.GRADE: S IN ECON1 WHERE S.GRADE NOT = 1)
```

```
/*gpa of students taking more than 4 courses*/
avgGPA(S.GRADE: S IN ECON1 WHERE countClasses(S) > 4)
```

These examples illustrate the power and convenience of generator expressions and generators as arguments to procedures. AvgGPA is an example of a programmer-defined aggregate function.

The implementation of this module is shown in Figure 15.4. Lines 8 to 12 complete the view declaration. The view mapping is specified by a generator expression which produces the tuples in the abstract relation. The particular course for which this module defines a view is specified as a constant in the mapping specification. Obviously, a better way to structure this module would be to make the course a module parameter so that one module could be used for all courses rather than having to define a separate module for each one.

CountClasses takes a view tuple and accesses the ENROLLMENT base relation to find the number of classes in which the student is enrolled. AvgGPA takes a generator argument and calculates the grade point average of the grades returned by the generator. ToGPA is an array that maps grades to the obvious numerical ranking. AddStudent is a procedure which causes a new tuple to be inserted into the view by performing an update on the ENROLLMENT base relation. The implementation of these operations could be expressed directly on the base relations without reference to the base relation tuples that produced a specific view tuple.

DropStudent takes a view tuple as an argument and deletes the tuple in the ENROLLMENT base relation that represents the student's enrollment. The problem is how to access the ENROLLMENT tuple given a view tuple. One solution would be to execute a query to find the tuple, e.g.,

```
UPDATE E IN ENROLLMENT FOR C IN COURSE
  WHERE STUDENT.S#=E.S# AND C.C#=E.C#
  AND C.TITLE="ECON1" DO
    DELETE E;
END;
```

where student is the argument to the procedure dropStudent. This solution is intolerably inefficient. Additionally, this implementation of the update implies an update to the ENROLLMENT relation as each student is dropped rather than deferring the change until all students to be dropped have been processed. In other words, these semantics of the view update differ from the deferred update semantics for a physically existing relation. A better solution would be to allow dropStudent to access the base tuples directly. This solution is achieved by allowing the base relation tuples used to construct the view tuple to be accessed given a base relation tuple.

Associated with each view tuple is a record, called the "view tuple base

```
courseView: module =
public
   . . .
private
   /*view mapping specification*/
   ECON1: view=
      <S#:E.S#, NAME:S.NAME, GRADE:E.GRADE>:
   E IN ENROLLMENT, S IN STUDENT, C IN COURSE
   WHERE C.TITLE = "ECON1" AND C.C# = E.C# and S.S# = E.S#;
   countClasses: procedure=
   begin
      return COUNT(X IN ENROLLMENT WHERE X.S#=STUDENT.S#);
   end;
   /*initialize grade point mapping */
   toGP: array gradeType of real:=[4, 3, 2, 1, 0, 0];
   avgGPA:procedure=
   begin
      return AVG(toGP[S.GRADE]: S IN STUDENT WHERE S.GRADE
         NOT = l;
   end;
   addStudent: procedure=
   begin
      if(S IN STUDENT, C IN COURSE
         WHERE S.NAME=STUDENT AND C.NAME="ECON1")
      then
         APPEND<S#: S.S#, NAME: STUDENT, GRADE:l> TO
            ENROLLMENT;
      else
         print("No such course or student");
      fi;
   end;
   assignGrade: procedure=
   begin
      REPLACE STUDENT'base.E BY
         STUDENT'base.E<GRADE:courseGrade>;
   end;
   dropStudent: procedure=
   begin
      DELETE STUDENT'base.E;
   end;
end; /* Course view */
```

FIGURE 15.4. Private Section of CourseView Module

record," which has a field that holds the current value for each iteration-variable bound in the mapping specification for the view, e.g., the base record declared for ECON1 view tuples is

```
record
    E: tuple ENROLLMENT'type;
    S: tuple STUDENT'type;
    C: tuple COURSE'type;
end
```

To access this record given a view tuple, say STUDENT, one applies the BASE attribute-function to STUDENT, i.e., STUDENT'base. Thus, to access the ENROLLMENT base relation tuple, one writes

```
STUDENT'base.E
```

Because this is just a value of type tuple in a relation, DELETE is a legal operation. In this way, dropStudent can delete the appropriate base tuple directly. AssignGrade also uses this feature to replace the grade stored in the ENROLLMENT tuple.

This section has illustrated the language constructs provided in RIGEL to support the disciplined use of views. The approach to views taken here is very different from that taken in other languages. An explicit specification is given for the type of the abstract relation that the view simulates and for the update operations that are allowed on the view. Another important difference is that it is possible to separate the view declaration from the view implementation in accordance with the principles of information hiding by defining the view inside a module. Recall that a module is the language construct used to specify the database interface to a program.

6.0. CONCLUSION

The main contribution of this paper is to show how various programming language concepts can be generalized and used together to provide a good environment for writing database applications. First, the language type system was extended to allow definition of objects of type relation, view, and tuple and to support their disciplined use. Second, generators were introduced as a notation to specify complex retrievals and updates on tuples in views and relations. Finally, the use of modules, along with relations and views, was shown to provide a convenient notation for specifying program interfaces to databases.

## CHAPTER SIXTEEN

A Form Application Development System

Lawrence A. Rowe / Kurt A. Shoens

ABSTRACT

This paper describes FADS − a Form Application Development System which is an interactive system for the development of form-based database applications. FADS reduces the amount of work required to implement a forms application by suppressing much of the detail which would be required by conventional tools (e.g., a screen definition system, a database system, and a programming language). FADS provides direct access to a relational database, a standard model of the user interface, built-in forms constructs, and an integrated development and debugging environment. Using FADS, form applications can be developed quickly and the resulting systems are easy to modify. A prototype implementation of the FADS kernel has been completed.

1.0. INTRODUCTION

A form application is one in which users interact with a computer through a form displayed on a video terminal. These applications often involve several people sending and receiving forms to communicate and accomplish some goal. An on-line inventory control system, a student enrollment system, a software bug report system, and a purchase order system are examples of form applications.

The Form Application Development System (FADS) is an interactive system for developing form applications. It provides built-in facilities to display and enter data through forms and to execute high-level operations

---

L. A. Rowe, K. A. Shoens, *ACM-SIGMOD Conference Proceedings*, ACM-SIGMOD International Conference on Management of Data, Orlando, Florida, June 1982. Copyright 1982, Association for Computing Machinery, Inc.; reprinted by permission.

coded in a set-oriented query language. These high-level operations correspond to the actions that an end-user performs (e.g., "hire" an employee) when using the application. FADS applications are defined by filling in forms using a similar interface to that seen by a user of an application. An integrated development environment is provided that includes an application editor, a screen layout editor, a relation editor, and a debugger.

The goal of FADS is to shorten the time required to develop form applications that involve several users. This goal is accomplished by suppressing the detail that an application designer must specify, by having the system automatically fill in defaults (e.g., screen layout), and by providing an interactive development environment similar to that provided for LISP [TEIT81].

Previous work on tools for developing form applications can be divided into screen definition systems [TAND80, HEWL79], and office automation systems [DEJO80, LUO81, ZLOO81]. Screen definition systems such as Screen COBOL [TAND80] provide embedded language constructs to define screen layouts (i.e., position of fields on a screen) and display attributes (e.g., labels and integrity checks) and to do screen input/output. However, applications are still coded in a conventional programming language and the screen definitions do not access the data definitions stored in the data dictionary even though the same data is being described and manipulated. Consequently, changing an application often requires changes to the screen definition, the database definition, and the program which can be time-consuming and error prone.

Interactive screen definition systems, such as VIEW/3000 [HEWL79] allow the application programmer to design and edit screen layouts while they are displayed on the terminal. These systems provide a better tool to define screens than embedded languages because the designer can change the screen while looking at it rather than having to compile, link, and run a program to see what the screen looks like. Nevertheless, they have the same problems as embedded languages because they deal only with screen definition. They are not integrated with the database system and, in some cases, the interface between the program and the screen run-time system is not type checked.

Office automation systems address the same kinds of applications as FADS but they either do not provide a complete application development environment or were designed with a different idea of how applications will be developed. FOBE [LUO81] is a nonprocedural query language based on the form data model [SHU81] that was designed to specify office procedures. In contrast to FADS, it does not have an interactive development environment and, as described in [LUO81], it cannot be used to produce applications that are used interactively by an end-user.

SBA [DEJO80] and OBE [ZLOO81] are programming systems for end-users who gradually automate their activities. FADS is designed for programmers who develop interactive applications for many users. As with FOBE, SBA and OBE do not provide a complete programming environment.

The remainder of this paper is organized as follows. Section 2.0

describes the primitives on which the FADS system is based. Section 3.0 presents an overview of the application development environment, describes the interface that the user of a FADS application sees, and presents an example of application definition. Section 4.0 describes the application debugging tools. Section 5.0 describes the current implementation and extensions to the system. Finally, Section 6.0 summarizes the paper.

The examples below are taken from a bug report system that keeps track of the bug reports handled by a software support group. A relational database design for the system is shown in Figure 15.1. The BUGS relation contains a tuple for each reported bug. BUG is a short name for the bug and is the logical key of the relation. The PEOPLE relation contains information about the programmers and the BUGASSIGN relation represents the relationship of bugs assigned to programmers.

The users of the system include a secretary, a manager, and the maintenance programmers. The secretary screens incoming bug reports and enters data about each report into the system (e.g., who submitted the report and a description of the problem). The manager assigns a report to a programmer and sets a date by which the bug should be fixed. If the programmer does not complete the investigation by the due date, first the programmer and later the manager will be notified. After the bug has been fixed, the report is sent back to the manager. The manager then passes it back to the secretary who sends a response to the person who submitted the report.

2.0. FADS PRIMITIVES

This section describes the primitives used to define a FADS application, including: frames, forms, data types, operations, and roles. The primitive objects that comprise an application are stored in the data dictionary.

A FADS application consists of a collection of "frames" that the users of the application interact with and move between. A "frame" is what a user

---

BUGS (BUG, PROGRAM, VERSION, STATUS,
        DATE-SUBMITTED, SUBMITTER, AFFILIATION,
        DATE-FIXED, DESCRIPTION, RESPONSE)

PEOPLE (NAME, JOB-TITLE, ...)

BUGASSIGN (BUG, NAME, DATE-DUE, DATE-ASSIGNED)

FIGURE 16.1. Bug Report System Database Design

sees on the terminal display. It is composed of one or more forms in which data can be entered or displayed and a list of operations that a user can execute. Figure 16.2 shows a frame that contains one form (a bug report) and five operations (listed at the bottom of the frame).

A user of this frame can enter a bug report into the system by entering data into the fields in the form and executing the ENTER operation. A conventional data entry facility is provided in FADS for entering data into a form. An operation is invoked by typing an escape character and a unique prefix of the operation name.

```
┌─────────────────────────────────────────────────────────────┐
│                    BUG REPORT SYSTEM                          │
│                                                               │
│    BUG:                          DATE SUBMITTED: dd/mm/82     │
│                                                               │
│    PROGRAM:                      SUBMITTER:                    │
│                                                               │
│    VERSION:                      AFFILIATION:                  │
│                                                               │
│    STATUS: ASSIGNED              DATE FIXED: dd/mm/82          │
│            FIXED                                               │
│            REPORTED                                            │
│                                                               │
│                       DESCRIPTION                             │
│    ┌─────────────────────────────────────────────────────┐  │
│    │                                                       │  │
│    │                                                       │  │
│    │                                                       │  │
│    └─────────────────────────────────────────────────────┘  │
│                        RESPONSE                              │
│    ┌─────────────────────────────────────────────────────┐  │
│    │                                                       │  │
│    │                                                       │  │
│    └─────────────────────────────────────────────────────┘  │
│        ENTER    FIND    LIST    MODIFY    QUIT               │
└─────────────────────────────────────────────────────────────┘
```

FIGURE 16.2. A Frame

FADS supports two built-in kinds of forms: tuple and relation. A "tuple form" contains one or more fields that can display a tuple in a relation. The form in Figure 16.2 is a tuple form with a field for each attribute in the BUGS relation. This form corresponds to a paper form and is called the bug report form.

A "relation form" can display a relation. The tuples in the relation are displayed in a table format. Each row in the table corresponds to a tuple in the relation. Figure 16.3 shows a second frame that contains two forms: a relation form (labeled "Bug summary") that displays a summary of a collection of bug reports and a tuple form with only one field (labeled "bugs").

BUG SUMMARY

PROGRAM	BUG	STATUS	DATE DUE
RIGEL	scalar types	ASSIGNED	10/2/82
EQUEL	attributes	REPORTED	
C compiler	symbol table overflows	ASSIGNED	1/3/82

BUG:

DETAILS   RETURN

FIGURE 16.3. A Frame That Contains a Relation Form

Tuple and relation forms are primitives that can be used to define more complex forms. For example, a master-detail form, such as a purchase order, contains a tuple form that displays the data about the purchaser and a relation form that displays the items purchased. This example illustrates how non-normalized data can be displayed.

Each field in a tuple form and column in a relation form has a data type and display attributes. FADS supports a variety of built-in "data types" including: integers, reals, fixed and variable length strings, dates, times, and enumerated types.[1] Display attributes describe how the data should be displayed (e.g., the label, output format, and display enhancement) and entered (e.g., edit checks, default values, data formats, and input masks such as "dd/mm/82" for dates).[2]

In addition to the simple data types described above, FADS supports two structured data types: tuple and relation. These types describe the values that a tuple and relation form can hold. In a typical FADS application, a tuple type is defined for each entity in the application (e.g., a bug report). This type is then used to define a relation to store entities in the database and forms to display the entities. A tuple form is defined to display a single entity and a relation form is defined to display several entities. If there is a single type definition that is shared by the relation and form definitions, the application designer can add an attribute to the type definition and FADS will automatically extend the relation to include the attribute and the form definition to include an extra field.

Operations listed at the bottom of a frame are defined in an extended set-oriented query language. The language allows a query to access data entered into a form or to display in a form data retrieved from a database. The language also provides statements to call and return from another frame. Arguments such as the output of a query can be passed to a called frame. Lastly, the language includes statements to alter control-flow (e.g., a conditional statement).

Form applications often involve several people sending forms to each other. The extended query language does not provide an explicit statement to send data and a form from one user to another. Communication is accomplished by sharing access to a database. Data is entered into the database by the sender and a condition is set which causes the receiver to retrieve the data. For example, the secretary enters a bug report with status REPORTED. The manager retrieves all REPORTED bug reports, which effectively sends it from the secretary to the manager.

Using the database to implement communication has several advan-

---

[1] An enumerated type has a fixed number of values that are represented by identifiers. For example, the status attribute in the BUGS relation is an enumerated type with values: REPORTED, ASSIGNED, and FIXED.

[2] In addition to field level edit checks, FADS supports form and frame level integrity checks (e.g., cross field checks).

tages. First, only one copy of the bug report data is maintained which reduces the problem of maintaining consistent copies. Second, a database system provides crash recovery and concurrency control which would have to be implemented for an explicit send statement. And lastly, by storing all data in the database system other tools, such as an ad hoc query language and report writer can be used to access all data controlled by an application.

Different users of a form application typically require access to different data and operations. The data and operations that a particular user requires are defined by their role in the organization. For example, the secretary needs access to the details of all bug reports and operations to enter and correct reports. In contrast, the manager is interested only in summary information (e.g., the number of bug reports assigned to each programmer) and details about selected reports (e.g., bugs which have been reported but have not been assigned to a programmer).

Each user of a FADS application has a "role" that determines what frame is displayed when they run the application. This initial frame is called the user's "home frame." Figure 16.2 is the secretary's home frame for the bug report system.

This section described the primitives from which FADS applications are built. An application is composed of frames which allow users to enter and display data stored in a database. Each frame has a list of operations, specified in an extended query language, that a user can execute. These operations correspond to the actions that the user performs as defined by their role in the organization.

3.0. APPLICATION DEVELOPMENT

This section describes how a FADS application is developed. An overview of the application development environment is given in Section 3.1. Section 3.2 shows how a frame is defined and describes the extended query language that is used to define operations. Section 3.3 shows how forms are defined.

3.1. Application Development Overview

An application is defined by moving between frames, filling in forms, and executing operations to define the "objects" (i.e., frames, forms, relations, roles, and data types) that comprise the application. Figure 16.4 shows the frames in the application development environment (the boxes) and how the designer can move among them to define an application (the arrows).

The frame titled "application editor" is the top-level description of an application (i.e., it is the home frame for application designers). This frame allows the designer to enter the definition of a new FADS application or to modify the definition of an existing application. It has operations to list the names of objects in this application, to edit an object, or to enter the debugger to test the application.

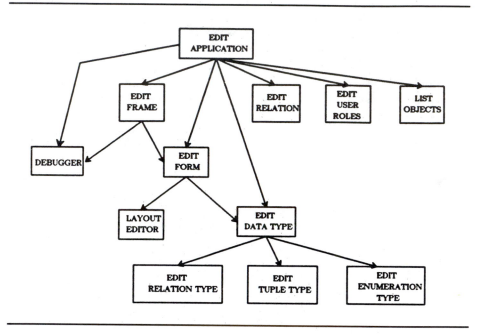

FIGURE 16.4. Application Development Environment

The "list objects" frame displays the names of all existing objects. It helps the designer to recall what objects are defined and it can be used to look up the name of an object.

The frames provided to edit the different kinds of objects (i.e., "edit frame," "edit form," "edit data types" including relations, tuples, and enumerated types, "edit relations," and "edit user roles") contain forms to define or modify a specific object. For example, the frame for editing frames is used to define the secretary's home frame shown in Figure 16.2. Examples of defining frames and forms are presented in Sections 3.2 and 3.3.

Since frames contain forms and forms are defined in terms of the data types they can display, the designer can move directly from defining a frame to defining a form, and from there to defining a data type. Objects can be defined in any order and the system accepts partial definitions. For example, if the designer is defining a frame and specifies that it contains a form which has not been defined yet, he can either complete the frame definition and then define the form or suspend work on the frame definition, define the form, and then complete the frame definition. A CHECK operation, described in Section 4.0, is provided so the designer can check the consistency of an application (e.g., that all forms contained in a frame are defined).

From the "application editor" frame, the designer can also call the relation editor or enter the FADS debugger. The relation editor is a simple form-based query system in which the designer can examine, modify, enter, and delete tuples in relations to verify the operations of an application. The relation editor is also used to set up test data for an application. The debugger allows the designer to set breakpoints, to run an application (i.e., call an application frame), to examine the state of a running application, and to switch back and forth between editing the application and running it. The debugger is described in more detail in Section 4.0.

Application definitions are stored in system catalogs in the database. This representation enhances the modularity of an application. For example, type definitions stored in the system catalogs are used throughout the application definition (e.g., to define the attributes in a relation and data types of fields in a form). This representation also encourages the designer to reuse pieces of an application (e.g., frames and forms) which provides a more consistent user interface because information is displayed and entered in the same way throughout the application. If frames and forms are reused the size of an application is reduced because fewer objects are defined.

This subsection presented an overview of the frames in the application development environment. They allow a designer to move easily between defining and testing the frames that comprise an application.

3.2. Frame Definition

This subsection describes how frames are defined. It also describes the extended query language used to define the operations in a frame.

A frame is defined by specifying the title, the forms, and the names and definitions of operations in the frame. Figure 16.5 shows an "edit frame" filled in to define the bug report frame shown in Figure 16.2. The name of the frame is BUGREPORT. The frame title is "Bug Report System" which is centered on the first line of the BUGREPORT frame. The frame contains one form, named BUGFORM, which is defined in the next subsection.

Operation definitions are coded in an extended query language based on QUEL [HELD75b]. The language includes statements to retrieve and update values in relations, a notation to reference values in forms, and statements to alter the control-flow of an application (e.g., to call and return from a frame, to execute a statement if a condition is true, and to exit an application). The remainder of this subsection illustrates the features of the language by describing the definitions of the BUGREPORT frame operations.

The first operation shows how data values in a form are referenced. The ENTER operation takes the data entered into the BUGFORM form and appends it to the BUGS relation. The expression "BUGFORM.ALL" references the values entered into the form. Each form holds the value which has been entered or displayed through it. Tuple forms hold tuple values and relation forms hold relation values. Individual fields in a tuple form can be

```
EDIT FRAME


NAME: BUGREPORT

TITLE: BUG REPORT SYSTEM

                                FORMS
                          ┌─────────────────────┐
                          │      BUGFORM         │
                          ├─────────────────────┤
                          │                      │
                          ├─────────────────────┤
                          │                      │
                          └─────────────────────┘


                            OPERATIONS
```

NAME	DEFINITION
ENTER	APPEND BUGS (BUGFORM.ALL)
FIND	BUGFORM = (RETRIEVE (BUGS.ALL) WHERE BUGS.BUG = BUGFORM.BUG)
LIST	CALL BUGSUM(SUMFORM = (RETRIEVE (BUGS.PROGRAM, BUGS.BUG, BUGS.STATUS,BUGASSIGN.DATE-DUE) WHERE BUGS.STATUS <> FIXED AND BUGS.BUG = BUGASSIGN.BUG))
MODIFY	REPLACE BUGS (BUGFORM.ALL) WHERE BUGS.BUG = BUGFORM.BUG
QUIT	QUIT

```
DEBUG  DELETE  ENTER  FIND  FORM  LAYOUT  MODIFY  RETURN
```

FIGURE 16.5. Definition of Bug Report Frame

referenced by using the selection operator (e.g., FORMNAME.FIELDNAME).
In this example, the fields in BUGFORM have the same names as the

attributes in the BUGS relation so the system can determine which field should be assigned to each attribute in the relation. If the names had been different, explicit assignments would be required. For example, suppose the field in the form which contained the name of the bug was named BUG-NAME. The assignment of a field in a form to an attribute in a relation could be specified as follows

APPEND BUGS(BUG = BUGREPORT.BUGNAME,...)

The second operation shows how queries are parameterized and how the result of a query is displayed in a form. The FIND operation takes the value entered into the BUG field and retrieves that bug report. The RETRIEVE-expression on the right-hand side of the assignment returns a tuple which is assigned to, hence displayed in, the form. The relation attributes are assigned to the form fields with the same names and are automatically converted to the appropriate data type and edited for output as specified for the form field. If the attribute names and fields were different, explicit assignments would be required.

In this example, only one tuple could be returned by the query because BUG is the logical key of the BUGS relation. If the query were different and more than one tuple were returned, FADS prints a message to that effect and allows the user to step through the values. Because this facility is built into FADS, the application designer does not have to write code to test whether more than one value was returned and to step through them.

The third operation shows how a frame is called and a value is passed to a form in the called frame. The LIST operation calls the frame shown in Figure 16.3 and passes to it the bug reports that have not yet been fixed. The definition of the operation shown in Figure 16.5 calls the frame named BUG-SUM and passes to it the bug report data retrieved from the database. The data passed to the frame is displayed in the form, named SUMFORM, which is the relation form in the BUGSUM frame. Notice that the retrieve statement includes a join and that data from both relations is displayed.

The MODIFY operation shows an example of a REPLACE statement that updates a bug report and the QUIT operation shows the QUIT statement that exits the bug report application.

This subsection showed how a frame is defined and described the extended query language for defining operations in frames.

3.3. Form Definition

This section shows how forms are defined. The definition of the bug report form (BUGFORM) contained in the BUGREPORT frame defined in Section 3.2 is used as an example.

A form is defined by specifying the title, the kind of form it is (i.e., tuple or relation), the data type that can be entered or displayed through it, and information specific to each kind of form.

An "edit form" frame filled in with the definition of BUGFORM is shown in Figure 16.6. This form is a tuple form defined for the data type BUGTYPE. BUGTYPE is used to define the relation BUGS and this form.

The form layout (i.e., the placement and order of the fields on the terminal display) is defined by a layout format. In this example, the format is "2 columns" which indicates that the fields should be arranged into two columns as shown in Figure 16.2. Other formats provided for tuple forms are: "packed" (pack as many fields on a line as possible) and "tabbed" (separate fields by tabs). Relation forms have only one layout format − the table format shown in Figure 16.3.

Layout formats are useful when building a prototype frame or when a frame will only be used a few times because the forms are easy to specify. A layout editor is provided that gives complete control over the form layout to the application designer. It displays a form or frame as it would appear on a terminal display and allows the designer to move fields around and to change

---

EDIT FORM

NAME: BUGFORM

TITLE:

DATA TYPE: BUGTYPE   FORM KIND: TUPLE
                                                RELATION

TUPLE FORM FORMAT: 2 COLUMNS

RELATION FORM NUMBER OF ROWS:

DELETE   ENTER   FIND   LAYOUT   MODIFY   RETURN   TYPE

FIGURE 16.6. Definition of the BUGFORM Form

labels and other display attributes. This combination of layout formats and a layout editor allows the designer to get a frame running quickly and to have complete layout control.

The data type BUGTYPE that is used to define BUGFORM is a tuple type. A tuple type is defined by specifying the name, type, and display attributes of each of its fields. Data types are defined by filling in forms in the same way frames and forms are defined.

Figures 16.5 and 16.6 and the BUGTYPE data type define the bug report frame shown in Figure 16.2. BUGTYPE is also used to define the BUGS relation and, in the complete definition of the bug report system, BUGFORM would be used in several different frames.

Section 3.0 has described the application development environment for FADS. The development environment includes tools to edit an application definition and the database on which the application runs.

Application definitions are specified by filling in frames that describe the frames, forms, data types, operations, relations, and user roles that make up an application. Using a form-based interface to define applications makes defining an application easy because the form indicates to the designer what information is required and input integrity checks can detect errors when the definition is entered.

FADS applications can be defined quickly because entering data (i.e., an application definition) into a form is fast and because the system provides reasonable defaults for much of the detail that would be required if the application were coded in a programming language. For example, default display attributes (e.g., labels, formats, and input integrity checks) are supplied for fields based on the name and type of the field and default screen layouts are supplied for forms.

FADS provides a standard frame organization (e.g., operations listed at the bottom) and built-in facilities for recognizing which operation was requested and for calling the appropriate operation definition. These definitions are coded in a high-level, nonprocedural query language that does not require redundant declarations of the data types, forms, and relations used in an operation. Because the number of lines of code required to define an operation is reduced and because the data types in the form fields are checked against the database data dictionary, the operation definitions are quicker to write, less prone to errors, and easier to debug when an error is made.

The next section describes the debugging tools for FADS applications.

4.0. APPLICATION DEBUGGING

This section describes the CHECK operation that checks the semantic consistency of a FADS application and the debugging frame which is called by the designer to test an application or by the system when a run-time error is encountered.

The CHECK operation performs many consistency checks on an application. It ensures that

1) all called frames exist,

2) all forms used in frames are defined,

3) operations are legal (e.g., form, field, and attribute names used in an operation are valid), and

4) data types used to define forms are defined and valid.

The CHECK operation warns the designer of possible problems, but does not stop him from running the application. The FADS system is designed to allow applications to be developed incrementally. The purpose of the CHECK operation is to remind the designer of incomplete or inconsistent specifications.

If a FADS application is running and an error is encountered (e.g., a frame called in an operation is not defined), the system takes different actions depending on whether the person running the application is a user or the designer. If it is a user, the system prints an appropriate error message (e.g., "Error in the operation definition."), and returns to a consistent state (e.g, returns control to the user).

If the user is the application designer, the BREAK frame is called (Figure 16.7). The BREAK frame displays the error message that caused the break and the list of active frames. The BREAK frame contains operations to control subsequent execution of the application, including breakpoint control; operations to examine or modify the values in any active frame; and an operation to edit an active frame with the application editor described in Section 3.0.

Breakpoints are controlled through a separate frame, called the BREAK-POINT frame, which contains a relation form with the breakpoint list. Breakpoints can be set on the execution of a frame or procedure, or on the access or modification of a relation. A breakpoint is set by entering a new row in the breakpoint table and removed by deleting an existing row.

One of the frames in the active list can be selected by entering its name in the FRAME-NAME field. Then, the DISPLAY operation will display the selected frame and allow the values inside to be modified using the standard form entry editing functions.

The definition of an active frame can be examined or modified with the application editor by selecting one of the frames for DISPLAY and executing the EDIT operation.

The QUERY operation calls the relation editor described in Section 3.0 so that the application designer can examine or modify the contents of the database. The CONTINUE operation resumes the application after a breakpoint. The RESTART operation restarts the application from scratch.

These application debugging facilities allow the designer to develop an

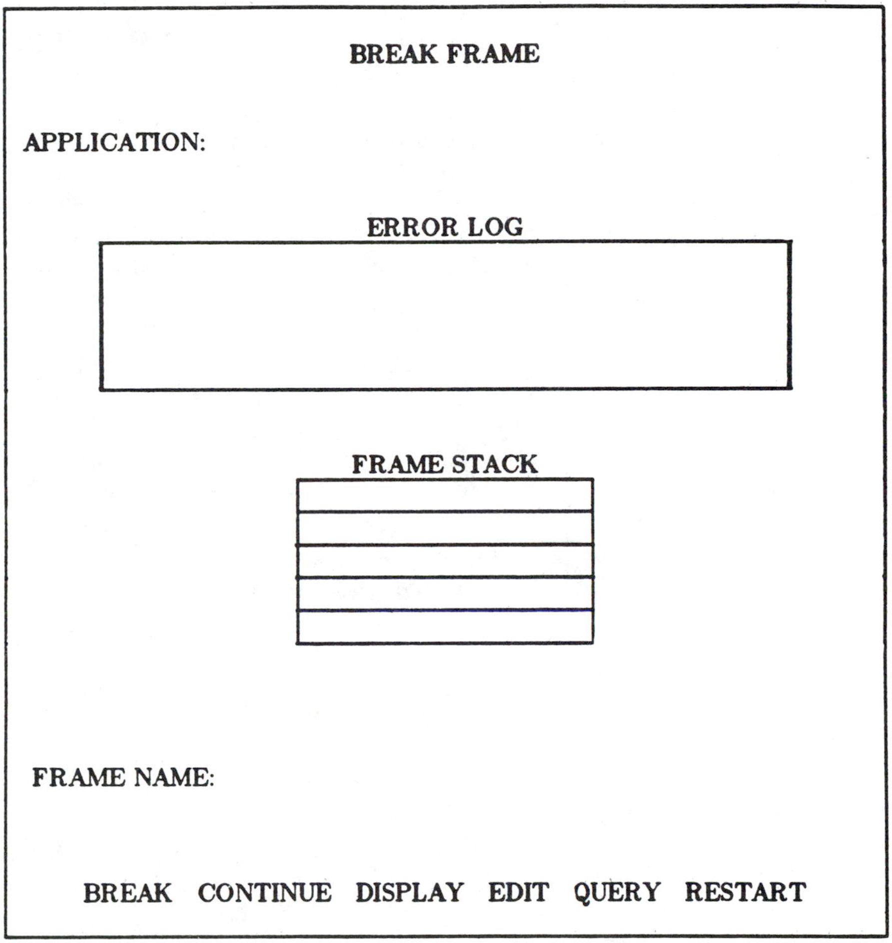

FIGURE 16.7. The BREAK Frame

application incrementally. It is not necessary to write the entire application before testing a portion of it. A piece as small as a single-frame can be written separately and tested. If the frame references an undefined object, the definition of the object can be specified using the EDIT operation of the BREAK frame, and the application resumed. This section described the facilities provided for testing and debugging a FADS application. These facilities provide convenient access to all the tools a designer will need: a relation editor, an application editor, a break point package, and access to the intermediate values in the application.

5.0. CURRENT IMPLEMENTATION AND FUTURE EXTENSIONS

This section briefly describes the implementation of FADS, the current status of the system, and the extensions we plan to make to it.

The FADS system runs as two processes: the database system (INGRES) and the FADS kernel. The kernel has three components: the frame driver, the executive, and the frame cache. The "frame driver" uses a terminal independent abstraction [ARNO81] which handles all input/output between a user and a terminal. This terminal abstraction allows FADS applications to run on any alphanumeric terminal with cursor addressing. The frame driver displays frames and the values in the forms inside, accepts input into forms, and passes operation requests to the FADS executive.

The "FADS executive" controls a running application. It loads and runs frames, executes queries, calls compiled procedures, and other control flow statements. The "frame cache" maintains an in-core copy of object definitions from the database to improve system performance.

The system is coded in C (approximately 15,000 lines) and runs on DEC VAX-11's [DIGI76] under the Virtual Memory UNIX[3] operating system [BABA79]. The INGRES interface is coded in EQUEL [ALLM76].

The current system has implemented the features described in the previous sections for running FADS applications. These features include: entering and displaying data through forms (tuple and relation forms), executing frames and operations, and executing the internal representation of an operation (running parameterized queries, displaying the output of a query in a form, and calling frames and procedures with arguments). The application development frames have been implemented and we are currently experimenting with the system.

The current system can be extended and improved in three general directions: adding new kinds of forms, using a personal computer for the user-interface, and providing more application development tools. These directions are discussed in the remainder of this section.

Many applications have forms which change depending on the data entered into a field. A simple example is an employee form with a marital status field. Depending on the marital status, different information is required (e.g., for married employees the spouse's name may be required while for divorced employees only the children's names, if any, are required). Popup forms which are displayed only if a specified condition is met (e.g., status is married) provide good feedback to the application user indicating

---

[3] UNIX is a trademark of Bell Laboratories.

what fields require values. The problem with popup forms is that the frame definitions which contain them are harder to understand because the forms displayed vary. Nevertheless, we plan to experiment with popup forms and frames for displaying their definitions.

Another kind of form which is currently being added to the system is graphical forms. These forms allow graphs, bar and pie charts, and scatter plots to be displayed. We are using a color graphics terminal so we will also be looking at display enhancements based on color.

The second set of extensions involves using a personal computer with a bit-mapped display and a mouse for the user interface. Besides using the mouse to select operations, values in enumerated type fields, and tuples in relation forms, we want to allow more user control of the amount of screen space used by a field or form. We also want to move the frame driver component, and possibly the entire FADS kernel described above, into the personal computer.

The last area to explore is in the development of more application development tools. Because the application description is stored in the data dictionary in the database, it will be very easy to develop tools which show the application at varying levels of detail. For example, a graph showing what frames call which other frames can be displayed. Or, the designer could ask questions like "what frames have operations which can update relation R?"

Another possibility is to display in real-time where each entity (e.g., bug report) is in the system. These higher level abstractions will make applications easier to write and maintain because the developers will not have to wade through as much detailed code to discover what the system is doing.

6.0. SUMMARY

This paper has described the Form Application Development System and shown how it can be used to develop interactive, form-based database applications quickly. FADS provides an integrated development environment that includes an application editor, a screen layout editor, a relation editor, and an interactive debugger.

ACKNOWLEDGEMENTS

We would like to thank Joe Cortopassi, Tom Morgan, John Ousterhout, and Mike Stonebraker for their comments on an earlier draft of this paper.

5

Extended Semantics for the Relational Model

This section presents four papers that explore extended semantics for the relational model. The conventional relational model is well suited to business data processing applications, but has limitations when used for nonbusiness applications. Most of the papers in the literature use examples from this domain of discourse, such as SUPPLIER, PART, SUPPLY, EMPLOYEE, DEPT, and so forth. Services provided by current database systems appeal to this application area. For example, the programming language interface and transaction management system are designed around the needs of business transaction processing applications.

Several years ago, the Defense Advanced Research Projects Agency (DARPA) started a new program in VLSI design. Several universities, including Berkeley, became involved in that program and devoted substantial effort to building VLSI design tools such as compacters, layout editors, routers, and so forth. It became clear to me that a VLSI circuit is a LARGE database; moreover, the VLSI tool builders were hard at work inventing special purpose database systems. At Berkeley, these were largely built on top of the UNIX file system. The VLSI folks often asked for some form of transaction management, protection, views, and access methods. These services are already provided by a database management system for the business data processing arena.

What I perceived was a tendency for special purpose applications to invent their own database facilities. Over time, such facilities tend to grow in an ad-hoc fashion until they resemble general purpose database systems in size and function. Several current Computer Aided Design (CAD) vendors find their software in exactly this situation today.

In my opinion, special applications should attempt to use a general purpose database system, extended if necessary with functions specific to the application at hand. There are two reasons for this opinion:

1) Most applications have at least some ordinary business data. For example, a CAD application containing a schematic for a printed circuit board would probably also have information on outside suppliers for components on that board. Such data is the standard SUPPLIER, PARTS, SUPPLY database, which is naturally handled by a relational system. A query such as, "find me the total parts cost of a particular board" requires constructing a join between business data (presumably relational) and CAD data. To answer such queries, a database system must have at least the power of a relational one. Moreover, it seems most natural to extend a relational database system with extra facilities appropriate to CAD rather than constructing a new database system from scratch.

2) Special purpose database systems tend to grow like a cancer over time and end up as unwieldy, unmaintainable packages.

Consequently, many researchers (including myself) have been looking for ways to allow current relational database systems to be more effective in various new application areas. These areas include:

1) CAD applications,
2) Applications with a lot of textual data (e.g., text editors),
3) Applications with pictorial data (e.g., satellite images),
4) Applications with spatial data (e.g., maps),
5) Applications with waveform data (e.g., voice),
6) Applications with large arrays (e.g., seismic systems).

Most of these require facilities not found in current relational systems. We discuss the requirements of CAD data to illustrate the problem.

CAD systems are almost always built upon the concept of versions. Hence, there is a "current" version of the database and, perhaps, several parallel groups making exploratory changes. For example, an airplane wing might have a group working on the cowling and another group working on the flaps. Each group has its own "hypothetical" version of the database which is undergoing modification. When the group is satisfied with its design changes, it makes public its version to other groups. Hence, at any time there may be several different "hypothetical" versions of the database, some of which may eventually be "committed." Moreover, some of the hypothetical changes may conflict.

It is almost impossible to model this environment with a conventional transaction management system. Write commands hold locks until the end of a transaction. If a user wishes to back out his work then he must specify transactions that last for days or weeks. The concurrency control system of all current database systems will refuse two updates that conflict and is not set up to expect transactions which last for a long time.

Another problem is that CAD data is often spatial in nature. An airplane wing has large portions which are coordinates of components. In addition, many parts are three dimensional objects. It is tedious to model such objects by the data types appropriate to business data processing applications (e.g., floating point numbers, integers, character strings, and so forth). Moreover, standard CAD tasks, such as, "find me all the parts that are contained in a particular geographic region of the airplane wing" become exceptionally difficult to express with conventional relational operators.

A last problem is that CAD designers often have a private workstation on which to perform their design modifications. Hence, it is practical to perform database functions on their workstation computer. This is much less prevalent in transaction processing environments where a 3270-class terminal is the standard operator's console. In addition, a design engineer tends to browse over large quantities of data making a few updates. This contrasts with an order-entry clerk who examines only a few records and updates many. Hence, buffering requirements may be substantially different in CAD environments.

It is clear that current conventional relational database systems do not perform well in CAD environments. This same statement appears to hold in the other example applications mentioned. The research issue is to cleverly extend relational systems and overcome these disadvantages. The relational model enjoys great acceptance because it is a small set of very powerful concepts. In my opinion, one should strive for extensions that have this same theme: namely great power at very small cost in intellectual complexity. The problem with older database systems is excessive complexity, and one should not fall into the same trap again.

In my opinion, the correct extensions have not yet been discovered because the current collection of possibilities is not yet of "spartan simplicity." This section offers four papers that propose various extensions in the theme of the above discussion. These are:

- Columns of relations can be of a user defined type (1st paper),
- An approach to versions (2nd paper),

- Ordered relations (3rd paper),
- QUEL commands as values of a column of a relation (4th paper).

I look forward to considerably more research in this area over the next few years.

## CHAPTER SEVENTEEN

Application of Abstract Data Types and Abstract Indices to CAD Data

Michael Stonebraker / Brad Rubenstein / Antonin Guttman

ABSTRACT

This paper explores the use of one form of abstract data types in CAD databases. Basically, new data types for columns of a relation, such as boxes, wires and polygons, become possible. Also explored is the possibility of secondary indices for new data types that can support existing and user-defined operators. The performance and query complexity considerations of these features are examined.

1.0. INTRODUCTION

It has been pointed out [HASK82, KATZ82b] that Computer Aided Design (CAD) applications are not particularly well suited to current relational database management systems. Extensions or modifications appear desirable to deal with the following issues:

1) Support for new data types such as polygons, rectagons, text strings, etc.

2) Support for efficient spatial searching.

3) Support for complex integrity constraints.

---

4)   Support for design hierarchies and multiple representations.

The first issue arises because CAD applications are not well served by the integers, floating point numbers and character strings prevalent in business data processing applications. Moreover, spatial searching is needed for design operations that involve objects which fall in a specific area, such as the display of a portion of a VLSI design on a CRT screen. Spatial searching is not effectively supported by existing general purpose DBMSs. The third issue arises because CAD designers often wish complex integrity constraints, such as integrated circuit layout rules, to be enforced for their data.

The last issue arises because many design environments have hierarchical levels of detail. For example, a VLSI integrated circuit might have several intermediate levels of detail between one containing the whole chip as a single black box and the one containing detailed spatial masks for circuit cells at the lowest level. These intermediate levels suppress details irrelevant to that particular level, and a designer can use whatever level of detail fits his particular needs. In addition, more than one view of the design may exist simultaneously, giving multiple overlapping representations for database objects. An example would be a bit-slice design for a CPU. For purposes of describing its physical construction, the design is made up of several parallel bit-slices, but a functional block diagram may consist of separate boxes for the ALU, register file, etc.

In [KATZ82b] several approaches are suggested for various of the above issues. In this paper we report on the success observed using one approach, abstract data types, as a solution to issue 1) and issue 2) above.

The remainder of this paper is organized as follows. In Section 2.0 we briefly review our use of abstract data types. A more complete discussion appears in [STON82a]. Then in Section 3.0 we describe extensions to secondary index facilities to support abstract data types. Extended secondary indices can provide efficient spatial searching as well as other kinds of indexing. Next, in Section 4.0 we apply abstract data types to a database of VLSI design information used in [GUTT82]. Lastly, in Section 5.0 we report on the performance implications of abstract data types by redoing the performance comparison between a relational database system and a special purpose CAD system reported in [GUTT82] and performing other experiments.

2.0. ABSTRACT DATA TYPES

Abstract data types (ADTs) [LISK74, GUTT77] have been extensively investigated in a programming language context. Basically, an ADT is an encapsulation of a data structure (so that its implementation details are not visible to an outside client procedure) along with a collection of related operations on this encapsulated structure. The canonical example of an ADT is a stack with related operations: new, push, pop and empty.

ADTs have been considered extensively in the context of semantic data modeling and as a central theme in database system implementation [LOCK79]. Moreover, the use of ADTs in a relational database context has been discussed in [ROWE79b, SCHM78, WASS79]. In these proposals a relation is an abstract data type whose implementation details are hidden from application level software. Then, allowable operations are defined by procedures written in a programming language that supports both database access and ADTs. One use of this kind of abstract data type is suggested in [ROWE79b] and involves an EMPLOYEE abstract data type with related operations hire-employee, fire-employee and change-salary. This use of ADTs can also limit access to a relation in prespecified ways, thereby guaranteeing a higher level of data security and data integrity. Also, a view [STON75] can be defined as an ADT. Consequently, the algorithm that transforms updates on views into updates on relations actually stored in the database can be encapsulated in the ADT, thereby providing a high degree of data independence.

This section presents a different use of ADTs, in particular for individual columns of a relation. The goal is to extend the semantic power of a relational database system by providing for the definition of new data types and related operators on these data types by means of defined procedures obeying a specialized protocol. This use of ADTs is a generalization of database experts [STON80c]. We explain our use of ADTs with an extended example concerning geometric objects.

In computer aided design of integrated circuits, objects are often made up of small rectangular pieces called "boxes." For a VLSI database one would like to be able to define a column of a relation of type "box." For example, one might define a boxes relation as follows:

> CREATE BOXES (OWNER = i4,
>   LAYER = c15,
>   BOX-DESC = BOX-ADT)

Here, the BOXES relation has three fields: the identifier of the circuit of which each box is a part, the processing layer for the box (polysilicon, diffusion, etc.) and a description of the box's geometry. All fields are represented by standard built-in types except BOX-DESC which is a data type added by an ADT implementor.

Tuples can be added to this relation using QUEL [STON76a] as follows:

> APPEND TO BOXES (OWNER = 99,
>   LAYER = "polysilicon",
>   BOX-DESC = "0,0,2,3")

Clearly, all fields can be correctly converted to an internal representation and stored in a database system with the exception of the string "0,0,2,3", which represents the box bounded by $x=0$, $y=0$, $x=2$, $y=3$. In order to be interpreted as the description of a box, special recognition code is required. Basically an input procedure must be available to the DBMS to perform the conversion of the character string "0,0,2,3" to an object with data type BOX-ADT. Such a routine is analogous to the procedure ascii-to-float which converts a character string to a floating point number. A DBMS has a collection of built-in conversion routines for standard types, and our proposal entails allowing additional conversion routines to be supplied by an ADT implementor.

One would also like to use standard DBMS operators on the BOX-ADT domain, e.g.,

```
RANGE OF B IS BOXES
REPLACE B (BOX-DESC = B.BOX-DESC * "0,0,4,1")
    WHERE B.OWNER = 99
```

The intended effect of this command is to replace the box by its intersection with another box. The intended semantics of * are those of intersection; consequently, the data manager must be instructed how to interpret the multiplication of two objects of type BOX-ADT. In this case "0,0,4,1" will be converted to an object of type BOX-ADT to match the type of B.BOX-DESC, and a procedure must be available to perform the appropriate multiplication.

Next one would like to define new functions on the BOX-ADT column. Numerical columns have sin, cos, log, etc. defined as built-in functions. Each of these accepts an integer or floating point number as input and returns a floating point number. Similarly, one might want to define a function that calculates the area of a box and use it in data manipulation commands, e.g.,

```
RETRIEVE (B.OWNER)
WHERE AREA(B.BOX-DESC) > 100
```

One must define for the database manager the function AREA which accepts a BOX-ADT as input and returns an integer.

In addition, one might want to define new comparison operations. For example, one might wish to define the concept "overlaps" for boxes, and to have a corresponding operator, "| |", defined for this purpose. The overlap operator could then be used to ask if there were any box overlapping the unit square based at the origin as follows:

```
RANGE OF B IS BOXES
RETRIEVE (B.BOX-DESC)
    WHERE B.BOX-DESC | | "0,0,1,1"
```

Not surprisingly, a procedure defined by the ADT implementor for the | | operator is required.

Lastly, one would like to be able to define aggregate functions for the new type. For example, one would like to be able to find the owner of the box with the largest vertical dimension on the polysilicon layer:

> RETRIEVE (B.OWNER) WHERE B.BOX-DESC =
>   TALLEST(B.BOX-DESC WHERE B.LAYER = "polysilicon")

Again, a routine is required to define the TALLEST function for the new data type.

As a result an ADT is the following abstraction:

1) a registration procedure whereby a DBMS is informed of the existence of the new type and given the length of its internal representation.

2) a collection of routines which define the semantics of operators for this type and perform conversions to other types. These routines must obey a prespecified protocol for accepting arguments and returning results. Once defined by the ADT implementor, the new type and operators become available to other users of the DBMS.

3) small changes to the parser and query execution engine to correctly parse commands with new operators and call the routines defined by the ADT implementor when appropriate during execution.

This abstraction has been implemented in the INGRES relational database system and is about 2500 lines of code. Details on implementation issues concerning parser tables, overloading of operators, security and dynamic loading of routines are addressed in [FOGG82, ONG82]. It appears to execute with modest performance degradation [FOGG82]. It should be noted that the implementation also allows definition of new operators and functions for ordinary data types.

3.0. EXTENDED SECONDARY INDICES

The preceding section has indicated a mechanism for adding new data types and new operators to a relational database system. This section explores the possibility of supporting secondary indices in this more general environment.

Traditionally, secondary indices provide a fast access path to required data items when a query specifies an exact match with a user specified value or a comparison operator applied with a specified value. For example, if secondary indices exist for the NAME and SALARY fields of an EMP relation, then the queries

> RANGE OF E IS EMPLOYEE
> RETRIEVE (E.SALARY) WHERE E.NAME = "Jones"
> RETRIEVE (E.NAME) WHERE E.SALARY > 1000

can be answered by using indices.

Since new operators can be defined for normal data types and for new ADT data types, one would want the following capabilities:

1)   Indices on ADT columns with existing operators.

For example, consider the situation where salaries of employees are stored as packed decimal numbers. Since this is not one of the built-in data types in many systems, an ADT is required. One would want to index salary so that the above query could be answered effectively. In this case extending an indexed sequential access method to support the new data type will be adequate.

2)   Indices on normal columns using new operators.

For example, consider the query:

        RANGE OF E IS EMP
        RETRIEVE (E.NAME) WHERE E.NAME !! 7

which requests the names of employees whose names are exactly 7 characters long. The new operator !! counts the number of non-blank characters in a name and compares the result to an integer operand. One would want a secondary index for the !! operator so that this query could be efficiently answered. Clearly, an index which provided a bin for each possible length would be appropriate.

3)   Indices on ADT columns with new operators.

Consider the query from Section 2 to find all the boxes that intersect the unit square at the origin:

        RANGE OF B IS BOXES
        RETRIEVE (B.BOX-DESC)
            WHERE B.BOX-DESC | | "0,0,1,1"

We need an index that will allow retrieval of only the boxes that qualify, or will at least restrict the search to a small subset of the BOXES relation.

The objective of this section is to propose a scheme which supports all three capabilities above. It has always been our position that an appropriate collection of access methods should be provided by any DBMS and that it should be easy to add new ones [STON76a]. Hence, our goal is to allow any access method to operate in the more general context of ADTs. Hashing and indexed-sequential (ISAM) are the access methods currently supported by INGRES, and we focus the discussion on extending these. As a running example, we use the BOXES relation defined above.

An index can be created using the INGRES index command:

INDEX ON BOXES IS B-INDEX (BOX-DESC)

This will create a relation of the following form which will be used as a secondary index:

B-INDEX (BOX-DESC, POINTER-TO-TUPLE)

A row exists in B-INDEX for each row in the BOXES relation and contains the BOX-DESC field along with a pointer to the given tuple in boxes. The index B-INDEX is initially stored as a heap and must be modified to hash or ISAM to be useful. For example:

MODIFY B-INDEX TO HASH ON BOX-DESC USING My-function

The only change to the current MODIFY command is the inclusion of a US-ING clause. INGRES normally builds hashed secondary indices by allocating a number of buckets, then reading the tuples one by one, calling its internal hash function to obtain a bucket number and storing the tuple in the correct bucket. In this context INGRES calls My-function instead of its built-in hash-ing function to obtain bucket numbers. My-function must be a valid func-tion registered through the ADT registration facility which expects a BOX-ADT as an argument and returns an integer. No other modifications are re-quired to the code if My-function returns a single integer.

However, suppose we have a grid in the x-y plane as shown in Figure 17.1, and we want My-function, when passed a box, to return the numbers of all the grid cells that it intersects. Grid cell zero is reserved for boxes which extend outside the boundary of the above structure. In this situation My-function returns a list of buckets instead of a single bucket number and INGRES must insert a row in the appropriate bucket in B-INDEX for each

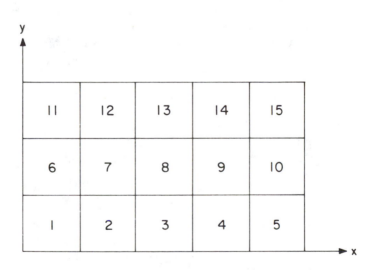

FIGURE 17.1. A Grid Structure for My-function

value in the list. The MODIFY command for this structure is

> MODIFY B-INDEX TO HASH ON BOX-DESC
>   USING My-function (param-list)

Here param-list is a character string containing necessary information such as the number and size of the grid squares and the location of the grid in the plane. These values could be hard-wired into My-function, but it is preferable that they be settable for each index.

We now illustrate how to use an ISAM structure with new columns and operators. Again, we could run the following MODIFY command:

> MODIFY B-INDEX TO ISAM (BOX-DESC) USING <+

Normally, an ISAM structure is built by sorting the values for BOX-DESC using the built-in operator < to define the sort order. In this case the index can be built in an analogous way by substituting the operator <+ to define some ordering on boxes, for example by comparing their areas. <+ would be expected to compare two box descriptions and return true or false if one was "less than" the other. The ISAM structure would then support the ordering determined by <+.

Once a hashed or ISAM secondary index is created for the boxes relation, one must specify to INGRES how the index can be used in processing queries. INGRES has a built-in function, FIND, for hashed structures which will return the hash buckets which must be inspected for tuples which satisfy a particular query. In the current implementation a hash bucket is identical to a UNIX page, so FIND returns a collection of pages. An analogous FIND function returns a collection of pages for an ISAM structure. These functions are called by specifying the value used in a qualification and the operator involved. For example, for the qualification

> WHERE E.SALARY > 1000

FIND is called with parameters > and 1000. In our extended environment, a FIND function must be provided for each possible operator for which the index can be used. We propose a new INGRES command for the purpose, i.e.,

> USE B-INDEX WITH Find-function
>   FOR (| | BOX-ADT, BOX-ADT | |)

This command specifies the circumstances under which the routine, Find-function, should be called to provide the required collection of pages to search. The above example indicates that this function is appropriate when the intersection operator | | is encountered connecting a variable and a value of type BOX-ADT. Moreover, the value can be on either side of the | | operator. For example, suppose one submitted the query:

> RANGE OF B IS BOXES
> RETRIEVE (B.ALL)
> WHERE B.BOX-DESC | | "0,0,1,1"

The string on the right is converted automatically to an object of type BOX-ADT because | | is defined to take BOX-ADT arguments. After the conversion, the qualification is of the form

> WHERE B.BOX-DESC | | BOX-ADT

and therefore B-INDEX can be used to process the query. The ADT function Find-function is called to return a list of pages which must be examined. Then, INGRES simply iterates over the list examining each index entry, following the appropriate pointer, obtaining a tuple from boxes and finally evaluating the user's qualification to ascertain if it is satisfied for the tuple in question.

It is possible to define different FIND routines for different operators as illustrated below. Suppose one defines a new operator "#|" which compares a box and a line and returns true if the box is "to the left of" the line. The index B-INDEX can be used to process queries involving the #| operator; however, a new FIND function must be used:

> USE B-INDEX WITH Second-fn FOR (#| LINE-ADT)

A user can submit a query such as

> RETRIEVE (B.ALL)
> WHERE B.BOX-DESC #| "0,0,1,3"

whereby he wants to see all boxes which are to the left of the line from (0,0) to (1,3). If the grid structure for B-INDEX from Figure 17.1 is one unit long on each side, then the boxes which qualify must lie in grid cells 1, 6, 11 or 0 and the others can be excluded. The function Second-fn can provide the needed semantics.

When more than one index can be used to process an INGRES query, e.g.,

> WHERE B.BOX-DESC | | "0,0,1,1"
>   AND B.BOX-DESC #| "0,0,1,3"

then INGRES must choose which index to use in processing the query. This is currently done by a hard-wired strategy routine. To be able to choose in the above context, this routine must be generalized to call both Find-functions to obtain lists of pages and then compare the sizes of the results, choosing the smaller list for iteration.

▩▩▩▩ 4.0. APPLICATION OF ABSTRACT DATA TYPES

In [GUTT82] we described a CAD database consisting of integrated circuit descriptions as stored by a special purpose graphics editor, KIC [KELL81]. A KIC database consists of a collection of circuit "cells." Each cell can contain mask geometry and subcell references. Circuit designs are hierarchical; a complete design expands into a tree, with a single cell at the root and instances of other cells, used as subcells, for the non-root nodes. Cells are the building blocks used to construct a circuit and include such objects as buffers, NOR gates and at a higher level, PLAs and arithmetic logic units.

In [GUTT82] we also described a relational schema which models this database consisting of five main relations:

CELL-MASTER (NAME, AUTHOR, MASTER-ID)

BOX (OWNER, LAYER, X1, X2, Y1, Y2)

WIRE (OWNER, LAYER, WIRE-ID, WIDTH, X1, Y1, X2, Y2)

POLYGON (OWNER, LAYER, POLYGON-ID, VERTNUM, X, Y)

CELL-REF (PARENT, CHILD, CELL-REF-ID, T11-T32)

In the CELL-MASTER relation, NAME is the textual name given to the cell and AUTHOR is the name of the person who designed it. MASTER-ID is a unique identification number assigned to each cell. It is used for unambiguous references to the cell within the database.

The BOX relation describes mask rectangles. OWNER is the identifier of the cell of which the box is a part. LAYER specifies the processing layer, e.g., "polysilicon" or "diffusion." X1 and X2 are the x-coordinates of the left and right sides of the box while Y1 and Y2 are the y-coordinates of the top and bottom.

A "wire" is a set of lines that serves to make an electrical connection between different parts of a circuit. Each tuple in the WIRE relation describes one line segment, giving the coordinates of its centerline (X1, Y1, X2, Y2) and its WIDTH. WIRE-ID is a unique identifier for a particular wire. OWNER and LAYER mean the same as in the BOX relation.

A polygon is a closed figure with any number of vertices. One vertex is stored in each tuple of the POLYGON relation. X and Y are the coordinates of the vertex, and VERTNUM orders the vertices (tuples) within one polygon.

Each CELL-REF tuple describes the use of one cell as a part of another, i.e., as a subcell. For example, suppose that the cell REGISTER contained several LATCH subcells. Then, there would be several CELL-REF tuples, each containing the identifier of the REGISTER cell in the PARENT field, and the identifier of the LATCH cell in the CHILD field. T11 through T32 are a 3 X 2 matrix of floating point numbers specifying the location, orientation and scale of each subcell with respect to its parent. This representation of a spatial transform is the one generally used in computer graphics [NEWM79].

To apply abstract data types to this application, we suggest the following:

1) A data type BOX-ADT.

   The internal representation of a box can be four integers representing the locations of the top, bottom and side boundaries. The external representation can be a character string consisting of numbers separated by commas, e.g., "0,0,1,1".

2) A data type POLYGON-ADT.

   The internal representation can be a fixed length string of integers if a maximum number of vertices is specifiable. For example, if 25 vertices are allowable, then 50 integers can represent any polygon. If no upper bound is possible, then ADTs can still be used. One can allocate a polygon file external to the database system which will be used to store polygon descriptions. When a new polygon is inserted, it will be physically placed in the external file (say using a first fit or best fit placement algorithm). The input conversion routine will then return a byte offset and length which will be stored as a fixed length object in the database.

3) A data type WIRE-ADT.

   If all segments of a wire are the same width, then the internal representation can be one integer for the width and four integers for each segment giving the coordinates of the endpoints.

4) A data type "array of floats."

   The internal representation is the obvious one for the required 3x2 matrix, T11, .., T32.

With these new data types we can simplify the schema above to:

> CELL-MASTER (NAME, AUTHOR, MASTER-ID, DEFINED)
>
> BOX (OWNER, LAYER, BOX-DESC)
>
> WIRE (OWNER, LAYER, WIRE-DESC)
>
> POLYGON (OWNER, LAYER, POLYGON-DESC)
>
> CELL-REF (PARENT, CHILD, CELL-REF-ID, ORIENTATION)

Notice that BOX-DESC, WIRE-DESC, POLYGON-DESC and ORIENTATION are all new types.

The performance experiments in [GUTT82] involved three common operations on VLSI data, namely retrieval of the top level geometry for a given circuit cell, full expansion of a design tree and retrieval of the top level geometry which falls in a particular geographic area. We express the first and third queries for the original INGRES schema below. Then, we introduce new operators for our abstract data types which will simplify the description of these queries.

In the following set of queries which retrieve the top level geometry, CELLID identifies the cell to be displayed. The first two queries simply retrieve all the boxes and wire segments belonging directly to the designated cell in any order. The third query, which retrieves polygon vertices, is more complicated because the vertices must be produced in the correct order and grouped by POLYGON-ID and LAYER in order to simulate the operation of KIC. All polygon data belonging to the given cell is first gathered into a temporary relation, which is then sorted, and finally the data is retrieved from the temporary and passed to the user. In the actual performance tests data was retrieved separately for each layer to accurately emulate the operation of KIC.

```
RANGE OF B IS BOX          /* repeated for each layer */
RETRIEVE (B.X1, B.Y1, B.X2, B.Y2)
WHERE B.OWNER = CELLID AND B.LAYER = value

RANGE OF W IS WIRE         /* repeated for each layer */
RETRIEVE (W.LAYER, W.X1, W.Y1, W.X2, W.Y2)
WHERE W.OWNER = CELLID AND W.LAYER = value

RANGE OF P IS POLYGON
RETRIEVE INTO PTEMP (P.LAYER, P.POLYGON-ID, P.VERTNUM,
    P.X, P.Y)
WHERE P.OWNER = CELLID AND P.LAYER = value

MODIFY PTEMP TO HEAPSORT ON LAYER, POLYGON-ID,
    VERTNUM

RANGE OF PT IS PTEMP       /* repeated for each layer */
RETRIEVE (PT.LAYER, PT.POLYGON-ID, PT.X, PT.Y)
```

The query below retrieves polygons from the top level geometry which fall in a specific geographic window. Left, Right, Bottom and Top are numbers giving the boundaries of the window. Again, the MODIFY command is required to correctly order polygon vertices.

```
RANGE OF P IS POLYGON
RETRIEVE INTO PTEMP (P.LAYER, P.POLYGON-ID, P.VERTNUM, P.X,
    P.Y)
WHERE P.OWNER = CELLID

MODIFY PTEMP TO HEAPSORT ON LAYER, POLYGON-ID, VERTNUM
RANGE OF PT IS PTEMP
RETRIEVE (PT.LAYER, PT.POLYGON-ID, PT.X, PT.Y)
WHERE MAX(PT.X BY PT.POLYGON-ID) > Left
AND   MIN(PT.X BY PT.POLYGON-ID) < Right
AND   MAX(PT.Y BY PT.POLYGON-ID) > Bottom
AND   MIN(PT.Y BY PT.POLYGON-ID) < Top
```

With our abstract data types, we can rewrite the queries for top-level geometry as

RANGE OF B IS BOX
RETRIEVE (B.LAYER, B.BOX-DESC)
WHERE B.OWNER = CELLID AND B.LAYER = value

RANGE OF W IS WIRE
RETRIEVE (W.LAYER, W.WIRE-DESC)
WHERE W.OWNER = CELLID AND W.LAYER = value

RANGE OF P IS POLYGON
RETRIEVE (P.LAYER, P.POLYGON-DESC)
WHERE P.OWNER = CELLID AND P.LAYER = value

This version will run faster because the detailed representation of each kind of geometric object will be handled by special routines instead of the general purpose query interpreter. Polygon retrieval will be much faster, since it is no longer necessary for the database system to put the vertices in the correct order.

If we also use a polygon overlap operator $<>$ similar to the box overlap operator defined above, then we can rewrite the query for polygons in a specific window as

RANGE OF P IS POLYGON
RETRIEVE (P.LAYER, P.POLYGON-ID, P.POLYGON-DESC)
WHERE P.OWNER = CELLID
AND P.POLYGON-DESC $<>$ make-poly("Left,Right,Bottom,Top")

The new query has several advantages over the original one. First, it is much clearer once the meaning of $<>$ is understood, because we avoid the awkward collection of clauses in the qualification. Moreover, it will be faster because the test for overlap with the window can be done more efficiently in a special routine. Also, if an index using the $<>$ operator exists for POLYGON-DESC then INGRES can use it automatically to limit the number of polygons inspected. Since the original form of the qualification contained aggregates, no index could be effectively used and a search of all polygons was required.

5.0. PERFORMANCE COMPARISON

As noted in Section 4.0, performance improvement from the use of ADTs can be realized from four sources:

1) Manipulation of a smaller number of columns. For example, a box can be retrieved as a single column rather than as four constituent parts.

2) Manipulation of fewer tuples, for example when polygons are represented by single fixed-size tuples with vertex lists stored externally.

3) Simplification of queries due to the introduction of new operators. This is especially noticeable in spatial windowing.

4) Use of abstract indices.

In this section we report on three different experiments. First, we redo the performance comparison between KIC and INGRES noted in [GUTT82]. This shows the effect of sources 1, 2 and 3. Since abstract indices are not yet operational, our second experiment simulates abstract indices in INGRES in order to predict the performance improvement which we expect from source 4 with a full implementation. Our last experiment consists of retrieval of VLSI data represented as polygons instead of boxes. This shows the improvement from sources 2 and 3 and puts our current implementation in its best light.

In [GUTT82] a performance comparison was reported between KIC and INGRES for the operations mentioned in Section 4.0. This comparison was performed for databases corresponding to two VLSI circuits under development at Berkeley.

KIC stored the layout in virtual memory on a VAX 11/780 computer system using its own specially designed data structures. The test machine had enough main memory so that the layout could be entirely resident in primary memory. On the other hand INGRES stored the design as disk resident relations with only small portions in a main memory buffer pool. Hence, the performance comparison was between a system using special data structures mostly in main memory and a system using general purpose data structures mostly on disk. The two systems also differed in that KIC clipped geometries to fit an appropriate window on a graphics terminal while INGRES did not simulate this operation.

Figure 17.2 summarizes the results of the first experiment. The first two columns show the performance difference between KIC and INGRES. KIC is assigned unit response time and unit CPU usage while the performance of INGRES is indicated relative to the KIC time. Note that INGRES performs about a factor of 3 worse in CPU time and 5 worse in response time for the top level geometry and the tree expansion queries. For the spatial retrieval it is a factor of 20 worse in CPU time and 45 slower overall.

The reason for the poor performance on spatial windowing is that KIC contains a geographic bin structure for spatial indexing similar to that in Figure 17.1. No such indexing is present in INGRES. Consequently KIC does a restricted search while INGRES must perform an exhaustive one.

Figure 17.2 also shows the performance of ADT-INGRES, a version of INGRES with the addition of the abstract data types mentioned in Section 4.0 and an overlap operator. Notice that ADT-INGRES is about 10 percent slower than regular INGRES on the top level and tree expansion tests. This represents about half of the 20 percent extra overhead needed to run the more general environment according to the results reported in [FOGG82]. Source number 1 apparently accounts for the 10 percent difference. We anticipated that the addition of an overlap operator would improve performance

	KIC	INGRES	ADT-INGRES
Top level geometry			
-CPU	1	3.2	3.6
-response time	1	5.5	5.8
Tree expansion			
-CPU	1	3.5	3.9
-response time	1	5.1	5.6
Spatial window			
-CPU	1	20	24
-response time	1	45	51

FIGURE 17.2. Relative INGRES Performance

considerably on the spatial windowing test. However the results show no improvement, probably because the extra overhead incurred by loading the overlap routine dynamically at run time cancels out the time saved during the actual processing of tuples. Source 2, the processing of fewer tuples for ADTs, has almost no effect because the design data consists mostly of boxes, where the number of tuples is the same. Unfortunately, the test data included only one polygon in the top level geometry, and the polygon portion of the benchmark consumed almost no time. The designers of the circuit in question chose to rely primarily on boxes as a representation vehicle and not on polygons. All complex shapes in the circuit except one are made up of overlapping boxes.

The second experiment is intended to predict the improvement we can expect from abstract indices. We preprocessed the box, wire and polygon data to compute a spatial bin for each object. This bin was stored explicitly in the database and used as a key for a normal INGRES secondary index. The spatial windowing benchmark was redone with this simulated bucketing and the results are presented in Figure 17.3. Simulated bucketing should closely mimic an actual implementation of abstract indices and a performance improvement of nearly a factor of 2 should be realizable.

The third experiment illustrates the performance improvement that can be realized with ADTs when the data is in the form of polygons instead of boxes. Polygons offer an important advantage over boxes for representation of complex geometric objects, namely that each object can be stored explicitly as a single unit instead of being made up of many apparently separate boxes which may overlap. This advantage is clearly illustrated in design rule checking. When large shapes are composed of many boxes, an overlap may or

	KIC	INGRES	INGRES with bins
Spatial window			
-CPU		1	20
-response time	1	45	25

FIGURE 17.3. Performance of Simulated Spatial Index

may not be an error, but with single polygons an overlap is a clear error.

For the third experiment we converted the boxes of the design data into appropriate polygons, and compared the performance of normal INGRES with ADT-INGRES when retrieving top level polygons for a single cell. Without ADTs the query is

```
RANGE OF P IS POLYGON
RETRIEVE INTO PTEMP (P.ALL) WHERE P.OWNER = CELLID
RANGE OF PT IS PTEMP
MODIFY PTEMP TO HEAPSORT
ON LAYER, POLYGON-ID, VERTNUM
RETRIEVE (PT.X, PT.Y)
```

With ADTs the query becomes

```
RANGE OF P IS POLYGON
RETRIEVE INTO PTEMP (P.POLYGON-DESC)
    WHERE P.OWNER = CELLID
RANGE OF PT IS PTEMP
```

	INGRES	ADT-INGRES
Top level geometry		
-CPU	1	.57
-response time	1	.64

FIGURE 17.4. Polygon Retrieval

> MODIFY PTEMP TO HASH ON LAYER
> RETRIEVE (PT.POLYGON-DESC)

The results of the test are shown in Figure 17.4 on page 332.

These latter two tests suggest that our tactics can save nearly half of the INGRES overhead for CAD data that is polygon-rich. It is entirely possible that a more efficient version of ADT-INGRES coupled with abstract indices could be made attractive for CAD data from a performance viewpoint.

6.0. CONCLUSIONS

We have identified several issues that are important in the ongoing effort to improve the usefulness and performance of database systems for use in CAD applications, and have shown how ADT columns in relations and abstract secondary indices can solve some of these problems. We have described an implementation of ADT columns in INGRES and have presented measurements of performance improvement. Further work is in progress in the area of access methods to support multi-dimensional spatial searching and the implementation of abstract data type secondary indices.

## CHAPTER EIGHTEEN

An Implementation of Hypothetical Relations

John Woodfill / Michael Stonebraker

ABSTRACT

In this paper we present a new approach to implementing hypothetical relations. Our design borrows ideas from techniques used in processing views
and differential files and offers several advantages over other schemes. A
working implementation is described and performance statistics are presented.

1.0. INTRODUCTION

Hypothetical relations [STON80c, STON81, AGRA82] have been suggested as
a mechanism to allow users to generate alternate versions of real relations.
Each version can be updated as if it were a real relation; however, only
differences between the hypothetical relation (HR) and the real relation on
which it is defined are actually stored. Previous papers have concentrated on
data structures for representing these differences and algorithms for processing data manipulation commands addressed to HR's.

HR's correspond closely to the notion of versions [BONA77] used in
systems which manage iterations of computer programs. On the other hand,
HR's differ fundamentally from views in that updates to HR's should NOT
cause changes to the relation on which they are defined. An update to a
view is reflected through to the base relation(s) underneath it.

Consider for example, a university financial officer who is in charge of
research assistants' salaries. Suppose she is trying to balance her budget and
wants to know whether her accounts would balance under the hypothetical
scenario that salaries of senior employees were cut by 20%. She could make
a new copy of her database, actually perform the appropriate updates, and

---

J. Woodfill, M. Stonebraker, *Proceedings of the Ninth Very Large Data Base Conference*, Florence, Ita-
ly, December 1983. Reprinted with permission of the VLDB Endowment; copyright © 1983.

then survey the results. This procedure would be slow and require considerable disk space. Alternatively she could define an HR on the employee relation, perform her updates on the HR, and then survey the results.

Another use of database HR's might be in debugging a database application program. The programmer might not want to test his program on "live" data because a logical error could corrupt the database. He could define an HR on the live data and test the program on this HR.

The implementation suggested in [STON80c] involves a single differential file [SEVR76]. A more elegant solution [STON81] suggests supporting HR's by using the view mechanism [STON75] already present in many relational systems. A hypothetical relation, W, for a real relation R would be defined as a view of the form W = (R UNION S) DIFFERENCE T. To support this implementation of HR's, one need only extend a relational DBMS and its associated view mechanism with the UNION and DIFFERENCE operators. A possible advantage of this implementation is that R can be a read-only relation while S and T are append-only. This leads to the possibility of implementation on an optical disk.

Unfortunately, there are problems with defining HR's as views. We first examine these problems and show general solutions in Section 2.0. Then in Section 3.0 we combine these solutions into a new mechanism for supporting HR's. Our implementation of this solution is described in Section 4.0. Finally, we present performance statistics from our running prototype in Section 5.0.

2.0. PROBLEMS AND SOLUTIONS

Proposals for implementing hypothetical relations as views contain various flaws which must be removed before a realistic implementation can be attempted.

2.1. The Re-Insertion Problem

[STON81] points out that the implementation of hypothetical relations as W = (R UNION S) DIFFERENCE T is flawed in the case where one wants to re-append a tuple which has been deleted, as shown by the example in Figure 18.1. Initially there is a tuple in relation R corresponding to Eric. Following the algorithm in [STON81], the tuple can be deleted by inserting it into relation T. Lastly a user re-appends Eric and an appropriate tuple is inserted into S. Unfortunately, the resulting hypothetical relation, W, does not contain the re-appended tuple since (R UNION S) is the same as R, and R DIFFERENCE T is empty.

R			S			T		
NAME	SALARY		NAME	SALARY		NAME	SALARY	
eric	10000		eric	10000		eric	10000	

FIGURE 18.1. A Re-Appended Tuple

2.2. A Solution Using Timestamps

As noted in [AGRA82], this problem can be solved by adding a timestamp field to the relations S and T, and modifying the semantics of the DIFFER-ENCE operator. Tuples in R do not require a timestamp field and can be thought of as having a timestamp of zero.

The timestamp field is set to the current time (from a system clock, or any other monotonically increasing source of timestamps) whenever a tuple is appended to S or T. For any relations A and B with timestamps as described, A DIFFERENCE B is defined as all tuples a in A for which there is no tuple b in B such that

1)   DATA(a) = DATA(b), and

2)   TIMESTAMP(a) < TIMESTAMP(b)

The definition of R UNION S is unchanged, except that a timestamp field must be added to the result, which contains either the timestamp of a tuple in S, or a zero timestamp for a tuple in R. If tuples with identical DATA appear in both R and S, the newer timestamp (from S) is chosen for the result tuple.

In the above example, the timestamp of Eric's tuple in T would be newer than that of Eric's tuple in R (zero), but would be older than the timestamp of Eric's tuple in S; hence, (R UNION S) DIFFERENCE T would be equivalent to S, and W would contain the re-appended tuple.

[KATZ82c] suggests solving the problem of re-appended tuples by adding a unique identifier (termed a Surrogate) to each tuple. Thus if a tuple is deleted from an HR, the appended tuple in T has the same Surrogate as the tuple to be deleted. If a tuple with the same DATA is subsequently appended, it will have a new Surrogate, and hence be distinct. Neither [AGRA82] nor [KATZ82c] deals with the multi-level HR's to be discussed next.

2.3. The Multiple-Level Problem

The addition of timestamps solves the re-insertion problem. However, this solution does not work for multi-level HR's. Consider the case of a second level hypothetical relation, W' = (W UNION S') DIFFERENCE T', as shown in Figure 18.2. Suppose Eric has been given a 20 percent raise in W' at timestamp 10 which caused the indicated entries in S' and T'. Since no updates have occurred in W, S and T are empty. Now suppose a user gives Eric a 50 percent raise in W at timestamp 20, which results in the entries for S and T shown in Figure 18.3. According to the algorithm above, W' would contain two tuples for Eric, one with salary 15,000, and one with salary 12,000. The problem is that the tuple in T' no longer functions to exclude Eric from W UNION S' and hence an unwanted Eric tuple is present.

There are at least two choices for the proper semantics for W' under this update pattern:

1)   Eric's salary is set to the latest value, in this case the 15,000 from W.

2)   Eric's salary is set to 12,000, corresponding to the original update of W'.

We make the latter choice, and specify the following semantics:

Once a tuple has been changed at level N, changes to this tuple at levels < N cannot affect tuples at levels ≥ N.

R

NAME	SALARY
eric	10000

S

NAME	SALARY	TIMESTAMP

T

NAME	SALARY	TIMESTAMP

S'

NAME	SALARY	TIMESTAMP
eric	12000	10

T'

NAME	SALARY	TIMESTAMP
eric	10000	10

FIGURE 18.2. Eric's 20% raise in W'

R

NAME	SALARY
eric	10000

S

NAME	SALARY	TIMESTAMP
eric	15000	20

T

NAME	SALARY	TIMESTAMP
eric	10000	20

S'

NAME	SALARY	TIMESTAMP
eric	12000	10

T'

NAME	SALARY	TIMESTAMP
eric	10000	10

FIGURE 18.3. Eric's 50% raise in W

As a result further modifications to the HR algorithms are required.

2.4. A Solution With Identifiers

These semantics can be guaranteed by the addition of a tuple identifier, and modification of the DIFFERENCE operator. A tuple identifier, TNAME, must be added to each tuple in R. Any inserts to S or T, which are used to replace or delete a tuple in W, must be marked with the identifier for the original tuple in R or S which they replace or delete. Each tuple inserted into W (and thereby added to S) must be given a new identifier. For any relations A and B with timestamps and TNAMES as described, A DIFFERENCE B is defined to be all tuples a in A for which there is no tuple b in B such that

1) TNAME(a) = TNAME(b), and
2) TIMESTAMP(a) < TIMESTAMP(b)

To guarantee that our chosen update semantics hold, tuples in A DIFFERENCE B must be given timestamps of zero. Hence, at a second level, each tuple in S' and T' will have a newer timestamp than its corresponding tuple in W.

In our example the identifier of all of the five Eric tuples from Figure 18.3 will be identical. Since the timestamp of the tuple in W is treated as being older than that of the tuple in T', only Eric's tuple from S' will be contained in W'.

Timestamps alone have been shown to be insufficient for solving the problems of multi-level HR's. Identifiers alone are also insufficient, since in multi-level HR's, identifiers must remain constant in REPLACES and hence multiple tuples with the same identifier must be distinguishable (timestamps can distinguish the multiple tuples).

3.0. A MECHANISM

Given these modifications to the composition of S, T and the meaning of DIFFERENCE, an HR of the form W = (R UNION S) DIFFERENCE T no longer has its original conceptual simplicity. Moreover, support for HR's becomes considerably more complex than simply implementing UNION and DIFFERENCE as valid operators in a relational system. Consequently, we have designed a mechanism based on differential file techniques. The goal is to provide a single-pass algorithm with proper semantics that will support arbitrary cascading of HR's. The next two sections describe our data structure and algorithm in detail.

3.1. The Differential Relation

Each hypothetical relation W, built on top of a real or hypothetical relation B, has S and T merged into an associated differential file D, which contains all columns from B plus five additional fields. For example, the differential relation D for the base relation R from Section 2.0 is shown in Figure 18.4. NAME and SALARY are the attributes from R. The fields MINDATE and MAXDATE are both timestamps. MINDATE is the timestamp as defined in Section 2.0, while MAXDATE is another timestamp to be explained in Section 4.2. The fields LEVEL and TUP# are used to identify the tuple which this tuple replaces or causes the deletion of. Each hypothetical relation is assigned a level number as indicated in Figure 18.5. All real relations are at

NAME	c12
SALARY	i4
MINDATE	i4
MAXDATE	i4
LEVEL	i1
TUP#	i4
TYPE	i1

FIGURE 18.4. Attributes of the Differential Relation

level zero, and an HR built from a real relation is assigned a level of one. Then an HR built on top of a level one HR is given a level of two. Hence the column LEVEL identifies the level number of a particular tuple, while the column TUP# is a unique identifier at a particular level. Together TUP# and LEVEL comprise the unique identifier, TNAME, of a tuple. Values for TUP# are sequentially allocated integers. The last field in D, TYPE, marks what form of update the tuple represents; thus, it has three values, APPEND, RE-PLACE, and DELETE.

The following examples will illustrate the use of these extra fields. A precise algorithm is presented in Section 3.2. Suppose the relation R has the data shown in Figure 18.6. Initially W is identical to R, and D is empty.

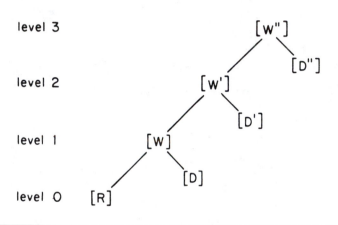

FIGURE 18.5. A Three Level Hypothetical Relation

NAME	SALARY	
fred	4000	TUP# of this tuple is 0
sally	6000	TUP# of this tuple is 1

FIGURE 18.6. The Initial Relation

Running the following QUEL command:

APPEND TO W (NAME = "nancy", SALARY = 5000)

would cause a single tuple to be inserted into D, as shown in Figure 18.7. The 30 stored in MINDATE is simply the current timestamp, and the TYPE is APPEND. Since there is no corresponding tuple at level 0, which the tuple replaces, the fields LEVEL and TUP# are set to identify the tuple itself (i.e., LEVEL = 1, TUP# = 0).

Suppose we now change the salary of Sally as follows:

RANGE OF W IS W
REPLACE W (SALARY = 8000) where W.NAME = "sally"

After this update, D looks like Figure 18.8. MINDATE is 40, the current timestamp. The tuple which we are replacing in R has an identifier of (LEVEL = 0, TUP# = 1) (see Figure 18.6).

Suppose we delete the tuple just replaced:

DELETE W WHERE W.NAME = "sally"

The resulting form of D is shown in Figure 18.9. Since this operation is a delete and NAME and SALARY are no longer important, they are set to null. TUP# and LEVEL are the same as in Figure 18.8, since they refer to the same tuple.

NAME	SALARY	MINDATE	MAXDATE	LEVEL	TUP#	TYPE
nancy	5000	30	————	1	0	APPEND

FIGURE 18.7. The Differential Relation After an Append

NAME	SALARY	MINDATE	MAXDATE	LEVEL	TUP#	TYPE
nancy	5000	30	————	1	0	APPEND
sally	8000	40	————	0	1	REPLACE

FIGURE 18.8. The Differential Relation After a Replace

NAME	SALARY	MINDATE	MAXDATE	LEVEL	TUP#	TYPE
nancy	5000	30	————	1	0	APPEND
sally	8000	40	————	0	1	REPLACE
		50	————	0	1	DELETE

FIGURE 18.9. The Differential Relation After a Delete

Suppose we now replace the tuple appended above; e.g.:

REPLACE W (NAME = "billy") WHERE W.NAME = "nancy"

The resulting form of D is shown in Figure 18.10. TUP# and LEVEL identify the original "nancy" tuple (see Figure 18.7). At this point, R is unchanged, and W looks like Figure 18.11.

3.2. The Algorithm

There are two parts to the algorithm for supporting hypothetical relations: accessing an HR, and updating an HR.

Accessing Hypothetical Relations

The algorithm for deriving a level N hypothetical relation W from a base relation R and a collection of differential relations D1, ..., DN is a one pass algorithm which starts with the highest level differential relation and proceeds

NAME	SALARY	MINDATE	MAXDATE	LEVEL	TUP#	TYPE
nancy	5000	30	————	1	0	APPEND
sally	8000	40	————	0	1	REPLACE
		50	————	0	1	DELETE
billy	5000	60	————	1	0	REPLACE

FIGURE 18.10. The Differential Relation After a Replace

NAME	SALARY	
fred	4000	unchanged
billy	5000	billy replacing nancy

FIGURE 18.11. The Final Hypothetical Relation

by examining all tuples at each level, passing through lower levels, and finally scanning through the level 0 base relation. Figure 18.12 shows this processing order more clearly. MaxLevel is the level N of the relation W.

An auxiliary data structure, which will be called "seen-ids," is maintained during the execution of this algorithm. This data structure has one associated update routine, "see(LEVEL, TUP#)," and a boolean retrieval function, "seen(LEVEL, TUP#)." The routine see(LEVEL, TUP#) inserts a TNAME (<LEVEL, TUP#>) into the data structure if it has not been seen before, while seen(LEVEL, TUP#) returns the value TRUE if <LEVEL, TUP#> is in seen-ids, FALSE otherwise.

The examine-and-process-tuple routine takes one or both of the following actions: it can "accept" the tuple for inclusion in W and it can call the routine "see" to place the identifier in "seen-ids." The algorithm for examining and processing of a tuple is shown in Figure 18.13. The choice of actions is summarized in Table 18.1. In applying Table 18.1 to a particular tuple T, "level0" is true if physlevel (from Figure 18.12) is zero, false otherwise. A

```
FOR physlevel := MaxLevel DOWN TO 0 DO
BEGIN
    WHILE (there are tuples at level physlevel) DO
    BEGIN
        tuple := get_next_tuple(physlevel);

        examine_and_process_tuple(tuple, physlevel);
    END
END.
```

FIGURE 18.12. HR Processing Order

	Conditions					Actions	
row	level0	newest	seen	type	samelevel	accept	see
1	yes	———	yes	———	———	no	no
2	yes	———	no	———	———	yes	no
3	no	no	———	———	———	no	no
4	no	yes	yes	———	———	no	no
5	no	yes	no	DELETE	yes	no	no
6	no	yes	no	REPLACE	yes	yes	no
7	no	yes	no	APPEND	yes	yes	no
8	no	yes	no	DELETE	no	no	yes
9	no	yes	no	REPLACE	no	yes	yes

TABLE 18.1. Processing Criteria for HR's

tuple T at physlevel N is "newest" if (as in Section 2.4) there is no tuple TB at physlevel N such that

1) (T.LEVEL = TB.LEVEL and T.TUP# = TB.TUP#), and

2) TA.MINDATE < TB.MINDATE

A tuple T has been "seen" when the pair <T.LEVEL, T.TUP#> has already been entered into "seen-ids." Fast tests for "newest" and "seen" are presented in Sections 4.2 and 4.3. The TYPE of tuple T is T.TYPE. "Samelevel" is true if T.LEVEL is the same as the current value of physlevel.

To demonstrate this processing we will generate W from D in Figure 18.10 and R in Figure 18.6. The starting configuration is shown in Figure 18.14. Processing starts with MaxLevel = 1 and physlevel = 1 in the differential relation D; hence, for all of this level, level0 will be false. Tuple (1) is not "newest", since tuple (4) has the same identifier, and a higher MIN-DATE. Since level0 is false, the tuple corresponds to line (3) of Table 18.1, and the tuple is neither "accepted" nor "seen."

Tuple (2) is not "newest" either, because tuple (3) has the same identifier, and a higher MINDATE, and so it also corresponds to line (3) of Table 18.1, and is neither "accepted" nor "seen."

Tuple (3) is "newest," because the only other tuple at this physlevel with the same identifier, tuple (2) has a smaller MINDATE. It has not been "seen," since seen-ids is empty and type is DELETE. We now determine "samelevel" by comparing the level field with physlevel. Physlevel is 1 and level is 0, so "samelevel" is false and line (8) is applied. Hence, the tuple is

```
examine_and_process_tuple(T, physlevel)
BEGIN
   level0   : BOOLEAN;
   newest   : BOOLEAN;
   seen     : BOOLEAN;
   type     : (APPEND, REPLACE, DELETE);
   samelevel : BOOLEAN;

   samelevel := TRUE; /* assume physlevel = datalevel */

   IF physlevel = 0 THEN
   BEGIN
        newest := NULL;
        seen := seen(T.LEVEL, T.TUP#);
        type := NULL;
        level0 := TRUE;
   END ELSE
   BEGIN
        newest := is_newest(T.MINDATE, T.LEVEL, T.TUP#);
        seen := seen(T.LEVEL, T.TUP#);
        type := T.TYPE;
        IF T.LEVEL <> physlevel THEN
                samelevel := FALSE;
        level0 := FALSE;
   END;
   IF table_accept(level0, newest, seen, type) THEN
        accept_tuple(T);

   IF table_see(level0, newest, seen, type, samelevel) THEN
        see(T.LEVEL, T.TUP#);
END;
```

FIGURE 18.13. Processing a Tuple

D

TUPLE	NAME	SALARY	MINDATE	MAXDATE	LEVEL	TUP#	TYPE
1	nancy	5000	30	————	1	0	APPEND
2	sally	8000	40	————	0	1	REPLACE
3			50	————	0	1	DELETE
4	billy	5000	60	————	1	0	REPLACE

R

5	fred	4000	tupnum of this tuple is 0
6	sally	6000	tupnum of this tuple is 1

seen-ids = { }

Tuples "accepted"

NAME	SALARY

FIGURE 18.14. Initial Structures for Processing W

"seen" but not "accepted." Tuple (4) is also "newest," has not been "seen," and type is REPLACE. Comparing level and physlevel, we find "samelevel" is true, since the level field is 1, and physlevel is still 1. Hence, (6) is the correct line in Table 18.1, and the tuple is "accepted" but not "seen." At this point, W and seen-ids look like Figure 18.15.

NAME	SALARY
billy	5000

seen-ids = {<0, 1>}

FIGURE 18.15.

Physlevel now changes to 0, "level0" becomes true, and we start to scan the base relation. Since "level0" is true, only lines (1) and (2) of Table 18.1 are relevant. The choice between them is determined by the value of "seen." To check whether a tuple has been "seen," at level 0, we look for

the pair <LEVEL = 0, TUP# = location> in seen-ids. For tuple (5) this pair
is <0, 0> (see Figure 18.14) which is not in seen-ids. . Hence, line (2) of
Table 18.1 is applied and we "accept" the tuple. The pair <0, location> for
tuple (6) is <0, 1>, which is in seen-ids. The corresponding line is (1), so
the tuple is not "accepted" and is not "seen." We have reached the end of
our scan, and have generated the relation W as follows in Figure 18.16.

NAME	SALARY
billy	5000
fred	4000

FIGURE 18.16.

Updating Hypothetical Relations

All updates to an HR of level N require appending tuples to the differential relation DN at level N. The contents of the different fields in the appended tuple are specified as follows:

(A) For APPENDS and REPLACES, the data columns of DN, are filled with
new data. For DELETES, the data fields are empty.

(B) MINDATE is assigned the current timestamp. (MAXDATE is discussed
in Section 4.2.)

(C) For APPENDS, TUP# and LEVEL are set to self-identify the inserted
tuple. For DELETES and REPLACES TUP# and LEVEL identify the tuple which we will call the "Affected Tuple." The Affected Tuple is the
tuple in R or in one of the differential relations DM (M <= N) which
is being deleted or replaced.

(D) TYPE is the type of the update, APPEND, DELETE or REPLACE.

4.0. IMPLEMENTATION

An implementation of HR's was done within the INGRES DBMS [STON76].
In order to create an HR, the following addition to QUEL was made:

DEFINE HYPREL newrel ON baserel

Once an HR has been defined, it can be updated and accessed just like an ordinary relation. Since, "baserel" can be either a regular relation, or an HR, a
practically unlimited number of levels is allowed.

4.1. DBMS Modifications

Within the INGRES access methods, a relation is accessed first by a call to "find" which sets the range for a scan of tuples, and then "get" is called repeatedly to access each tuple in this range. It is within "get" that most of the HR algorithm is implemented. "Get" returns "accepted" tuples from each differential relation, and finally the "accepted" tuples from the base relation. The routines which perform REPLACES, DELETES, and APPENDS are also modified to initialize and append the appropriate tuples to the differential relation.

4.2. Implementation of Newest

If tuples were appended to a differential relation at one end, and the relation were scanned from the other direction, it would be possible to tell when a tuple was the "newest" for a particular identifier by the fact that it was the first one encountered. Unfortunately, INGRES appends tuples and scans relations in the same direction. In order to be able to tell from a single pass whether a tuple is "newest", an additional timestamp field MAXDATE was added. When a tuple is appended, MAXDATE is set to infinity. When the tuple is REPLACED or DELETED at the same level, MAXDATE in the Affected Tuple is updated. Thus a tuple is the "newest" if the time of the current scan is between MINDATE and MAXDATE.

4.3. Implementation of Seen-Ids

The data structure, seen-ids, can be stored either in a series of main memory bit-maps, one for each level, or as a hashed table. For small relations or ones with many changes, the bit-map representation makes sense. Thus to "see" a tuple with tupnum Y at level L, bit Y in bitmap L is set. The boolean function "seen(L, Y)" tests whether the corresponding bit is set. For large relations with few changes a hash table is more efficient.

4.4. Performance Enhancement

If the base relation is organized as either a random hash structure or an ISAM structure, then the differential relations can be given a similar structure and a sequential scan of the differential relation can be avoided. To accomplish this, a correspondence must be established between the pages in a differential relation and those in the base relation. If a tuple would be placed on a certain page of the base relation, then the tuple in the hypothetical relation must be placed on the corresponding page in the differential relation.

　　If the base relation is structured so that the number of pages which must be scanned can be restricted for a particular query, then only the corresponding section of the structured differential relation need be scanned. For example, suppose the relation R(NAME, SALARY) is stored hashed on NAME and the differential relation D is stored likewise. Then, the query

RANGE OF W IS W
RETRIEVE (W.ALL) WHERE W.NAME = "billy"

only requires accessing the hash buckets corresponding to the hash value of "billy" in both R and D.

There is one complication with this performance enhancement, which stems from the fact that a replace can create a new tuple which differs from the Affected Tuple in the value of the column (or set of columns) which determine where a tuple is located. We will call this column (or set of columns) the Access Key of the relation. If the new version of a tuple has a different Access Key than the Affected Tuple it may go on a different page than it would if it had the same Access Key. This possible movement of the newest version of a tuple could have dire consequences. For example, consider the contents of R and D shown in Figure 18.17.

	R		D			
hashbucket	NAME	SALARY	NAME	SALARY	TYPE	OTHER
1	suzy	3000				
2	kelly	25				

FIGURE 18.17. R and D Hashed on Name

Then, suppose we do the following REPLACE:

RANGE OF W IS W
REPLACE W (NAME = "kelly") WHERE W.NAME = "suzy"

As a result, R and D would look like Figure 18.18:

	R		D			
hashbucket	NAME	SALARY	NAME	SALARY	TYPE	OTHER
1	suzy	3000				
2	kelly	25	kelly	3000	REPLACE	———

FIGURE 18.18. Problematic Hashed Replace

and the query:

RETRIEVE (W.ALL) WHERE W.NAME = "suzy"

would generate the result of Figure 18.19.

NAME	SALARY
suzy	3000

FIGURE 18.19. Result of a Query

Despite the fact that we changed Suzy's name, she appears in the result because the algorithm indicates searching the hashbucket corresponding to "suzy", hashbucket 1 of D, where there are no tuples, then searching hashbucket 1 of R, where Suzy's tuple appears. This tuple in hashbucket 1 of R is "accepted", because no tuples have been "seen." Unfortunately, the algorithm never searches hashbucket 0 of D to discover the replacement tuple.

     This problem can be solved by the addition of a fourth type of differential tuple, FORWARD. A FORWARD tuple is inserted in hashed and ISAM differential relations in the location indicated by the Access Key of the Affected Tuple whenever a REPLACE is done which changes the Access Key so that the new REPLACE tuple will go in a different hashbucket (or ISAM data page) than that of the Affected Tuple. With this correction, D of Figure 18.18 would look like Figure 18.20.

hashbucket	NAME	SALARY	MINDATE	MAXDATE	LEVEL	TUP#	TYPE
1		0	100	INFINITY	0	0	FORWARD
2	kelly	3000	100	INFINITY	0	0	REPLACE

FIGURE 18.20. The Differential Relation

The processing of the query would then start in hashbucket 1 of D in Figure 18.20, where a FORWARD tuple would be found, and the ordered pair <0, 0> would be added to seen-ids. Next, hashbucket 1 of R would be scanned, but since <0, 0> is in seen-ids, Suzy's tuple, tuple 0 of R, would not be accepted.

4.5. Functionality

With these enhancements, all QUEL commands have been made operational on HR's. Moreover, a type of "snap-shot" of the state of an HR at any point in the past can be accessed by setting the scan time (see Section 4.2) to a time prior to the current time. In this way the algorithm is run with some earlier timestamp than the normal current one.

Because differential relations are stored as standard relations, they can be restructured and manipulated using the full power of QUEL. Hence, a user can easily purge the differential relation of records which became invalid as of a certain date using the following QUEL command:

RANGE OF D IS D
DELETE D WHERE MAXDATE < "a given date"

Alternatively, if a user wanted to merge the HR back into the base relation, he can use a series of QUEL statements to update the base relation using the information in the differential relations. A simple utility could also be constructed to perform the same function.

4.6. Space Utilization

The secondary storage requirement for an unstructured HR is one differential tuple per updated tuple. For a structured relation, there is a significant initial overhead for the hashed or ISAM differential relation. This cost can be minimized by constructing the differential relation so that one of its pages corresponds to several in the base relation. If it is expected that 25% of the tuples in the HR will be updated, one page in the differential relation might correspond to four pages in the base relation.

The only primary storage requirement is temporary space for bitmaps for the duration of a scan. These bitmaps require roughly one bit per unique identifier. For example a million record relation would require a corresponding bitmap of 1 million bits, i.e., 125k bytes.

5.0. PERFORMANCE MEASUREMENT

Our performance study is aimed at comparing the performance of QUEL commands on standard relations versus the same commands on HR's. The tests were run on a single-user VAX-11/780. The three benchmarks in Figure 18.21 are used to measure update performance for a relation PARTS5000(P#, PNAME, PWEIGHT, PCOLOR) of 5000 tuples stored as a heap. MOREPARTS5000 is a source of 5000 additional parts tuples. At the beginning of each benchmark PARTS5000 is returned to its initial state. Table 18.2 indicates the results of running benchmarks (a) - (c) first with PARTS5000 as a real relation stored as a heap and then for PARTS5000 as an HR stored as a heap. In the latter case PARTS5000 consists of an empty differential relation, D, and a 5000 tuple real relation, R, stored as a heap. Notice that real and hypothetical relations perform comparably.

Table 18.3 shows the same update tests run against PARTS5000 hashed on P#. Benchmark (d) (shown in Figure 18.22) is added in order to test HR performance when Access Keys are changed and FORWARD tuples are

Benchmark (a)
        RANGE OF P IS PARTS5000
        RANGE OF M IS MOREPARTS5000
        APPEND TO PARTS5000 (M.ALL)
Benchmark (b)
        RANGE OF P IS PARTS5000
        DELETE P
Benchmark (c)
        RANGE OF P IS PARTS5000
        REPLACE P (WEIGHT = M.WEIGHT + 1000)

FIGURE 18.21. Update Benchmarks

CPU Time

benchmark	operation	HR cpu secs	real relation cpu secs	performance change
(a)	APPEND	26.57	24.47	8%
(b)	DELETE	19.78	24.38	-19%
(c)	REPLACE	25.03	26.03	-4%

Elapsed Time

benchmark	operation	HR elapsed secs	real relation elapsed secs	performance change
(a)	APPEND	36	32	12%
(b)	DELETE	25	26	-4%
(c)	REPLACE	35	28	25%

TABLE 18.2. Updates on 5000 Tuples Unstructured

Benchmark (d)
        RANGE OF P IS PARTS5000
        REPLACE P (P# = P.P# * 1000)

FIGURE 18.22. Hashed Update Benchmark

Benchmark (e)
        RANGE OF P IS PARTS
        RETRIEVE (M = MAX(P.WEIGHT))

FIGURE 18.23. Retrieval Benchmark

CPU Time

benchmark	operation	HR cpu secs	real relation cpu secs	performance change
(a)	APPEND	64.82	74.68	-14%
(b)	DELETE	21.32	20.15	5%
(c)	REPLACE	40.97	42.32	-4%
(d)	REPLACE	89.63	91.33	-2%

Elapsed Time

benchmark	operation	HR elapsed secs	real relation elapsed secs	performance change
(a)	APPEND	226	268	-16%
(b)	DELETE	37	31	19%
(c)	REPLACE	59	47	25%
(d)	REPLACE	422	345	22%

TABLE 18.3. Updates on 5000 Tuples, Hashed on P#

inserted in the differential relation (see Section 4.4).

To test retrieval performance we also ran benchmark (e) (shown in Figure 18.23) for a 10000 tuple real relation and a 10000 tuple HR. The hypothetical relations had sizes of differential relations, D, varying from 0 to 200% of the size of the R. (If every tuple has been replaced once in an HR, D is 100% of the size of R.) Table 18.4 shows the results of these tests.

Benchmark (e) was also run against a second level HR based on a first level HR with 50% of its tuples replaced. The results of this test are in Table 18.5.

Lastly, we ran benchmark (f) (shown in Figure 18.24) against a PARTS relation hashed on P#. Table 18.6 compares performance where PARTS5000 is either a 5000 tuple real relation hashed on P#, or a 5000 tuple HR hashed on P#, with 50% of its tuples replaced. MOREPARTS5000 is an unstructured 5000 tuple relation.

We can see that the performance of INGRES using hypothetical relations is comparable to its performance on real relations for a variety of

CPU Time

size of D	HR cpu secs	real relation cpu secs	performance change
0%	13.86	11.88	16%
10%	14.40	11.88	21%
25%	15.22	11.88	28%
50%	16.73	11.88	40%
100%	18.60	11.88	56%
200%	21.58	11.88	81%

Elapsed Time

size of D	HR elapsed secs	real relation elapsed secs	performance change
0%	15	13	15%
10%	15	13	15%
25%	16	13	23%
50%	18	13	38%
100%	21	13	61%
200%	30	13	130%

TABLE 18.4. Retrieval Performance with 10000 Tuple Base (Benchmark (e))

CPU Time

size of D	HR cpu secs	real relation cpu secs	performance change
0%	17.35	11.88	46%
10%	17.73	11.88	49%
25%	18.52	11.88	55%
50%	18.78	11.88	58%
100%	20.75	11.88	74%

Elapsed Time

size of D	HR elapsed secs	real relation elapsed secs	performance change
0%	18	13	38%
10%	19	13	46%
25%	19	13	46%
50%	21	13	61%
100%	24	13	84%

TABLE 18.5. Retrieval Performance 10000 tuples, 2 Levels (Benchmark (e))

Benchmark (f)

```
RANGE OF M IS MOREPARTS5000
RANGE OF P IS PARTS5000
RETRIEVE (M.WEIGHT, P.WEIGHT) WHERE M.P# = P.P#
```

FIGURE 18.24. Hashed Retrieval Benchmark

type	cpu time secs	elapsed time minutes
real relation	131	5.85
HR	185	9.88
performance change	68%	

TABLE 18.6. Hashed Access Performance (Benchmark (f))

commands including restrictions, aggregates, and joins. In some cases HR's cause additional overhead, however this penalty is usually small. Only in extreme cases is it more than a factor of the HR level number.

6.0. CONCLUSIONS

We have described a mechanism for supporting HR's which is shown to overcome the problems of previous proposals. We have described an implementation of this mechanism and provided data to show that performance of HR's is surprisingly good and has modest space requirements. Moreover, using our HR mechanisms, it is possible to make inquiries about HR's as of a particular time in the past. Hence, an additional benefit is an efficient implementation of "snapshots."

## CHAPTER NINETEEN

Document Processing in a Relational Database System

Michael Stonebraker / Heidi Stettner / Nadene Lynn / Joseph Kalash / Antonin Guttman

ABSTRACT

This paper contains a proposal to enhance a relational database manager to support document processing. Basically, it suggests support for data items which are variable length strings, support for ordered relations, support for substring operators, and support for new operators which concatenate and break apart string fields.

1.0 INTRODUCTION

Currently document processing is usually done by text editors which contain their own facilities to store and manipulate data. If documents could be stored as ordinary data in a database management system, then any available database services would automatically be available for documents. Such services include concurrency control, crash recovery and access control. Also, access methods and indexing facilities in a data manager would not need to be duplicated in a text editor. Moreover, inclusion of documents and normal database data within a single subsystem may expedite putting database data, such as figures and tables, into the middle of documents. Such facilities are supported by the records processing facilities of the Xerox Star [PURV82]. Lastly, the capabilities of the database query language can be used to advantage in certain kinds of document manipulation. For example, if a

M. Stonebraker, H. Stettner, N. Lynn, J. Kalash, and A. Guttman, *ACM Transactions on Office Information Systems*, vol. 1, no. 2, April 1983. Copyright 1983, Association for Computing Machinery, Inc.; reprinted by permission.

document is stored in a relation WORD-SENT-DOC as follows:

```
CREATE WORD-SENT-DOC    (SENTENCE# = i2,
                         WORD# = i2,
                         WORD = c40)
```

then the following QUEL [HELD75b] command counts the number of words in the document.

```
RANGE OF W IS WORD-SENT-DOC
RETRIEVE (WORD-COUNT = COUNT (W.word))
```

More generally, the following code produces a histogram of sentence length.

```
RANGE OF W IS WORD-SENT-DOC
RETRIEVE INTO TEMP (W.SENTENCE#,
        LENGTH = COUNT (W.WORD BY W.SENTENCE#))
RANGE OF T IS TEMP
RETRIEVE (T.LENGTH,
        FREQ = COUNT (T.SENTENCE# BY T.LENGTH))
```

Hence, many complex document analyses can be performed with simple relational aggregate operators.

Text editors, such as ex [JOY79a], manipulate documents which effectively have the format:

```
CREATE LINE-DOC (LINE# = i2, TEXT = c255)
```

Basically, each line of text is a variable length string and has an associated line number. In the above relation this string is limited to 255 bytes. The LINE# field supports two features of text editors. First, lines of a document are inherently ordered, and a line number supports such an ordering. In addition, many text editors allow one to jump to a specific line of a document. Such line-oriented commands must be supported by a LINE# field.

In order to effectively support both LINE-DOC and WORD-SENT-DOC and the ability to transfer a document from one format to the other, new database facilities are required. This paper proposes new mechanisms, including:

1) variable length strings

2) ordered relations

3) new substring operators

4) a new break operator

5) a generalized concatenate operator

Some general purpose data managers already include variable length strings; however, the remaining features constitute our proposed new extensions.

In Sections 2.0 through 6.0 we discuss these constructs in turn and give examples of their utility. Then, in Section 7.0 we discuss the extensions necessary to relational views [STON75] to support these extra mechanisms. The context in which we present our constructs is the INGRES database system [STON76a]. However, the features could easily be changed to apply in most relational environments.

One should keep in mind that we are not proposing that text editing of database documents be performed using the command languages of a relational DBMS. Rather, we are proposing DBMS facilities which can effectively support a text editor run as an application program making calls on extended DBMS facilities.

Since text editors are optimized for document processing, one should be concerned about the performance of a relational database system compared to that of a normal text editor. Consequently, Section 8.0 indicates the results of a performance study comparing INGRES as a document processor with that of the text editor ex.

2.0. VARIABLE LENGTH STRINGS

Our first extension is support for a field which is a variable length string. The syntax we propose is an extension of the CREATE statement as follows:

CREATE DOCUMENT (DOC# = i4, TEXT = c0)

Here a document relation would have a document number as the first field and then have the text of the document as a second field. The c0 indicates a character string field which is potentially larger than any fixed length.

There are two possible mechanisms which could be used to store such variable length fields. The first is to define them as a new type of column using an abstract data type facility [STON82a]. This paradigm supports constructing a code for the variable length string in the database and then storing the string external to the database. Any of the popular tactics to store and retrieve variable length stings could be used, (e.g., first fit, best fit, cyclic best fit, etc.). Using this technique, the database manager need never know about the variable length data.

The second method is to extend the access methods to allow variable length strings. This could be accomplished easily by placing a length descriptor at the front of each variable length field and another length descriptor at the beginning of the whole record. This approach has been used successfully by System R [ASTR76].

3.0. ORDERED RELATIONS

We first discuss simple one dimensional ordered relations. Then, in Section 3.2 we generalize the notion to multidimensional ordered relations.

3.1. Simple Ordered Relations

In order to support documents which are stored in the format of one line per record, we need a relational structure such as the following:

    CREATE LINE-DOC (LID = i4, TEXT = c0)

Here, we have a line number as the first field followed by the text for that line as a variable length string. However, one has the problem that adding a new line in the middle of the document is a tedious task; one must renumber all the subsequent lines. Also, renumbering is required any time one moves a line or lines to a different place in the document or deletes a line.

A more desirable approach is to have a database manager assist with line numbers. The notion of an ORDERED relation is required which is supported by a special storage structure. An unordered relation, S, can be ordered as follows:

    ORDER S WITH LID

This command would have the effect of converting the unordered relation at the top of Figure 19.1 into the ordered relation at the bottom. An unordered relation, S, with a single data field, TEXT, is shown with 5 tuples containing the first 15 words of the Gettysburg Address. All tuples in INGRES have an associated tuple identifier (TID) which is not visible to users but is shown in the figure. To convert the relation S to an ordered relation, any keyed primary structure (e.g., B-tree [COME79] or ISAM index) is discarded and the special data structure shown at the bottom of Figure 19.1 is built in its place. This structure is similar to one suggested in an exercise in [KNUT78] and used in assorted text editors. In this section we apply the structure to relational DBMSs and generalize it to multiple dimensions.

The auxiliary structure of Figure 19.1 is a B-tree containing TIDs as its leaf node data. These TIDs indicate the ordering of the tuples in the relation when traversed in top-to-bottom order. At higher levels of the tree one stores pointers to lower levels of the tree and a count field, $N(T)$ for each subtree T, indicating how many TIDS are present in the subtree. Figure 19.1 indicates higher level blocks as containing either one or two pointers and the associated count field for each. Momentarily we will discuss the updating and search of this structure.

The user view of an ordered relation S(TEXT) will have an LID field added as follows:

    S (LID, TEXT)

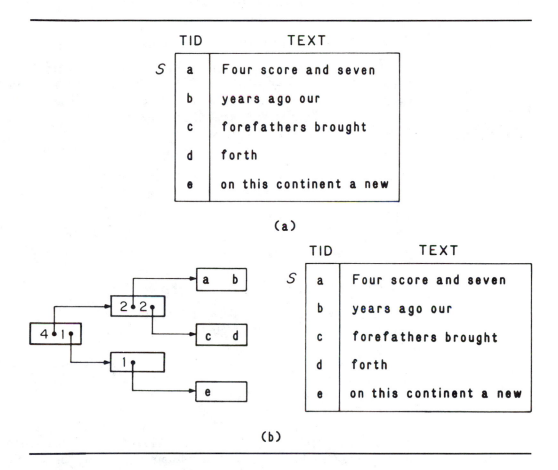

FIGURE 19.1. Ordered Relation With Access Path

This LID behaves exactly like an ordinary field; hence, one can query the line id field, e.g.

RETRIEVE (S.ALL) WHERE S.LID = 100

This command will retrieve line 100 of the relation S. By examining the root node of the B-tree one can discover in which subtree, Y, line 100 exists by performing the computation:

$$\min_{Y}\left[\sum_{T \le Y} N(T)\right] \ge 100$$

The computation is repeated at each level saving the lowest LID that is present in the current subtree as one descends. At the leaf level, TIDs are searched sequentially until a count equal to 100 minus the lowest LID on the block is reached. This is the TID for line 100.

A new line can be inserted as follows:

APPEND TO S (LID = 100, TEXT = "new words go here")

This will add a new tuple to S which can be physically located anywhere in the file containing this relation. The new TID, t, must then be inserted in the B-tree. One first finds the 100th line as above, incrementing by 1 the affected subtree count at each level of the tree. Then one inserts t before the 100th TID. If this insert causes a block split, the conventional B-tree algorithm is used and the subtree counts are adjusted as appropriate.

A line can be deleted as follows:

DELETE S WHERE S.LID = 100

First, the 100th line is found and removed from the B-tree. The subtree counts must be adjusted as the tree is descended. Subsequently, the row with the indicated TID is removed from the relation.

Lastly, a line can be moved as follows:

REPLACE S (LID = 50) WHERE S.LID = 100

This is implemented by a line delete followed by an insert if the new LID is smaller than the old one. If a higher LID is assigned, then the insert must be done first.

It should be noted that secondary indices can be created for ordered relations. Moreover, any QUEL commands which do not affect the LID have the identical semantics as in current QUEL.

One last point is that the LID must be considered the primary key of an ordered relation. Suppose one allowed an ISAM primary key for an ordered relation, e.g., EMP indexed on NAME. Then, assume one renamed Mr. Aardvark to Mr. Zoom. This will necessitate physically changing the TID of the tuple in question, and an auxiliary update to the B-tree must be performed. Without back-pointers from the relation to the B-tree, there is no way to do this auxiliary update efficiently.

One generalization of simple ordered relations is appropriate. It would be helpful to change an ordinary relation which has a user supported sequence field to an ordered relation. As such, the sequence field should define the ordering and should be suppressed as the same function is supported by a LID. The following extension supports this notion.

$$\text{ORDER R WITH field} - 1 \left[= \left\{ \begin{array}{c} \text{ASCENDING} \\ \text{DESCENDING} \end{array} \right\} \text{field} - 2 \right]$$

For example, given a relation R(A, B, C), one could execute:

ORDER R WITH MY-LID = ASCENDING A

This would have the effect of sorting R(A,B,C) by ascending values of A before building the structure of Figure 19.1. Also, A would be discarded as an attribute of R and replaced by an ordering field called MY-LID. Consequently, the structure of R becomes:

R(MY-LID, B, C)

If a user wishes the field A to remain in the relation in addition to the LID field, he can execute the following commands:

MODIFY R TO heapsort ON A
ORDER R WITH MY-LID

The first command instructs INGRES to sort R on field A. Then R can be ordered to achieve the desired effect. It should be noted that the "sort by" clause in SQL [CHAM74b] can perform the same function.

The inclusion of ordered relations and variable length strings as fields allows a relational database system to effectively support documents in the format of LINE-DOC from Section 1.0. We now turn to multidimensional ordered relations.

3.2. Ordered Relations in Two Dimensions

Although simple ordered relations are helpful in processing documents, there are cases where a two-dimensional ordering is required. For example, WORD-SENT-DOC from Section 1.0 needs to be ordered by SENTENCE# and then within each sentence it must be ordered by WORD#. Simple ordered relations cannot provide this multidimensional ordering.

A second example is the application package TIMBER [STON82b] which supports placement of icons representing data from a database on a graphics terminal in a manner similar to that of SDMS [HERO80]. These icons have a two dimensional position on the screen, and panning in both the vertical and horizontal direction is supported. Here, a two dimensional ordered relation is required.

To support such two dimensional structures we can expand the ordered relation concept in two different ways. First, one would want the possibility of having a relation such as WORD-SENT-DOC ordered by WORD# for each particular value of SENTENCE#. The syntax we propose is the following:

$$\text{ORDER R BY field} - 1 \left[\text{WITH field} - 2 = \left\{ \begin{array}{c} \text{ASCENDING} \\ \text{DESCENDING} \end{array} \right\} \text{field} - 3 \right]$$

For example, we could perform the desired ordering on WORD-SENT-DOC as follows:

ORDER WORD-SENT-DOC BY SENTENCE#
WITH LID = ASCENDING WORD#

The BY clause indicates that the ordering is produced for each value of SENTENCE#. The WITH clause specifies sorting by ascending WORD# and replacing that field with an LID field. Hence, the user view of WORD-SENT-

DOC becomes:

WORD-SENT-DOC (SENTENCE#, LID, WORD)

The auxiliary structure for this ordered relation is shown in Figure 19.2. Here a form of secondary index is created with one row of an INDEX relation for each possible sentence number. The example in Figure 19.2 shows sentences 1 to 3. For each sentence there is a pointer field which indicates the root of a B-tree structure of the form of Figure 19.1. For each value of SENTENCE#, the LID for the first word is 1 and increases for subsequent words.

Obvious extensions to the algorithms of Section 3.1 can support this structure. Hence, new words can be inserted and deleted and the LID field will be dynamically adjusted. However, we still have the problem that SENTENCE# must be a user supported field. Consequently, whenever a new sentence is added or dropped, the user must adjust his own sentence numbers.

The second syntactic extension corrects this deficiency:

$$\text{ORDER R WITH field} - 1 \left[= \left\{ \begin{array}{c} \text{ASCENDING} \\ \text{DESCENDING} \end{array} \right\} \text{field} - 2 \right]$$

$$\left[, \text{field} - 3 = \left\{ \begin{array}{c} \text{ASCENDING} \\ \text{DESCENDING} \end{array} \right\} \text{field} - 4 \right]$$

This syntax allows two ordering fields as follows:

ORDER WORD-SENT-DOC WITH
        LID-X = ASCENDING SENTENCE#,
        LID-Y = ASCENDING WORD#

This version of the order command allows a two dimensional ordering first by SENTENCE# and then by WORD# and a user sees the relation:

WORD-SENT-DOC (LID-X, LID-Y, WORD)

SENTENCE#	pointer
1	a
2	b
3	c

FIGURE 19.2. The Auxiliary Structure

The support structure we need is a generalization of Figure 19.1 in which the leaf nodes of the B-tree for LID-X do not contain TIDs of tuples in the relation WORD-SENT-DOC. Instead, each contains a pointer to a second B-tree as in Figure 19.2 which supports a LID-Y for each value of LID-X. Again obvious extensions of the algorithms of Section 3.1 will support such a structure. Lastly, it is clear that the structure can be generalized to N-dimensional orderings.

In the next three sections we turn to QUEL extensions which are useful in supporting document processing.

4.0. SUBSTRING OPERATORS

4.1. Extended Wild Cards

A common operation for text editors is to substitute a second string for each occurrence of a first string. For example, the text editor ex allows one to substitute lower case letters for the first occurrence of "THE" on each line with the following command:

> 1,$s/THE/the/

The "1,$" specifies the command is to affect lines between 1 and the last line in the document, noted by $. The command "s" specifies substitution for each occurrence of "THE" the string "the."

It is currently possible to find each tuple of LINE-DOC which has the string "THE" with the following QUEL command:

> RANGE OF L IS LINE-DOC
> RETRIEVE (L.ALL) WHERE L.TEXT = "*THE*"

Here, * is a wild card and matches any variable length string. In addition to *, INGRES currently supports special characters which match any single character, one of a set of characters, a range of characters, or a regular expression of the above. Currently, these wild cards can only appear in a qualification and not in the target list.

The extension proposed is the inclusion of *i as a "wild card" which matches any string. Values of i must be between 0 and some predetermined upper bound, say 9. Moreover, *i can also appear in the target list and has the same value for a tuple as it does in the qualification. Consequently the substitution of lower case letters for "THE" can be accomplished as follows:

> REPLACE L(TEXT = "*1the*2") WHERE L.TEXT = "*1THE*2"

With extended wild cards, we can do other text operations. For example, to delete a line up to the first instance of "the" we would perform:

> REPLACE L(TEXT = "the*2") WHERE L.TEXT = "*1the*2"

To flip the portion of the line after "the" with the portion before "the", we would perform:

REPLACE L(TEXT = "*2the*1") WHERE L.TEXT = "*1the*2"

However, there are a number of operations which are not possible with extended wild cards. These include deleting the first 10 characters on each line and changing the 7th word of a line to a specific pattern. To perform such functions, we require the substring operators in the next subsection.

4.2. Substring Operators

At the present time QUEL provides support for referencing a field in a relation as:

TUPLE-VARIABLE.FIELD

Moreover, the concatenate function allows one to combine fields from R(A,B,C) together as follows:

RETRIEVE INTO R2 (COMBINED = concat(R.A, R.B))

However, there is no way to break a field apart. This section proposes facilities to alleviate this weakness. We propose that a field can have one of five additional formats:

TUPLE-VARIABLE.FIELD [X]
TUPLE-VARIABLE.FIELD [X, Y]
TUPLE-VARIABLE.FIELD [X, Y)
TUPLE-VARIABLE.FIELD (X, Y]
TUPLE-VARIABLE.FIELD (X, Y)

The values for X and Y match a substring from the field indicated. Hence, the first format keeps only the substring matched by X while the second keeps the substring in between the strings matched by X and Y including the endpoints. In general, the curved bracket indicates excluding the string which marks the boundary of the field to be retained, while a square bracket means including it. In all cases X matches the first substring starting from the left side of the field while Y matches the first substring starting from the end of the substring matched by X. For example, if the text field of a tuple in LINE-DOC has the value:

the fox jumped over the log

then:

L.TEXT ["the"]	has value "the"
L.TEXT ["the", "the"]	has value "the fox jumped over the"
L.TEXT ("the", "over")	has value " fox jumped "
L.TEXT ["over", "fox"]	has a value of the empty string

Both X and Y are of the form AB where:

$$A = \begin{bmatrix} i \\ \$ \end{bmatrix}$$

$$B = \begin{bmatrix} \text{QUEL string} \\ s \\ w \\ c \end{bmatrix}$$

Both A and B are optional. B can be any valid string in QUEL including the extended wild cards from Section 4.1. Moreover, s stands for any sentence, w for any word and c for any character. Momentarily we discuss adding other user defined markers. If B is not specified, the default is ?, the wild card that matches any single character.

The first portion, A, can be any integer i from 0 to 9, meaning the i-th occurrence of a string matching B, or it can be $. The $ deals with changing the left-to-right search order for matching X and Y and is illustrated by example. Suppose LINE-DOC has a text field of

the boy and the girl like the man

The following constructs have the values indicated:

L.TEXT ("the", "the")	has value " boy and "
L.TEXT (1"the",1"the")	has value " boy and "
L.TEXT (1"the",2"the")	has value " boy and the girl like "

If we did not know how many "the" patterns existed on the line and wanted the pattern between the last two of them, we would use:

L.TEXT ($"the", $"the")

Here, $ specifies beginning at the end of the line and searching backwards. If Y has a $ specified, it is matched first and then X is matched. If neither i nor $ is specified for X and Y, then the default is i=1.

With these substring operators, we can perform the examples not possible with extended wild cards. For example to delete the first 10 characters in every line of LINE-DOC we would:

REPLACE L (TEXT = L.TEXT(10c,$])

In order to change the 7th word on each line to be "tuple" we would:

REPLACE L (TEXT = concat(L.TEXT[,6w],"tuple", L.TEXT[7w,$]))

Hopefully, an improved syntax for the last operation will be found in the future.

In order to support user defined markers to delimit the boundary of a string of interest, we require a definition facility. Such a facility would be used, for example, to support searching for the first occurrence of a digit in a string. The syntax used is the following:

DEFINE marker AS regular-expression

The allowed regular expressions are those allowed in ex [JOY79a] and include normal characters (which match that character), a string of characters inside square brackets (which matches any character in that string), two characters separated by a dash (which matches any character between the two endpoints), a * (which matches any string of zero or more characters) and ? (which matches any single character). The special meaning of *, -, and ? can be negated by preceding them with a backslash. For example:

DEFINE d AS [0-9]
DEFINE U AS [A-Z]
DEFINE u AS [a-z]

These definitions represent respectively markers consisting of digits, upper case letters, and lower case letters. Markers to delimit characters, words and sentences are given below.

DEFINE c AS ?
DEFINE w AS [,;.!\?]
DEFINE s AS [.!\?]

A user may freely redefine the built-in markers by using different definitions. Of course, markers longer than a single character are also allowed such as the one below for two digit numbers.

DEFINE n AS [0-9][0-9]

In our implementation the initial definitions and any user extensions are stored in a relation in the database and loaded into a main memory table at run time.

Now, suppose we wished to break a text field into all of its component words. The next section discusses an operator to accomplish this task.

5.0. THE BREAK OPERATOR

The syntax we propose to break apart a text field into its component parts is the following:

$$\text{BREAK} \left[\text{tuple} - \text{variable.field} - 1 \text{ by } X \left\{ \begin{array}{c} \text{ASCENDING} \\ \text{DESCENDING} \end{array} \right\} \text{field} - 2 \right]$$

This operator takes the field specified by FIELD-1 and fragments it into pieces. The value of X determines the endpoints of these fragments. In the previous section we indicated the legal specifications for X, and this operator uses the same ones. In order not to lose semantic information, we must retain the ordering of the fragments and the markers in between the fragments. Consequently, FIELD-2 has a sequence number to specify this ordering and it can either be ascending or descending. Moreover, the marker is automatically added to the end of a fragment. An example should clarify this operator.

Suppose we wished to store LINE-DOC in a relation with one word per row. We could accomplish this as follows:

> RETRIEVE INTO WORD-DOC (
> LINE# = L.LID
> WORD = BREAK[L.TEXT BY W ASCENDING WORD#])

This will create a new relation WORD-DOC with three fields as follows:

> WORD-DOC (LINE#, WORD, WORD#)

The field WORD# is added to the relation and orders the words on a given line. The field WORD stores the individual words along with the their ending marker. Removal of the marker can be accomplished, if desired with the substring operators of Section 4.0.

The last operator allows one to concatenate groups of records back together. In a sense it is the inverse of the BREAK operator.

6.0. THE CONCAT OPERATOR

The generalized concatenate operator which we require is the following:

> CONCAT [TUPLE-VARIABLE.FIELD-1
> BY TUPLE-VARIABLE.FIELD-2
> WHERE qualification
> WITH ASCENDING TUPLE-VARIABLE.FIELD-3]

Basically, CONCAT is an aggregate operator and is similar to the other QUEL aggregate operators such as SUM or AVERAGE. It groups together all fields which have a constant value for FIELD-2 keeping only those which satisfy the qualification. However, instead of performing a numerical computation, the values obtained are sorted on FIELD-3 and concatenated together.

Both the BY clause and the WHERE clause are optional, as is the case for aggregates. A few examples will explain the CONCAT operator further.

Suppose we wanted to restore WORD-DOC back to its original state as LINE-DOC. This is accomplished as follows:

> RANGE OF W IS WORD-DOC
> RETRIEVE INTO LINE-DOC(
> W.LINE#,
> TEXT = concat (W.WORD WITH ASCENDING W.WORD#))

Now consider the relation WORD-SENT-DOC from Section 1.0. We can form a relation SENT-DOC with one tuple for each sentence as follows:

```
RANGE OF W IS WORD-SENT-DOC
RETRIEVE INTO SENT-DOC(
    W.SENTENCE#,
    TEXT = concat (W.WORD BY W.SENTENCE#
WITH ASCENDING WORD#))
```

Applying another CONCAT operator would allow us to generate a relation that had the entire document as a single tuple as follows:

```
RANGE OF S IS SENT-DOC
RETRIEVE INTO DOC(
    TEXT = concat (S.TEXT WITH ASCENDING SENTENCE#))
```

It should be clear that two successive break operators could restore SENT-DOC and WORD-SENT-DOC respectively.

7.0. VIEWS

It should be clear that some of the representations which we have created for documents are space inefficient. For example, WORD-SENT-DOC has a word number and a sentence number for each word in a document. However, these representations are often easy for an end user or application program to process, as noted in Section 1.0.

   Consequently, one might like to actually store SENT-DOC (which is space efficient) and allow the user to manipulate WORD-SENT-DOC. This requires views involving the extended operators proposed earlier. In the next several subsections we consider the mapping of each operator in turn.

7.1. Ordered Views

Since ordered relations are supported by a physical access path, there is some difficulty with the implementation of ordered views. Clearly, ordered views for unordered relations cannot be supported. However, given an ordered relation R(LID, A, B, C) we can define a view as follows:

```
DEFINE VIEW V (R.LID, R.B) WHERE QUAL
```

where QUAL is an arbitrary qualification. If one applies standard query modification techniques [STON75], one can obtain an LID field for the view V. The problem is that V.LID is not sequenced 1,2,3... but will have gaps when a tuple of R does not satisfy the qualification QUAL. Defensive programming on the part of the user is required in order for a program on an ordered relation to work on an ordered view. In particular, one must never use

```
current LID + 1
```

to obtain the next row of an ordered relation. Rather, one must express this as:

> min (E.LID WHERE E.LID > current LID)

With this proviso, ordered views present no difficulty.

7.2. Substrings

Consider a view which contains a substring from a field in an existing relation. For example, suppose V is defined as

> DEFINE VIEW V (R.A, C = R.C[X,Y])

for some legal values of X and Y. We can map a REPLACE command such as

> REPLACE V (C = "new") WHERE QUAL

into the following command:

> REPLACE R (C = concat(R.C[,X), "new",R.C(Y,$]) WHERE QUAL

DELETES and APPENDS can be analogously transformed.

7.3. The BREAK Operator

Consider the view

> DEFINE VIEW V (R.A,
>   C = BREAK[R.C BY U ASCENDING j])

and the update

> REPLACE V (C = "new ") WHERE QUAL and V.j = k

This would be converted to:

> REPLACE R (C = concat(R.C[,k*U),
>   "new ",
>   R.C((k+1)*U,$])
>   WHERE QUAL

As long as the value k is explicitly given in the qualification, the above semantics work correctly. If multiple values are specified, e.g.,

> ...V.j < k

or if a comparison is made to another field, e.g.,

> ...V.j = F.H

for some field H in another relation, then there is considerable difficulty.

Not only do we have a non-functional update [STON76a] in which we are attempting to update the same tuple several times in a single command but also query modification in advance of execution fails to work.

7.4. The CONCAT Operator

Lastly, consider the view V(C, B)

> DEFINE VIEW V (C = concat (R.C BY R.B ASCENDING R.A),
>   B = R.B)

and the update

> REPLACE V (C = "new") WHERE QUAL and V.B = k

To support such a command we require the following algorithm. Let n = width (C) be the number of bytes in the fixed length field, C. Moreover, let !x! be the smallest integer greater than x and let "string"[i*n,(i+1)*n] be the substring between character positions i*n and (i+1)*n.

> For i = 0, ..., !width ("new" / width (C))!
> DO
>   RETRIEVE (R.ALL) WHERE R.A = i
>   if a tuple is returned then
>   REPLACE R (C = "new"[i*n,(i+1)*n]) WHERE R.A = i
>   else
>   APPEND TO R (C = "new"[i*n,(i+1)*n], A = i)
> END

Unfortunately, there is no single command which can perform this update and a collection of commands is required.

The conclusion of this section is that under some circumstances support for views containing our extended operators is possible. However, BREAK and CONCAT appear difficult to support except in very restricted circumstances.

8.0. A PERFORMANCE STUDY

In order to explore the performance which might be obtained by an editor built as an application program for a relational database system, we compared the performance of INGRES with that of the UNIX editor, ex, for a variety of editing commands. Ex was chosen because the UNIX command to obtain CPU time and elapsed time operates correctly with this editor. It would be desirable to redo this study for a screen-oriented editor, such as vi, when more sophisticated timing facilities are available.

For ex, the documents to be edited were placed in UNIX files, while they were stored as ordered relations with one line per tuple in INGRES. The corresponding ex and INGRES commands which were timed are given in Figure 19.3. Each command will be explained after the performance results

Timed Commands			
Command Number	ex	INGRES	Document Size (lines)
1	1,$p	RETRIEVE (R.text)	100
2	1,$p	RETRIEVE (R.text)	10,000
3	100p	RETRIEVE (R.text) where R.LID = 100	100
4	1,$s/line 60/ new line	REPLACE R(text = "new line") where R.text = "line 60"	100
5	same as 4	same as 4	10,000
6	change 10 lines, write at end.	10 REPLACEs	100
7	same as 6	same as 6	10,000
8	change 10 lines, write after each one.	same as 6	100
9	same as 8	same as 6	10,000
10	g/27/p	RETRIEVE (R.all) where R.NUMB = 27	2000

FIGURE 19.3. Commands Times on ex and INGRES

are given. Timings were obtained using the UNIX TIME command on a VAX 11/780 computer with no active jobs other than the benchmark commands. The results are shown in Figure 19.4. The times in Figure 19.4 indicate the CPU time spent executing the command in user space (user time), the CPU time spent by the operating system in support of the user command (system time), the total CPU time (user + system) and the elapsed time to process the command (execution time).

Commands one and two print entire documents of 100 and 10,000 lines respectively. Ex prints the smaller document faster by a factor of 2; however, INGRES wins on CPU time when the 10,000 line document is printed. Command three prints a single line from a 100 line document and ex is a clear winner in this case. The fourth and fifth commands substitute the string "new line" whenever "line 60" appears in the document. A sequential search of the entire document must be made by both ex and INGRES for the

Performance Results				
	ex			
Command Number	User Time	System Time	User + System	Exec. Time
1	0.2	0.1	0.3	:01
2	22.3	10.0	32.3	1:42
3	0.007	0.006	0.013	:0001
4	0.1	0.1	0.2	:01
5	10.5	2.2	12.7	:14
6	0.3	0.1	0.4	:01
7	6.8	2.4	9.2	:09
8	0.3	0.4	0.7	:01
9	20.9	6.6	27.5	:31
10	3.2	0.3	3.5	:04

	INGRES			
Command Number	User Time	System Time	User + System	Exec. Time
1	0.6	0.1	0.7	:05
2	17.0	13.4	30.4	5:04
3	0.253	0.075	0.328	:0035
4	0.6	0.4	1.0	:01
5	15.8	3.0	18.8	:33
6	3.6	1.5	5.1	:07
7	3.4	1.5	4.9	:10
8	3.4	1.5	4.9	:10
9	3.4	1.5	4.9	:10
10	1.7	1.0	2.7	:13

FIGURE 19.4. Times in Seconds for Benchmark Commands

100 and 10,000 line documents. In both cases, ex is faster than INGRES. Commands six through nine all perform a series of line changes by indicating the line number to be changed and the new text string. Tests six and seven have ex writing all changes to the permanent disk-based copy of the document only at the end of the editing session. In contrast, ex updates the

disk-based copy after each line is replaced in tests eight and nine. Since INGRES maintains only one disk-based copy of the document, this second approach more closely resembles its mode of processing. Once again, ex wins when the file size is 100 lines and INGRES' CPU time is smaller with the large document.

In order to demonstrate the effectiveness of a service available in INGRES, we performed test 10. Here, we assume that a numeric field, NUMB, is present for each line of the document. INGRES can put NUMB in a separate field and use the relation DOCUMENT (LID, text, NUMB). Additionally it can build a secondary index on the field NUMB to speed searches involving that field. On the other hand, ex must store the numeric field as part of the text field. The last command finds all lines of the document where the numeric field has a value of 27. The command in test 10 prints all lines containing the string "27." Because INGRES can use the secondary index to avoid a sequential search, it uses less CPU time than ex.

From these tests it is clear that INGRES uses less CPU time than ex when a large document is edited. The slower INGRES execution times for large documents are partially due to the number of bytes printed. At the time that these tests were performed INGRES could only use fixed length fields. Hence, documents in INGRES had each line blank-padded to a fixed size of 80 bytes. Text strings in ex are not blank-padded. As a result more characters are printed by INGRES than by ex for each command, leading to a slower total execution time. Variable length fields in INGRES would reduce the number of bytes printed to the length of the actual text.

A small document is usually processed faster by ex. INGRES has a high fixed overhead to process any command, and the fixed cost is not amortized over a large amount of work. Lowering the fixed overhead by optimizing INGRES would make it more competitive in this situation.

In summary, these tests indicate that a performance competitive text editor can probably be built on top of a relational database system that has been properly optimized and supports variable length strings.

9.0. CONCLUSIONS

This paper has proposed a small collection of facilities including ordered relations, substring operators, CONCAT and BREAK. These allow a relational database system to be substantially more useful in aiding text processing application programs by supporting ordered documents and the ability to decompose and compose text fields.

At the current time (August 1982) ordered relations, extended wild cards and substring operators are implemented in INGRES. An abstract data type facility is nearing completion which can support variable length character strings. Only CONCAT and BREAK have not yet been attempted.

## CHAPTER TWENTY

QUEL as a Data Type

Michael Stonebraker / Erika Anderson / Eric Hanson / Brad Rubenstein

ABSTRACT

This paper explores the use of commands in a query language as an abstract data type (ADT) in database management systems. Basically, an ADT facility allows new data types, such as polygons, lines, money, time, arrays of floating point numbers, bit vectors, etc., to supplement the built-in data types in a database system. In this paper we demonstrate the power of adding a data type corresponding to commands in a query language. We also propose three extensions to the query language QUEL to enhance its power in this augmented environment.

1.0. INTRODUCTION

Abstract data types (ADTs) [LISK74, GUTT77] have been extensively investigated in a programming language context. Basically, an ADT is an encapsulation of a data structure (so that its implementation details are not visible to an outside client procedure) along with a collection of related operations on this encapsulated structure. The canonical example of an ADT is a stack with related operations: new, push, pop and empty.

The use of ADTs in a relational database context has been discussed in [ROWE79b, SCHM78, WASS79]. In these proposals a relation is considered an abstract data type whose implementation details are hidden from application level software. Allowable operations are defined by procedures written in a programming language that supports both database access and ADTs. One use of this kind of data type is suggested in [ROWE79b] and involves an EMP abstract data type with related operations hire-employee, fire-employee and change-salary.

In [STON82a, STON83a] we presented an alternate use of ADTs.

M. Stonebraker, E. Anderson, E. Hanson, and B. Rubenstein, *ACM-SIGMOD International Conference on Management of Data*, Boston, Massachusetts, June 1984.

Instead of treating an entire relation as an ADT, we suggested that the individual columns of a relation be ADTs. This use of ADTs is a generalization of database experts [STON80c].

In Section 2.0 we briefly review our proposal and then in Section 3.0 we introduce QUEL as a data type and indicate desirable operators for this new type. Section 4.0 turns to a discussion of three extensions to the QUEL language that are useful in this environment. In Section 5.0 we consider optimization issues related to QUEL ADTs. Lastly, we indicate that several database problems including referential integrity, non-first normal form relations, and generalization hierarchies can be solved by defining QUEL as an abstract data type. Section 6.0 presents our approach to these problems. Section 7.0 concludes by summarizing the paper.

2.0. ABSTRACT DATA TYPES

We explain our use of ADTs with an example concerning geometric objects. In computer-aided design of integrated circuits, objects are often made up of rectangular boxes. For a VLSI database one would like to define a column of a relation as type BOX. For example, one might create a BOXES relation as follows:

```
CREATE BOXES (OWNER = i4,
              LAYER = c15,
              BOX-DESC = BOX-ADT)
```

Here, the boxes relation has three fields: the identifier of the circuit containing the box, the processing layer for the box (polysilicon, diffusion, etc.) and a description of the box's geometry. All fields are represented by built-in types except BOX-DESC, which is an ADT.

Tuples can be appended to this relation using QUEL [STON76a] as follows:

```
APPEND TO BOXES (OWNER = 99,
                 LAYER = "polysilicon",
                 BOX-DESC = "0,0,2,3")
```

The built-in data types are converted to an internal representation and stored in a database system. The string "0,0,2,3", represents the box bounded by x=0, y=0, x=2, y=3 and requires special recognition code. An input procedure must be available to the DBMS to perform the conversion of the character string "0,0,2,3" to an object with data type BOX-ADT. Such a routine is analogous to the procedure ascii-to-float which converts a character string to a floating point number.

It is desirable to have special operators for BOX-ADTs. For example, one would clip box dimensions as follows:

```
RANGE OF B IS BOXES
REPLACE B (BOX-DESC = B.BOX-DESC * "0,0,4,1")
        WHERE B.OWNER = 99
```

The * operator represents box intersection. In this case "0,0,4,1" will be converted to an object of type BOX-ADT, and a procedure must be available to perform box intersection between this ADT and B.BOX-DESC.

In addition, one might want to define new comparison operations. For example, one might wish to define | | as an operator meaning "overlaps." The | | operator could then be used to return the boxes overlapping the unit square based at the origin as follows:

```
RANGE OF B IS BOXES
RETRIEVE (B.BOX-DESC)
        WHERE B.BOX-DESC | | "0,0,1,1"
```

Again, a procedure is required for the overlap operator.

As a result an ADT contains the following elements:

1) a registration procedure to inform the DBMS of the new type, giving the length of its internal representation.

2) a collection of routines which implement operators for this type and perform conversions to other types. These routines must obey a prespecified protocol for accepting arguments and returning results. Once defined by the ADT implementor, the new type and operators become available to other users of the DBMS.

3) modest changes to the parser and query execution routines to correctly parse commands with new operators and call the routines defined by the ADT implementor during execution.

This abstraction has been constructed in about 2500 lines of code for the INGRES relational database system. Implementation details are addressed in [FOGG82, ONG82], and ADTs execute with a modest performance degradation [FOGG82]. Suggestions concerning how to integrate new operators into query processing heuristics and access methods are contained in [STON83a, ONG83].

3.0. QUEL AS A DATA TYPE

We turn now to utilizing the ADT mechanism to define commands in a query language as an ADT. Hence, a column of a relation can have values which are one (or more) commands in the data manipulation language, QUEL. We explain our proposal using the following relations:

```
EMP (NAME, SALARY-HISTORY, HOBBIES, DEPT, AGE, BONUS)
DEPT (DNAME, FLOOR)
SALARY (NAME, DATE, PAY-RATE)

SOFTBALL (NAME, POSITION, AVERAGE)
MUSIC (NAME, INSTRUMENT, LEVEL)
RACING (NAME, AUTO, CIRCUIT)
```

A tuple exists in the EMP relation for each employee in a particular company. Employees can have zero or more hobbies. For those employees who have softball as a hobby, a tuple in the SOFTBALL relation gives their position and batting average. If an employee plays an instrument, a tuple in MUSIC indicates the instrument he plays and his skill level. Lastly, those employees who race sportcars are listed in the RACING relation along with the type of car they drive and the circuit they race on.

The SALARY relation contains employees' salary histories. Each time the salary of an employee is modified, a tuple is appended to the SALARY relation indicating the date of the modification and the new PAY-RATE. The DEPT relation contains the floor number of each department. Lastly, the EMP relation contains three fields, SALARY-HISTORY, HOBBIES, and DEPT which are of type QUEL. The HOBBIES field holds a query (or queries) which, when executed, will yield information on the employee's hobbies. The DEPT field contains a query which will return the name of the department for which the employee works, and the SALARY-HISTORY field contains a query that finds all records in his salary history. An example insert to the EMP relation might be:

```
APPEND TO EMP (
  NAME = "Fred",
  SALARY-HISTORY = "RANGE OF S IS SALARY
                    RETRIEVE (S.ALL)
                    WHERE S.NAME = "Fred"",

  HOBBIES = "RANGE OF M IS MUSIC
             RETRIEVE (M.ALL) WHERE M.NAME = "Fred"
             RANGE OF R IS RACING
             RETRIEVE (R.ALL) WHERE R.NAME = "Fred"",

  DEPT = "RANGE OF D IS DEPT
          RETRIEVE (D.DNAME) WHERE D.DNAME = "toy"",
  AGE = 25,
  BONUS = 10)
```

The appropriate additional insertions are:

```
APPEND TO MUSIC(
        NAME = "Fred",
        INSTRUMENT = "piano",
        LEVEL = "novice")
APPEND TO RACING(
        NAME = "Fred",
        AUTO = "formula Ford",
        CIRCUIT = "SCCA")
```

This collection of inserts will append Fred as a new employee in the toy department with racing and music as hobbies.

In a later section we will propose an implementation of this data type. In this section we specify desirable operators for this type and their intended semantics.

The current implementation of ADTs [FOGG82, ONG82] allows operators to be overloaded. INGRES currently allows "." as an operator with two operands, a tuple variable and a column name, e.g., E.NAME. Our first ADT operator overloads the operator ".". First, we propose that "." allow a left operand which is a field of type QUEL and a right operand of type column name. For example:

```
RANGE OF E IS EMP
RETRIEVE (E.HOBBIES.INSTRUMENT)
        WHERE E.NAME = "Fred"
        AND E.HOBBIES.LEVEL = "novice"
```

In this case NAME is a column in the relation indicated by E while LEVEL and INSTRUMENT are columns in the relation (or relations) specified by the QUEL in E.HOBBIES. This command is interpreted as follows:

1) Find all values for E.HOBBIES which satisfy the qualification E.NAME = "Fred",

2) For each value found, ignore all commands which it contains except RETRIEVE and DEFINE VIEW. For each RETRIEVE command which the value contains, replace the keyword RETRIEVE with the keyword DEFINE VIEW and execute it to form a legal view. For each view definition which the value contains, execute it directly to form a legal view. Then, define T to be a tuple variable which will iterate over this collection of views. For each one, execute:

```
RETRIEVE (T.INSTRUMENT) WHERE T.LEVEL = "novice"
```

The result of the overall query is the union of the results of the individual commands executed in step 2.

In general, if X is a tuple variable, Y is a field of type QUEL, and Z is a field, then X.Y.Z is a field in a collection of views, one for each RETRIEVE and DEFINE VIEW command contained in a qualifying value for X.Y.

Moreover, "." can be arbitrarily nested and the above semantics apply recursively at each level. Also note that this use of "." is similar to that proposed in GEM [ZANI83], and we comment further on the relationship of our proposal to GEM in a later section.

Our second use of "." has a left operand which is a field of type QUEL and a right operand which is a QUEL statement, e.g.:

        RANGE OF E IS EMP
        RETRIEVE (E.SALARY-HISTORY.
              RETRIEVE (DATE, PAY-RATE) WHERE PAY-RATE < 400)
        WHERE E.NAME = "Fred"

Here, E.SALARY-HISTORY is a field of type QUEL and the inner RETRIEVE command is the right hand operand for the intervening ".". This use of "." is a short-hand notation for the equivalent expression:

        RANGE OF E IS EMP
        RETRIEVE (E.SALARY-HISTORY.DATE,
                E.SALARY-HISTORY.PAY-RATE)
        WHERE E.NAME = "Fred"
        AND E.SALARY-HISTORY.PAY-RATE < 400

In this nested retrieval context "." has a similar meaning to the one discussed above. In particular, the left hand operator evaluates to the collection of views mentioned earlier, and a range variable, say T, is created to iteratively span this set. The QUEL command which is the right hand operand is then executed for each view by appending T as the tuple variable to any field name which does not have an explicit variable.

When the right hand operand is a RETRIEVE command, the result of this operator is a collection of result relations. The semantics of "." when the right hand operand is a QUEL update command are unclear, and we expect to support this form of nesting only for RETRIEVEs.

We now turn to several other operators on QUEL data items. First, all the normal character string operators can be overloaded. For example:

        RANGE OF E IS EMP
        RETRIEVE (E.NAME) WHERE E.DEPT = "RANGE OF D IS DEPT
                                RETRIEVE (D.DNAME)
                                WHERE D.DNAME = "toy""

In this context, = simply implies character string equality between e.DEPT and the constant string containing the query.

Consider an operator, ==, which has two fields of type QUEL as operands and returns true if they specify the same collection of tuples. For example,

operator name	description	left operand	right operand	result
.	referencing	field of type QUEL	field-name	field
.	referencing	field of type QUEL	QUEL statement	relation
=	character string compare	*	*	boolean
==	relation compare	*	*	boolean
>>	relation inclusion	*	*	boolean
<<	relation inclusion	*	*	boolean
U	union	*	*	relation
!!	intersection	*	*	relation
JJ	natural join	*	*	relation
OJ	outer join	*	*	relation

* denotes a field of type QUEL, a QUEL statement,
a relation or a tuple variable

TABLE 20.1. Proposed Operators

```
RANGE OF E IS EMP
RANGE OF F IS EMP
RETRIEVE (E.NAME, F.NAME) WHERE E.SALARY-HISTORY ==
                         F.SALARY-HISTORY
```

This query will return pairs of employees with identical names and salary histories. A containment operator, <<, can be specified similarly for operands which are fields of type QUEL. Additionally, all operators in a relational algebra (e.g., join, union, intersection) can be easily defined between fields of type QUEL.

Any relational algebra operators will produce a result of type relation. Since QUEL allows cascaded operators, we require operators for data of type relation. It is straightforward to overload all operators for the QUEL data type to apply to data of type relation. For example to find pairs of employees with different names and the same salary history, we would execute

```
RANGE OF E IS EMP
RANGE OF F IS EMP
RETRIEVE (E.NAME, F.NAME)
      WHERE E.SALARY-HISTORY.
               RETRIEVE (DATE, PAYRATE)
      == F.SALARY-HISTORY.
               RETRIEVE (DATE, PAYRATE)
```

Here, == has relations as both operands and returns true if the two relations are equal.

The last generalization is to allow any operator for fields of type QUEL to be overloaded to apply to operands which are QUEL statements or tuple variables. For example, suppose a relation STANDARD contains a collection of dates and payrates. The following command would find all employees with the same salary history that appears in STANDARD:

```
RANGE OF E IS EMP
RANGE OF S IS STANDARD
RETRIEVE (E.NAME)
      WHERE E.SALARY-HISTORY.
               RETRIEVE (DATE, PAYRATE)
      == RETRIEVE (S.ALL)
```

Here the right hand operand of == is a simple QUEL statement. A short-hand for the above statement would have a tuple variable for the right operand of == as follows:

```
RANGE OF E IS EMP
RANGE OF S IS STANDARD
RETRIEVE (E.NAME)
      WHERE E.SALARY-HISTORY.
               RETRIEVE (DATE, PAYRATE)
      == S
```

Our complete set of proposed operators appears in Table 20.1. Most can be applied interchangeably to operands which are fields of type QUEL, tuple variables, QUEL statements, and relations.

4.0. EXTENSIONS TO QUEL

There are three main extensions which we propose for inclusion in QUEL to enhance its power in the ADT environment of Section 3. In addition, we endorse the proposal made in [ZANI83] to have default tuple variables. In this situation, a command such as:

RETRIEVE (EMP.AGE) WHERE EMP.NAME = "Fred"

would be interpreted as:

RANGE OF EMP IS EMP
RETRIEVE (EMP.AGE) WHERE EMP.NAME = "Fred"

This suggestion simplifies many QUEL commands and was inserted into one version of QUEL [RTI83b].

In addition to default tuple variables we propose three other extensions. First, we suggest the possibility of executing data in the database rather than retrieving or updating it. The syntax is as follows:

EXEC (EMP.HOBBIES) WHERE EMP.NAME = "Fred"

The target list must be a field of type QUEL and instances which satisfy the qualification are found and executed. In this case, the hobbies which Fred engages in are returned.

This extension frees a user from having to know the field names in the QUEL in E.HOBBIES. Also, it allows one to store updates in the database and execute them at a later time. Such database procedures are discussed in Section 6.0.

Notice that EXEC complicates the extended interpretation of "." in the previous section. For example, it is reasonable to have a value for E.HOBBIES which is an EXEC command. For example, one could change Fred's hobbies to be the same as John's by the following update:

RANGE OF E IS EMP
REPLACE E (HOBBIES =
    "RANGE OF F IS EMP
     EXEC (F.HOBBIES) WHERE F.NAME = "John"")
WHERE E.NAME = "Fred"

If X is a tuple variable, Y is a field of type QUEL and Z is a field, and if a qualifying value for X.Y contains an EXEC command, then the semantics of X.Y.Z from the previous section must be extended. In particular X.Y.Z can be a column in an additional set of views. For each EXEC contained in a qualifying value of X.Y, replace the EXEC by RETRIEVE and run the command. If the result contains values of type QUEL, then X.Y.Z must span any views which result from these values by executing DEFINE VIEW commands, replacing RETRIEVE commands by DEFINE VIEW commands and recursively applying the above meaning to EXEC commands.

The second extension is to generalize the RANGE statement. We propose to allow a tuple variable to range over a collection of one or more relations. Then we use this facility to support the further generalization illustrated below:

RANGE OF E IS
    EMP.SALARY-HISTORY WHERE EMP.NAME = "Fred"
RETRIEVE (E.DATE) WHERE E.PAY-RATE = 1000

The intent is to allow E to range over the result of a query specification. Because RETRIEVE is the only reasonable QUEL command to put in a RANGE statement, we leave it out of the syntax and include only the target list and qualification. Moreover, the query specification must return data items of type QUEL. The purpose of the second extension is to allow the above expression rather than the less natural equivalent command:

RANGE OF E IS EMP
RETRIEVE (E.SALARY-HISTORY.DATE)
    WHERE E.SALARY-HISTORY.PAY-RATE = 1000
    AND E.NAME = "Fred"

If X and U are tuple variables and Y a field of type QUEL, then the semantics of

RANGE OF U IS X.Y WHERE qualification

are the following:

1) Run the query

    RETRIEVE (X.Y) WHERE qualification

    to find qualifying data items of type QUEL.

2) For each RETRIEVE, DEFINE VIEW or EXEC command, perform the steps indicated earlier to define the appropriate collection of views, $C1,...,Cn$.

3) Replace the range statement by

    RANGE OF U is $C1,...,Cn$

The third extension is to allow update commands to have a generalized target relation as suggested by the following example:

APPEND TO EMP.SALARY-HISTORY
    (DATE = "6/81", PAYRATE = 2000, NAME = "Fred")
WHERE EMP.NAME = "Fred"

Currently QUEL only supports a target which is a relation. In this generalization, the target can also be a column of a relation in the database which is of type QUEL.

The intent of the third extension is to allow the above expression rather than the equivalent extended command:

RANGE OF E IS EMP.SALARY-HISTORY
WHERE EMP.NAME = "Fred"
APPEND TO E (DATE = "6/81", PAYRATE = 2000,
NAME = "Fred")

Notice that extended RANGE statements and extended targets automatically introduce views. The usual semantic problems occur in updating these views.

5.0. SPECIAL CASES OF QUEL AS A DATA TYPE

Three special QUEL data types will be suggested in this section to allow either increased performance or a more natural syntax. First we suggest relations as a special case of the QUEL ADT. Clearly, a value of type QUEL can be a relation, i.e.:

RANGE OF R IS ANY-RELATION
RETRIEVE (R.ALL)

Since the interpretation of the QUEL extensions in Section 4 required that the query be treated as a view, we must invoke view processing to support such functions. A data type of relation as a special case of a QUEL data type will allow such operators to be optimized by ignoring the view processing.

The internal representation of a QUEL data type may be anything from a text string for the command to a machine language procedure containing a compiled version of the access plan. The choice depends on trading off efficiency, flexibility and complexity of the underlying DBMS. Alternatively, it is also possible to precompute the answer to any RETRIEVE command. This collection of pointers to tuples would be stored as the value of the field. In the case that at most one tuple qualified, this value would be a pointer to a single tuple or the null pointer. This representation is exactly the data type "pointer to a tuple" suggested by Powell [POWE83] and by Zaniola [ZANI83]. More generally, the value could contain multiple pointers to tuples in different relations. Consequently, implementing the QUEL data type by precomputing answers for QUEL queries provides a generalized version of previous proposals. Storing such physical pointers in the database has a clear speed advantages over storing the query. However, it also has the disadvantage that a pointer can be left "dangling" if the tuple it points to is moved. Moreover, no consistency guarantee is made if the tuple which is pointed to gets updated.

A mechanism to overcome these deficiencies is to create a new lock mode. Besides conventional read and write locks, one could support a "materialize" lock. Such a lock would be placed on any object which was used to precompute another database object. Materialize locks would be compatible with read locks but not write locks. Moreover, any process which wished to set a write lock on an object for which a materialize lock had been previously set could "break" the materialize lock and invalidate the precomputed object. This procedure would succeed unless the precomputed object was locked. Such a policy has points in common with [BROW81] and can guaranteed database consistency in this environment.

The third special case of a QUEL data type can be illustrated by appending a tuple to the EMP relation, e.g.

APPEND TO EMP (NAME = "Joe", DEPT = "shoe")

In this case DEPT is a field of type QUEL and we would prefer to simply enter the value "shoe" and not the remainder of the query. If DEPT is defined to be a new ADT which is special version of the QUEL ADT, then the routine which converts from external to internal format for this ADT can change "shoe" to:

RETRIEVE (DEPT.DNAME) where DEPT.DNAME = "shoe"

Consequently, a user need not type all the extra pieces of the QUEL command.

6.0. USES OF QUEL AS A DATA TYPE

In this section we indicate several uses for the above facilities.

6.1. Unnormalized Relation

There has been much discussion surrounding normalization of relations, and several recent proposals have advocated unnormalized relations [HASK82, GUTT82, ZANI83]. One use of a QUEL ADT is to support hierarchical data as noted in the example use of SALARY-HISTORY.

6.2. Referential Integrity

The notion of referential integrity has been formalized for relational databases in [DATE81]. Basically, a data item must take on values from the set of values in a column of another relation. Notice that our example use of the DEPT field in the EMP relation automatically has this property. Although not all of the options suggested in [DATE81] can be easily supported using QUEL as a data type, several of the more common ones can be.

6.3. Variant Records

Our use of queries in the HOBBIES field corresponds closely to the notion of variant records in a programming language such as Pascal. Frames-oriented languages such as FRL [ROBE77] or KRL [BOBR77] also allow a slot in a frame to contain a value of an arbitrary type with arbitrary fields. Our use of QUEL queries with different ranges supports this notion.

6.4. Aggregation and Generalization

QUEL as a data type can support both generalization and aggregation as proposed in [SMIT77]. For example, consider:

>   PEOPLE (NAME, PHONE#)

where PHONE# is of type QUEL and is an aggregate for the more detailed values AREA-CODE, EXCHANGE and NUMBER. A simple APPEND to PEOPLE might be:

>   APPEND TO PEOPLE (NAME = "Fred", PHONE# =
>   "RETRIEVE (AREA-CODE = 415,
>   EXCHANGE = 999,
>   NUMBER = 9911)")

Generalization is also easy to support. If all employees have exactly one hobby, then the HOBBIES field in the EMP example relation will specify a simple generalization hierarchy. In fact, our example use of hobbies supports a generalization hierarchy with members which can be in several of the subcategories at once.

6.5. Database Procedures

Stored commands are easily supported with the facilities described above. For example, suppose an employee is allowed to have only one hobby and we want a general database procedure to change the hobby of an employee from playing softball to playing a musical instrument. Call this procedure SOFTBALL-TO-MUSIC and add it to a relation PROCEDURES as follows:

>   APPEND TO PROCEDURES(
>   NAME = "SOFTBALL-TO-MUSIC",
>   CODE = "DELETE SOFTBALL WHERE SOFTBALL.NAME = $1
>   APPEND TO MUSIC (NAME = $1,
>   INSTRUMENT = $2,
>   LEVEL = $3)
>   REPLACE EMP (HOBBIES =
>   "RETRIEVE (MUSIC.ALL)
>   WHERE MUSIC.NAME = $1")

Now suppose we define a new ADT operator, WITH, that will substitute a parameter list given as the right hand operator into a query which is the left hand operator. With this operator we can make Fred play the violin at skill level novice as follows:

>   EXEC (PROCEDURES.CODE WITH ("Fred", "violin", "novice"))
>   WHERE PROCEDURES.NAME = "SOFTBALL-TO-MUSIC"

In this way we can store collections of QUEL commands in the database and execute them as procedures.

6.6. Triggers

Triggers have been widely suggested as a possible mechanism for implementing consistency constraints and for producing side effects for commands. They can be supported by using the features discussed in previous sections. Consider a relation:

> TRIGGER (IF, RELNAME, COMMAND, THEN)

The field THEN is of type QUEL while IF is of type QUEL qualification. Both RELNAME and COMMAND are ordinary character string fields.

Currently INGRES performs deferred update [STON76a] and writes a "side file" containing proposed changes to the database as phase 1 of a command. In phase 2 the side file is processed and the changes are installed. Consider modifying the side file to be a relation SIDE and interrupting query processing at the end of phase 1 to perform:

> EXEC (TRIGGER.THEN) WHERE TRIGGER.IF
> > AND TRIGGER.COMMAND = user-command
> > AND TRIGGER.RELNAME = relation-from-user

Here, user-command is the type of command run by the user (e.g., REPLACE, DELETE) and relation-from-user is the name of the relation being updated. These constants are readily available from the run time DBMS.

An example tuple in the TRIGGER relation might be:

> APPEND TO TRIGGER(
> > IF = "SIDE.TID = EMP.TID AND EMP.NAME = "Fred"
> > > AND SIDE.AGE > EMP.AGE",
> > RELNAME = "EMP",
> > COMMAND = "REPLACE",
> > THEN = "APPEND TO ALARM
> > > (MESSAGE = "Fred got older")")

The TRIGGER relation is used to provide an alerting capability when Fred receives an update. Since TRIGGER may have a large collection of tuples, we require indexing on relname and command to restrict the set of TRIGGER.IF terms that must be evaluated. It may be reasonable to have other extra fields in TRIGGER to provide further efficiency in TRIGGER selection.

6.7. Storing Data as Rules

Consider the requirement that all employees over 40 years old must receive a bonus of 1000. The relation in Section 2 showed both AGE and BONUS as explicit data and an integrity constraint could easily be defined to enforce this constraint, e.g.:

```
RANGE OF E IS EMP
DEFINE INTEGRITY E WHERE E.BONUS = 1000 OR E.AGE <= 40
```

However, an alternative representation would be to remove BONUS as a stored field in EMP and add the following rule to TRIGGER:

```
APPEND TO TRIGGER(
        RELNAME = "EMP"
        THEN = "REPLACE SIDE(BONUS = 1000)
                WHERE SIDE.TID = EMP.TID AND
                EMP.AGE > 40")
```

If the QUEL parser was changed to allow queries that retrieve fields which are not stored, then this trigger will return the correct data by updating SIDE. Hence, the trigger mechanism can support storing data items as rules. Of course, the efficiency of this implementation is questionable, and it is awkward to ask questions about what rules are in effect.

6.8. Complex Objects

There has been substantial discussion concerning database support for complex objects [LORI83, STON83a]. Suppose a complex object is composed of text, lines, and polygons. It would be possible to construct the following relations:

```
OBJECT (OID, DESCRIPTION)
LINE (LID, DESCRIPTION, LOCATION)
TEXT (TID, DESCRIPTION, LOCATION)
POLYGON (PID, DESCRIPTION, LOCATION)
```

Here, the LINE, TEXT and POLYGON relations hold descriptions of individual objects and can make use of the abstract data types described in [STON83a]. Then, the description field in OBJECT would be of type QUEL and contain queries to assemble the pieces of any given object from the other relations. This representation allows clean sharing of lines, text and polygons among multiple higher level objects by allowing the same query to appear in multiple object descriptions.

Materializing an object from the OBJECT relation will be slow since it involves executing several additional QUEL queries. Hence, it is clearly desirable to precompute the value of frequently used objects and store the result in the OBJECT description field.

6.9. Transitive Closure

The facilities of this paper can be used to support transitive closure operations such as found in the "parts explosion" problem. Suppose one creates a PARTS relation as follows:

```
PARTS (PNAME, COMPOSED-OF)
```

Consider a car which is made up of a drivetrain and a body. These are made up in turn of other smaller parts. The car would be inserted as follows:

```
APPEND TO PARTS(
PNAME = "car",
COMPOSED-OF = "RETRIEVE (PNAME = "car")
                EXEC (PARTS.COMPOSED-OF)
                    WHERE PARTS.PNAME = "drive-train"
                EXEC (PARTS.COMPOSED-OF)
                    WHERE PARTS.PNAME = "body"")
```

The command

```
EXEC (PARTS.COMPOSED-OF) WHERE PARTS.PNAME = "car"
```

will find all the parts that make up a car.

7.0. IMPLEMENTATION

If INGRES had been designed to support internal multitasking, then it would be a simple matter to implement EXEC by stacking the INGRES processing environment and executing the new command in a single INGRES process. However, at this point it would be very costly to change our code to be reentrant and support this kind of recursion. Other systems (e.g., System-R [ASTR76]) do not have this shortcoming.

Hence, our operational code to implement EXEC spawns a separate copy of the INGRES code and passes the QUEL command to the spawned version for execution. Returned data is redirected through the INGRES which did the spawning to the user who ran the original command. Since the passed command can be another EXEC, the total number of spawned INGRES's can increase without bound. Currently, the command is passed to the spawned process as a character string and all query processing steps are performed at run time by the second process.

We are currently implementing QUEL as an ADT. This data type is internally represented as a character string. Storing a preprocessed version of the command would entail a great deal more code. Operators which return a result of type relation will store the result in the database and return the name of the object. This result can be involved in further processing or returned to the user. In the latter case, it is the responsibility of the internal-to-external conversion routine to accept the relation name, access the database and return tuples to the calling program or user.

No thought has been given on how to optimize QUEL commands extended with the operators of Table 20.1. Integrating these new functions into query processing heuristics is left for future research. The design of a programming language interface supporting the objects generated by our proposal also remains to be studied.

8.0. CONCLUSIONS

This paper has proposed a novel use of abstract data types and extended QUEL with three additional features. These extensions support added power, referential integrity, variant records, database procedures, generalization and aggregation in a single facility.

Our proposal has points in common with GEM, which supports new data types corresponding to "pointer to a tuple" and "set of values." Moreover, generalization hierarchies are supported and range variables can conveniently be defined over entities in this hierarchy. Our proposal effectively supports both of GEM's new data types as special cases of the QUEL ADT. Moreover, generalization is cleanly supported. Only GEM's use of range variables is not contained in our proposal.

Database Design

It appears that most designers of applications for relational database systems have difficulty designing relational schemas. Minimally, they have to simultaneously solve the following three problems.

1) A schema in 1st (or 2nd or nth) normal form for their data must be formulated.

2) Normal forms always "improve" the schema by dividing a single relation into two or more new ones. Hence, any command which spanned a single relation previously now spans two relations. Hence, a subset of an application is turned into join queries, which presumably execute at some performance penalty relative to single relation commands. Hence, there is a performance cost to normalization, and users may have to "denormalize" for performance reasons. This issue is studied in [SCHK82].

3) A physical database design must be done, i.e., storage keys for relations and appropriate secondary indexes must be specified. Again there are substantial performance consequences to the various possibilities.

Most relational systems give a user relatively little help with these three problems. Moreover, to accomplish the first task, a user must be able to generate an initial relational schema and then know enough normalization theory to understand how to obtain nth normal form, for some n. This requires that the user understand the concept of functional dependencies. Issues 2 and 3 require that the user understand data structures well enough to make an intelligent choice among the alternatives. The user must also know something about accessing patterns.

Accomplishing these steps requires either an intellectual guru or a mere mortal with substantial database experience. The tools that have been proposed to assist with these problems are very primitive. Moreover, this issue is an ideal example of an expert system, and the database community clearly needs to write one or more.

The two papers in this section have been chosen because they seem to shed some light on these problems. The first paper gives a simple methodology for designing databases which a "nonguru" can understand. In fact, this simple methodology yields 4th normal form without requiring the user to have a higher degree in mathematics. The second paper gives an intuitively understandable framework in which to view the choice of access paths. Again, no complex concepts must be understood to use the methodology.

## CHAPTER TWENTY-ONE

Logical Design and Schema Conversion for Relational and DBTG Databases

Eugene Wong / Randy H. Katz

ABSTRACT

The objective of this paper is three-fold: first, a variant of the Entity-Relationship model is proposed as the data model for logical design. In terms of the constructs of the model "update anomalies" as the goal for logical design, mapping rules will be proposed for transforming a design schema into a corresponding schema of either relational or DBTG type. Third, it is shown that with relatively minor semantic augmentation of DBTG and relational data models, the mapping is reversible. As a consequence, reversible schema conversion between DBTG and relational models becomes possible.

1.0. INTRODUCTION

The semantic sparseness of the relational data model, while responsible for much of its power in retrieval and data manipulation, works against it in update operations. This defect has long been recognized [CODD71], and the problem has given rise to a theory of "normal forms" [BERN76, FAGI77a, FAGI77b]. With a substantial and growing literature, the theory of relational normal forms has acquired a life of its own, and most of the recent results do not directly address problems of update difficulties. While logical design for databases of the CODASYL-DBTG type has received comparatively little attention, problems of update anomalies are no less important there. The first motivation for the work reported in this paper is to provide a unified

E. Wong and R. H. Katz, in *Entity-Relationship Approach to Systems Analysis and Design*, P. P. Chen, editor, North-Holland Publishing Company, Amsterdam, The Netherlands, 1980.

framework for designing relational and DBTG schemas that are free of update anomalies.

Our work is also motivated by the realization that coexistence of DBTG and relational data models in the same system may well be necessary in many instances. A distributed database system, for example, may result from the integration of existing databases of both types. Consequently, we believe that algorithms for DBTG-Relational schema conversion that are semantics-preserving are needed. We propose that a test for semantics-preservation be reversibility of the conversion process.

Our approach to both of these problems is to introduce as an intermediary a "design data model" which is a variant of the Entity-Relationship model. Specifically, we shall do three things: define "update anomalies" in terms of the constructs of the design mode; present mapping rules for producing anomaly-free schemas of both DBTG and relational types, and by semantic augmentation make these mappings reversible and consequently render a reversible schema conversion between DBTG and relational data models possible.

2.0. A DESIGN MODEL

We shall use the term "data model" in a generic sense to mean a collection of data object types, and a "schema" to mean a specific choice of data objects to represent a database. For example, the relational data model consists of the data object types domains and relations, while a relational schema would comprise a specific collection of relations, each with specified domains.

Our point of departure is to choose a basic semantic data model to be used to specify a design schema. The model as such is not new, being a simplified version of both the Entity-Relationship model [CHEN76] and the semantic data model introduced in [SCHM75].

For each instance of time t, let $E_1(t), E_2(t), \ldots, E_n(t)$ be n distinct sets, which we shall call "entity sets." An entity set, usually referenced by name, is in reality a family of sets which change as members are inserted and deleted.

A "property" of an entity set $E(t)$ is a one-parameter family of functions f_t, mapping at each t $E(t)$ into some set V of values. Observe that implicit in this definition are the requirements that: (a) at each t f_t is defined on all of $E(t)$, and (b) for every e in $E(t)$ the value $f_t(e)$ is unique.

As an example, consider the following entity sets and properties:

entity set	properties
EMP	ENAME, BIRTHYR
DEPT	DNAME, LOCATION
JOB	TITLE, STATUS, SALARY

A relationship R_t among entity sets $E_1(t)$, ..., $E_n(t)$ is a time-varying relation, i.e., at each t R_t is a subset of the cartesian product $E_{(t)}XE_2(t)X...XE_n(t)$. For example, the following two relationships specify respectively the employees qualified to hold each job, and the jobs allocated to each department:

QUALIFIED (JOB, EMP)
ALLOCATION (DEPT, JOB)

A relationship may optionally have a property defined on it. For example, NUMBER ALLOCATED is such a property for ALLOCATION. We assume that the relationships specified in a design schema are independent and indecomposable. Independence means that no relationship is derivable from other relationships, and indecomposability means that no relationship is equal to the join of two of its projections for all time.

We shall say that a binary relationship R_t on entity sets $E_1(t)$ and $E_2(t)$ is "single-valued" in $E_1(t)$ if each entity of $E_1(t)$ occurs in at most one instance of R_t. If each entity in $E_1(t)$ occurs in exactly one instance of R_t, we shall call R_t an "association." At each t an association $R_t(E_1(t),E_2(t))$ is a function which maps $E_1(t)$ into $E_2(t)$. For example, consider the binary relationship MGR (EMP). If each department is required to have one and only one manager at all times, then MGR(EMP) is an association. If a department can be temporarily without a manager, then MGR(EMP) is a binary relationship, single-valued in DEPT, but is not an association. As we shall see, the distinction between an association and other relationships is important for both relational and DBTG schemas. The distinction between single-valued relationships and other relationships is important in the DBTG data model, where the set construct provides a natural support for "single-valued" relationships.

We shall assume that neither an association nor a single-valued relationship has a property defined on it. A property of an association is necessarily a property of the domain entity set of the association so that the concept is superfluous. A single-valued relationship cannot enjoy automatic integrity support through the set construct if it has a property defined on it.

The design model that we have outlined distinguishes among the following semantic objects:

1) entity set,
2) properties of entity sets,
3) associations,
4) single-valued binary relationships,
5) relationships,
6) properties of relationships.

An example of a design schema is the following:

entity set	properties
EMP	ENAME, BIRTHYR
DEPT	DNAME, LOCATION
JOB	TITLE, SALARY

associations
WORKS-IN (EMP, DEPT)
ASSIGNMENT (EMP, JOB)

relationship	status	properties
MGR (EMP)	single-valued	–
QUALIFIED (EMP, JOB)	general	–
ALLOCATION (DEPT, JOB)	general	number

3.0. DESIGN FOR ANOMALY-FREE UPDATES

Roughly speaking, "update anomalies" take the form of either "fragmentation of an atomic operation" or "uncontrolled side effects." A data model used for logical design must make these issues clear. We think that the design model we have introduced is particularly well suited for this purpose.

We shall define an "atomic update operation" as one of the following:

1)   inserting or deleting an entity,

2)   inserting or deleting an instance in a relationship,

3)   changing the value of a function (property or association) of an entity.

An atomic update operation may cause inconsistencies in the database. For example, suppose the job-entity ENGINEER is deleted, what happens to employees who are engineers? For consistency to be maintained, one or more additional atomic updates may have to be undertaken. These induced updates will be referred to as "side-effects."

Observe that only updates of type (1) have side-effects, and these can be described as follows:

1)   Deleting an entity e causes

   a)   the deletion of any instance of a relationship in which e participates, and

   b)   the deletion of any entity that has e as its range value in an association.

2)   Insertion of an entity e requires any entity that is the value of any association of e to already exist.

We note that side-effects of the type (1b) propagate, so that deleting one entity may spawn a large number of additional entity deletions. The type "association" exists precisely to allow automatic propagation of deletions. Whether one designates a single-valued binary relationship as an association or not is a design choice used to control side-effects. The concept of "dependent entities" can be modeled by an association in this way.

We also note that the insertion side-effect (2) means that the order of insertion of entities may be constrained by associations, and no cycle of associations can exist.

Our approach to logical design can now be stated. First, one specifies a schema (design schema) in terms of the design data model. In so doing, one completely determines the atomicity and side-effects of all update operations. To design schemas of the relational and DBTG types, one needs mapping rules that would transform the design schema into one of the appropriate types, while preserving both atomicity and side-effects of updates. What we mean by this is expressed by the following goals for the mapping rules:

Preservation of Atomicity

One atomic update affects a single tuple in the corresponding relational schema and a single record (plus possibly some set membership changes) in the DBTG schema.

Preservation of Side-Effects

The additional atomic operations induced are exactly the same as in the design model case.

The DBTG data model provides the possibility of automatic integrity support for the constructs "association" and "single-valued relationship." We wish to take advantage of this possibility. Hence, the mapping rules for the DBTG case should provide:

Automatic Integrity Support (for "association" and single-valued relationships)

This support will be achieved through the feature of set-membership-option on insert/delete provided in the DBTG definition facility.

4.0. MAPPING RULE FOR A RELATIONAL SCHEMA

We define an "identifier" as a one-to-one property of an entity set, designated to represent the entities. As such, the value of the identifier for a given entity cannot be changed [HALL76]. A "primary" function is a property or an association specified in the design schema. A "primitive object" is either a relationship, or an entity set in its role as the domain of a primary function. We propose the following rules for mapping a design schema into a relational schema.

1) Each entity set has an explicit identifier which represents it globally in the relational model.

2) The identifier(s) of a primitive object together with all the primary functions of the primitive object are grouped in the same relation of the relational schema.

3) There is one and only one primitive object per relation of the relational schema.

Comments:

1) Often, an entity can be identified by a combination of associations and/or properties. For example, (DNAME, MGR) may well identify a department uniquely. We shall assume that even in such cases, an explicit identifier is assigned. Arguments in favor of an explicit identifier are many and to us persuasive: (a) Values of properties and associations can change, and such changes can propagate if they are used in identifiers, thus violating the minimal update design objective. (b) An identifier is an incarnation of an entity and as such should only be inserted and deleted, not changed. (c) Finally, it usually takes more than one association and/or property to uniquely identify an entity set. For global representation, such a combination is too verbose.

2) The concept of an identifier is not the same as that of a "key" in the framework of normalization. A key is defined in terms of the attributes of a specific relation, while we have defined an identifier in terms of an entity set and nothing else. An identifier is more than a one-to-one function; its role is to stand for the corresponding entity.

3) Mapping rule (2) is clearly designed to minimize updates. By choosing to represent an association as a relationship, a designer can circumvent the automatic deletion property of an association, but at the price of sacrificing some economy in expression for updates.

4) We believe that mapping rule (3) by itself captures the essence of normal forms. A violation of any one of the normal forms can be interpreted as a violation of rule (3).

Example:

Consider the design schema given in the previous example. Let us introduce the following identifiers for the entity sets: ENO for EMP, DNO for DEPT, and JID for JOB. The primitive objects for this example together with their functions are given as follows:

primitive object	function
EMP	ENAME,BIRTHYR,WORKS-IN,ASSIGNMENT
DEPT	DNAME,LOCATION
JOB	TITLE,SALARY
MGR	–
ALLOCATION	NUMBER
QUALIFIED	–

These are mapped into five relations according to the mapping rules as follows:

    EMP(ENO, ENAME, BIRTHYR, ASSIGNMENT, WORKS-IN)
    DEPT(DNO, DNAME, LOCATION, MGR)
    JOB(JID, TITLE, SALARY)
    ALLOC(DNO, JID, NUMBER)
    QUAL(JID, ENO)

5.0. NORMAL FORMS

A violation of one of the normal forms can always be interpreted as a violation of mapping rule (3). Different ways in which (3) are violated correspond to different normal forms, and these can be classified as follows:

(A) Putting two primitive objects which have no entity set in common in the same relation. This violation of (3) results in a relation not in 2NF.

Example: Cartesian product of JOB and DEPT

(B) Putting a function of an entity set and a relationship involving it in the same relation. This too results in a relation not in 2NF.

Example: Equijoin of JOB and QUAL on JID

(C) Putting two functions with different entity sets as their domains in the same relation. If this violation is not one of category (A) then it must involve function f_1 and f_2 of the form

$$E_1 \xrightarrow{f_1} E_2 \xrightarrow{f_2} S$$

Example: The equijoin EMP (ASSIGNMENT = JID)JOB

(D) Putting two relationships with a common entity set together in the same relation. This violation results in a relation not in 4NF.

Consider the equijoin AQ of ALLOC with QUAL. As it stands, AQ is not in 2NF because of the partial dependence of NUMBER on the key (DNO, JID, ENO) of AQ. The projection AQ[DNO, JID, ENO] is in 3NF (and hence also 2NF), but not 4NF. There are two multivalued dependencies: "ENO on JID" and "DNO on JID" in AQ[DNO, JID, ENO].

Theorem 5.1: A relational schema resulting from applying the mapping rules (1) - (3) to a design schema is in 4NF.

Proof: By rule (3), there is one and only one primitive object per relation. One possibility is that the primitive object is an entity set E serving as the domain of a collection of primary functions. In this case its identifier is a key of the relation, and every attribute, being a representation of a primary function of E, is a full function of the identifier. There can be no multivalued dependency in such a relation.

The other possibility is that the primitive object is a relationship. The identifiers of the entity sets making up the relationship comprise a key of the relation, and every non-key attribute is a function of the key. Suppose that contrary to the assertion of the theorem the relation is not in 4NF, then it is equal to the join of two relations [FAGI77a]. Either the identifiers making up the key are split between these two relations or they are not. If they are split then the relationship must be decomposable, contradicting the assumption that each relationship in the design schema is indecomposable. If the key resides entirely in one of the component relations, then attributes of the other component relation cannot be functions of the key, contradicting mapping rule (2).

6.0. MAPPING RULES FOR A DBTG SCHEMA

The following mapping rules are introduced to convert a design schema into a DBTG schema so as to achieve our design goals:

1) Each entity set has an explicit identifier.

2) For each entity set E define a record type r(E). The data items of r(E) are made up of the identifier of E and the properties of E.

3) For an association or single-valued relationship $R(E_1, E_2)$ where $E_1 \neq E_2$, define a set type s(R) with $r(E_2)$ as the member record type.

4) For an association or single-valued relationship R(E,E) define a record type r(R) having no data item, and a pair of set types $s_1(R)$ and $s_2(R)$ forming a cycle between r(E) and r (R). The assignment is depicted in Figure 21.1.

5) For a general relationship $R(E_1, E_2,...,E_n)$ define a confluent hierarchy, consisting of a record type r (R) with only the properties of R as its data items, and n set types $s_1(R), s_2(R),...,s_n(R)$ as shown in Figure 21.2.

All the object types in the design model have now been mapped into object types in the DBTG data model. Two kinds of record types have resulted from the mapping; ones which contain an identifier data item and those which do not. We shall call the former "self-identified" record types, and the

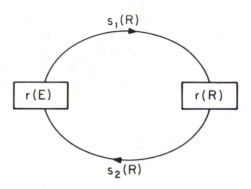

FIGURE 21.1. A Single Valued Relationship or Association

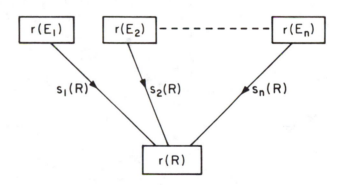

FIGURE 21.2. A Confluent Hierarchy

latter "link" record types. Self-identified record types represent entity sets while link record types represent relationships and possibly associations.

For set types the logical concept of total membership would be useful in our context. A record type r is a "total" member of a set type s if every occurrence of r is a member of an occurrence of s. A member that is not total is said to be "partial." The membership of a link record type in any set type should always be total. The membership of a self-identified record type should be total in any set which represents an association but not otherwise.

The concept of "total" membership in sets does not exist in the current version of the DBTG model although a related concept appears to have been suggested by [NIJI75].

Natural enforcement for "total" membership is provided by the mandatory/automatic option for delete/insert in DBTG, except when a sequence of set types forms a cycle. In that case one set type in the cycle is required to be "manual" on insertion. Under our mapping rules a cycle of set types each having a total member can arise in only two ways: (i) a two-set cycle representing a self-association, (ii) a cycle of associations. In the first case we shall make the set types $s_2(R)$ mandatory/manual. In the latter case we choose any one of the set types to be mandatory/manual.

Summarizing our discussion on set membership, we have the final mapping rule for DBTG:

6) The membership of a link record type in any set type is total. The membership of a self-identified record type in any set that represents an association (or is a part of the representation of a self-association) is total, but not otherwise. All set membership that are not total are optional/manual. All total memberships are mandatory/automatic, except for a self-association or a cycle of associations. For the exceptions one of the set types in the cycle must have a mandatory/manual membership option, and the property of being "total" must be supported procedurally.

Application of these six rules to the first example yields the DBTG schema shown in Figure 21.3. Except for the partial membership of DEPT in MGR, all memberships are total.

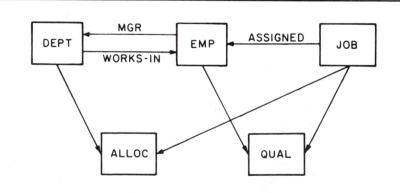

FIGURE 21.3. A DBTG Schema

▄▄▄ 7.0. SCHEMA TRANSLATION AND EQUIVALENCE

The mapping rules indicate which objects of the target model schema have been derived from design model constructs. If the schema is augmented with additional semantic information that distinguishes among similar objects derived from different design model objects, the mapping rules of Sections 4.0 and 6.0 can be used to formulate inverse mappings.

For example, in Section 6.0 we introduced a distinction between self-identified records and link records, and between total and partial memberships in a set in a DBTG schema. Although these distinctions can be deduced from existing constructs of the DDL, it is desirable to make them explicit in the DBTG schema. Similarly, the relational schema can be augmented with identification of key and foreign key domains (ID domains).

The equivalent relational and DBTG constructs for each design model construct are shown below:

Entity Set	Record Type(SI)	Relation(E)
Identifier	Data Item(ID)	Key Domain(ID)
Property	Data Item	Domain(value)
Association	Set Type(Total)	Domain(ID)
S.V. Relationship	Set Type(Partial)	Relation(S)
E_1 (S.V.)	Member	Key Domain(ID)
E_2	Owner	Domain(ID)
Relationship	Record Type(L)	Relation(R)
Property	Data Item	Domain(value)
	+ Set Types(Total)	
$E_1, E_2, ..., E_n$	Owners	Domains(ID)

We note that there is a certain difficulty in distinguishing between a single-valued relationship and a general binary relationship within a derived relational schema without distinguishing between the types of relations. This is why we have introduced E,S, and R relations.

It follows that DBTG schema derived from a design schema by following our mapping rules can be translated into a relational schema which is the same as what would be obtained by directly mapping the design schema. The rules of translation are rather simple and given below.

For a self-identified record, define its "key" to be its identifier. For a link record, define its "key" to be collection of the keys of the owner of all sets in which the link record is a member. For a DBTG schema obtained from using our mapping rules, link records can only be owned by self-identified records, so that the definition of key is not circular. We propose the following rules for DBTG to relational schema translation.

1)   For each self-identified record type r, define a relation R(r). Each data item of r is a domain of R(r). The key of the owner of every set in which r is a total member is also a domain of R(r).

2) For each link record type k that is the member of two or more set types, define a relation R(k). The domains of R(k) consist of the data items of k plus the keys of the owners of the sets in which k is a member.

3) For each set type s which has a partial member, define a binary relation R(s). The domains of R(s) are the keys of the owner and the member of s.

In terms of the constructs of the design model, the first rule identifies an entity set, the second a relationship, and the third, a single-valued relationship.

Similarly, we can formulate the rules for mapping a relational schema directly into a DBTG schema. Identifier domains are drawn from the key values of the associated E-relation. We propose the following rules for relational-to-DBTG schema transformation:

4) For each E-relation R define a self-identified record type r whose identifier is the key domain of R. Each value domain of R is a data item of r. The representation of the E-relations associated with the identifier domains of R are owners of sets for which r is a total member.

5) For each R-relation R define a link record type 1. Each value domain of R is a data item of 1. The representation of the E-relations associated with the identifier domains of R are owners of sets for which 1 is a total member.

6) For each S-relation R, the representation of the E-relation associated with the key domain of R is the partial member of a set owned by the representation of the E-relation associated with the identifier domain of R.

Rule 4 identifies an entity set, rule 5 a relationship, and rule 6 a single-valued relationship.

We have identified a collection of DBTG schemas that can be mapped into corresponding relational schemas while preserving the design goals. The translation procedure can be applied in general, but in doing so, we impose a semantic interpretation on the schema to be translated. The success of the translation depends on the extent to which the interpretation is correct.

8.0. CONCLUSION

The focus of this paper is semantics of data models, but semantics with a purpose. The purpose is two-fold: logical design to avoid update anomalies, and semantic comparison between data models to achieve schema translation that is reversible. We believe that in the process the semantics of both relational and DBTG models are elucidated. Issues of performance have not been addressed. For the relational case, issues of performance relate only to the storage schema and are rightly avoided in the design of the conceptual schema. The situation is somewhat more complex in the DBTG case. There are constraints as to how sets are implemented, so that logical design bears an impact on performance. We shall try to explain this issue through an example.

Consider a design schema containing entity sets: SUPPLIERS and PARTS, and a relationship INVENTORY (SUPPLIERS, PARTS). Following the mapping rules of Section 6.0 results in a DBTG schema as depicted in Figure 21.4, where INVENTORY is a link record type. It can be argued with some cogency that if the only accesses are through suppliers, then the design shown in Figure 21.5 would be better for performance.

The latter design can, in fact, be obtained with our procedure by modifying the design schema. Instead of PARTS, introduce an entity set PARTS-OF-SUPPLIERS, the same part supplied by different suppliers being separate entities. The INVENTORY relationship is now single-valued in PARTS-OF-SUPPLIERS, so that an application of the third mapping rule in Section 6.0 results in precisely the second design. The design goals are still

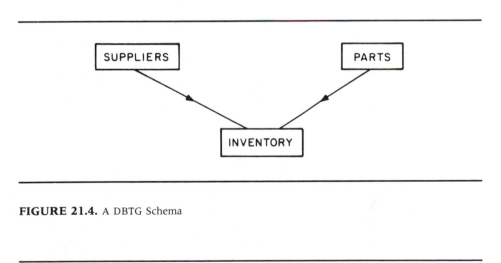

FIGURE 21.4. A DBTG Schema

FIGURE 21.5. Another DBTG Schema

satisfied but now have a different interpretation. For example, changing the property of a part is no longer an atomic update operation, because a part is no longer an entity. Hence, atomicity, though preserved, no longer guarantees that only a single data-item value be changed. In short, one can change the DBTG design by manipulating the design schema, but there are consequences of doing so on redesign and updates, and these can be made explicit by a careful examination of the design goals.

## CHAPTER TWENTY-TWO

An Access Path Model for Physical Database Design

R. H. Katz / Eugene Wong

ABSTRACT

Design and Access Path Data Models are presented to form an integrated framework for logical and physical database design in a heterogeneous database environment. This paper focuses on the physical design process. First, a physical design is specified in terms of general properties of access paths, independent of implementation details. Then, a design is realized by mapping the specification into the storage structures of a particular database system. Algorithms for assigning the properties to logical access paths and for realizing a 1978 CODASYL DBTG schema are given.

1.0. INTRODUCTION

As the trend towards distributed database systems continues to gain in momentum, the problem of database design in a heterogeneous environment is becoming crucial. We view a distributed database system as being built on top of existing systems available at the local sites of a computer network. If a distributed database is to evolve naturally, there must be support for extending it to the underlying heterogeneous systems.

Database design is complicated by the difficulty in designing physical databases for a variety of storage structures supported by the underlying systems. We follow [CARD75] in partitioning the physical design process into its implementation-oriented (access path selection) and implementation-dependent (storage structure choice) aspects. A physical design is specified in terms of basic properties of storage structures without making a commitment to an actual implementation. A design is "realized" by mapping the system-independent specification into the storage structures available in a particular database system. Analytic methods, such as [CARD73, GOTL74, CARD75, YAO75, SILE76, DUHN78, SCHK78], can be used in the latter step. Our contribution is to provide an integrated framework for logical and physical design, and to provide design tools with a high degree of independence from the underlying data models and systems.

In this paper, we propose the concept of an access path data model for physical design. The access path model has grown out of the attempts to extend our work with the Design Model [WONG79] to problems of physical database design. The term "data model" is used in a generic sense to mean a collection of data object types, such as attributes and relations in the relational model. "Schema" is used to mean a specific choice of data objects to represent a database, such as a choice of specific relations and associated attributes.

The access path model can be viewed as an interface between the logical view of data and the access methods and storage structures chosen to support that view. In terms of the language of the ANSI/X3/SPARC report [TSIC77b], it mediates between the conceptual and internal schemas.

We are not the first to exploit the usefulness of an access path model. The DIAM (Data Independent Access Model) framework [SENK73] is structured into four levels consisting of entity set, string, encoding, and physical device models. The string model is most closely associated with our notion of access path model. Although the DIAM model is a significant contribution, we believe that our formulation of access path is more natural and easy to understand. In addition, the access path schema is oriented towards the problem of physical design, rather than a general model of data management systems.

The paper is organized as follows. A semantic data model is presented which is the basis for our approach to database design. Logical access paths are represented by functional interrelationships between objects. The access path model is defined to capture those functions which can be used to efficiently access objects in the physical realization of the database. A methodology for specifying an implementation-oriented physical design is given which is based on assigning the highest level support for the most frequently traversed access paths. A simple-minded approach for mapping a design specification into the storage structure of CODASYL DBTG systems is included, we conclude the paper with a discussion on future directions.

2.0. THE DESIGN MODEL

The design model is the starting point for our approach to database design. It has been formulated to capture the kinds of integrity constraints supported by the relational and DBTG models, yet remains independent of them. The model is based on a variation of the entity-relationship model [CHEN76] and has been influenced by the semantic data model of [SCHM75]. A more complete discussion of the design model and its application to logical design and schema conversion can be found in [WONG79].

For each instance of time t, let $E_1(t)$, $E_2(t)$, ... , $E_N(t)$ be n distinct sets, which are called *entity sets*. A *property* of an entity set $E(t)$ is a one-parameter family of functions f_t, mapping at each t $E(t)$ into a set V of values. Because f_t is defined for every element of the domain, it is a total function. As an example, consider the following entity sets and properties:

ENTITY SETS	PROPERTIES
EMP	ENAME, BIRTHYR
DEPT	DNAME, LOCATION
JOB	TITLE, STATUS, SALARY

A relationship R_t among entity sets $E_1(t)$, $E_2(t)$, ... , $E_N(t)$ is a subset of the cartesian product $E_1(t)$ X $E_2(t)$ X ... X $E_N(t)$ at each time t. Properties of relationships may be defined in an analogous way to properties of entity sets. Relationships are assumed to be independent, i.e., not derivable from other relationships, and nondecomposable, i.e., not equal to the join of their projections into subrelationships. For example, the following two relationships specify the employees qualified to hold each job, and the jobs allocated to a given department. "Number allocated" may be specified as a property of "allocation":

RELATIONS	PROPERTIES
QUALIFIED (JOB, EMP)	- - -
ALLOCATION (DEPT, JOB)	NUMBER

We further distinguish the types of relationship recognized by the design model. A binary relationship R_t on entity sets $E_1(t)$ and $E_2(t)$ is *single-valued* in $E_1(t)$ if each entity of $E_1(t)$ occurs in at most one instance of R_t. Intuitively, we may think of R_t as representing a function from $E_1(t)$ into $E_2(t)$, because each entity in $E_1(t)$ can be related to no more than one entity in $E_2(t)$. If each entity in $E_1(t)$ occurs in exactly one instance of R_t, R_t is called an *association*. We may think of R_t as representing a total function. Single-valued relationships which are not associations can be thought of as partial functions, because at a given point in time, the function need not be defined over all entities in $E_1(t)$. Associations are used to model the situation in which the domain object can exist only if it is related to some range object. If an object in the range of an association is deleted, then the objects in the domain no longer occur in an instance of R_t. Therefore, they must be deleted to maintain the totality of the function. Examples of associations include:

WORKS-IN (EMP, DEPT)
ASSIGNMENT (EMP, JOB)

which represent the facts that an employee must work-in some department at all times and must be assigned to some job at all times. An example of a single-valued relationship which is not an association is:

MGR (DEPT, EMP)

which associates a managing employee with a department, although a department can exist without a manager.

Explicit provisions for value set definitions have been omitted in our model. A subsystem such as that proposed in [MCLE76] could be included, but existing systems do not support sophisticated domain definition. A simpler approach is to use the primitive data types supported by most systems for the domain definition (e.g., integer, char(10), etc.).

Our design model can be reformulated to represent logical access paths in terms of total and partial functions between objects. This is similar to the

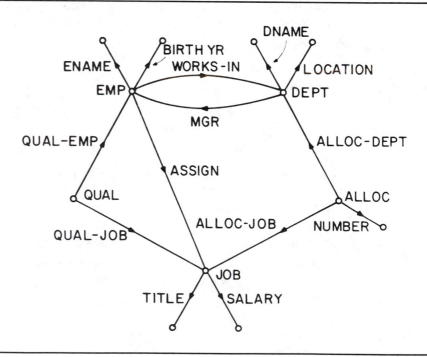

FIGURE 22.1. Graphical Representation of Schema

approach taken in the functional data models of [BUNE79] and [SHIP80]. The objects of the schema are the value sets, entity sets, and relationships. Single-valued relationships are partial functions, while associations and properties are total functions. In addition, total functions can be defined to map a relationship object into the entity set objects over which it is defined.

The above example is reproduced here in terms of the functional viewpoint (some abbreviation has taken place):

> TOTAL FUNCTIONS
>   ENAME: EMP → char(20)
>   TITLE: JOB → char(15)
>   BIRTHYR: EMP → integer
>   SALARY: JOB → integer
>   DNAME: DEPT → char(10)
>   WORKS-IN: EMP → DEPT
>   LOCATION: DEPT → char(20)
>   ASSIGNMENT: EMP → JOB
>   QUAL-EMP: QUAL → EMP
>   QUAL-JOB: QUAL → JOB
>   ALLOC-DEPT: ALLOC → DEPT
>   ALLOC-JOB: ALLOC → JOB
>   NUMBER: alloc → integer
> PARTIAL FUNCTIONS
>   MGR: DEPT → EMP

A design schema can be represented graphically. Let I = (V,E) be a directed graph with set V of vertices and set E of edges. For each object in the schema, there is a vertex in V. For each function from $object_1$ to $object_2$, there is a directed edge from the vertex for $object_1$ to the vertex for $object_2$. Value objects are represented by black vertices, non-value objects by white. The graphical representation of the example schema is shown in Figure 22.1.

3.0. THE ACCESS PATH MODEL

The functions of the design model represent logical access paths that can be used to navigate among the objects of the schema. For example, WORKS-IN(ENAME^{-1}("fred")) gives us the department that Fred works in. The access path schema is concerned with those functions and inverses that are "supported" for efficient access by the underlying database system. "Support" is used in an operational sense to mean that the time to perform a supported access is less than the time to perform an unsupported one.

When used to access objects, logical access paths are called *access mappings*. An access mapping may be defined for either a function or its inverse. To make it possible to compose access mappings, we extend the definition to allow them to be applied to sets of domain objects. An access mapping is *supported* in the storage structure if the database system can efficiently perform the desired access, i.e., the time to access an object via a supported access map is less than the time to scan the object set exhaustively for the desired object(s). If an access mapping is not supported, it is an *unsupported* access mapping. Supported access mapping is our terminology for the usual notion of access path.

An access path schema consists of the objects of the design schema and the supported access mappings. A graphical representation similar to the one proposed in the previous section can be used to represent an access path schema. The schema must continue to represent all logical interrelationships, whether or not they are efficiently supported. For example, WORKS-IN associates with each employee a single department. If WORKS-IN is not supported, we must still be able to access the associated department, albeit not as efficiently as if the mapping had been supported. To accomplish this, we introduce the concept of *identifier*. An identifier is a 1-to-1 property of an entity set which is used to uniquely represent each entity in the set. An unsupported access mapping between employees and departments can be represented instead as an access mapping between employees and the identifier value set of department.

(supported)   WORKS-IN: EMP → DEPT
(unsupported) WORKS-IN: EMP → identifiers of DEPT

The access path schema, together with the assigned storage structure properties (introduced in Section 4.1), captures the effects of storage structure support without committing the schema to a particular implementation and without sacrificing any of the interrelationships of the design schema. WORKS-IN can be used to navigate directly between employees and departments only if the mapping is supported by the underlying system. It is immaterial whether this support is furnished by a physical pointer between employee records and department records, an index that maps employee identifiers into department records, or some other technique.

4.0. PHYSICAL DATABASE DESIGN

The access path schema provides a useful interface between the user's logical view of the data and its physical implementation. In this section, we will describe an implementation-oriented physical design methodology which is largely independent of the specific database system and data model. The implementation-dependent aspects will be discussed in Section 5.0.

The approach is to generate designs which provide the best possible support for the most travelled access paths, without conflicting with the support for other paths. A specification of the user's expected access patterns is used to direct the design process. A system specific mapping is then invoked to implement the access path schema by choosing storage structures sup‹ ported by the target system.

4.1. Algebraic Structure for Physical Design

For the purposes of implementation-oriented design, we shall use the logical access paths of the design schema. An access path schema may be used to represent those paths actually chosen for support. Properties of an access mapping can be formulated to capture desirable characteristics of traversing the mapping in either the functional or inverse functional direction. Consider the schema function f: A → B. The following properties of the mapping can be defined:

1) *Evaluated:* given a in A, f(a) can be found without an exhaustive scan of B, i.e., the cost to access f(a) is less than the cost to access every element of B.

2) *Indexed:* given b in B, $f^{-1}(b)$ can be found without an exhaustive scan of A.

3) *Clustered:* the elements of $f^{-1}(b)$ are in close proximity, i.e., the cost to access the elements in the inverse is less than the cost to access an arbitrary subset of the same cardinality.

4) *Well Placed:* a and f(a) are stored in close proximity, i.e., the cost to access both is less than the cost to access them separately.

We make the critical assumption that each object of the schema, be it a value, an entity, or a relationship instance, is assigned to a single stored record. Replication, e.g., the replication of data values to record instances, will be made explicit by introducing new objects into the schema. The usual concept of "record" can be represented as a concatenation of the stored records of the values that make up the fields of the record. Our approach does not preclude the record segmentation and allocation techniques described in [SCHK78]. Given this assumption, certain implication rules can be formulated:

(i) *well-placed → evaluated*

By placing f(a) near a, a fast way to get from the domain to the range is automatically provided. It is no longer necessary to scan the entire set of range objects to find the desired one.

(ii) *clustered → indexed*

By placing elements of $f_{-1}(b)$ together, an exhaustive scan of all the domain objects of f is not necessary. The scan is considerably speeded up by placing the objects together.

(iii) *well placed → clustered*

Let b = f(a). Well placed means that a and b are stored together. Since there is one record for each b instance, all A objects with b in the range of f will be placed near b and hence near each other. Thus clustering is achieved.

For systems without index storage structures, it is possible to have a mapping which is evaluated but not indexed. For example, an employee's name may be stored in the record that represents the employee, with no storage structures available to access the record via an employee name. The opposite is possible as well. Some inverted file systems allow access to a record through a value that is not stored in that record. For example, an employee's name may not be stored with the record that represents the employee, but an index on employee name is available. Thus evaluated need not imply indexed and vice versa.

The implication rules can be used to impose a partial ordering among the properties shown in Figure 22.2. A *label* is an assignment of properties to an edge of the integrity schema. There are six distinct labels: W, <C,E>, <I,E>, C, I, and E. Our algorithm will generate schemas with maximally supported access paths. We assume that all access paths are at least evaluated. Therefore we deal only with the first three labels, denoted as "W", "C", and "I". A *labelling* is an assignment of a label to each edge of the schema, denoted as an n-tuple $(1_1, 1_2, \ldots, 1_n)$ where n is the number of edges in the schema. The assignment is subject to constraints which are shown below. The partial ordering among properties induces a partial ordering among labels as well: "W" > "C" > "I". A partial ordering can be defined for labellings. Let L_1 and L_2 be two labellings over the same schema. We say that $L_1 = L_2$ if for each edge in the schema, L_1's assigned label is the same as L_2's assigned label. We say that $L_2 > L_1$ if for each edge in the schema, either L_1's assigned label is the same as L_2's or L_2's label > L_1's, and $L_1 \neq L_2$. Note that under this definition, some labellings are incomparable,

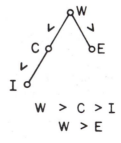

$$W > C > I$$
$$W > E$$

FIGURE 22.2. A Partial Ordering of Properties

e.g., $L_1 = ($ "W", "C"$)$ and $L_2 = ($ "C", "W"$)$.

An obvious approach to achieving a maximal labelling is to assign "W", the label that represents the highest degree of support, to each edge. Unfortunately, certain labellings represent a choice of properties which cannot be supported simultaneously within a schema. There are four constraints which *conflict-free* labellings must meet.

(i)   *cluster constraint:* It is not possible to label more than one outedge of a node with a "C" or "W." Clustering places together all domain objects which are mapped into the same range object. It is not possible to partition the domain on more than one function and still achieve this advantageous placement. Note that 1-to-1 properties do not cause a conflict because a 1-to-1 function partitions the domain objects into clusters of size one. This can always be supported regardless of additional clustering. (See Figure 22.3.)

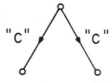

FIGURE 22.3. A Cluster Contraint

(ii) *placement constraint:* It is not possible to label more than one inedge of a node with "W." Well-placement places clusters of domain objects with a common range object near that range object. It is not possible to achieve this advantageous placement simultaneously for domain objects from more than one function. (See Figure 22.4.)

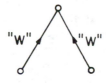

FIGURE 22.4. A Placement Constraint

(iii) *placement-cluster constraint:* It is not possible to simultaneously label an inedge of a node "W" while labelling an outedge "C." The placement of X object clusters near their associated Y objects destroys the advantageous clustering of the Y objects. 1-to-1 functions do not cause the constraint to be violated. (See Figure 22.5.)

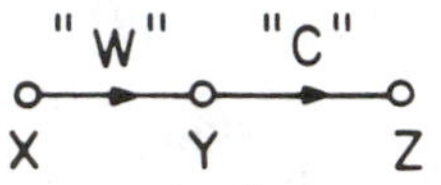

"W"   "C"

X   Y   Z

FIGURE 22.5. A Placement-Cluster Constraint

(iv) *implied constraints:* Certain compositions of functions and their properties result in the violation of one of the above constraints. For example, this schema would cause a violation of an implied cluster constraint. (See Figure 22.6.)

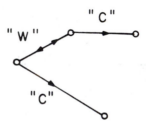

FIGURE 22.6. An Implied Constraint

The above constraints are conservative in the sense that the desirable properties of placement and clustering can be achieved, even if the constraints are violated. However, this tends to be sensitive to the parameters of a particular system. For example, in constraint (ii), if clusters from both domain object sets can fit on the same page, then simultaneous well placement can be achieved.

The *degree* of a schema is the number of violations of placement or cluster constraints that may be made during the labelling process. Each of these violations can be resolved if we introduce the replication of objects. Assume that the schema is labelled as in (i). A *conflict* is a violation of a cluster or placement constraint. A cluster conflict can be resolved by one of the following methods shown in Figure 22.7. In (A), a copy of the domain object is made, and both the original and the copy are clustered on the appropriate ranges. In (B), a copy of the range is made and placed in one-to-one

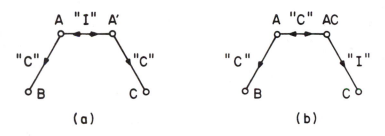

FIGURE 22.7. Cluster Conflict Resolution

correspondence with the original domain object. To illustrate this, consider the entity set employees and the value set integers, interrelated by the property function age. Schematically, the following situation can arise:

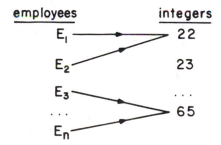

The effect of type (B) cluster resolution is to replicate the age values so there is one age value per employee:

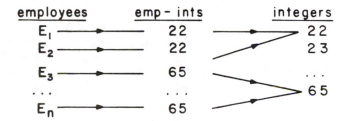

A placement conflict is resolved in an analogous way in Figure 22.8.

The degree of a schema is a measure of the amount of replication we are willing to tolerate during the labelling process. Replicated information introduces increased costs for storage and update while reducing retrieval costs. A degree of 0 ensures that no replication will result, i.e., the cluster and placement constraints are never violated; a degree of $n > 0$ will allow

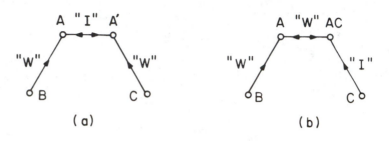

FIGURE 22.8. Placement Constraint Resolution

up to n replicated objects to be created.

A *maximal labelling* is a labelling L for which there exists no labelling L' such that L' > L. Our objective is to generate maximal conflict-free labellings. Because not all labellings are comparable, it is possible to generate many such labellings for the same schema. Rather than generate all the possible labellings for a given schema, usage information can be used to restrict the enumeration to those that best support the expected usage patterns of the database.

4.2. A Labelling Algorithm

In this subsection, we present an algorithm for generating a maximal labelling that specifies superior support for the access paths most heavily travelled. Assume that the degree of replication is n. This means that up to n placement or cluster conflicts will be tolerated while labelling the schema. These conflicts will later be resolved using the techniques of the previous subsection.

The input to the algorithm is a schema to be labelled and a ranking of the edges (access mapping) according to frequency of traversal. The algorithm only enforces cluster and placement constraints. Initially all edges are labelled "I." We begin by assigning the next most favorable label ("C") to the heaviest used edge. We continue assigning labels in this manner until either n cluster conflicts have been detected or all edges have been examined. Then we assign the most favorable label ("W") to the most heavily used edge that is already labelled "C". We continue until a total of n cluster or placement conflicts is detected. The edge that causes the n+1th conflict is not relabelled. The algorithm to assign labels is given in Figure 22.9. When all edges have been assigned a label, resolution is performed for each vertex which does not meet the placement and cluster constraints. Type (A) placement resolution is chosen for conflicts involving association and single-valued relationship edges and type (B) for conflict involving property edges.

Algorithm LabelSchema
        # conflicts ← O
        for each edge do label edge "I"
        for each edge
                (in frequency of access order) do
                label edge "C"
                if cluster conflict then
                        if *# conflicts* = n
                                then relabel edge "I"
                        else *# conflicts* ← *# conflicts* + 1
        for each edge labelled "C"
                (in frequency order) do
                label edge "W"
                if placement conflict then
                        if *# conflicts* = n
                                then relabel edge "C"
                        else *# conflicts* ← *# conflicts* + 1

FIGURE 22.9. Labelling Algorithm

The algorithm can be illustrated with an example. Consider the sample schema shown in Figure 22.10. Consider the following ranking of access mappings, from most to least heavily used.

1) S-SP
2) SNO
3) P-SP
4) QTY
5) PNO
6) PNAME
7) SNAME

This ranking could have been derived from a set of user queries in conjunction with an indication of relative frequency, or simply specified by the designer. For a degree of replication = 1, the algorithm proceeds as follows:

initial labelling: all edges labelled "I"

C-labelling:

STEP 1: label S-SP with "C"

STEP 2: label SNO with "C"

S(SNO, SNAME)
P(PNO, PNAME)
SP(S, P, QTY)

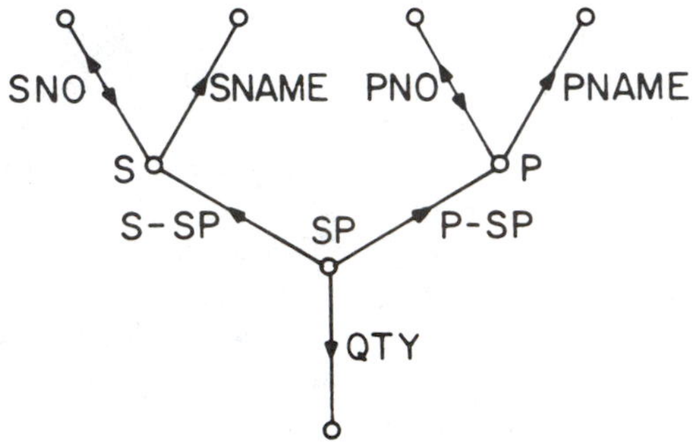

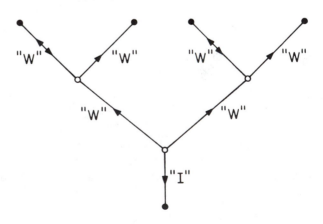

FIGURE 22.10. A Sample Schema

STEP 3: P-SP cannot be labelled "C" without a conflict. Label it "C". No additional conflicts are allowed.

STEP 4: QTY cannot be labelled "C" without a conflict.

STEP 5: label PNO with "C."

FIGURE 22.11. A Labelling

STEP 6: label PNAME with "C" (does not conflict with PNO).

STEP 7: label SNAME with "C" (does not conflict with SNO).

W-labelling: all edges labelled "C" can be relabelled "W" without conflict.

The resulting labelling is shown in Figure 22.11.

  Placement resolution must be performed for SP. The more frequently used edge will emanate from the original SP while the less frequently used edge will emanate from the replicated SP'. Type (A) resolution is used because the conflicting edge, P-SP, involves nonvalue vertices, as shown in Figure 22.12.

  We note that fully constrained labelling can be formulated in terms of an integer linear program with an objective function that maximizes the sum of the frequencies of the edges labelled "W" and "C." Further details can be found in [KATZ80].

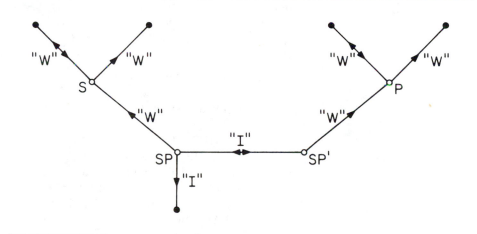

FIGURE 22.12. Resulting Labelling

5.0. IMPLEMENTING A SCHEMA

Up to this point, the design has been independent of the actual data model and system. In this section we briefly discuss the considerations involved in mapping a labelled schema into DBTG storage structures.

  The quality of the mapping depends on the detail of usage information specified. In the following, we assume that information has been specified at the level of the previous section. All property mapping are "evaluated," i.e., supported by placing the range value in the record that represents the entity or relationship instance.

In the new CODASYL proposal [CODA78], many aspects of the physical database design have been removed from the schema DDL and localized in data storage definition. The DSDL provides facilities for the specification of the pagination of the storage media, schema to storage record mapping, record pointer implementation, set representation, and storage record placement. We do not deal with the specification of the storage media, and assume that all sets are represented by chains with direct pointers. Additional usage information could be used to make a more sophisticated choice for these parameters.

Algorithm CodasylPhysicalDesign
FOR EACH nonvalue node DO
    IF node is entity set THEN
        i ← identifier outedge
        j ← other outedge labelled "W" or "C"
        IF $f_i > f_j$
            THEN calc on key data item
            ELSE
                IF j is association or
                    s.v. relationship
                    THEN cluster on set membership
                        IF label = "W"
                            THEN place near owner
                      ELSE /* property outedge */
                        sort & index on data item
                FOR EACH property edge labelled "I" DO
                    index on data item
        ELSE /*relationship*/
            j ← outedge labelled "W" or "C"
            IF association
                THEN cluster on set membership
                  IF label = "W"
                    THEN place near owner
                ELSE sort & index on data item
                FOR EACH property edge labelled "I" DO
                  index on data item

FIGURE 22.13. CODASYL Design

The DSDL provides three choices for the record placement strategy. A record may be calc'd (hashed) on a key specified in the DDL, clustered by set membership and optionally placed near the owner, or stored in sequential sorted order. Indexes can be specified separately for keys specified in the DDL.

At most one nonidentifier outedge of a node can be labelled "W" or "C." This edge should be used to determine the primary structure of the record type if its traversal frequency exceeds that of the identifier outedge. Otherwise, the identifier outedge (which can always be labelled "W") should be used. In the latter case, the record type is calc'd on the related key data item. In the former, if the outedge is a property, then the record type is stored sequentially and sorted and indexed on the appropriate data item. Otherwise the outedge represents an association or single-valued relationship, and the record type is clustered on the associated set. If "W" is specified, the records are placed near their owners. Indexes are created for data items whose associated property mappings are labelled "I." The algorithm of Figure 22.13 can be used to determine the record type's structure.

The DSDL also provides facilities to allow a single schema record to be represented by multiple stored records. This corresponds closely to our formulation of replication. Consider the degree 1 labelling and its associated

CODASYL schema, shown in Figure 22.14. The DSDL specification for the schema would be:

    MAPPING FOR S
        STORAGE RECORD IS S

    MAPPING FOR P
        STORAGE RECORD IS P

    MAPPING FOR SP
        STORAGE RECORDS ARE SP, SP'

    STORAGE RECORD NAME IS S
        PLACEMENT IS SEQUENTIAL ASCENDING SNAME
        SET S-SP ALLOCATION IS STATIC
            POINTER FOR FIRST, LAST RECORD SP
                IS TO SP

    STORAGE RECORD NAME IS P
        PLACEMENT IS SEQUENTIAL ASCENDING PNAME
        SET P-SP ALLOCATION IS STATIC
            POINTER FOR FIRSTR, LAST RECORD SP
                IS TO SP'

```
STORAGE RECORD NAME IS SP
   LINK TO SP'
   PLACEMENT IS CLUSTERED
         VIA SET S-SP NEAR OWNER S
   SET S-SP ALLOCATION IS STATIC
      POINTER FOR NEXT, PRIOR
      POINTER FOR OWNER

STORAGE RECORD NAME IS SP'
   LINK TO SP
   PLACEMENT IS CLUSTERED
         VIA SET S-SP NEAR OWNER P
   SET P-SP ALLOCATION IS STATIC
      POINTER FOR NEXT, PRIOR
      POINTER FOR OWNER
```

record types   *sets*

S(SNO, SNAME)   S-SP, Owner S, Member SP
P(PNO, PNAME)   P-SP, Owner P, Member SP
SP(QTY)

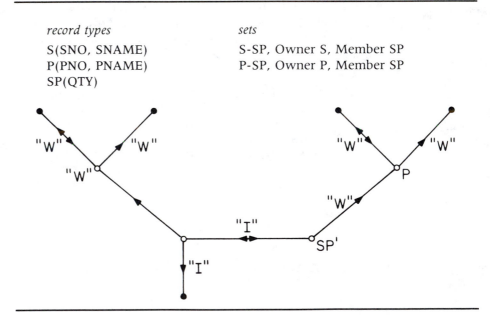

FIGURE 22.14. A Degree 1 Labelling

plus specification for INDEXES for each data item not covered in the above. The access schema for the above is shown in Figure 22.15. All access mapping are maximally supported. Usage information may indicate that certain paths are not worth the overhead of supporting them.

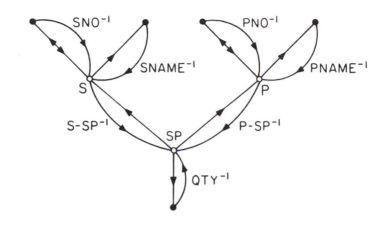

FIGURE 22.15. An Access Schema

6.0. CONCLUSIONS AND FUTURE WORK

In this paper we have proposed an access path model for physical database design as an extension of our original work with a semantic model for logical database design and schema conversion. The properties of access paths were discussed and a methodology which generates maximally supported schemas was proposed and illustrated with examples. We believe that this approach to qualitative physical design is new and unique.

We have briefly discussed the applications of our methodology for designing CODASYL physical databases. More work is required on usage specification in order to improve the quality of the design.

The access path model also has applications to problems of program translation. A generalized query processing algorithm can be formulated to "compile" nonprocedural queries, e.g., relational calculus, into the access paths supported in the access schema. Primitive operations on the access schema can be defined in a way that facilitates implementing these operations in terms of CODASYL DML. In addition, we have been investigating how to reverse the process, i.e., "decompiling" programs that access data at the level of DML into nonprocedural queries, with the aid of the access schema. These problems are further explored in [KATZ80].

References

[AGRA82]   Agrawal, R., and D. DeWitt, "Updating Hypothetical Data Bases," unpublished working paper, 1982.

[ALLM76]   Allman, E., G. Held, and M. Stonebraker, "Embedding a Data Manipulation Language in a General Purpose Programming Language," *Proceedings of the 1976 ACM-SIGPLAN-SIGMOD Conference on Data Abstraction, Definition, and Structure*, Salt Lake City, UT, March 1976, pp. 25-35 (also in this volume).

[ALLM82]   Allman, E., and M. Stonebraker, "Observations on the Evolution of a Software System," *IEEE Computer*, Vol. 15, No. 6, June 1982, pp. 27-32.

[ALSB76]   Alsberg, P., and J. Day, "A Principle for Resilient Sharing of Distributed Resources," *Proceedings of the Second International Conference on Software Engineering*, San Francisco, CA, October 1976.

[ARNO81]   Arnold, K., *Screen Updating and Cursor Movement Optimizations: A Library Package*, Department of Electrical Engineering and Computer Sciences, University of California, Berkeley, CA, 1981.

[ASTR76]   Astrahan, M., et al., "System R: A Relational Approach to Database Management," *ACM Transactions on Database Systems*, Vol. 1, No. 2, June 1976, pp. 97-137.

[BABA79]   Babaoglu, O., W. Joy, and J. Porcarj, "Design and Implementation of the Berkeley Virtual Memory Extensions to the Unix Operating System," *UNIX Programmer's Manual*, Seventh Edition, University of California, Berkeley, CA, December 1979.

[BAYE70]   Bayer, R., "Organization and Maintenance of Large Ordered Indices," *Proceedings of the 1970 ACM-SIGFIDET Workshop on Data Description, Access and Control*, Houston, TX, November 1970.

[BELL73]   Bell, J., "Threaded Code," *Communications of the ACM*, Vol. 16, No. 6, June 1973.

[BELL78]   "The UNIX Time-Sharing System," *Bell Systems Technical Journal*, Vol. 57, No. 6, July 1978.

[BERN76]   Bernstein, P. A., "Synthesizing Third Normal Form Relations from Functional Dependencies," *ACM Transactions on Database Systems*, Vol. 1, No. 4, Dec. 1976, pp. 277-298.

[BERN79]   Bernstein, P., and D. Chiu, *Using Semi-joins to Solve Relational Queries*, Technical Report CCA-01-79, Computer Corporation of America, Cambridge, MA, January 1979.

429

[BHAR80]   Bhargava, B., "An Optimistic Concurrency Control Algorithm and its Performance Evaluation Against Locking," *Proceedings of the International Computer Symposium*, Taipei, Taiwan, December 1980.

[BIRS77]   Birss, E., Hewlett-Packard Corporation, General Systems Division, private communication, 1977.

[BIRT73]   Birtwistle, G., et al., *SIMULA BEGIN*, Petrocelli, 1973.

[BITT83]   Bitton, D., D. DeWitt, and C. Turbyfil, *Benchmarking Database Systems: A Systematic Approach*, Technical Report 526, Computer Sciences Department, University of Wisconsin, Madison, WI, December 1983.

[BLAS76]   Blasgen, M., and K. Eswaran, *On the Evaluation of Queries in a Relational Data Base System*, IBM San Jose Research Report RJ-1745, April 1976.

[BLAS77]   Blasgen, M., and K. Eswaran, "Storage and Access in Relational Data Base Systems," *IBM Systems Journal*, December 1977.

[BLAS79a]   Blasgen, M., et al., "The Convoy Phenomenon," *Operating Systems Review*, April 1979.

[BLAS79b]   Blasgen, M., et al., *System R: An Architectural Update*, IBM San Jose Research Report RJ-2581, July 1979.

[BOBR77]   Bobrow, D., and T. Winograd, "An Overview of KRL, a Knowledge Representation Language," *Cognitive Science*, Vol. 1, No. 1, 1977.

[BONA77]   Bonanni, L., and A. Glasser, *SCCS/PWB User's Manual*, Bell Telephone Laboratories, November 1977.

[BOUR78]   Bourne, S., "The UNIX Shell," *The Bell System Technical Journal*, Vol. 57, No. 6, July-August 1978, pp. 1971-1990.

[BOYC73]   Boyce, R., et al., *Specifying Queries as Relational Expressions: SQUARE*, IBM San Jose Research Report RJ-1291, October 1973.

[BOYC74]   Boyce, R., and D. Chamberlin, "SEQUEL: A Structured English Query Language," *Proceedings of the 1974 ACM-SIGFIDET Workshop on Data Description, Access and Control*, Ann Arbor, MI, May 1974, pp. 219-261.

[BRAT77]   Bratsbergsengen, K., and O. Risnes, "ASTRAL - a Structured Relational Applications Language," *Proceedings of the SIMULA Users Conference*, September 1977.

[BROD78]   Brodie, M., and J. Schmidt, "What is the Use of Abstract Data Types in Data Base?" *Proceedings of the Fourth International Conference on Very Large Data Bases*, West Berlin, Germany, October 1978, pp. 140-141.

[BROD80]   Brodie, M., (ed.), *Proceedings of the Workshop on Data Abstraction, Databases, and Conceptual Modelling*, Pingree Park, CO, June 1980.

[BROD84]   Brodie, M., (ed.), *On Conceptual Modelling*, Springer-Verlag, New York, NY, 1984.

[BROW81] Brown, M., "The Cedar Database System," *Proceedings of the 1981 ACM-SIGMOD Conference on the Management of Data*, Ann Arbor, MI, June 1981.

[BUNE79] Buneman, P., and R. Frankel, "FQL: A Functional Query Language," *Proceedings of the 1979 ACM-SIGMOD Conference on the Management of Data*, Boston, MA, June 1979.

[CARD73] Cardenas, A., "Evaluation and Selection of File Organization - A Model and a System," *Communications of the ACM*, Vol. 16, No. 9, September 1973.

[CARD75] Cardenas, A., "Analysis and Performance of Inverted Data Base Structures," *Communications of the ACM*, Vol. 18, No. 5, May 1975.

[CATT80] Cattell, R., "An Entity-based Database User Interface," *Proceedings of the 1980 ACM-SIGMOD Conference on the Management of Data*, Santa Monica, CA, May 1980.

[CHAM74a] Chamberlin, D., et al., *A Deadlock-Free Scheme for Resource Locking in a Data Base Environment*, IBM San Jose Research Report, June, 1974.

[CHAM74b] Chamberlin, D., and R. Boyce, "SEQUEL: A Structured English Query Language," *Proceedings of the 1974 ACM-SIGFIDET Workshop on Data Description, Access and Control*, Ann Arbor, MI, May 1974, pp. 219-261.

[CHAM75] Chamberlin, D., J. Gray, and I. Traiger, "Views, Authorization and Locking in a Relational Data Base System," *Proceedings of the 1975 AFIPS National Computer Conference*, Vol. 44, Anaheim, CA, May 1975, pp. 425-430.

[CHAM76a] Chamberlin, D., "Relational Data Base Management: A Survey," *Computing Survey*, Vol. 8, No. 1, March 1976.

[CHAM76b] Chamberlin, D., et al., "SEQUEL2: A Unified Approach to Data Definition, Manipulation, and Control," *IBM Journal of Research and Development*, Vol. 20, No. 6, November 1976, pp. 560-575.

[CHEN76] Chen P., "The Entity-Relational Model: Towards a Unified View of Data," *ACM Transactions on Database Systems*, Vol. 1, No. 1, March 1976, pp. 9-36.

[CHU76] Chu, W., "Performance of File Directory Systems for Data Base in Star and Distributed Networks," *Proceedings of the 1976 AFIPS National Computer Conference*, Vol. 45, AFIPS Press, Montvale, NJ, 1976.

[CODA71] *CODASYL Data Base Task Group Report*, 1971.

[CODA73] CODASYL Programming Language Committee, *CODASYL COBOL Data Base Facility Proposal*, March 1973.

[CODA78] CODASYL Data Description Language Committee, *Journal of Development*, 1978.

[CODD70] Codd, E., "A Relational Model of Data for Large Shared Data Banks," *Communications of the ACM*, Vol. 13, No. 6, June 1970, pp. 377-387.

[CODD71]   Codd, E., "A Data Base Sublanguage Founded on the Relational Calculus," *Proceedings of the 1971 ACM-SIGFIDET Workshop on Data Description, Access and Control*, San Diego, CA, November 1971, pp. 35-68.

[CODD72]   Codd, E., "Relational Completeness of Data Base Sublanguages," *Courant Computer Science Symposium 6*, Prentice-Hall, Englewood Cliffs, NJ, May 1972, pp. 65-90.

[CODD74]   Codd, E., and C. J. Date, "Interactive Support for Non-programmers, the Relational and Network Approaches," *Proceedings of the 1974 ACM-SIGFIDET Workshop on Data Description, Access and Control*, Ann Arbor, MI, May 1974.

[COME79]   Comer, D., "The Ubiquitous B-Tree," *Computing Surveys*, Vol. 11, No. 2, June 1979.

[DATE74]   Date, C. J., and E. Codd, "The Relational and Network Approaches: Comparison of the Application Programming Interfaces," *Proceedings of the 1974 ACM-SIGFIDET Workshop on Data Description, Access and Control*, Ann Arbor, MI, May 1974, pp. 85-113.

[DATE76]   Date, C. J., "An Architecture for High-Level Language Database Extensions," *Proceedings of the 1976 ACM-SIGPLAN-SIGMOD Conference on Data Abstraction, Definition, and Structure*, Salt Lake City, UT, March 1976.

[DATE81]   Date, C. J., "Referential Integrity," *Proceedings of the Seventh International Conference on Very Large Databases*, Cannes, France, September 1981.

[DATE84]   Date, C. J., "A Critique of the SQL Database Language," to appear in *ACM-SIGMOD Record*.

[DAYA78]   Dayal, U., and P. Bernstein, "On the Updatability of Relational Views," *Proceedings of the Fourth International Conference on Very Large Data Bases*, West Berlin, Germany, October 1978, pp. 368-377.

[DEJO80]   DeJong, S., "The System for Business Automation (SBA): A Unified Development System," *Information Processing*, 1980.

[DENN68]   Denning, P., "The Working Set Model for Program Behavior," *Communications of the ACM*, Vol. 11, No. 5, May 1968, pp. 323-333.

[DEWA75]   Dewar, R., "Indirect Threaded Code," *Communications of the ACM*, Vol 18, No. 6, June 1975.

[DEWI78]   Dewitt, D., "DIRECT - A Multiprocessor Organization for Supporting Relational Data Base Management Systems," *Proceedings of the Fifth Annual Symposium on Computer Architecture*, 1978.

[DEWI84]   Dewitt, D., et al., "Implementation Techniques for Main Memory Database Systems," *Proceedings of the 1984 ACM-SIGMOD Conference on Management of Data*, Boston, MA, June 1984.

[DIGI76]   Digital Equipment Corporation, *VAX-11/780 Architecture Handbook*, 1976.

[DIGI77]   Digital Equipment Corporation, *DBMS-11 Data Base Administrator's Guide*, DEC-11-ODABA-A-D, 1977.

[DUHN78]   Duhne, R., and D. Severance, "Selection of an Efficient Combination of Data Files for a Multiuser Database," *Proceedings of the 1978 AFIPS National Computer Conference*, Vol. 47, New York, NY, June 1978.

[EPST77]   Epstein, R., *Creating and Maintaining a Database Using INGRES*, Memo No. M77-71, Electronics Research Laboratory, University of California, Berkeley, CA, December 1977.

[EPST78]   Epstein, R., M. Stonebraker, and E. Wong, "Query Processing in a Distributed Data Base System," *Proceedings of the 1978 ACM-SIGMOD Conference on the Management of Data*, Austin, Texas, May 1978 (also in this volume).

[EPST80a]   Epstein, R., and M. Stonebraker, "Analysis of Distributed Data Base Processing Strategies," *Proceedings of the Sixth International Conference on Very Large Data Bases*, Montreal, Canada, October 1980.

[EPST80b]   Epstein, R., and P. Hawthorn, "Design Decisions for the Intelligent Database Machine," *Proceedings of the 1980 AFIPS National Computer Conference*, Anaheim, CA, May 1980.

[ESWA76]   Eswaran, K., J. Gray, R. Lorie, L. Traiger, "On the Notions of Consistency and Predicate Locks in a Data Base System," *Communications of the ACM*, Vol. 19, No. 11, November 1976.

[FAGI77a]   Fagin, R., "Multivalued Dependencies and a New Normal Form for Relational Databases," *ACM Transactions on Database Systems*, Vol. 2, No. 3, September 1977, pp. 262-278.

[FAGI77b]   Fagin, R., "The Decomposition Versus the Synthetic Approach to Relational Database Design," *Proceedings of the Third International Conference on Very Large Data Bases*, Tokyo, Japan, October 1977.

[FOGG82]   Fogg, D., *Implementation of Domain Abstraction in the Relational Database System INGRES*, Masters Thesis, Department of Electrical Engineering and Computer Science, University of California, Berkeley, CA, September 1982.

[FURT78]   Furtado, A., "A View Construct for the Specification of External Schemas," Series: *Monografias em Ciencia da Computacao*, 1978.

[GO75]   Go, A., M. Stonebraker, and C. Williams, "An Approach to Implementing a Geo-data System," *Proceedings of the 1975 ACM-SIGGRAPH-SIGMOD Conference for Data Bases in Interactive Design*, Waterloo, Ontario, Canada, September 1975, pp. 67-77.

[GOOS78]   Goos, G., and U. Kastens, "Programming Languages and the Design of Modular Programs," *Constructing Quality Software*, P. Hibbard and A. Schuman, (eds.), North-Holland, Amsterdam, 1978.

[GOTL74]   Gotlieb, C., and F. Tompa, "Choosing a Storage Schema," *Acta Informatica*, Vol. 3, 1974, pp. 297-319.

[GOTT75]   Gottlieb, D., et al., "A Classification of Compression Methods and Their Usefulness in a Large Data Processing Center," *Proceedings of the 1975 AFIPS National Computer Conference*, Vol. 44, Anaheim, CA, May 1975, pp. 453-458.

[GRAY75]   Gray, J., R. Lorie and G. Putzolu, "Granularity of Locks in a Shared Data Base," *Proceedings of the First International Conference of Very Large Data Bases*, Framingham, MA, September 1975, pp. 428-451.

[GRAY76]   Gray, J., R. Lorie, G. Putzolu, and I. Traiger, "Granularity of Locks and Degrees of Consistency in a Shared Data Base," *Proceedings of the IFIP Working Conference on Modelling of Data Base Management Systems*, Freudenstadt, Germany, January, 1976.

[GRAY78]   Gray, J., "Notes on Data Base Operating Systems," *Operating Systems: An Advanced Course*, Springer-Verlag, New York, NY, 1978, pp. 393-481.

[GRIF76]   Griffiths, P., and B. Wade, "An Authorization Mechanism for a Relational Data Base System," *ACM Transactions on Database Systems*, Vol. 1, No. 3, September 1976.

[GUTT77]   Guttag, J., "Abstract Data Types and the Development of Data Structures," *Communications of the ACM*, Vol. 20, No. 6, June 1977.

[GUTT82]   Guttman, A., and M. Stonebraker, "Using a Relational Database Management System for Computer Aided Design Data," *Data Base Engineering*, June 1982.

[HAGG83]   Hagmann, R., private communication, 1983.

[HALL76]   Hall, P., J. Owlett, and S. Todd, "Relations and Entities," *Proceedings IFIPTC-2 Working Conference on Modelling in Database Management Systems*, North-Holland, Amsterdam, 1976.

[HAMM76a]   Hammer, M., "Data Abstractions for Databases," *Proceedings of the 1976 ACM-SIGPLAN-SIGMOD Conference on Data Abstraction, Definition, and Structure*, Salt Lake City, UT, March 1976, pp. 58-59.

[HAMM76b]   Hammer, M., and I. Chan, "Index Selection in a Self Adaptive Data Base System," *Proceedings of the 1976 ACM-SIGMOD Conference on the Management of Data*, Washington, DC, June 1976.

[HAMM79]   Hammer, M., and D. Shipman, *Reliability Mechanisms for SDD-1: A System for Distributed Databases*, Computer Corporation of America, Cambridge, MA, July 1979.

[HASK82]   Haskings, R., and R. Lorie, "On Extending the Functions of a Relational Database System," *Proceedings of the 1982 ACM-SIGMOD Conference on the Management of Data*, Orlando, FL, June 1982.

[HAWT79] Hawthorn, P., and M. Stonebraker, "Use of Technological Advances to Enhance Data Base Management System Performance," *Proceedings of the 1979 ACM-SIGMOD Conference on the Management of Data*, Boston, MA, June 1979 (also in this volume).

[HELD75a] Held, G., and M. Stonebraker, "Access Methods in the Relational Data Base Management System INGRES," *Proceedings of ACM-Pacific-75*, San Francisco, CA, April 1975.

[HELD75b] Held, G., M. Stonebraker, and E. Wong, "INGRES: A Relational Data Base Management System," *Proceedings of the 1975 AFIPS National Computer Conference*, Vol. 44, Anaheim, CA, May 1975, pp. 409-416.

[HELD75c] Held, G., *Storage Structures for Relational Data Base Management Systems*, Ph.D. Thesis, Department of Electrical Engineering and Computer Science, University of California, Berkeley, CA, 1975.

[HELD78] Held, G., and M. Stonebraker, "B-trees Re-examined," *Communications of the ACM*, Vol. 21, No. 2, February 1978.

[HERO80] Herot, C., "SDMS: A Spatial Data Base System," *ACM Transactions on Database Systems*, Vol. 5, No. 4, December 1980.

[HEWL77] Hewlett-Packard Corporation, *IMAGE Reference Manual*, 1977.

[HEWL79] Hewlett-Packard Corporation, *HP 3000 Computer System VIEW/3000 Reference Manual*, 32209-90001, 1979.

[IBM66] IBM Corporation, *OS ISAM Logic*, GY28-6618, IBM Corporation, White Plains, NY, June 1966.

[IBM74] IBM Corporation, *IMS-VS General Information Manual*, GH20-1260, IBM Corporation, White Plains, NY, April 1974.

[IBM81] IBM Corporation, *SQL/Data System, Terminal User's Reference*, SH24-5017-1, IBM Corporation, White Plains, NY, 1981.

[JOHN74] Johnson, S., "YACC, Yet Another Compiler-Compiler," *UNIX Programmer's Manual*, Bell Telephone Laboratories, Murray Hill, NJ, July 1974.

[JOY79a] Joy, W., "The Text Editor EX," unpublished working paper, 1979.

[JOY79b] Joy, W., "The VI Text Editor," unpublished working paper, 1979.

[JOY80] Joy, W., "Comments on the Performance of UNIX on the VAX," unpublished working paper, 1980.

[KAPL80] Kaplan, J., *Buffer Management Policies in a Data Base System*, Masters Thesis, Department of Electrical Engineering and Computer Science, University of California, Berkeley, CA, 1980.

[KASH80] Kashtan, D., "UNIX and VMS: Some Performance Comparisons," unpublished working paper, SRI International, Menlo Park, CA, 1980.

[KATZ78]   Katz, R., "Compilation in Data Base Systems," *Proceedings of the 1978 AFIPS National Computer Conference*, Vol. 47, New York, NY, June 1978.

[KATZ80]   Katz, R., *Database Design and Translation for Multiple Data Models*, Ph.D. Thesis, Department of Electrical Engineering and Computer Science, University of California, Berkeley, CA 1980.

[KATZ82a]   Katz, R., *Support for Alternative Views of CAD Data*, Technical Report 27, Computer Science Department, University of Wisconsin, Madison, WI, October 1982.

[KATZ82b]   Katz, R., (ed.), Special Issue on CAD Data Bases, *Data Base Engineering*, June 1982.

[KATZ82c]   Katz, R., and T. Lehman, *Storage Structures for Versions and Alternatives*, Computer Science Technical Report 479, University of Wisconsin, Madison, WI, July 1982.

[KEEH74]   Keehn, D., and J. Lacy, "VSAM Data Set Design Parameters," *IBM Systems Journal*, September 1974.

[KELL81]   Keller, K., *KIC, A Graphics Editor for Integrated Circuits*, Masters Thesis, Department of Electrical Engineering and Computer Science, University of California, Berkeley, CA, June 1981.

[KNUT78]   Knuth, D., *The Art of Computer Programming, Volume 3: Sorting and Searching*, Addison-Wesley, Reading, MA, 1978.

[KNUT84]   Knuth, D., *The TeXbook*, Addison-Wesley, Reading, MA, 1984.

[KUNG81]   Kung, H., and J. Robinson, "On Optimistic Methods for Concurrency Control," *ACM Transactions on Database Systems*, Vol. 6, No. 2, June 1981.

[LAMP76a]   Lampson, B., and H. Sturgis, "Crash Recovery in a Distributed System," working paper, Xerox PARC, Palo Alto, CA, 1976.

[LAMP76b]   Lamport, L., *Time, Clocks and Ordering of Events in a Distributed System*, Massachusetts Computer Associates Report CA-7603-2911, March 1976.

[LANG77]   Lang, T., C. Wood, and E. Fernandez, "Database Buffer Paging in Virtual Storage Systems," *ACM Transactions on Database Systems*, Vol. 2, No. 4, December, 1977.

[LAUE79]   Lauer, H., and R. Needham, "On the Duality of Operating System Structures," *Operating Systems Review*, April 1979.

[LIND79]   Lindsay, B. G., et al., *Notes on Distributed Databases*, IBM Research Report No. RJ2571, July 1979.

[LIPS76]   Lipson, W., and Lapezak, *LSL User's Manual*, Technical Note No. 9, Computer Systems Research Group, University of Toronto, Toronto, Ontario, Canada, August, 1976.

[LISK74]   Liskov, B., and S. Zilles, "Programming With Abstract Data Types," *ACM-SIGPLAN Notices*, April 1974.

[LISK77]   Liskov, B., et al., "Abstraction Mechanisms in CLU," *Communications of the ACM*, Vol. 20, No. 8, August 1977, pp. 564-576.

[LOCK79]   Lockmann, P., et al., "Data Abstractions for Data Base Systems," *ACM Transactions on Database Systems*, Vol. 4, No. 1, March 1979.

[LORI77]   Lorie, R., "Physical Integrity in a Large Segmented Data Base," *ACM Transactions on Data Base Systems*, Vol. 2, No. 1, March 1977.

[LORI83]   Lorie, R., and W. Plouffe, "Complex Objects and Their Use in Design Transactions," *Proceedings of the Engineering Design Applications of ACM-IEEE Data Base Week*, San Jose, CA, May 1983.

[LUO81]   Luo, D., and S. Yao, "Form Operation by Example: A Language for Office Information Processing," *Proceedings of the 1981 ACM-SIGMOD Conference on the Management of Data*, Ann Arbor, MI, June 1981, pp. 212-223.

[LYNN82]   Lynn, N., *Implementation of Ordered Relations in a Data Base System*, Masters Thesis, Department of Electrical Engineering and Computer Science, University of California, Berkeley, CA, September 1982.

[MACR76]   Macri, P., "Deadlock Detection and Resolution in a CODASYL Based Data Management System," *Proceedings of the 1976 ACM-SIGMOD Conference on the Management of Data*, Washington, DC, June, 1976.

[MARY80]   Maryanski, F., "Query By Forms," unpublished presentation, 1980.

[MATT70]   Mattson, R., et al., "Evaluation Techniques for Storage Hierarchies," *IBM Systems Journal*, June 1970.

[MCDO75a]   McDonald, N., *CUPID: A Graphics Oriented Facility for Support of Nonprogrammer Interactions with a Data Base*, Ph.D. Thesis, Department of Electrical Engineering and Computer Science, University of California, Berkeley, CA, 1975.

[MCDO75b]   McDonald, N., and M. Stonebraker, "Cupid: The Friendly Query Language," *Proceedings of the ACM-Pacific-75*, San Francisco, CA, April 1975, pp. 127-131.

[MCLE76]   McLeod, D., "High Level Domain Definition in a Relational Data Base System," *Proceedings of the 1976 ACM-SIGPLAN-SIGMOD Conference on Data*, Salt Lake City, UT, March 1976.

[MERR77]   Merrett, T., *Aldat: Augmenting the Relational Algebra for Programmers*, Technical Report SOCS-78.1, School of Computer Science, McGill University, Montreal, Quebec, Canada, November 1977.

[METC76]   Metcalf, R., and D. Boggs, "Ethernet: Distributed Packet Switching for Local Computer Networks," *Communications of the ACM*, Vol. 19, No. 7, July 1976.

[MYLO78]   Mylopoulos, J., et al., *A Preliminary Specification of TAXIS: A Language for Designing Interactive Information Systems*, Technical Report CCA-78-02, Computer Corporation of America, Cambridge, MA, January 1978.

[NEWM79]   Newman, W., and R. Sproul, *Principles of Interactive Computer Graphics*, McGraw-Hill, 1979.

[NIJI75]   Nijssen, G.M., "Set and CODASYL Set or Coset" in *Data Base Description*, B. C. M. Douque, G. M. Nijssen, (eds.), North-Holland, Amsterdam, 1975, pp. 1-70.

[ONG82]   Ong, J., *The Design and Implementation of Abstract Data Types in the Relational Database System INGRES*, Masters Thesis, Department of Electrical Engineering and Computer Science, University of California, Berkeley, CA, September 1982.

[ONG83]   Ong, J., et al., "Implementation of Data Abstraction in the Relational Database System INGRES," *ACM-SIGMOD Record*, April 1983.

[OSSA79]   Ossanna, J., "Nroff/Troff User's Manual," *Unix Programmer's Manual*, Seventh Edition, Vol. 2A, Jan. 1979.

[OZKA77]   Ozkarahan, E., S. Schuster, and K. Sevcik, "Performance Evaluation of a Relational Associative Processor," *ACM Transactions on Database Systems*, Vol. 2, No. 2, June 1977.

[POWE83]   Powell, M., and M. Linton, "Database Support for Programming Environments," *Proceedings of the Engineering Design Applications of ACM-IEEE Database Week*, San Jose, CA, May 1983.

[PREN77]   Prenner, C., *A Uniform Notation for Expression Queries*, Memo No. M77-80, Electronics Research Laboratory, University of California, Berkeley, CA, September 1977.

[PREN78]   Prenner, C., and L. Rowe, "Programming Languages for Relational Data Base Systems," *Proceedings of the 1978 AFIPS National Computer Conference*, Vol. 47, New York, NY, June 1978, pp. 849-855.

[PURV82]   Purvy, R., et al., "The Design of Star's Records Processing," *Proceedings of the SIGOA Conference on Office Information Systems*, Philadelphia, PA, June 1982.

[REDE80]   Redell, D., et al., "Pilot: An Operating System for a Personal Computer," *Communications of the ACM*, Vol. 23, No. 2, February 1980.

[RIES77]   Ries, D., and M. Stonebraker, "Effects of Locking Granularity in a Database Management System," *ACM Transactions on Database Systems*, Vol. 2, No. 3, September 1977.

[RIES79]   Ries, D., and M. Stonebraker, "Locking Granularity Revisited," *ACM Transactions on Database Systems*, Vol. 4, No. 2, June 1979 (also in this volume).

[RIET81]	van de Riet, R., et al., "High Level Programming Features for Improving the Efficiency of Relational Database System," *ACM Transactions on Database Systems*, Vol. 6, No. 1, March 1981.
[RITC74a]	Ritchie, D., *C Reference Manual*, Bell Telephone Laboratories, Murray Hill, NJ, 1974.
[RITC74b]	Ritchie, D., and K. Thompson, "The UNIX Time-sharing System," *Communications of the ACM*, Vol. 17, No. 7, July 1974, pp. 365-375.
[ROBE70]	Roberts, L., and B. Wessler, "Computer Network Development to Achieve Resource Sharing," *Proceedings of the 1970 AFIPS Spring Joint Computer Conference*, AFIPS Press, Montvale, NJ, 1970.
[ROBE77]	Roberts, R., and I. Goldstein, *The FRL Manual*, Memo No. 409, Massachusetts Institute of Technology, Artificial Intelligence Laboratory, Cambridge, MA, September 1977.
[RODR76]	Rodriguez-Rosell, J., "Empirical Data Reference Behavior in Data Base Systems," *IEEE Computer*, Vol. 9, No. 11, November 1976, pp. 9-13.
[ROTH75]	Rothnie, J., "Evaluating Inter-Entry Retrieval Expressions in a Relational Data Base Management System," *Proceedings of the 1975 AFIPS National Computer Conference*, Vol. 44, Anaheim, CA, May 1975.
[ROTH77a]	Rothnie, J. B., Jr. and N. Goodman, "A Survey of Research and Development in Distributed Database Management," *Proceedings of the Third International Conference on Very Large Databases*, Tokyo, Japan, October, 1977.
[ROTH77b]	Rothnie, J., and N. Goodman, "An Overview of the Preliminary Design of SDD-1: A System for Distributed Databases," *Proceedings of the Second Berkeley Workshop on Distributed Data Management and Computer Networks*, Lawrence Berkeley Laboratory, May 1977.
[ROWE78]	Rowe, L., and K. Shoens, *Rigel: Preliminary Language Specification*, Department of Electrical Engineering and Computer Science, University of California, Berkeley, CA, December 1978.
[ROWE79a]	Rowe, L., and K. Birman, "Network Support for a Distributed Data Base System," *Proceedings of the Fourth Berkeley Workshop on Distributed Data Management and Computer Networks*, San Francisco, CA, August, 1979.
[ROWE79b]	Rowe, L., and K. Shoens, "Data Abstraction, Views and Updates in RIGEL," *Proceedings of the 1979 ACM-SIGMOD Conference on the Management of Data*, Boston, MA, June 1979 (also in this volume).
[ROWE82]	Rowe, L., and K. Shoens, "FADS - A Forms Application Development System," *Proceedings of the 1982 ACM-SIGMOD Conference on the Management of Data*, Orlando, FL, June 1982 (also in this volume).
[ROWE83]	Rowe, L., "An Introduction to the Relational Model," *Symposium on Database Management Systems*, Sydney, Australia, November 1983.

[RTI83a]   Relational Technology Inc., *EQUEL C User's Guide*, Version 2.0 VAX/UNIX, Berkeley, CA, January 1983.

[RTI83b]   Relational Technology Inc., *INGRES Reference Manual, Version 1.4*, Berkeley, CA, 1983.

[SCHA78]   Schapiro, R., and R. Millstein, "Failure Recovery in a Distributed Database System," *Proceedings of the 1978 COMPCON Conference*, September 1978.

[SCHK78]   Schkolnick, M., "A Survey of Physical Database Design Methodology and Techniques," *Proceedings of the Fourth International Conference on Very Large Data Bases*, West Berlin, Germany, October 1978.

[SCHM75]   Schmid, H., and J. Swenson, "On the Semantics of the Relational Data Model," *Proceedings of the 1975 ACM-SIGMOD Conference on the Management of Data*, San Jose, CA, May 1975.

[SCHM77]   Schmidt, J., "Some High Level Language Constructs for Data of Type Relation," *ACM Transactions on Database Systems*, Vol. 2, No. 3, September 1977, pp. 247-261.

[SCHM78]   Schmidt, J., "Type Concepts for Database Definition," *Proceedings of the International Conference on Data Bases*, Haifa, Israel, August 1978.

[SCHO75]   Schoenberg, I., *Implementation of Integrity Constraints in the Relational Data Base Management System INGRES*, Masters Thesis, Department of Electrical Engineering and Computer Science, University of California, Berkeley, CA, 1975.

[SELI79]   Selinger, P., et al., "Access Path Selection in a Relational Data Base System," *Proceedings of the 1979 ACM-SIGMOD Conference on the Management of Data*, Boston, MA, June 1979.

[SENK73]   Senko, M., et al., "Data Structures and Accessing in Data-Base Systems," *IBM Systems Journal*, Vol. 12, No. 1, 1973.

[SEVR76]   Severance, D., and G. Lohman, "Differential Files: Their Application to the Maintenance of Large Databases," *ACM Transactions on Database Systems*, Vol. 1, No. 2, June 1976.

[SHAW74]   Shaw, A., *The Logical Design of Operating Systems*, Prentice-Hall, Englewood Cliffs, NJ, 1974.

[SHER76]   Sherman, S., and B. Brice, "Performance of a Database Manager in a Virtual Memory System," *ACM Transactions on Data Base Systems*, Vol. 1, No. 4, December 1976, pp. 317-343.

[SHIP80]   Shipman, D., "The Functional Data Model and the Data Language DAPLEX," *ACM Transactions on Database Systems*, Vol. 5, 1980.

[SHOE82]   Shoens, K., *A Form Application Development System*, Ph.D. Thesis, Department of Electrical Engineering and Computer Science, University of California, Berkeley, CA, November 1982.

[SHU81]   Shu, N., V. Lum, F. Tung, and C. Chang, *Specification of Forms Processing and Business Procedures for Office Automation*, IBM San Jose Research Report RJ-3040, February 1981.

[SILE76]   Siler, K., "A Stochastic Model for Database Organizations in Data Retrieval Systems," *Communications of the ACM*, Vol. 19, No. 2, February 1976.

[SKEE81a]   Skeen, D., and M. Stonebraker, "A Formal Model of Crash Recovery in a Distributed System," *IEEE Transactions on Software Engineering*, Vol. SE-9, No. 3, May 1983.

[SKEE81b]   Skeen, D., *Crash Recovery in a Distributed Database System*, Ph.D. Thesis, EECS Dept., University of California, Berkeley, August 1981.

[SKEE82]   Skeen, D., "A Quorum-Based Commit Protocol," *Proceedings of the Sixth Berkeley Workshop on Distributed Data Management and Computer Networks*, Pacific Grove, CA, February 1982.

[SMIT76]   Smith, A., *Sequentiality and Prefetching in Data Base Systems*, IBM San Jose Research Report RJ-1743, March 1976.

[SMIT77]   Smith, J., and D. Smith, "Database Abstractions: Aggregation and Generalization," *ACM Transactions on Database Systems*, Vol. 2, No. 2, June 1977.

[STAL81]   Stallman, R., "EMACS: The Extensible, Customizable Self-Documenting Display Editor," *Proceedings of the 1981 ACM-SIGPLAN-SIGOA Symposium on Text Manipulation*, June 1981.

[STEA76]   Stearns, R., et al., "Concurrency Control for Data Base Systems," *Proceedings of the 1976 ACM Symposium on the Foundations of Computer Science*, October 1976.

[STON74a]   Stonebraker, M., "A Functional View of Data Independence," *Proceedings of the 1974 ACM-SIGFIDET Workshop on Data Description, Access and Control*, Ann Arbor, MI, May 1974.

[STON74b]   Stonebraker, M., *High Level Integrity Assurance in Relational Data Base Systems*, Memo No. M74-3, Electronics Research Laboratory, University of California, Berkeley, CA, August 1974.

[STON74c]   Stonebraker, M., and E. Wong, "Access Control in a Relational Data Base Management System by Query Modification," *Proceedings of the 1974 ACM National Conference*, San Diego, CA, November 1974, pp. 180-187.

[STON75]   Stonebraker, M., "Implementation of Integrity Constraints and Views by Query Modification," *Proceedings of the 1975 ACM-SIGMOD Conference on the Management of Data*, San Jose, CA, May 1975, pp. 65-78.

[STON76a]   Stonebraker, M., E. Wong, P. Kreps, and G. Held, "The Design and Implementation of INGRES," *ACM Transactions on Database Systems*, Vol. 1, No. 3, September 1976, pp. 198-222 (also in this volume).

[STON76b]   Stonebraker, M., and P. Rubinstein, "The INGRES Protection System," *Proceedings of the 1976 ACM National Conference*, Houston, TX, October 1976.

[STON77]   Stonebraker, M., and E. Neuhold, "A Distributed Database Version of INGRES," *Proceedings of the Second Berkeley Workshop on Distributed Data Management and Computer Networks*, Lawrence Berkeley Laboratory, May 1977.

[STON79a]   Stonebraker, M., "Concurrency Control and Consistency of Multiple Copies in Distributed INGRES," *IEEE Transactions on Software Engineering*, Vol. SE-5, No. 3, May 1979.

[STON79b]   Stonebraker, M., "MUFFIN: A Distributed Data Base Machine," *Proceedings of the First International Conference on Distributed Computing*, Huntsville, AL, October 1979.

[STON80a]   Stonebraker, M., "Operating System Support for Data Base Management Functions," *Communications of the ACM*, Vol. 24, No. 7, July 1981 (also in this volume).

[STON80b]   Stonebraker, M., "Retrospection on a Data Base System," *ACM Transactions on Database Systems*, Vol. 5, No. 3, September 1980 (also in this volume).

[STON80c]   Stonebraker, M., and K. Keller, "Embedding Hypothetical Data Bases and Expert Knowledge in a Data Manager," *Proceedings of the 1980 ACM-SIGMOD Conference on the Management of Data*, Santa Monica, CA, May 1980.

[STON81]   Stonebraker, M., "Hypothetical Data Bases as Views," *Proceedings of the 1981 ACM-SIGMOD Conference on the Management of Data*, Ann Arbor, MI, June 1981.

[STON82a]   Stonebraker, M., "Adding Semantic Knowledge to a Relational Database System," *Proceedings of the NSF Workshop on Semantic Modeling*, Intervale, NH, June 1982.

[STON82b]   Stonebraker, M., and J. Kalash, "TIMBER: A Sophisticated Relation Browser," *Proceedings of the Eighth International Conference on Very Large Data Bases*, Mexico City, Mexico, September 1982.

[STON83b]   Stonebraker, M., et al., "Support for Document Processing in a Relational Database System," *ACM Transactions on Office Information Systems*, April 1983 (also in this volume).

[STON83a]   Stonebraker, M., et al., "Application of Abstract Data Types and Abstract Indices to CAD Databases," *Proceedings of the Engineering Design Applications of ACM-IEEE Database Week*, San Jose, CA, May 1983.

[STON84]   Stonebraker, M., et al., *Problems in Supporting Data Base Transactions in an Operating System Transaction Manager*, Electronics Research Laboratory, University of California, Berkeley, CA, September 1984.

[SVOB79]   Svobodova, L., "Reliability Issues in Distributed Information Processing Systems," *Proceedings of the Ninth IEEE Fault Tolerant Computing Conference*, Madison, WI, June 1979.

[TAND79]   Tandem Computers, *Enscribe Reference Manual*, Tandem Corporation, Cupertino, CA, August 1979.

[TAND80]   Tandem Computers, *Tandem 16 Pathway Reference Manual*, 82041, Tandem Corporation, Cupertino, CA, February 1980.

[TEIT81]   Teitelman, W., and L. Masinter, "The Interlisp Programming Environment," *IEEE Computer*, Vol. 14, No. 4, April 1981.

[THOM75]   Thomas, R., *A Solution to the Update Problem for Multiple Copy Databases Which Use Distributed Control*, Report 3340, Bolt Beranek and Newman, Inc., Cambridge, MA, July 1975.

[TSIC75]   Tsichritzis, D., *A Network Framework for Relational Implementation*, Report CSRG-51, Computer Systems Research Group, University of Toronto, Toronto, Ontario, Canada, February 1975.

[TSIC77a]   Tsichritzis, D., "Research Directions in Data Base Management Systems," *SIGMOD Record*, Vol. 9, No. 3, 1977, pp. 26-41.

[TSIC77b]   Tsichritzis, D., and A. Klug, (eds.), *The ANSI/X3/SPARC DBMS Framework - Report of the Study Group on Data Base Management Systems*, 1977.

[TUEL76]   Tuel, W., Jr., "An Analysis of Buffer Paging in Virtual Storage Systems," *IBM Journal of Research and Development*, Vol. 20, No. 5, September 1976.

[WASS78]   Wasserman, A., et al., *Report on the Programming Language PLAIN*, TR-34, University of California, San Francisco, CA, 1978.

[WASS79]   Wasserman, A., "The Data Management Facilities of PLAIN," *Proceedings of the 1979 ACM-SIGMOD Conference on Management of Data*, Boston, MA, June 1979.

[WEBE78]   Weber, H., "A Software Engineering View of Data Base Systems," *Proceedings of the Fourth International Conference on Very Large Data Bases*, West Berlin, Germany, October 1978, pp. 36-51.

[WEGB71]   Wegbreit, B., "The ECL Programming System," *Proceedings of the 1971 AFIPS Fall Joint Computer Conference*, Vol. 39, AFIPS Press, Montvale, NJ, 1971, pp. 253-262.

[WIRT77]   Wirth, N., "Modula: A Language for Modular Multiprogramming," *Software: Practice and Experience*, Vol. 7, 1977, pp. 3-35.

[WONG76]   Wong, E., and K. Youssefi, "Decomposition: A Strategy for Query Processing," *ACM Transactions on Database Systems*, Vol. 1, No. 3, September 1976, pp. 223-241.

[WONG77]   Wong, E., "Retrieving Dispersed Data from SDD-1: A System for Distributed Databases," *Proceedings of the Second Berkeley Workshop on Distributed Data Management and Computer Networks*, Lawrence Berkeley Laboratory, May 1977, pp. 217-235.

[WONG79]   Wong E., and R. Katz, "Logical Design and Schema Conversion for Relational and DBTG Databases," *Proceedings of the International Conference on the Entity-Relationship Approach to Systems Analysis and Design*, Los Angeles, CA, December 1979.

[WONG84]   Wong, E., *The Design of Representation Schema*, Tech. Report, Honeywell Corporation Computer Science Center, Bloomington, MN, July 1984

[YAO75]   Yao, S., and A. Merten, "Selection of File Organization Using an Analytic Model," *Proceedings of the First International Conference on Very Large Data Bases*, Framingham, MA, September 1975.

[YAO77]   Yao, S., "Approximating Block Accesses in Database Organizations," *Communications of the ACM*, Vol. 20, No. 4, April 1977, pp. 260-261.

[YAO78a]   Yao, S., "Optimization of Query Evaluation Algorithms," *ACM Transactions on Database Systems*, Vol. 4, No. 2, June 1979, pp. 133-155.

[YAO78b]   Yao, S., and D. DeJong, "Evaluation of Database Access Paths," *Proceedings of the 1978 ACM-SIGMOD Conference on the Management of Data*, Austin, TX, May 1978.

[YOUS78]   Youssefi, K., *Query Processing for a Relational Database System*, Memo No. M78-3, Electronics Research Laboratory, University of California, Berkeley, CA, January 1978.

[ZANI83]   Zaniola, C., "The Database Language GEM," *Proceedings of the 1983 ACM-SIGMOD Conference on the Management of Data*, San Jose, CA, May 1983, pp. 207-218.

[ZLOO81]   Zloof, M., "QBE/OBE: A Language for Office and Business Automation," *IEEE Computer*, Vol. 14., No. 5, May 1981, pp.13-22.

[ZLOO82]   Zloof, M., "Office-by-Example: A Business Language That Unifies Data and Word Processing and Electronic Mail," *IBM Systems Journal*, Fall 1982.

[ZOOK75]   Zook, W., et al., *INGRES Reference Manual*, Memo No. M75-19, Electronics Research Laboratory, University of California, Berkeley, CA, April 1975.

Index